Vengeance and Justice

Vengeance and Justice

*Crime and Punishment
in the 19th-Century
American South*

EDWARD L. AYERS

New York   Oxford
OXFORD UNIVERSITY PRESS
1984

Library of Congress Cataloging in Publication Data
Ayers, Edward L. 1953—
   Vengeance and justice.
   Bibliography: p.   Includes index.
   1. Criminal justice, Administration of—Southern
States—History—19th century.   2. Crime and criminals
—Southern States—History—19th century.   3. Punishment
—Southern States—History—19th century.   4. Revenge
—Southern States—History—19th century.   I. Title.
HV9475.A13A96   1984   364'.975   83-17472
ISBN 0-19-503383-3

Printing (last digit): 9 8 7 6 5 4 3 2 1

Printed in the United States of America

For Abby

Acknowledgments

I have long looked forward to the day when I could thank the people whose help has meant so much to me.

Yale University, the Whiting Foundation, the University of Virginia Summer Grants Program, and the Carter G. Woodson Institute for Afro-American and African Studies at the University of Virginia gave me essential financial support. Without the aid of the Alabama Department of Archives and History, the Atlanta Historical Society, the Georgia Department of Archives and History, the Georgia Historical Society, the Mississippi Department of Archives and History, the Tennessee State Library and Archives, the Library of Congress, the Massachusetts State Library, the University of Georgia Library, the Greene and Whitfield County, Georgia, courts, and the Whitfield-Murray Historical Society this book would have been impossible. The interlibrary loan and reference librarians at Yale University and the University of Virginia proved invaluable allies.

This book began in Yale University's American Studies Program, where many people taught me a great deal about scholarship and friendship. I particularly want to thank Joel Bernard, Gerald Burns, Steven Hahn, Jane Hunter, Jackson Lears, David Lubin, Michael McGerr, Michael Smith, and Christopher Wilson. C. Vann Woodward, in the last graduate seminar he taught at Yale, revealed to me in his person and his work the potential of Southern history; Richard W. Fox and Paul E. Johnson, then just beginning their careers as professors, introduced me to social history and inspired me with their example and encouragement. Kai T. Erikson read my dissertation with the insight of a sensitive sociologist, and John Blassingame never failed to pose challenging problems or offer help in figuring them out. I count myself extraordinarily lucky, above all, to have had David Brion Davis as my adviser. Interested in and knowledgeable about an incredibly broad range of subjects, willing to let younger scholars take chances, demanding yet thoroughly supportive, he helped me more than I can say.

I found yet another congenial scholarly community at the University of Virginia. The secretaries of the History Department, especially Ella Wood and Lottie McCauley, kindly helped me with typing and mastering the word processor. Two graduate students, Lou Tanner and Kevin Thornton, cheerfully assisted me in the boring work of gathering crime statistics from dusty and remote records; a host of other students, particularly Stuart McGehee, raised important questions. The close readings of several of my colleagues— Fred Carstensen, Paul Gaston, Michael Holt, Joseph Kett, and Olivier Zunz—helped make this a more polished and precise book. William W. Abbot performed an editing job that gave credence to legends I had heard of his skill and generosity. Thomas Noble, too, supplied good will and good advice as he brought his considerable grammatical and analytical abilities to bear. Stephen Innes commented in great and perceptive detail on two entire drafts and inspired the book's title. I deeply appreciate his help and his friendship.

When Professor Bertram Wyatt-Brown and I discovered a few months before I completed this manuscript that he was on the verge of publishing a book that explored one of my book's major themes, he rushed me the galleys of his important study, *Southern Honor*. His provocative and far-ranging exploration helped focus and clarify the ideas on honor I had suggested in the dissertation from which this book developed. Professor Wyatt-Brown's generosity exemplifies the scholarly spirit at its best.

Sheldon Meyer, Tessa DeCarlo, and Leona Capeless of Oxford University Press turned my manuscript into a book with the skill and helpfulness I had expected from such a distinguished house.

Despite the prodigious and generous efforts of all these people, they of course are not to be held accountable for errors I insisted upon making. I thank them sincerely and absolve them completely.

One group of people, however, must shoulder responsibility. My parents must be held to account because they have for so long shared with me the fruit and example of their hard work; my grandparents must accept blame, too, for instilling in me a fascination with and respect for the rural South. Marsha and Tom McNeer also must share culpability, for they housed and fed me in Atlanta for week after week with unfailing hospitality and humor. Nathaniel, for his part, pretended to accept the repeated explanation that I could not play because I was "working," when any two-year-old could plainly see that I was merely looking at books. My wife, Abby, has lived with this endeavor for as long as I have. She helped bring it into being with her diligence and camaraderie during a long, low-budget research trip and has sustained it in the years since with a grace and understanding I can scarcely repay.

Charlottesville   E.L.A.
October 1983

Contents

Vengeance and Justice

Introduction

Violence permeates the most potent and indelible images of the American South: eye-gouging free-for-alls at the rural courthouse; men of aristocratic mien and pretension solemnly dueling at ten paces; rebellious slaves writhing under the lash; chain gangs, bloodhounds, and grisly lynchings. These images can never be far from our conception of what made the South "the South," of what made that tortured region so often at odds with itself and with the rest of nineteenth-century America.

The causes of these cruelties and barbarities have long seemed common knowledge, common sense. Racism, the frontier, war, political conflict, and social dislocation seem more than sufficient to explain the South's tragic history of crime and punishment. Because these forces seem so obvious, in fact, no one has thought to take a look at how the patterns of Southern crime and punishment fit together, how they changed before and after the Civil War, how they differed within the subregions of the South, how they were resisted by Southerners of both races.

We have been blinded by our preconceptions. Southern crime and punishment were not the simple, almost elemental, phenomena they have long seemed. The nineteenth-century South, more than most societies, saw itself divided by conflicting interests, loyalties, economies, races, and classes. The patterns of crime and punishment reveal those patterns of conflict in subtle as well as obvious ways; the

3

incongruities, puzzles, and quandaries of the South are as important as the sometimes undeniable simplicities of the region.

Most of the South's conflicts and complexities grew out of the region's unique position in the nineteenth-century world. No other society experienced a history as the world's most powerful slave society within an Anglo-American civilization that saw itself as the antithesis of everything slavery embodied. Although white Southerners waged a war against the North in large part to preserve slavery, the South shared many ideals and dreams with the North, dreams it would not, could not renounce. White Southerners defined themselves in the same political language as other Americans; they believed, in fact, that the slave South alone preserved the freedom won by America's founding fathers. They spoke of the justice of slavery and the necessity for black subordination at the same time they extolled the South's heritage of freedom. The white South adhered to its version of republicanism before, during, and after the Civil War with a tenacity born of self-righteous conviction. The unstable compound of a political ideology based on equality mixed with a biracial society based on inequality helps account for much of the nature of Southern punishment in both the antebellum and postbellum periods.

On another level, much of Southern crime and punishment— including black theft, white lynching, and the convict lease system— can be understood only by looking at something besides political ideology that the South shared with the rest of America: involvement in the international market economy. The rewards and values of that economy beckoned the South before and after the Civil War, and many people in the region could not remain deaf to its siren call. But just as the past left the South a cursed inheritance of slavery, violence, and injustice, so the future that Southerners belatedly welcomed in the form of railroads and merchants helped breed new sources of theft, conflict, and bloodshed. Southerners of both races wore shackles not entirely of their own making, shackles that help explain their tragic history of crime and punishment.

I have tried to find out what kinds of crimes and punishments marked the different areas and eras of the South in order to offer an interpretation of nineteenth-century Southern justice that is coherent and yet faithful to the complexity of the region. The study explores the proportions of people prosecuted and imprisoned for various types of crimes, tries to find out who they were and how their punishments were arrived at, investigates the workings of prisons and police forces, judges and juries, lynch mobs and moonshiners. I have defined crime broadly, as broadly as various groups of Southerners defined it: this account includes not only criminal cases tried in courts but also extrajudicial acts as disparate as duels, stealing by slaves, offenses of church members against their congregation, and the terrorism of the Ku Klux Klan. Each of these "crimes" led to widely varying consequences, of course, yet each mattered a great deal to large numbers of nineteenth-century Southerners. The formal courts are therefore only a partial—if crucial—element of the story this book attempts to tell.

So large and amorphous a subject does not lend itself to a simple linear organization. Part One establishes the major themes of the book as it examines in turn the most important cultural and structural components of crime and punishment in the slave South. Then Part Two, which begins with secession and ends with the turn of the century, shows how those components were transformed as Old South became New South. The histories of three specific communities—a city, a plantation county, and an upcountry county—are woven into the narrative to provide focus and a sense of scale. I have attempted, in other words, to combine relatively sweeping theoretical discussions with portrayals of the place of crime and punishment in everyday life. To ignore the broad questions about Southern uniqueness and identity, economy and state, that crime and punishment can illuminate would be to ignore something valuable. To ignore what the region's various transgressions and retributions can reveal of the emotions, struggles, and even triumphs Southerners experienced, however, would be an equal loss.

PART ONE

1

Honor and Its Adversaries

Southern violence had become legendary even before the nineteenth century began. Isaac Weld, after visiting the new United States in the 1790s, recounted stories of fighting and eye-gougings he had witnessed in Maryland and Virginia—stories that were already familiar features of Southern travel accounts. Weld had been "credibly assured" that in the Carolinas and Georgia "the people are still more depraved in this respect than in Virginia, and that in some particular parts of these states, every third or fourth man appears with one eye." Weld did not risk visiting these far reaches of the South to verify the troubling rumors, but Charles William Janson, an Englishman, did make the trip to Georgia and the Carolinas several years later and found the violence even more bloody and widespread than earlier writers such as Weld had led him to expect: "The eye is not the only feature which suffers on these occasions. Like dogs and bears, they use their teeth and feet, with the most savage ferocity, upon each other."[1]

But not all Southern violence exhibited such unrestrained passion. While backwoodsmen brawled and disfigured one another, planters and politicians solemnly faced each other upon the dueling grounds. In 1826 a victorious duelist rushed to his fallen foe: "White, my dear fellow," he said quietly, "I am sorry for you." "I do not blame you," his bleeding opponent answered, and the two duelists clasped hands. The wounded man recovered, and the other was elected governor of Tennessee a few months later. Twenty-five years after this duel a

9

student wrote home that college life in Virginia presented certain dangers: "challenges are continually passing; fights are had almost every day." Another student assured concerned faculty members that the bowie knife he carried would be used only "against a person who should insult him and refuse to give him honorable satisfaction."[2]

Even after the South's fall in the Civil War, one thing remained constant. "Self-respect, as the Southerners understand it, has always demanded much fighting," a Connecticut native serving in the Freedmen's Bureau explained to fellow Northerners. "A pugnacity which is not merely war paint, but is, so to speak, tattooed into the character, has resulted from this high sentiment of personal value." As in the colonial and antebellum period, all classes seemed touched with violence: "It permeates all society; it has infected all individualities. The meekest man by nature, the man who at the North would no more fight than he would jump out of a second story window, may at the South resent an insult by a blow, or perhaps a stab or pistol shot."[3]

Nor was the pervasive violence confined to the turbulent years of Reconstruction. Even in the 1890s, the bloodshed was still a sign of Southern distinctiveness. "People who have never visited the Southern States but only read of these deeds of violence, are not infrequently inclined to smile when the principals are referred to as 'members of prominent families' or 'leading citizens,' " a Southern writer admitted. But, in fact, "farmers, merchants, bankers, physicians, lawyers, even ministers of the gospel, often slay their fellow-man in private warfare, and often after a mock trial are set at liberty, not only with no serious detriment to their reputation, but in many instances with increased popularity."[4] Every statistical index—police, court, and prison records, tabulations from newspapers, census figures—corroborates this eyewitness testimony.[5] The context of Southern violence changed in dramatic ways, but the evidence suggests strong continuities in the archetypal violence of the nineteenth-century South: fistfights, shooting affrays, and duels between individual men.

Explanations for Southern violence have never been lacking. As early as the 1790s Thomas Jefferson observed that the unbridled authority wielded by slaveholders tended to breed impetuous behavior and shortness of temper, characteristics passed from one generation of masters to the next. Emily Burke, a New England schoolteacher who taught in Georgia in the 1840s, also located the origins of slaveholders' violence in the patterns of their upbringing: "The manner of training children at the South accounts for that pugilistic spirit and uncontrollable temper, when excited, we all know is a characteristic of the Southerner. At that tender age when the earth is in its most plastic state, no attempts are made to subdue his will or control the passions, and the nurse, whether good or bad, often fosters in her bosom a little Nero, who is taught that it is manly to strike his nurse in the face in a fit of anger." The wife of a Georgia planter told C. G. Parsons that "slaveholders' children, instead of being taught to govern their tempers, are encouraged to indulge their passions; and, thus educated, they become the slaves of passion."[6]

Southerners did indeed pass on, consciously and unconsciously, their propensity for violence through the lack of restraint and the encouragement of self-assertion these commentators described.[7] On the other hand, slaveholders enjoyed no monopoly of command over other people, and wealthy children raised by servants in other contexts have not been noted for their violence and lack of self-control. Perhaps nineteenth-century Southerners would have also pointed out that the great responsibility of owning slaves actually nurtured the virtues of patience and self-restraint—not childish impetuosity. White men from the North and Europe, Frederick Law Olmsted thought, "would all and each lose patience with the frequent disobedience and constant indolence, forgetfulness and carelessness, and the blundering, awkward brute-like manner of work of the plantation slave. The Southerner, if he sees anything of it, generally disregards it and neglects to punish it. Although he is naturally excitable and passionate, he is less subject to impatience and anger with the slave, than is, I believe, generally supposed, because he is habituated to regard him so completely as his inferior, dependent and subject." Slaveholders could and did point to the procedural fairness often granted slaves in Southern courts of justice as evidence of their coolheadedness. Furthermore, an explanation of Southern violence based solely on the personality characteristics created by slaveholding does not explain either the apparent violence of the great majority of Southerners who never owned slaves or the persistence of Southern violence for more than a century after the end of slavery. There can be little doubt that slaveholders often seemed haughty and touchy, but there was obviously more than this alone to Southern violence.[8]

The frontier's corrosive effect on the power of the law has often been offered as another explanation of Southern violence. The frontier, this argument runs, breeds lawlessness, and the frontier was, in effect, built into the South in the form of plantations. Our national mythology assumes violence to be a natural outgrowth of the frontier; the explanation seems almost commonsensical to most Americans.[9] But in other English colonies such as Canada and Australia frontier challenges similar to those of the United States did not breed notoriously high levels of violence among the settlers. Recent studies of the American West and Midwest challenge the stereotypes of rampant violence on these frontiers of the United States as well. The violence that did erupt in Western cattle towns and on the open range in the post–Civil War years may well have been Southern violence transplanted, especially by way of Texas.[10] If earlier Souther frontier areas did suffer from violence—and from all accounts, they did—then we need to look beyond the mere setting of the frontier to explore the character of the people who lived and died there. Bloodshed was the product of a culture Southern frontiersmen brought with them, not something they found waiting in the wilderness. The frontier of the South did witness violence, but primarily because the frontier exaggerated cultural traits already in existence.

Several historians, recognizing the key role of culture in violent behavior, isolate various fatal flaws within Southern culture: a brooding and pervasive sense of grievance and displaced frustration, an undue affection for guns, and a pessimistic evaluation of human nature that automatically assumed violence to be the inevitable—if unfortunate—recourse in the face of intractable problems.[11] Each of these interpretations holds much truth, and each offers another clue toward the solution of an obviously complex puzzle. But none of them can explain why Southerners saw the world in such ways; all these explanations seem to mistake the symptom for the disease. In fact, the metaphor of cultural pathology and dysfunction may mislead us. Without condoning the killing, we should look at the South and its violence on its own terms and without censure of cultural habits we find abhorrent. In doing so we are led to reexamine white Southerners' own often-repeated explanation of why they killed each other with such frequency and regularity. They, of course, said they did it for honor's sake.

The mere word "honor," though, puts us on our guard and conjures up images of pretentious self-proclaimed aristocrats shooting each other in ridiculous displays of their own insecurity. That is because honor has no resonance, no meaning, in our culture today, where values antithetical to honor rule. Yet, just as they claimed, many Southern men recognized the dictates of honor: a system of values within which you have exactly as much worth as others confer upon you. Women, children, and slaves had no honor; only adult white males had the right to honor—and even they, if challenged, had to prove their worth through their courage.[12] In a culture of honor, anthropologist Pierre Bourdieu explains, "the being and truth about a person are identical with the being and truth that others acknowledge in him." Thus, according to Charles Sydnor, in the antebellum South "it was considered as brutal and uncivilized to call a man a liar as it was to bruise or cut his body."[13]

That Southern men responded passionately when their honor was questioned has long been recognized. Contemporaries repeatedly said as much. Twentieth-century Americans, however, have been reluctant to take Southerners at their word, and even if we do it remains difficult to learn just how many Southerners gave allegiance to honor, how honor operated in day-to-day life, how it appeared in the flesh.

In reconstructing the workings of Southern honor and violence, it is crucial to understand that Southern white men among all classes believed themselves "honorable" men and acted on that belief. Honor did not reside only within the South's planter class. All knew that the failure to respond to insult marked them as less than real men, branded them, in the most telling epithets of the time, as "cowards" and "liars." A coward tolerated insult, a liar attacked honor unfairly. To call a Southern man either one was to invite attack. Any man living in the South had trouble if he chose not to respect honor's dictates; he might find it difficult to convince other men his stance was not mere cowardice. "The barbarous baseness and cruelty of public opinion, dooms a young man, when challenged to fight," English traveler William Faux noted in 1823. "They must fight, kill or be killed, and that for some petty offense beneath the notice of the law. Established names only . . . may refuse to fight, but this is rarely done; to refuse is a stain and a high dishonour." Honor and "public opinion" came to seem synonymous, an overwhelming force that compelled men to wage fights for which they had little heart. Public opinion meant different things in different classes; to many poor men it meant the respect of a few drinking friends; to local luminaries it meant the judgment of nearby planters and professional men; to politicians it meant the verdict of the press. But to men of all classes, public opinion dictated that they not tolerate affront.[14]

Just as men of different classes played to different audiences of honor, so the exact form of violence generated by conflicts between two unyielding claimants of honor varied from class to class. While some men faced each other under elaborate ritual on dueling grounds, many more combatants fought in obscure taverns and streets. Aggression flourished most democratically where gambling and drinking flourished. One who had lived in Southern communities, as had H. V. Redfield, "could hardly fail to be impressed with the prevalence of whiskey-drinking and the frequency of fighting with deadly weapons." On the days men congregated in town, "when the whiskey begins to work, it very often happens that there is 'a fight' between parties having what is locally called 'a grudge' and the chances are that deadly weapons will be used. Perhaps several parties will be drawn in from kinship or partiality, and then the 'difficulty' assumes such proportions that the solitary town constable or sheriff, or both, can do little towards quelling it."[15]

Southern grand juries and newpapers blamed much of the region's violence on liquor, and there is no reason to doubt them. Southerners apparently drank prodigious amounts of alcohol throughout the nineteenth century. Alcohol, criminologists agree, is "the one factor in crime that can be neither argued down or dismissed." Antebellum Northerners drank great amounts as well and alcohol fueled many fights there, yet Northern alcohol-related violence was never the problem it was in the South, where alcohol and honor combined to create a volatile mixture. The cultural expectations of how drunken men are supposed to act obviously shape intoxicated behavior, and the Southern men who attacked companions or adversaries in drunken rage were acting in ways understandable, even expected, by others in their culture. A drunken man seldom literally "loses his head"; he knows which insults will hurt the most and whom he can afford to taunt. Alcohol dissolved the barriers of self-restraint that kept honor under control, heightened the thirst for the respect and admiration of others, loosened the tongue.[16]

Southern violence might erupt in less predictable arenas of conflict, as well, when men were stone sober. In fact, the major danger of homicides in the South, a Northern editor told his middle-class readers, lay not so much in their frequency as in the fact "that any one of any class in society is exposed to them." If in "the South you should get into a quarrel with a neighbor, and he should announce his intention of killing you, you would get no support from the public in appealing to the police for protection . . . . You may live at the South for forty years without having this experience, but you may have it any day, if your boy kills a strange turkey or your neighbor's cow breaks into your corn."[17] What is missing from this account, however, is the recognition that it required two unyielding parties to spark lethal violence from such mundane conflict. If the "offending" party were willing to apologize and make restitution, the matter would likely be dropped—if not forgotten. Southern newspapers did indeed relate instances where men killed others over trivial matters, but the specific incident often seems to have been merely the trigger, after a longer period of frustration or series of conflicts. As a nineteenth-century observer noted, "in by far the greater number of 'difficulties' it is known beforehand just what is about to happen, intimations of an impending struggle being whispered on the streets or in the country store, and everybody is listening for the reports of firearms that are to send one or more citizens into eternity." Southern violence possessed its own rules and unfolded on its own schedule.[18]

Had the broad stratum of Southerners who were neither rich nor poor not considered themselves men of honor, Southern violence would have seemed much less threatening and puzzling to outsiders than it did. Had common men not resisted indignity "even at the expense of their life or that of those who venture to insult them," as a Scottish traveler in the early 1840s observed with surprise, Southern violence would never have attained the levels it did. As unusual as the violence of the respectable farmers of the South seemed, however, the violence of the higher social strata over more rarefied conceptions of honor attracted more attention.[19]

Dueling constituted not merely a pseudo-aristocratic affectation, but the most rationalized manifestation of a set of values accepted in every part and by every class of the antebellum South. In fact, the duel came to the South long after the code of honor; it was not until the 1770s, when English and French army officers made it the fashion within the American army, that duels appeared with any frequency in the New World. For a few decades, Northerners as well as Southerners fought on the field of honor, but by 1830 dueling and the South had become virtually synonymous. Even England, to whom wealthy Southerners looked for the validation of their culture, saw dueling come under concerted and effectual attack by ministers and intellectuals who preached a code of "Christian commerce." By the last antebellum decade, the South stood alone in the Anglo-American world in its toleration of dueling.[20]

The bellicose posture of the South's wealthy seemed inexplicable to those outside the South except as a symptom of a deformed moral constitution. When prominent Southern politicians bridled at "insult" in the halls of Congress, Northern audiences ridiculed their brittleness and deplored their lack of self-control. When wealthy planters who seemed to have no reason to fear anyone's having a poor opinion of them risked their lives over a drawing room *faux pas*, critics in North and South could only shake their heads in disbelief. "About certain silly abstractions that no practical business man ever allows to occupy his time or attention, they are eternally wrangling," Hinton Rowan Helper sarcastically observed in the 1850s, "and thus it is that rencounters, duels, homicides, and other demonstrations of personal violence, have become so popular in all slaveholding communities." It seemed that Southern aristocrats actually wished to put their honor at risk, wished to live in a charged atmosphere where insult and conflict flourished.[21]

And they did. Since the heart of honor was the respect of others, public life offered the opportunity to garner honor from the broadest of all audiences. Politics raised the stakes of honor: nowhere was the possible esteem higher, nowhere the danger of assault on one's honor greater. It required manliness to put one's reputation at risk in such an arena.[22] Public life might not have been so dangerous had only a relatively few "gentlemen" sought its rewards, but the South was a political democracy for white men. Men of modest background could and did become lawyers, editors, and politicians, and all of them coveted the respect their new station seemed to demand. Southern gentlemen felt that their class towered "above the cloud of laws that blanket and hold in place the lower orders. Therefore, gentlemen would challenge only gentlemen." The problem was that the lower boundary of the gentleman's class was so poorly drawn. Pretenders and outsiders convinced themselves they could prove their worthiness of inclusion in the circle of the elect by fighting a duel.[23]

Timothy Flint, a Northerner who lived in the Mississippi Valley for many years, described how honor could become a commodity purchased with blood: "Many people without education and character, who were not gentlemen in the circles where they used to move, get accommodated here from the tailor with something of the externals of a gentleman, and at once set up in this newly assumed character. The shortest road to settle their pretensions is to fight a duel. Such are always ready for the combat."[21] Fittingly enough, the published insult constituted the only American contribution to the ritual of the duel; the affronted party printed his "card" in a newspaper so that as many people as possible, including strangers, would know of his willingness to defend his honor—and know also that he possessed honor worthy of defense. It seems no accident, either, that most duels were fought not between established planters, but between young men in the professions dependent upon the manipulation of language and image: law, journalism, and politics. An ambitious young man might make a name for himself by challenging the right opponent in the fluid society of the Old Southwest.[25]

Joseph G. Baldwin characterized with scorn and sarcasm the business of the courts of the cotton frontier of Alabama and Mississippi in the 1830s: "The major part of criminal cases, except misdemeanors, were for killing, or assaults with intent to kill. They were usually defended upon points of chivalry. The iron rules of British law were too tyrannical for free Americans, and too cold and unfeeling for the hot blood of the sunny south." A young lawyer from Alabama engaged in a revealing exchange with Alexis de Tocqueville, who asked:

> "Is it then true that the ways of the people of Alabama are as is said?"
>
> "Yes. There is no one here but carries arms under his clothes. At the slightest quarrel, knife or pistol comes to hand. These things happen continually; it is a semi-barbarous state of society."
>
> Q. "But when a man is killed like that, is his assassin not punished?"
>
> A. "He is always brought to trial, and always acquitted by the jury, unless there are greatly aggravating circumstances.... This violence has become accepted. Each juror feels that he might, on leaving the court, find himself in the same position as the accused, and he acquits."

The young lawyer then admitted that he too had fought, and exhibited four deep scars on his head. Tocqueville, incredulous, asked, " 'But you went to law?' *A.* 'My God! No. I tried to give as good in return.' "[26]

Honor and legalism, as students of other honor-bound societies have observed, are incompatible: "to go to law for redress is to confess publicly that you have been wronged and the demonstration of your vulnerability places your honor in jeopardy, a jeopardy from which the 'satisfaction' of legal compensation in the hands of secular authority hardly redeems it." Such attitudes are clearly reflected in the famous dictum given to young Andrew Jackson by his mother: "The law affords no remedy that can satisfy the feelings of a true man." And when a man who had taken the law into his own hands was placed before the jury, the result was predictable. "Almost any thing made out a case of self-defense—a threat—a quarrel—an insult—going armed, as almost all the wild fellows did—shooting from behind a corner, or out of a store door, in front or from behind—it was all self-defense!" And it probably *was* self-defense, given the inexorable way insult bred violence. Even Blackstone, from whom Southern lawyers worshipfully learned their craft, admitted that honor was "a point of nature so nice and delicate that its wrongs and injuries escape the notice of the common law, and yet are fit to be redressed somewhere." That "somewhere" was the Southern dueling ground, tavern, and street.[27]

It is easy to allow colorful accounts from the frontier of the Old Southwest, from travel writers looking for the interesting anecdote, and from angry Southerners themselves to dominate a portrayal of Southern honor and violence. If we do, it is easy to exaggerate the ferocity and frequency of that violence. Rarer are accounts—such as Frederick Law Olmsted's—that show the way honor could actually be a laughing matter in the South. Riding on a Kentucky train in 1853, Olmsted and his traveling companions, including his brother, saw a "modest young man" walking through the car with a Colt revolver protruding through the back of his jacket. Several of the passengers laughed, and one of Olmsted's Southern friends called out, " 'You'll lose your Colt, Sir.' The man turned and after a moment joined the laugh and pushed the handle into the pocket." Olmsted's brother wondered if there might not have been " 'danger in laughing at him.' 'Oh, no,' replied our companion, evidently supposing him serious, 'he would not mind a laugh. It's the best place to carry your pistol, after all,' said he. 'It's less in your way than anywhere else. And as good a place for your knife as anywhere else is down your back, so you can draw over your shoulder.' "[28]

Although the South appears to have had its share of fight-provoking bullies, men sensitive to insult did not necessarily seek violence. David Macrae had seen armed and touchy men in his tour of the South soon after the Civil War and recognized the volatility of honor, but he estimated "as very slight the danger which any man runs even in the worst parts of the South-west, who is engaged in honest work and attends to his own business." Southern violence was triggered only by a limited number of specific cues, particularly insult. And although an outsider might offend a Southerner, the insult had to be considered an intentional affront before it would provoke violence. It was not as if men whose conception of honor meant they thought violence was sometimes unavoidable felt compelled to fight each other every day. Accounts of duels reveal that seconds and even principals made every effort to avoid actual bloodshed. More than one duel was a pro forma exercise in etiquette that injured the reputation of neither man.[29]

Contemporaries who described Southerners as gracious and hospitable described men who adhered to honorable conduct, but so did those who described Southerners as touchy and even belligerent. Honor, the overweening concern with the opinions of others, led people to pay particular attention to manners, to ritualized evidence of respect. When that respect was not forthcoming between men, violence might be the result. A culture of honor thus tended to breed the extremes of behavior for which nineteenth-century Southerners were famous. Yet Southern culture was not so brittle that it could not absorb the usual range of human foibles and quirks. Honor did not create one temperament, one personality, any more than does any other culture. A sense of noblesse oblige and disciplined rectitude, as well as violence, could and did grow out of honor.[30]

Any accurate description of Southern honor must be couched in qualified language and described with care, for it was simultaneously potent and elusive. No contemporary visitor saw the entirety of Southern honor, no Southern poet or philosopher described its workings from the inside. Historians must therefore reconstruct it out of fragments, glimpsed encounters, passing comments. Southern honor was an anomaly, a strange hybrid of Old World and New World.

But so was Northern culture, and by the mid-nineteenth century the Northern United States had generated the core of a culture antagonistic to honor. This Northern culture celebrated "dignity"— the conviction that each individual at birth possessed an intrinsic value at least theoretically equal to that of every other person.[31] In practice, of course, this ideal was qualified, violated, and under-mined. Women, blacks, and Irish immigrants, to name the most obvious examples, were not treated as equals by native white men. Even those white men found their supposedly equal worth mocked by class distinctions. Nevertheless, from the perspective of world history few can fail to be struck at the public allegiance awarded dignity at every turn in the American North in the mid-nineteenth century. Dignity stood as the ideal, the goal, however often it was violated in practice. Deviations had to be explained away, ration-alized.

[In a culture of dignity, people were expected to remain deaf to the same insults that Southern men were expected to resent) "Call a man a liar in Mississippi," an old saying went, "and he will knock you down; in Kentucky, he will shoot you; in Indiana, he will say "You are another.""[32] Dignity might be likened to an internal skeleton, to a hard structure at the center of the self; honor, on the other hand, resembles a cumbersome and vulnerable suit of armor that, once pierced, leaves the self no protection and no alternative except to strike back in desperation. Honor in the Southern United States cannot be understood without reference to dignity, its antithesis and adversary to the north.

Both honor and dignity had roots in Old World cultures but developed new strains in the bracing environment of the New World. Almost from the very beginning a subtle and reinforcing sifting process created regional cultures in North America. Once British settlers arrived in America in the seventeenth and eighteenth centuries, they inevitably drew upon different elements of their diverse and changing culture as increasingly different economies led the Northern and Southern colonies further and further apart. Just as Northern settlers tried to reestablish the "English ways" of the counties and towns from which they came, so did the slaveholding gentry of colonial Virginia consciously adopt the culture of the English aristocracy.[33]

Lawrence Stone has carefully described that culture, and he finds violence at its core. His description of English society has a familiar ring: "In the sixteenth and seventeenth centuries tempers were short and weapons to hand. The behaviour of the propertied classes, like that of the poor, was characterized by the ferocity, childishness, and lack of self-control of the Homeric age. . . . The educational and social system of the age inculcated ideals of honour and generosity. Impulsiveness was not reproved, readiness to repay an injury real or imagined a sign of spirit, loyalty to a friend in a quarrel was a moral duty. . . . Moreover, a gentleman carried a weapon at all times, and did not hesitate to use it."[34]

The Southern gentry of the colonial era adopted the values of a proud and domineering English ruling class, a class whose power and authority they planned to replicate in the New World. When, by the middle of the eighteenth century, the planting class in each of the major Southern colonies had assumed social, political, and cultural dominance, honor and its violence were a part of the culture they regarded as their own, as the only culture worthy of emulation. The style of the American colonial slaveholding gentry, argues Rhys Isaac, is "best understood in relation to the concept of honor—the proving of prowess. A formality of manners barely concealed adversary relationships; the essence of social exchange was overt self-assertion." Horses, clothing, and betting displayed this self-assertion, but so did the "conventional forms of aggression—in banter, swearing, and fighting."[35]

Lower-class English and Scots-Irish emigrants carried their own experiences with violence to America, expectations and tendencies that soon combined with the aristocratic ideals of honor to spark violence on every level of colonial Southern society. Philip Vickers Fithian, a tutor from New Jersey who kept a journal of his sojourn in Virginia in the 1770s, described the forms honor took among the common folk. One combatant might have offended another when he "has in a merry hour call'd him a *Lubber*, or a *thick-Skull*, or a *Buckskin*, or a *Scotchman*, or perhaps one has mislaid the other's hat, or knocked a peach out of his Hand, or offered him a dram without wiping the mouth of the Bottle; all these, & ten thousand more quite as trifling & ridiculous, are thought & accepted as just Causes of immediate Quarrels, in which every diabolical Stratagem for Mastery is allowed and practised."[36]

Another traveler, Elkanah Watson, witnessed the battles of honor among the lower class. At a Virginia courthouse on election day in 1778 Watson watched "a fight between two very unwieldy, fat men, foaming and puffing like two furies, until one succeeded in twisting his forefinger in a side-lock of the other's hair, and was in the act of thrusting, by this purchase, his thumb into his adversary's eye, when he bawled out 'King's cruse,' equivalent, in technical language, to 'enough.' " Such fights strictly followed rules previously agreed to. Combatants fought not to the point of death or even disfigurement, but to the dishonor of the weaker. In some fights, however, the physical loss seemed less painful at the time than the loss of honor. Watson came "near being involved in a boxing-match" himself when he rebuffed "with little respect" an Irishman who wanted to swap horses. The immigrant from Ireland, his pride wounded, swore belligerently that the Englishman did not " 'trate him like a jintleman.' "[37]

A particularly virulent strain of violence entered the South in the culture of the Scots-Irish, the majority of whom chose the South for their home in the eighteenth century. In Carl Bridenbaugh's language, the Scots-Irish were "undisciplined, emotional, coura- geous, aggressive, pugnacious, fiercely intolerant, and hard- drinking." All observers agreed that the Scots-Irish had little patience for legal forms and found quick recourse in their guns, knives, or fists. "It appears to be more difficult for a North-of-Irelander than for other men to allow an honest difference of opinion in an opponent," a contemporary and sympathetic biographer of Andrew Jackson argued, "so that he is apt to regard the terms opponent and enemy as synonymous." Southern mountain culture, indelibly dyed by the Scots-Irish origins of so many early settlers, became famous for its sensitivity, as Horace Kephart observed, "to any disparaging remark or imagined affront."[38]

Many of the Scots-Irish settled in Pennsylvania as well as in the South, and Benjamin Franklin spoke for many other Pennsylvanians when he denounced the Scots-Irish in the Quaker State as violent, narrow-minded drunkards—"white savages." The Middle Colonies, marked by an ethnic and economic diversity not found either to their south or to their north, apparently shared some of the violence of their Southern neighbors. In the first decades of the eighteenth century, for example, the courts of New York and North Carolina recorded similar proportions of assaults among the crimes on their dockets.[39] But, ironically, the same early diversity that bred dissen- sion in the Middle Colonies paved the way for the eventual strengthening of the law. Conflict between rival ethnic and economic groups created a widely perceived need for a system of law that stood above the conflict. Even seventeenth-century Puritan Massachusetts evolved its generalized respect for the secular law, as David Konig has shown, only after slow and painful attempts to reassert the older form of "informal communal pressures" that had sufficed in the past. Massachusetts saw the convergence of too many "competing value systems that would have to be reconciled. As the New World economy developed and became more complex, new and competing interests would collide and require balancing. With no group or interest able to assert unchallengeable control, some type of modus vivendi would have to be synthesized and elaborated as a new social ideal." The written law emerged as that modus vivendi. By 1700 the people of Massachusetts were, in Konig's ironic phase, "a contentious and well-ordered people." They argued, they prosecuted people in the courts, but they generated exceedingly little of the kind of violent crime common in the South.[40]

Southerners, by contrast, could be called "an agreeable and violent people." Without the disunity engendered by immigrant groups of widely varying background, without the social diversity generated by economic diversity, without any long-term challenge to its slaveholding oligarchies, the South maintained into the nineteenth century a pattern of local and personal power the Northern colonies and states did not, indeed could not, perpetuate. The formal written law never attained the weight it assumed in the North. Just as the apparent weakness of New England agriculture fostered the necessity for economic diversification in the North, so did early social tensions generate a tradition of a law that stood above society. The techniques of Southern agriculture, on the other hand, recreated themselves wherever Southerners went, and so did the Southern preference for personal rather than impersonal justice when honor was at stake.

At the same time that the Puritans developed new conceptions of legal order, they perpetuated a sense of themselves directly and self-consciously opposed to worldly honor. Where honor celebrated display, the ideal **Puritan called for restraint.** Where honor demanded wealth as a means to command man's respect, the ideal Puritan valued wealth only as evidence of God's grace. Where honor needed the respect of others, the ideal Puritan spurned the opinions of men. Where honor existed in the constant assertion of self, the ideal Puritan gloried in the abnegation of self. Where honor looked outward, the Puritans looked inward. Ironically, Puritanism ultimately elevated the self far more than honor ever could: by making the self the focus of mastery, of control, of restraint, the Puritan self assumed a separateness, an inviolability the self of honor could never attain. The origins of dignity in America seem to lie here, within Puritanism.[41]

And yet had the only advocates of dignity been the Puritans, an isolated and alienated sect doomed to extinction, dignity could never have attained the position of dominance it eventually assumed in the

Anglo-American world. [Dignity triumphed because it was inextricably tied to the transformations of society and personality that accompanied the growth and development of capitalism. The ideal of the inherent value of the autonomous individual grew up simultaneously with the new ideals of character, of self-control, of discipline, of delayed gratification that have come to be the hallmark of the bourgeoisie. Dignity was not a mere by-product or residue of capitalism, but it seems doubtful that dignity would have so quickly conquered centuries-old patterns of human behavior had it not partaken of the power of this new economic and social order. And conversely, the new economic order could not have attained its enormous power to transform human relations in America without the drive and legitimation of the ideals of dignity.]

Dignity contained a political as well as a religious and an economic dimension. The ideals of discipline, "progress," moderation, and impersonal legalism strongly appealed to Northern men who voted for the the Whigs and the Republicans. Their ideal government was an active one, a government that created opportunities for freedom by creating prosperity. Many men in the North, especially immigrants, remained skeptical of such government-sanctioned development, however, and these men tended to vote for the Democrats. The North was no more unanimous in its devotion to dignity than the South was in its devotion to honor. But the most self-conscious and active ministers, intellectuals, reformers, labor leaders, and politicians pursued dignity in the North, and increasingly established its dominance.[42]

The various elements of dignity did not come together to form a coherent set of ideals until the 1830s—and even then dignity was constantly changing, growing, asserting itself, investing first commercial and then industrial capitalism with its moral power and authority. The spread of the gospel of dignity took on the dimensions of a crusade. Through educational and religious organizations, through publications and speaking tours, and through mass migration, New England colonized much of the North with the ideal.[43] Similarly, the extension of dignity to previously outcast groups provided the impetus behind much of the reform impulse of the antebellum North. To many, the deepest horror slavery was that it violated the slaves' selfhood, destroyed their capacity for moral choices, made them less than human. To advocates of temperance, alcohol had the same corrosive effect on self-control and thus on dignity. To supporters of the penitentiary, the new institution offered a way to remake the criminal's character, to replace a faulty self with a new one. To Southerners at the time and to many subsequent historians, the element of coercion that lay behind so many of these reforms seems to make a mockery of dignity. Reformers maintained all sorts of class, gender, and racial prejudices. They did not achieve universal dignity; by their own lights, however, they were seeking to extend dignity's reach, seeking to free people from outside constraints and replace them with inner constraints.

Ironically, dignity's intense concern with the self may have taken its toll: since at least 1860 the North has witnessed many more suicides than has the violent South. The same forces that made the dignified self a source of tremendous controlled energy also made it vulnerable to its own constant questioning, probing, measuring. The dignified self was the focus of antagonism as well as esteem.[44]

The dramatic emergence of dignity left behind it a legacy of monuments, of causes, of philosophies. Honor, by contrast, dyed so deeply with the coloring of the past, seemed largely "invisible" in the mid-nineteenth century. To contemporary Northerners, the South's culture could only be identified by what it was not: disciplined, controlled, productive of progress and change. The principal Southern characteristic, thought Ralph Waldo Emerson, was "wildness." Abolitionists portrayed the region as a caldron of sexual depravity; white Southern men gave their selves up to all that their bodies commanded. Their baser natures also told Southerners to quarrel and fight, and in their childish impetuosity they had not the strength of character to resist. Honor was just another word for lack of self-control.[45]

For antebellum Northerners, honor was an epiphenomenon of slavery. Without the obscene wealth made possible by slavery, they argued, no white Southerner could claim to be an "aristocrat," or have either the incentive or the means to emulate the archaic aristocratic code of the Old World. Without the scattered settlement demanded by plantation agriculture, the law and its officials would be able to exercise their proper power. Without the degrading effect of slavery on manual labor, ordinary white Southerners would work harder and develop the universally extolled virtues of Northern farmers and artisans. Without the opportunities for indulgence offered by slavery, white men would be forced to restrain themselves sexually. Without the force of violence which always lurked behind the benevolence of slavery, the South's "best" people would not be tainted with violence by their very upbringing. Given the real insights of these commonplace charges, it was no wonder that Northerners were blind to the internal logic and autonomy of honor.[46]

Bertram Wyatt-Brown, who has portrayed Southern honor with sensitivity and imagination, stresses the internal logic and autonomy of that culture instead of its ties to the South's economic, ideological, and religious context—especially slavery. In Wyatt-Brown's view, "honor existed before, during, and after slavery in the Southern region. Bondage was the answer to an economic need. The South was not founded to create slavery; slavery was recruited to perpetuate the South. Honor came first." Wyatt-Brown, drawing upon much of the same anthropological work which informs this discussion, argues for "the distinct existence of honor apart from a particular system of labor, a special region of the country, and a specific time in history."[47]

There can be no doubt that cultures of honor existed for centuries before the South, or the New World, were known to Europeans; that cultures of honor flourished independently of slavery; and indeed that cultures of honor survive to the present. Nevertheless, it seems certain that honor would have died in the South without the hothouse atmosphere provided for that culture by slavery.

Despite honor's ancient lineage and broad geographical distribution, it thrives only in certain kinds of societies, ones that are economically undiversified, localized, explicitly hierarchical—societies where one standard of worth can reign. Slavery and the scattered patterns of settlement that accompanied slavery fostered a society where the opinions of a relatively few people mattered more than in the North, where a multitude of paths to respectability and prosperity developed. Honor presupposes undisguised hierarchy, and a slave society builds an incontrovertible hierarchy into basic human relations. Even more than this, slavery by its very nature dishonored all members of one class and bestowed honor on another; in the American South, race codified and reified this class distinction. In slave societies throughout world history, Orlando Patterson has discovered, "the nonslaveholding free group came to adopt elements of the timocratic [honorable] character of the master class. The poorest free person took pride in the fact that he was not a slave. By sharing in the collective honor of the master class, all free persons legitimized the principles of honor and thereby recognized the members of the master class as those most adorned with honor and glory." Slavery generated honor. There seems little reason to doubt, in other words, that had the South not made the "unthinking decision" to adopt slavery the region would have followed a path of cultural development similar to that of the rest of North America. Just as the ancient patterns of personalized subordination and patronage that antedated and paralleled slavery in the Northern colonies were eventually replaced by the new patterns of depersonalized, market-oriented, contractual relationships, so too would the early South have changed.[48]

Slavery was the key: slavery insulated the colonial and antebelleum South—including those large and numerous areas where subsistence farming rather than slave-based plantations dominated—from the economic and cultural forces so bound up with dignity. Ruralness alone did not perpetuate honor, for the farmers who settled the North were deeply imbued with dignity by their religion and their upbringing. Northern farmers brought expectations and values to the frontier distinct from their Southern counterparts—ideals that fostered dignity and eased the way for market values. The conflict between the rural cultures of North and South appeared in antebellum southern Illinois, where migrants from both regions settled. A Southerner who moved to Illinois later recalled that settlers from his native region scarcely saw notes, receipts, mortgages or bonds until the Northerners arrived in Illinois, and when the newcomers "sought to introduce their system of accounts, written notes, and obligations, they were looked upon with great suspicion and distrust, and their mode of doing business regarded as a great and unwarrantable innovation upon established usage." As one historian of the Midwest observes, "To the Southerner his own way of doing business affirmed confidence and personal honor. To the Yankee it was a lack of proper system, a sinful inefficiency." Such divisions reflected others. As the Northern-based *Home Missionary* noted in 1856, the Yankee settlers, in their zeal to spread what seemed their obviously superior culture, built schools and libraries, founded colleges and newspapers; the upland Southerners just got along. In fact, the Southerners were known primarily for "intemperance, profanity, and *fisticuffs* on all public days."[49]

The origins and power of dignity lay in Protestant religion as well as in capitalism, however, and the potent Southern evangelicalism of the antebellum era could act as a bridge between honor and dignity. Southern evangelicalism, like dignity, demanded self-control and restraint. Further, honor was necessarily a secular system of values and was directly at odds with the spiritual frame of reference of evangelical Christianity. The Anglicanism of the colonial era had made its peace with honor, but it did so at the cost of religion's autonomy and ability to meet the needs of the white poor and the black slaves who had no worldly honor. Evangelicalism met the needs of a broad range of nonelite Southerners so well that it transformed the South between the 1760s and the 1830s. After that transformation the mind of the South became divided against itself in a way it had not been during most of the colonial era, when honor had no organized opposition. As a result of the evangelical transformation, the most powerful critique of honor eventually came from within the South itself.[50]

From its earliest days, Southern evangelicalism defined itself in opposition to the culture of honor. Not merely violence, but the entire culture of display, ostentation, worldly hierarchy, sport, and amusement fell prey to its wrath. This defiant tone lessened somewhat after the 1830s, as evangelicalism grew into the religion of "respectable" slaveholders as well as the faith of their slaves and poor neighbors. And Southern evangelicalism took on the coloration of its society: Protestantism in the South stressed the harsher, fatalistic, patriarchal, Old Testament side of the Bible and Christianity, even as Northern Protestantism increasingly took on a rational, optimistic, "feminized," New Testament emphasis. Yet the differences between Northern and Southern evangelicalism were scarcely greater than the differences between Southern evangelical piety and Southern honor. Southern men who had undergone a conversion experience discarded the equation of manliness with boastfulness and pride, replaced honor's vulnerable strengths with an inner strength that could resist the scorn of the worldly. Southern evangelicalism became stronger with every passing decade of the antebellum era. Newly prosperous Southern men increasingly turned to religion as a "respectable" alternative to honor. As Donald G. Mathews has argued, these men "were trying to replace class distinctions based on wealth and status—they called it wordly honor—with nonclass distinctions based on ideological and moral purity."[51] Respected Southern men, especially politicians, defended their honor and received publicity for their violence, but other respectable Southern men spurned honor and left no historical record other than their names in one of the membership books of the evangelical churches established wherever several families lived near one another in the rural South.

The names of Southern women also appeared in those books. Southern women embraced evangelicalism in ever-growing numbers and with ever greater fervor throughout the nineteenth century. **Many women found the strength of piety their greatest refuge in a** patriarchal society. Piety gave women a system of belief which undermined the secular conception of females as mere bearers of children, household laborers, or mannequins of finery. Piety stressed not merely woman's supposedly emotional nature, but also her ability to discipline herself, to reject the world of fashion and prestige. The evangelical church gave women a new strength. This strength, it was true, was not to be an end in itself, but rather a force women were to use to nurture piety in their children and in their husbands; the churches preached the conscious submission of women. Nevertheless, the evangelical churches held out an autonomy for women found nowhere else, and in turn women constituted the churches' greatest power.[52]

Honor, on the other hand, offered women nothing except prestige by association with a male relative. Women played the crucial roles of audience and reward for conflict between honorable men, but nothing more. A true woman would supposedly refuse to give herself to a man who would not or could not defend his honor; no woman wanted to share in a dishonored name. Southern ministers recognized this fact and admonished Christian women to help destroy this wordly and false system of values. "We would have every Christian young woman speak to these men of blood in the words of the patriarch, 'Instruments of cruelty are in their habitation. Oh! my soul come not thou into their secret,'" a Charleston pastor cried in the 1850s. "The mothers and daughters of Carolina are involved in a fearful responsibility on this subject. It is in their hands to stop this bloodshed, and in the name of God, I call upon them to do so."[53]

The South's clergy, who usually refrained from speaking on "secular" issues, excoriated the ritualized bloodshed of the duel, the very symbol of honor among the worldly elite. Delivering a sermon in Charleston in 1856 after the dueling death of a promising young man, the Reverend Arthur Wigfall made clear his agreement with other Southern churchmen that the pulpit was not the place to discuss "all the topics which agitate the public mind. Long distant be the day when the Southern pulpit shall become that mere 'drum ecclesiastic' which in some denominations, at the North especially, it has been made." But "another bright and gifted son of Carolina" had been sacrificed to dueling, and all Southern Christians had to denounce the "bloody monster." The Reverend Wigfall, invoking the most damning language he could muster, laid bare the secular, hierarchical basis of "the Pagan temple of Honour," ruled "by the same spirit which teaches the Hindoo to throw himself beneath the car of Juggernaut. . . . There exists in our country a privileged class, *soi disant* men of honor, who have established for themselves 'a higher law.' They put their foot upon the criminal code and trample it in the dust. They may and they do commit murder with impunity." The Presbyterian minister had no objection to "an aristocracy built upon virtue and intelligence. But we do protest, and shall with our dying breath protest against an aristocracy of crime."[54]

Wigfall did not stand alone in his attack upon honor. Nearly a decade earlier another minister had leveled the same attack against a self-proclaimed aristocracy: "Is the crime redeemed of its ignominious wickedness, because it is introduced with all the punctilios of etiquette, and perpetrated according to all the rules of polished gentility?" Yet another pastor put the matter even more bluntly: "duelling is opposed in spirit and practice to the Law of God. It is, therefore, a sin, a crime. No circumstances can make it right. No one except an atheist can, consistently with his principles, advocate it."[55]

Dueling presented such a profound problem for the South, its Christian ministers felt, primarily because the practice received at least the tacit approval of others besides the aristocracy's "silken scoundrels." "Is our hope then in public opinion?" asked Arthur Wigfall. "Nay, this is the very Demon that is driving its murderous car over our mangled bodies." Another minister agreed that dueling persisted because of "the false principles of honor which enter deeply into the whole structure of public sentiment." The ministers conceded that denunciation of dueling did not come easily to Southern Christians; Wigfall admitted that anyone unwilling to denounce dueling in the strongest language might be suffering, "unconsciously perhaps," from sympathy with the practice. Other preachers were less charitable: they ascribed Christians' acquiescence to a "fear of man," "an indefinable dread of averted looks and cold salutations." "The Code of Honor," preachers charged, constituted a form of slavery. Honorable men "submit themselves to be bound hand and foot, and delivered over to its tender mercies, no matter what obligations of prior and more sacred authority may be violated." Nevertheless, they argued, the public's silence on dueling did not signal Christians' widespread support of the bloodshed. It was merely that no one believed objections would do any good. As a commentator on Reverend Wigfall's sermon remarked, "The mass of our intelligent community do not approve of duelling, but neither do they positively and earnestly disapprove it, nor speak out boldly and loudly against it." That matter-of-fact statement seems to capture the fundamental ambivalence of the antebellum South as a whole towards honor.[56]

Few men consider themselves lawless, and Southerners, as Charles Sydnor has suggested, adhered faithfully to what they perceived to be the law of the Constitution and the Bible—and believed that Northerners did not. Southerners received a reputation for lawlessness largely because they believed that injured honor could not receive satisfaction through the third party of the state. As Wilbur J. Cash observed, the Southern tradition maintained "as its ruling element, an intense distrust of, and indeed, downright aversion to, any actual exercise of authority beyond the barest minimum essential to the existence of the social organism." And yet, "when the Southern backwoodsman moved out into the new cotton country west of the Appalachians, he immediately set up the machinery of the State, just as his fathers before him had done in the regions east of the mountains; everywhere he built his courthouse almost before he built anything else. And here in the South, as in all places in all times, the State, once established, inevitably asserted its inherent tendency to growth, to reach out and engross power."[57]

Cash was right: the state was by no means the nonentity commentators on Southern violence might lead us to believe. After all, without victims who prosecuted, without constables and sheriffs who arrested, without magistrates who arraigned, without grand juries who indicted, without petit juries who convicted, and without judges who sentenced, we would not have the court and prison records to prove how violent the South was. Honor worked against the state, but did not render it powerless.

It is significant that lawyers made up a large portion of state legislators and won great wealth and respect through their profession; even someone who turned so readily to violence when honor was involved as Andrew Jackson spent much of his life as a lawyer. The citizen of the most remote backwoods county, wrote Edward Phifer, "was remarkably aware of his legal rights and was ready to go to court on the slightest provocation." Courthouses throughout the

South were crowded with cases, and with spectators whenever court was in session. Anyone who has ever looked into the huge dusty volumes of court records in rural Southern courthouses can only be struck at how much litigation Southerners waged against each other over rights to property. Three or four time-consuming and expensive civil cases are recorded there for every criminal case, which are plentiful enough in themselves.[58]

Fredrick Law Olmsted came closest, it seems, to describing the true role of the law in the South. Poorer whites adhered to honor and remained "habitually a law to themselves, while they are accustomed, from childhood, to the use of the most certain deadly weapon"; slavery, too, undermined the law, for it was its own "barbarous, patriarchal system of government." But the barbarous government of slavery "exists within another Government—as far as possible, with this circumstance, of the most republican and enlightened form." Indeed, given honor and slavery, Olmsted thought, "it is really wonderful that Law has so much power, and its deliberate movements and provisions for justice to accused parties are so much respected, as, [in] spite of calumny and occasional exceptions, is usually the case in our Slave States." As Charles Sydnor has argued, while honor, slavery, and scattered patterns of settlement meant that the "segment of life that was controlled by law" was circumscribed in the plantation South, this "is not equivalent to saying that law, within its restricted zone, was held in disrespect."[59]

Southern judges and juries apparently wielded the power of the state with great care—not merely because honor caused them to hold law in contempt, but also because their political ideology made them wary of the state's power, whatever form it took. In their eyes, such an attitude constituted the very opposite of lawlessness, of a callous disregard for citizens' rights. A nineteenth-century historian of Mississippi was proud that the courts of that state had always operated under the fundamental premise, enunciated by none other than Sir William Blackstone, "that it is better that ninety-nine guilty men should escape, than that one innocent man should suffer." A lawyer from the same state remembered that "in courts, of that period, all the technicalities of the common law were rigidly observed," and told how he had quashed eighty indictments at one time over one such technicality.[60]

Moreover, the inefficiency of Southern courts may not have been as uniquely Southern as it has sometimes seemed. Inefficiency, in a sense, was built into the entire American system of criminal justice. According to Lawrence Friedman, in the nineteenth century "judge was played off against jury, state against citizen, county against state, state against federal government. Every master had to submit to another master." Many of the same complaints raised against Southern judges and juries were also leveled at their counterparts in the North and West, in cities as well as in the countryside—and in the present as well as in the past. American fiction in the antebellum period portrayed all American justice as inefficient: jurors, David Brion Davis has found, appeared as "gullible, ignorant men, who, if not susceptible to bribes, were easily swayed by subtle misrepresentation, sensationalism, and demagoguery. Public opinion, stirred to excitement by gossip and newspapers, was quick to condemn the innocent or to justify the guilty without adequate evidence." Well-meaning judges were powerless, governors too ready to pardon.[61]

The position of the law has always been problematical in a republican democracy; the law has always seemed too weak in the eyes of some, while to others it has seemed in danger of becoming too strong, of subverting American liberties. Nineteenth-century white Southerners, as the history of the penitentiary in the Old South reveals, were far more afraid of the second threat than of the first. They consciously kept their state weak.[62] Complaints about Southern justice, therefore, cannot automatically be taken as evidence of honor, of contempt for written law in general. Factors other than honor have to be taken into account.

Southern honor did exist, did breed violence among men of every class, did cut against evangelical Christianity and the law of the state. Without the concept of honor, Southern violence remains inexplicable. Honor was the catalyst necessary to ignite the South's volatile mixture of slavery, scattered settlement, heavy drinking, and ubiquitous weaponry. Honor thus served to set the South apart from the North, and once established honor became an integral part of the Southern identity. But it was never more than a part. Southern honor, like Northern dignity, grew out of a historical conjunction of economic system and received culture. When these forces changed, honor and dignity changed. Honor increasingly came under attack from within and without the South that nourished it, incongruous and anomalous in the century of dignity's triumph.

2

The Penitentiary
in the Old South

The institutional buildings must have looked out of place in the Old South. The penitentiary—the "black flower of civilized society," in Nathaniel Hawthorne's phrase—seemed to flourish only in the soil that produced cities and factories. Without an urban and industrial backdrop in the distance, the Southern penitentiary appears out of context, isolated. The institution seems incongruous, too, on the ideological landscape of the slave South; honor overshadowed dignity in the South, and the penitentiary was in many ways the archetypal institution of dignity, of internalized control. The zealous reformers who made the North's penitentiaries centers of world attention had little contact with the South, and found no counterparts there. Further, slavery kept the great majority of the South's poor under tight control. The South, it would seem, simply had little objective or subjective need to build penitentiaries.[1]

Yet the South did build penitentiaries, of the same kind and at the same rate as most Northern states. American prisons appeared in two distinct waves, in the 1790s and in the 1820s, and Southern states participated in both. In the more dramatic and widespread second wave, initiated by famous penitentiaries in New York and Pennsylvania, Northern and Southern states at similar stages of settlement built new sorts of institutions almost simultaneously. Maryland and Massachusetts opened penitentiaries in 1829, Tennessee and Vermont in 1831, Georgia and New Hampshire in 1832. Between 1834 and 1837 Louisiana and Missouri built penitentiaries, as did Ohio and New Jersey. Within the next five years, Mississippi and Alabama did the same, along with Michigan, Indiana, and Illinois. Only the Carolinas and Florida, the latter virtually empty throughout the antebellum era, managed to resist the innovation, and Carolinians fiercely debated the issue for decades.

In their bitter disputes over the penitentiary Carolinians resembled their fellow Southerners. Southerners of every state, whether they actually built penitentiaries or not, never ceased to debate the justice and utility of the institution. In every decade between the 1790s and the 1850s there were Southerners who argued that the penitentiary constituted an essential part of any enlightened government; for just as long, other Southerners warned that the penitentiary posed a real and direct threat to American freedom, to the ideals of the American Revolution. To both sides, the debate over the penitentiary was in effect a debate over the meaning of republican government. Southerners attuned to the cosmopolitan concerns of "advanced" republican thinking linked to dignity labored for decades to build centralized state penal institutions. Southerners who wanted to keep power closer to home launched the most sustained opposition the penitentiary has ever confronted. The prolonged battle over the Southern penitentiary can help chart the ideological terrain of the South, help highlight the channels of power in the region, help define the problematic nature of the state in the slave South.

The penitentiary, despite the shortcomings so obvious to its Southern critics, has long been viewed by most people as an unfortunate yet indispensable part of modern society. Historians have traced its origins over centuries and in different countries to find out how the penitentiary came to dominate our conception of punishment. Some see the penitentiary's creators as enlightened humanitarians, striving to end the torture, humiliation, and suffering of public executions and barbaric prisons. Other historians see the penitentiary as part of the subtle and repressive social control apparatus of the modern state.[2] Still others, struck by the simultaneous rise of prison and factory, stress the interconnectedness of the penitentiary and industrial capitalism.[3] The fact that the rural slave South built penitentiaries at the same time as the people in the Northern United States and Europe were building theirs makes the origins of the institution even more puzzling. Precisely because the penitentiary appears to be such an anomaly in the South, in fact, its history there may allow us to isolate the truly essential conditions for its birth and survival.

The exact moment of the institution's birth, like so much else about the penitentiary, remains uncertain, a question of debate. Incarceration, after all, had been used for centuries to isolate the poor, the insane, and the criminal. Houses of correction appeared in sixteenth-century Holland, and during the next two centuries most European governments built and then discarded similar institutions. Eighteenth-century prisoners languished in ships, in abandoned palaces, in old barns, and in penal colonies; no philosophy lay behind these haphazard prisons—only the determination to be rid of criminals or troublemakers. In America, poorhouses and work-houses fulfilled similar utilitarian functions in Northern and Southern colonies, but few magistrates or judges expected that these institutions would manufacture reformed inmates. As late as the 1770s, there seemed little reason for people in the Old World or the New to believe that any radical change would disrupt the patterns of the past.[1]

But in the last quarter of the eighteenth century a series of events transformed the meaning of incarceration. England suddenly lost its major dumping ground for criminals—the American colonies—and began to look for new places to put its rapidly growing criminal population. In America, the Revolution accelerated the social dislocation generated by burgeoning cities and trade. Leaders increasingly worried about controlling what appeared to be a rising tide of poverty and crime while remaining true to their revolutionary ideals. Social tensions created a receptive audience for the growing number of religious and secular thinkers in Europe, England, and America who attacked the inefficient and inhumane dungeons and corporal punishment of the past. The most insistent and compelling religious voice was that of Englishman John Howard, who, after years of exploring the decaying prisons of England and the Continent, published in 1777 an immensely influential account of the misery and waste he found. Howard proposed a new program for prisons, one institutionalizing the precepts of his evangelical faith. Howard argued that after a period of isolation at night and moral nurture and silent labor during the day, the criminal's own conscience would lead him to see the error of his ways. He would find the path to a better life through hard work, self-control, and penitence. Decent food, health care, and concerned chaplains would show the criminal that he had only himself to blame for his situation, that society was just and humane.[6]

Many of the best minds of the age in England and on the Continent, drawing upon the secular Enlightenment instead of religious teachings, found other reasons to champion legal and penal reform. The penitentiary, they realized, offered a more efficient, reasonable, precise way to punish criminals than did the outmoded means of lash, stocks, and dungeon. Montesquieu, Voltaire, Beccaria, and Bentham demanded carefully measured laws and punishments, laws that depended upon "reason," not the mere perpetuation of past prejudice and barbarities. These secular reformers' ultimate purpose was the same as Howard's: to prevent the criminal from becoming a bitter, hardened, and ruined enemy of the social order.[7]

American Quakers and American devotees of the Enlightenment, especially in Pennsylvania, quickly seized upon penal reform; the gallows and dungeon had no place in their conception of a Christian and republican nation. The restriction of capital punishment to only the most serious offenses marked their first task, and this they accomplished in the 1780s and 1790s. Instead of death as punishment for serious crimes, Pennsylvania lawmakers turned to "hard labor," not only in prisons, but also "publicly and disgracefully imposed . . . in streets of cities and towns, and upon the highways of the open country and other public works." The reform of the criminal law did not automatically lead reformers to advocate the creation of prisons; in fact, prisons were looked upon with disapproval by reformers as places where the state's injustice toward prisoners could be hidden from the eyes of the people. Public punishment seemed the more enlightened route. But Thomas Jefferson believed that the Pennsylvania experiment had unintended consequences: "exhibited as a public spectacle, with shaved heads and mean clothing, working on the high roads produced in the criminals such a prostration of character, such an abandonment of self-respect, as, instead of reforming, plunged them into the most desperate and hardened depravity of morals and character." Further, reformers had not anticipated the objections of citizens who resented the unpleasant spectacle and the noise the convicts created, who insisted that prisoners be kept out of sight and hearing. The prison, whatever its defects, seemed the only solution.[8]

Philadelphia reformers looked to the old Walnut Street Jail for a remedy. In 1790 they ordered a new cell house built where felons

could be isolated from other prisoners and kept busy with productive labor. For a few years it seemed that this makeshift
institution might provide humane yet effective and unobtrusive
punishment. During the next decade, before it became clear that the
Walnut Street Jail had failed to reform its inmates or support itself
financially, neighboring New York and New Jersey built similar
prisons—and so did Virginia.[9]

In 1796 Virginia became the first state after Pennsylvania to reduce
dramatically the number of crimes punished by death; only first-
degree murder remained a capital offense. The legislators called for
"a gaol and penitentiary house" to contain the state's felons.
Benjamin Henry Latrobe drew the plans, which resembled Jeremy
Bentham's famous "Panopticon": cells surrounded a central area in
a semicircle, so that a few guards would be able to keep an eye on a
large number of prisoners. When convicted criminals first arrived at
the Virginia penitentiary, they all underwent a period of solitary
confinement—anywhere from one-twelfth to one-half of their
sentence—to give them an opportunity to mull over their crime and
become penitent. But in Richmond the penitentiary was built near a
stagnant pool where the sewage of the city accumulated, the cells had
no heat, and prisoners could not work in their dark isolation. The
time spent in solitary confinement was a hellish introduction to
reformation. Water oozed from the walls, men's feet froze, and
several prisoners went mad. Others died. The surviving inmates
emerged from their solitary cells to join other prisoners in the
workshops, where they made leather goods for the state militia and
nails and shoes for sale outside the walls. The workshops failed to
turn a profit, however. Disorder reigned, and several bold escape
attempts proved successful. After six years the keeper of the
institution became despondent, because most prisoners were "insensible to favour and admonition"—the penitentiary was a "truly
disagreeable and dangerous" place.[10]

Despite the dismal examples of Pennsylvania and Virginia, most of
the other early states, including the Southern states of Kentucky,
Maryland, and Georgia, built prisons before 1820. Overcrowding
invariably destroyed, usually within a few years, the mixture of
solitary penitence and careful moral nurture John Howard and
American reformers had envisioned. Warden after warden resorted
to brutal means to keep the prisoners under control or showed
prisoners what investigators considered undue leniency. The object
of the penitentiary in Georgia, noted one of its governors, had been

to reform the criminal by "confinement and hard labor—a system which is constantly exhibited in contrast to the bloody one of England, and which from its congeniality with the American character and feeling, it would be desirable to perpetuate." But the reform proved defective "in its theoretical detail. . . . We passed at once from the extreme of severity to the extreme of lenity. . . . There is not even the appearance of punishment connected with our Penitentiary establishment, unless the restraint upon the liberty of roaming at large for the commission of crime be considered so." Critics in Georgia and in the North called for a quick return to corporal punishment or transportation of inmates to deserted reaches of the world.[11]

But at this juncture the American penitentiary experienced a subtle but ultimately far-reaching transformation. In Auburn, New York, obscure officials pieced together a prison program that was to be copied throughout America and Europe. Rather than resort to total solitary confinement or to indiscriminate mixing of inmates, the two extremes of earlier practice, the "Auburn system" confined prisoners to separate cells at night and brought them together to work in total silence during the day. Character reformation, brought about by the daytime silence and nocturnal isolation, seemed possible at last; profits and labor control, created by the combined labor of many hands under constant supervision, seemed assured as well. No contamination could spread, but budget-conscious legislators could be mollified. The long-unfulfilled dream of a workable penitentiary apparently had come to pass.[12]

After visiting Auburn, Alexis de Tocqueville and Gustave de Beaumont commented upon the eerie effect of the new system: "the silence within these vast walls . . . is that of death. . . . We felt as if we traversed catacombs; there were a thousand living beings, and yet it was a desert solitude." Despite Auburn's austerity, a school of reformers in Pennsylvania steadfastly maintained that the New York prison was not austere enough, that only the silence of total physical solitude, day and night, could effect the true reformation of criminals. These crusaders tirelessly championed the Eastern State Penitentiary of Pennsylvania as the model penal institution, but only neighboring New Jersey followed this more demanding path. The rest of America seemed content with the more practical Auburn system.[13]

The leading authority on American penal history, David Rothman, argues that these innovations of the 1820s marked the

"discovery" of the penitentiary by a generation of Americans
nostalgic for a stable, familial colonial past. And yet, as we have seen,
virtually every feature of the penitentiary had been articulated and
implemented for decades before the 1820s; the Auburn plan was as
much a culmination as a new beginning. In typical American
fashion, Auburn's "inventors" were actually tinkerers, assembling
the old pieces of the penitentiary into a basic and durable machine.
Without this new improved version of the penitentiary, the institution probably would not have spread as far and as fast as it did. But it
remains the case that the fundamental ideas and impetus behind the
penitentiary were not a product of the 1820s. Nor was the institution
a novel creation of the Northern United States.[14]

The core of the ideology that made the penitentiary seem logical,
even essential, came to fruition in the eighteenth century in both
regions of America. That ideology, republicanism, rested upon the
conviction that individuals, voluntarily joined together, constituted
the only rightful source of government's power. The theorists of
both the penitentiary and the republican state assumed that the
social contract involved the sacrifice of the least possible amount of a
citizen's freedom—just enough to guarantee the rights of others. The
penitentiary appealed to the early advocates of republicanism
because it could measure, in the universally valued and universally
owned units of years, months, and days, the precise amount a
criminal owed others in the society. Further, the penitentiary took
away from the criminal that possession citizens of a republic were
thought to value above all: freedom. Finally, in a republican society
held together, in theory at least, primarily by mutual consent and
invisible market forces, a single standard of behavior seemed crucial
if society were not to fragment and collapse into anarchy. The
penitentiary, along with the other asylums of a republican society—
workhouses, orphanages, mental institutions, schools—set apart in
institutions those who did not maintain the necessary autonomy and
self-regulation and at the same time inculcated those virtues through
the very institutions that segregated them from society.[15]

As long as people voluntarily obeyed the rather strict rules of
virtuous republican society, their freedom was assured. But those
who violated the single fragile, even brittle, standard of behavior had
to be isolated from the law-abiding to be re-formed into the
universal moral mold. It was this tension between the ideal of total
freedom and the desire for a uniformity enforced through public
opinion and institutions that Tocqueville found at the heart of

American society. The penitentiary played a crucial role in this conflict. "While society in the United States gives the example of the most extended liberty," Tocqueville remarked, "the prisons of the same country offer the spectacle of the most complete despotism." Nonrepublican governments could rely upon a strong state, tradition, a loyal clergy, and sharply defined codes of class behavior to restrain its citizens; a republic had only self-control, contracts—and penitentiaries.[16]

Every antebellum American man believed in "the republic," but the republic was different things to different men. Not surprisingly, the various regions and classes of Americans tended to develop differing conceptions of the ideal republic. To influential New Englanders, for example, republicanism required that the government maintain individual freedom through constant vigilance and active involvement in the society. An active state also appealed to the powerful merchants of New York and Philadelphia, who longed for a stable and uniform business environment. To Northern artisans and farmers, republicanism meant egalitarianism—equal freedom for all productive members of society. The state, these men believed, should guarantee that no monopoly or conspiracy undermined equality.[17]

To most Southerners, republicanism simply meant freedom from the will of anyone: centralized power, even in the name of an activist republican government, promised more evil than good. The abstract good of "social improvement" did not seem worth the risk of giving up concrete liberties. This Southern republicanism took its particular shape from slavery. Not only did slavery perpetuate a rural, localized culture in which men distrusted strangers' claims to power, but slavery actually constituted, in the words of one South Carolinian, "the cornerstone of our republican edifice." Slavery, claimed its defenders, guaranteed that no white man needed to be dependent upon another for his bread or his self-esteem—dependencies which corrupted republican freedom and self-control. Further, because slavery embodied and displayed the antithesis of republicanism, it served to make white Southerners, slaveholding and nonslaveholding alike, particularly mindful that no one undermined their liberty. In this assertion of white male autonomy, localistic Southern republicanism and Southern honor reinforced each other, fueled each other. Both made men determined that they would not be infringed upon in any way by any one. Most white Southern men, justified both by honorable and republican ideals, found little difficulty in justifying the fact that they alone possessed liberty. For them, slaves—along with women, children, and the insane—were dependents for whom they as free white men assumed responsibility. These dependents had neither the need nor the right to participate in government. Thus Southern republicanism, like all other variants of the ideology, perpetuated freedom of a particular kind for particular people. Few beneficiaries of early republicanism, whatever their region or class, were embarrassed by its restrictions; its gifts seemed too precious and fragile to be shared indiscriminately.[18]

A shared belief in republicanism, though, did not prevent strong disagreement among Southern men over which state policies best guaranteed their freedom. The debates over the Southern penitentiary—whether in Georgia in 1829, in Alabama in 1834, in North Carolina in 1846, or in Virginia in 1858—revolved around the same broad questions: What was the role of the state in a republic? What was the place of the Southern republic in the "civilized world"? Southern state legislators and anonymous citizens who wrote letters to newspapers waged the debate, often with great skill and insight. Some of these Southerners believed freedom could grow best under the protection of an enlightened state government that made laws more effective by making them less brutal and offered the possibility of restoring the ex-criminal to society. Others believed, just as strongly, that such an innovation threatened the liberty of citizens and even of convicted criminals. Both sides used the same rhetoric, but with visions of a different republic in mind.

The criminal law of the era before the penitentiary depended upon an assemblage of fines, imprisonment in local jails, whipping, branding, and death. In 1826, Tennessee State Representative Thomas Fletcher remarked with wonder and indignation that he had seen "penal statutes of England enforced in the courts of this state, which were enacted by the British parliament, even before this nation was born—even before the continent of America was discovered." Common law and colonial statutes of North Carolina had been thoughtlessly thrown in with the antique enactments of England to form Tennessee's criminal law. "Thus we present to the world the strange feature in government of a people living under the operation of laws cut and made without reference to our size." The result: "With us the body of a citizen may be suspended from a tree, and his neck dislocated amidst the melting agonies of suffocated life—the back, laid bare to public gaze, is torn and lacerated—the face branded with burning irons—the ears severed from the head, and left nailed to the pillory—and the legs and arms begirt with handcuffs and chains." All this the justice for white citizens of "a christian people in an enlightened age!"[19]

Mississippi legislators echoed Representative Fletcher's incredulous fury. "Will the pillory still disgrace a civilized age?" asked one. "Will the branding iron still be exhibited in the courts of justice to the dishonor of humanity, giving to the villain letters in *hand* and *body*, which will carry his hatred to the human race?" Another Mississippian raged that "only a savage land, where dwells the cruel, barbarous, and bloody brute barbarism" would perpetuate such torture. A Georgia legislator warned that branding an *M* into a murderer's cheek or cropping a thief's ears made a criminal unable to go elsewhere and start anew, and thus created a permanent criminal class. "The mark of his infamy is fixed and visible to all—let him remove from the scenes of his past crimes—go where he will—he is regarded, shunned and pointed at as a villain—excluded thus forever from society." Indeed, on the Kentucky frontier respectable citizens who suffered disfiguring injuries made certain the local court clerk recorded the innocent nature of their accident so that they could prove they were not criminals if ever challenged to do so.[20]

The criminal law of states without a penitentiary, argued the institution's sponsors, undermined itself because its penalties were so bloody and so inhumane that few jurors would convict. "Our penal code is like a clap of thunder," observed a correspondent to a North Carolina newspaper, "terrific if it hits, but it misses its intended object oftener than it hits." An Alabama critic argued that the "present laws by their very severity, do in effect license a large class of crimes." Although, for example, a man might be convicted of fraudulently obtaining through forgery only fifty cents, "the law punishes the offender with *death.* . . . Is this the amount of our boasted advancement in civilization? But no; the offender is not so punished." Invariably the criminal escapes, due either to "the sympathy of the Jury of the ingenuity of the Judge"; if not, the governor unfailingly pardons him.[21]

Observing with disgust that before the advent of the penitentiary Georgia law levied the death penalty for more than 160 offenses, a legislator compared law and medicine: "What should we think of the skill or ability of that Physician who would prescribe the same treatment for all kinds of disease, who instead of healing a flesh

wound, or removing a fever by proper application, would amputate
the limb, or kill the patient? Would not this be curing disease with a
vengeance?" "A dead man is forever useless," observed a Virginia
legislative committee, but "the very worst living man, who can exist,
may be turned to some account."[22]

(One of the greatest attractions the penitentiary offered was the
precision of its punishment—the law could wield a scalpel rather
than a bludgeon.) A letter to a North Carolina newspaper in 1846
invoked a frequent metaphor: the institution as a beautiful self-
adjusting machine. "The Penitentiary graduates not only the *quantity*,
but the *quality* or *degree of intensity*, which depends on the grade of the
crime, the age of the criminal, his conduct after conviction, his
degree of depravity which is indicated by his obedience or disobedience, his livelihood or penitence." Barbaric physical punishment ruins a man forever. "But shut the offender up in solitary
confinement—there to commune with the silent monitor of his
heart—his conscience—he there reflects on his crimes—the scenes
of the past—the hopes of the future—all at a single moment rush to
his recollection, and overwhelm him with feelings of remorse."[23]

The penitentiary depended upon self-imposed psychological
terror as a means of reformation. When juries and judges decreed
that a brand must be burned into felon's thumb or his back whipped
in public, the truly hardened criminal merely scoffed, claimed one
contemporary. The prospect of confinement in the penitentiary,
however, would put fear in his heart. "The criminal is generally a
man of unbridled passions, and little sense of character," observed a
correspondent to the Raleigh *Register*. "Pain and shame are less
dreadful to him than restraint. His reckless habits generate a brutal
hardihood, which bids defiance to corporal punishment and
depriving him of character, render him insensible to shame. But
restraint he most cordially hates and dreads." "A Planter" in North
Carolina eschewed abstract philosophy and drew a homey analogy
to explain the Enlightenment argument that certainty of punishment
mattered more than its severity. "Whip a dog every time he enters
your parlor and kitchen and you will soon be unable to coax him to
put his nose inside the door. But if he is sometimes allowed to lie by
the fire and sometimes severely lashed, he will take ten thousand
stripes and be a house dog in spite of them."[24]

(Free governments required citizens who had in effect internalized
government.) A republic simply could not tolerate what a Kentucky
official in 1860 called the "ignorant, drunken, vicious, or suffering

class." Such "an element in society . . . will always be a disturbing one, and has no business there; it must be remedied in order to have peace, order, and comfort. Now as it cannot be removed bodily, as the men and women composing it cannot be put out of the world, the only and the best way of removing the disturbing element is to change them, if possible, into intelligent, virtuous, and enjoying persons; then there will be harmony." This offered one of the most alluring promises of the penitentiary: criminals would, in effect, disappear—if not permanently through reformation, at least temporarily through incarceration.[25]

A republic necessarily rested upon a fragile base, citizens of the new nation constantly told one another, and a "disturbing" class might, if it grew fast enough, bring down the entire edifice of freedom—especially since crime and immorality seemed dangerously contagious in a republic. "Is it not better to pluck from a quiet community a riotous individual, who bids defiance to his country's laws," asked a Georgia legislator in 1828, "and thereby arrest the destructive influence of his misguided conduct, and confine him with convicts alike base and unprincipled with himself, and whose morals he cannot corrupt?" The answer was obvious.[26]

In every way, then, advocates of the Southern penitentiary couched their arguments in the language and concerns of republicanism. Their desire to make the law more equitable, reasonable, and predictable tapped the concerns of all architects of republicanism, for only law that won popular respect and approval would command people's willing obedience. Their insistence that prisoners be segregated from the body politic and reformed before they could return reflected republican fears that disorder and vice were contagious. The deprivation of freedom emerged as the ultimate penalty precisely because freedom stood as the most prized gift of a republican society. And since all men supposedly owned the same amount of freedom, the ideal penitentiary, unlike a monetary fine, would penalize the rich as much as the poor. On the other hand, Southern advocates of the penitentiary also unmasked the power and coercion that often remained disguised or hidden in a republican government. The penitentiary, unlike older forms of punishment, promised to cleanse society by segregating and hiding its deviants, a practice that once initiated led to the incarceration in various institutions of all who did not measure up in a broad variety of ways: age, "sanity," or means of subsistence. The penitentiary claimed to reconstitute prisoners' personalities to make them conform to a universal ideal. Such was the despotism Tocqueville found joined to American freedom.)

Alexis de Tocqueville was not the only one to perceive this coercion; many Southern opponents of the penitentiary saw it as well, and ridiculed the proposed "reform." To Louis Reneau, a state representative from the mountains of eastern Tennessee, time in a penitentiary threatened to be a far less humane punishment than the physical punishment it would replace. In fact, the penitentiary smacked of slavery. "How is this pretended humanity to be exercised?" he asked in 1826. "It is by taking a man who by the present law can only be sentenced to have a few stripes, and a few weeks imprisonment, and shutting him up in the penitentiary, there to be kept at hard labour, and to be whipped and driven at the whim and pleasure of his master." A North Carolina legislator, Theophilus Lacey, agreed: "I cannot believe this Penitentiary is calculated for humane purposes, since it proposes that an unfortunate criminal shall drag out, in some cases ten or twenty years, and in others the whole of his life, in prison; whereas if an offender was punished with death at once, he would be forgotten, and not be a living monument of misery and distress."[27]

In fact, Southern opponents of the penitentiary countered every argument its sponsors offered. Did the backers of the penitentiary want republican law? Then preserve public executions. In 1859 Georgia Representative Delany declared he "wanted no Bastille in Georgia—he wanted the trials in public and so ought to be the executions." Another champion of tried and true methods pronounced that "the influence of one public flagellation, would have ten times more powerful effect in deterring others from falling into the same terrors, than if applied in private." Did reformers complain that the laws were too severe to punish effectively? "If any punishment can be pointed out which is too severe, it is easy to make it more mild," observed one critic, "but it would seem, from the arguments of gentlemen, that there was no other possible remedy than that, which is afforded by the penitentiary system. . . . An ordinary act of legislation is all sufficient for the purpose, without running the risk of experiments." Did the penitentiary, unlike physical punishment, possess the beauty of a finely tuned machine? "If a man is disposed to give way to conscience, he will yield as soon at one place as another; but if his conscience has left him . . . , you had as well argue in machinery the utility of the fly-wheel of

perpetual motion, as to talk of reclaiming him in the Penitentiary."[28]

When penitentiary advocates, in order to convince skeptics that
the penitentiary would not let villains off with too little punishment,
stressed the terrors of imprisonment, opponents turned this argument against them: "The quantity of suffering under the penitentiary
system, will in the aggregate, far exceed that, which is experienced
under the criminal laws now in force amongst us, and jurors will be
equally disposed to acquit." Indeed, asked a Southern minister, if
"solitary imprisonment for life is the most terrible and the most
frightful of all punishments, and in this respect more terrific, as a
warning, than death itself—then where is the honesty or the
propriety of such reasoners in denouncing the punishment of death,
because IT is so awful and severe?"[29]

But surely opponents of the penitentiary system would be impressed with the cosmopolitan host of witnesses one Georgia
lawmaker invoked: Montesquieu, Blackstone, the prophets of the
Bible, even Catherine II of Russia—all testified that mere cruelty of
punishment did not deter crime. Surely, claimed an ally, the
principles of penal reform were those of "the wisest and best of men
that have lived—they are now the principles of the world." Who were
these wisest of men? "There, sir, (*pointing to the portrait of Franklin*) is
the shade of one, mild, benevolent Philosophic, who has been the
active and able advocate of those principles—there sir (*pointing to the
portrait of Lafayette*) is another, the friend of man, and the soldier of
chivalry, who was proud to urge upon the world, the adoption of
those principles." Skeptics in the Georgia House were not impressed
with the dramatic flourish of their colleague. One commented that
Lafayette's portrait "might appear pretty in a ladies magazine, but
argued nothing in favor of penitentiary confinement."[30]

Concerns about living up to "the principles of the world" took on
particular urgency in Georgia, because after a fire in 1829 opponents
of the penitentiary tried to abolish the institution rather than rebuild
it. Such a move threatened to make Georgia the first republican
government in the world to renounce this embodiment of "progress." When proponents of the penitentiary argued that to turn
away from the institution back toward physical punishment was to
"make a retrograde movement in civilization, and that by this act we
would incur and draw down upon ourselves the censure of other
States," one Georgia legislator asked, "can it justly be said that after

sufficiently trying an experiment, which we have found by experience not to be congenial with the interests and character of our State,
that we are going backwards in . . . civilization? It cannot sir."
Opposition to the penitentiary in Georgia could no more be
criticized "than an agriculturist could be censured for abandoning
the culture of any plant, when he had sufficiently learned by
experience that its growth was not congenial with the soil and
climate of the country." And even when Southerners did look to
other states for an example of the penitentiary's beneficent effects,
what did they find? "The sad experience of other states has taught
us," a Tennessee lawmaker had warned as early as 1821, "that the
refinements of civilization, the strength of moral conduct, and the
stability of our Holy religion, all shudder and tremble for the
prosperity of a state possessing within its limits a Penitentiary Wall."
In the same year, the governor of Kentucky admitted that his state's
faltering institution was a mere "mansion of guilt."[31]

One critic of the penitentiary denied that the penitentiary was a
republican institution at all, charging it was, rather, a usurper of
basic rights. "In surrendering individual rights to society," Sylvanus
argued, "it is reasonable to suppose that the right to remain with his
wife and children, and to labour for their benefit was retained; and
that the very principle of Penitentiary punishment is an encroach-
ment on individual rights." Not only republican ideals but
"humanity" to the "afflicted innocence" of the criminal's family
dictated that "it is much better to chastise the man soundly" and let
him go. The remedy of the penitentiary threatened to inflict more
pain on society than did the disease it purported to cure.[32]

"What are *inalienable* rights?" asked Bertie, another participant in
the North Carolina newspaper debate of 1846. "In the time of the
Revolution it was admitted that by taking away any part of our labor,
without our consent, amounted to slavery, and that any such slavery
was worse than death; but under the Penitentiary system the free-
born citizen is made to labor directly under the lash as a slave, and is
not this worse than death?" This opponent of the penitentiary
turned the very language of the innovation's sponsors against them:
"What legal or moral right has a State to inflict upon them this horrid
tyranny, which would disgrace the most barbarous and savage
times?" Quoting New York and New Jersey penitentiary reports
which admitted some of the failures of the institution, Bertie asked
"how a person can repent and reform in a state of constant
punishment, the mind strained to a state of endurance and the
person in duress?"[33]

A republican people, Bertie thundered, made their own decisions and accepted no practice merely because other governments might adopt it. "I protest against this question being decided by precedents from other states or governments. We should know the princples upon which we act." In fact, Bertie slyly concluded, North Carolina, one of only two settled American states without a penitentiary in 1846, could stand as a beacon to other republican governments. "I think instead of adopting the Penitentiary system we should rather increase our Christian humanity and benevolence in the abolition of Penitentiary slavery in other States and governments; for, in my opinion, a free-born American sovereign to be placed in this degrading institution is far worse than death by any torture whatsoever."[34]

Apparently such stirring rhetoric reflected the general, if less articulate, convictions of a majority of Southerners. In the only two times voters in the South were given the opportunity to express their opinions on the penitentiary system, the institution went down to overwhelming defeat. The first test came in the young state of Alabama in 1834, after legislative sponsors had introduced unsuccessful penitentiary bills in 1831 and 1832. When the 1833 session began, a Mobile newspaper reported, "The Penitentiary System seems to be popular, and it is not unlikely one will be established at the present session." The next issue of the paper carried an endorsement of the penitentiary by Governor Gayle. But two weeks later, the paper had discovered that "the Penitentiary System has many advocates and some violent opponents." The legislature debated the issue for several days, but could not reach a decision. Finally, in January 1834, the lawmakers determined to allow the public to decide. After months of editorials, letters, and reports from other penitentiaries printed in Alabama newspapers, voters went to the polls in August. The early returns from the cities seemed encouraging to backers of the penitentiary. Both Mobile and Huntsville expressed overwhelming approval, 2,613 votes to only 511. But when all the rural returns were in, "a large and decided majority" of the state's population had voted against the penitentiary. As Governor Gayle glumly reported, "Whatever opinions we may entertain on this interesting subject, the question has been settled in a manner, and by a tribunal, that commands implicit acquiescence." The people had spoken.[35]

A similar referendum in North Carolina twelve years later provoked even more heated discussion—perhaps because by that time the Carolinas seemed so isolated by their failure to build a penitentiary. The failure was not for lack of trying: proposals to build a penitentiary were introduced in twenty-three sessions of the legislature between 1791 and 1845. The vote was often close. In 1812 a penitentiary bill passed the House of Commons and lost in the Senate only by the vote of the Speaker. The surplus of $60,000 in state funds in 1812 could have been used to build a penitentiary that would have long served the state, complained a newspaper in 1845, but instead it had been squandered on an internal improvements scheme. In other years, the penitentiary lost only because its supporters could not agree which part of the state should win the privilege of having the institution located there. Little wonder that in 1845 the Raleigh *Star* fumed, "We believe in the expediency of establishing a Penitentiary in North Carolina, and of doing it *now*. We have been dilly-dallying about it long enough." In the months before the referendum, state newspapers published reports from the penitentiaries of other states and letters from citizens, including some of those quoted in the preceding pages, so that the people could make an informed decision. In September 1845, nearly a year before the vote, the *Highland Messenger* of Asheville observed, "The subject is beginning to excite some little attention, and judging from the opinions of our immediate neighbors, a majority of this portion of the State, are opposed to the measure."[36]

As it turned out, these residents of mountainous western North Carolina were not the only voters who opposed the penitentiary. Only three of the state's seventy-four counties returned a majority for the institution in the 1846 referendum. In fact, a mere 28 percent of the state's voters expressed approval of the penitentiary. In exactly half of the reporting counties, fewer than one-fifth of the county voters approved the innovation. Indeed, the vote was so over-whelmingly negative that no clear patterns of support emerge from the numbers. The fragmentary evidence from the earlier referendum in Alabama suggests that counties with large towns formed the primary locus of penitentiary support in that state. The counties of North Carolina's five largest towns, however, returned an average vote almost identical to that of the state at large, although returns at the district level do show that in several counties townsmen voted for the penitentiary, while voters in outlying districts in those counties voted heavily in the negative.[37]

We might expect, too, that counties that voted strongly Whig would also have voted for the penitentiary—since Whigs generally offered more support for social welfare expenditures than did Democrats—

but no such connection appeared. In the same election in which the penitentiary suffered such a heavy loss, in fact, the Whigs won majorities in over half the counties and elected their candidate for governor. Both parties in North Carolina seemed unsure about the penitentiary; neither party publicly identified itself as for or against the institution. From the very earliest debates over the referendum, newspapers had urged that the penitentiary issue "be kept entirely free from party politics." And it was, on the state level. But two months before the vote the Democratic *North Carolina Standard* of Raleigh reported that a Whig state senator in the western part of the state had in fact preached against the penitentiary, charging that the Democrats were for the institution and that it would cost an "enormous sum." The *Standard* asked, "Are the Whig leaders indeed playing a double game upon the Penitentiary? *We warn our friends to be on their guard.*" In the days before instant mass communication, urban Whigs may have well called for a penitentiary while their rural counterparts denounced it as Democratic folly. Nevertheless, after the election even the *Standard* admitted that the referendum had been "kept free from contact with party politics" and that "there were many able advocates of the Institution in both parties."[38]

As a matter of fact, the penitentiary, perhaps because politicians recognized its unpopularity, did not receive the consistent support—or opposition—of either party in any Southern state. A Whig from eastern North Carolina cautioned the governor against taking a public stance on the penitentiary: "I am satisfied that a determined opposition to the measure exists in the minds of the people, and that the better course for the Whig party will be to make no issue about it and to suffer none to be made." Alliances on the penitentiary issue tended to be temporary and fragile coalitions shaped as much by personal inclination and immediate expediency as by party ideology. Both parties portrayed themselves, saw themselves, as the true defenders of republican values, but neither was sure the penitentiary helped in that defense. The party out of power could always unearth reports of the inefficient and unprofitable administration of the penitentiary to portray its opponents as betrayers of the public trust. This ploy, frequently resorted to and well publicized, helped confirm the electorate's distaste for the penitentiary. Usually the attacks fastened upon the administrators of the penitentiary, who often conducted themselves with obvious and indefensible incompetence. One A. Fulcher, for example, assistant keeper of the Georgia penitentiary, went into nearby Milledgeville while on duty, "getting drunk and neglecting the necessary attention to business from one to six o'clock." He was dismissed. At other times the line between political and personal attacks disappeared. The Athens *Southern Whig* lambasted Democratic warden Charles H. Nelson as "totally deficient in financial ability" and the perpetrator of "an inhumanity and cruelty that would have disgraced a brute"—a cruelty that "is enough by itself to warrant his dismissal, independent of the many bad qualities he possesses and the numerous good ones he never adorned." Nelson immediately dispatched a letter to the editor of the *Whig*, demanding to know the author of the editorial. He received no answer, and so he wrote again, charging that the editor had uttered a *"Libel*, the *only weapon of the Coward*; and in your *subsequent course* you are *employing* the *shield* of the *dastard.* However, neither shall avail you, as I shall publish the correspondence to correct the former, and when we meet, which I hope will be this Summer, I will correct the latter, as I have been forced to do with others, under similar circumstances." As far as is recorded, no duel ever resulted, but the shortcomings of the penitentiary were broadcast nevertheless.[39]

The only consistent and enthusiastic support the public heard for the penitentiary came from state governors, regardless of their party. Confined to short terms of office by rigid constitutional limits, governors had little real power. But they did receive the state's attention and columns of newsprint once a year when they delivered their annual message. For decades the strongest calls for penitentiaries appeared in those messages. Governors seem to have gloried in their brief role as the state's conscience by calling for a broad range of "improvements," including the building and support of a penitentiary. A more cynical interpretation might point to governors' desire for scarce patronage plums—of which the penitentiary was often the largest. Governor George W. Crawford of Georgia complained half-jokingly to a political ally during a campaign in 1845 that the fruits of the office were poor: "You have my plan and I implore your friendly aid, to the end that I may be rid of a vexatious canvass—or what may be worse—of an office, whose chief pleasure is to watch the rogues in and *out* of the Penitentiary." The patronage of the penitentiary did not long go unused by any governor: between 1817 and 1868, for example, only one principal keeper of the Georgia penitentiary served as long as four years.[40]

Governors, whatever their motives, could only make recommendations that penitentiaries be created and maintained; the

ultimate decision lay with state legislators. These men, not known for
their bold and active legislation, created penitentiaries in state after
state, sometimes over the known opposition of the voters. Seven years
after the Alabama electorate rejected the penitentiary, for example,
state lawmakers established an expensive institution. Legislators
certainly recognized the political liabilities of calling a penitentiary
into being. In the Alabama House of Representatives in 1834, a Mr.
Lee from Perry County "asked with much emphasis, how we can
return to our constitutents, and inform them, we have imposed a tax
of $2000 upon each county for the purpose of erecting a Penitentiary
for the punishment of offenders?"[41]

Many lawmakers thought they knew what was best for the
people—whether or not the people agreed. In Georgia's legislative
halls in 1829, when the fate of the burned penitentiary hung in the
balance and some legislators called for a referendum, a Mr.
Crawford of Columbia County "rose and observed that he was as
much devoted to the people and their interests as the gentleman
from Pike . . . or any other gentleman on the floor. He respected
their opinions—He knew they were competent to give a correct
decision where they had correct information." Nevertheless, his
antipenitentiary opponents wanted to leave the question "to the
people, when they have not the requisite intelligence respecting it,
and know nothing of its management." And then Crawford indulged
in language that betrayed deep frustration with what he perceived to
be the popular opposition to progress: "The people perhaps would
wish to bring us back to a state of nature, destroy all tracks of
civilization, let the weaker be borne down by the stronger." Supporters of the penitentiary seem to have known from the beginning
that they must count on the influential and well-educated to bring
the innovation to the South. When, in 1826, Governor William
Carroll of Tennessee wrote letters of inquiry to states which had
already built penitentiaries, he closed with a revealing question: "Is it
the general opinion of the most experienced and thinking part of
your state that penitentiaries afford the best means of obtaining the
great ends of justice: the prevention of crimes and the reformation of
criminals?"[42]

The state legislators who initiated penitentiaries numbered themselves among "the best people" from their counties. They were
wealthier than most of their constituents, of course, and owned a
greater stake in social order. This may have been incentive enough
for many lawmakers to vote for a penitentiary. "A Planter" from

North Carolina cited a hypothetical case that appealed directly to the concerns of the propertied: "I have an unprincipled, mischievous, thievish neighbor who trades with my negroes, lets down my fences, and turns his stock into my fields, steals my lambs and pigs, etc. What shall I gain by having him convicted in our courts? Conscience will not allow me to have his life taken on account of a little pelf; and if I have him whipped, what do I or the community gain by it?" But if North Carolina built a penitentiary, "where he could be kept at work and out of the way of doing mischief, for five or ten years, then there would be a strong motive for me to have him caught in his villainy and convicted." And as a Mississippi planter, denouncing white men who were too lazy to work and who encouraged slaves to steal, told Frederick Law Olmsted, "When I get to be representative, I'm going to have a law made that all such kind of men shall be took up by the State and sent to the penitentiary, to make 'em work and earn something to support their families." Such self-interest and class bias have always been powerful motives behind the penitentiary. Every proponent of the institution would have readily admitted that he acted to protect property by making the law stronger. In this sense, the penitentiary was undoubtedly the product of self-conscious class legislation. But the penitentiary served class interests in a less obvious way: it "proved" the benevolence of the men who ruled, demonstrated that fair and equitable punishment flourished under their aegis, showed to the world that the slave south was not the barbaric land its detractors claimed.[13]

Southern legislatures, too, may have been predisposed to support the penitentiary when they would not support other state innovations because so many of their members were lawyers. One historian has estimated that seven out of ten of the representatives in Alabama's lower house in 1859 began their careers as lawyers, and such training characterized a large portion of all state legislators. Many planters, too, although never intending to practice, read law and prided themselves on their legal knowledge. All these men learned their law from Sir William Blackstone's *Commentaries on the Laws of England*, which first appeared in America in 1771–72. Blackstone offered a convenient, conservative, comforting presentation of the law congenial to propertied Southerners—except that he championed the penitentiary. In his chapter entitled "Of the Nature of Crimes, and Their Punishment," Blackstone, citing Beccaria and Montesquieu, presented a powerful case for the penitentiary. His argument against harsh punishments accorded with the experience of Southern lawyers in remote county courts: the long list of capital punishments for relatively minor offenses, "instead of diminishing, increases the number of offenders. The injured through compassion, will often forbear to prosecute; juries, through compassion, will often forget their oaths . . . , and judges, through compassion, will respite one half of the convicts." The penitentiary could remedy this defect in the law. Blackstone's measured language, backed by his universally respected authority, spoke to Southern lawyers in a way mere reform tracts never could.[44]

Southern legislators, governors, and newspaper editors were representative of the most cosmopolitan elements of their society. They shared many of the values and concerns of the outside world, and they were aware that the rest of the Anglo-American world increasingly looked upon their slave South as a throwback to a part of a common past best forgotten. This may help account for the frequency with which the dualism of "barbarism" and "civilization" recurs in Southern pleas for the penitentiary. "It is notorious that throughout this country and perhaps the civilized world," one proponent of the penitentiary observed, "there is a growing opposition to the infliction of the punishment of death." Virginia officials argued that the penitentiary represented nothing less than "one of the distinct lines of separation between a barbarous and an enlightened age." It seems no accident that cosmopolitan planters and lawyers, disappointed by the inefficiency of justice in their own neighborhoods, turned to the penitentiary as the "civilized" solution to the problem.[15]

As the referendum in North Carolina suggested, support for the penitentiary resided in relatively small groups within each county around the state. Sometimes the group of supporters made up no more than 3 percent of the voters in a county, and seldom more than 30 percent. There are reasons to suspect that the educated and propertied elite made up most of this minority in each county. Grand juries, drawn from the most "respectable" citizens of each county, repeatedly petitioned for penitentiaries in states where they did not exist. In South Carolina, for example, eighty-two grand juries made such pleas between 1846 and 1857. Virtually every Southern newspaper editor who made his opinion known—even those from remote rural counties—also spoke in favor of penitentiaries. In fact, the repeated calls for penitentiaries by prominent people have led earlier students of the institution in the South to conclude that "the people" wanted penitentiaries while stingy legislators thwarted their desires. In fact, the situation seems to have been the opposite. As letters and legislative votes revealed, some influential men did oppose the penitentiary—perhaps in an effort to maintain their local and personal power, or from a desire to keep their offices, or from convictions they shared with their constituents that the penitentiary was simply unnecessary in the slave South. And yet sufficient numbers of the powerful favored the institution to bring it to life in most Southern states despite strong and widespread opposition.[16]

One group of educated and influential Southerners, however, was conspicuous for its lack of support for the Southern penitentiary— the ministers of evangelical Christian churches. Individual ministers called for penal reform and visited the penitentiaries and others served as chaplains in the prison, but from all indications Southern evangelicals as a group had little use for the penitentiary. One minister invoked the very language penitentiary advocates so often used—but to attack the penitentiary. William Plumer of Virginia denounced the institution as "the greatest monument of barbarism and cruelty" in America, "and the more likely to be perpetuated and be mischievous, because its friends evidently had very good intentions and were philanthropic in their feelings." Francis Lieber, a German refugee and reformer living in South Carolina, was filled with despair when he wrote to Dorothea Dix in 1851 that, despite his best efforts, he had "not yet been able to interest one solitary minister in the cause of prison discipline or penal law reform." Southern ministers particularly distrusted the attempt of penal reformers to do away with the death penalty in favor of the penitentiary. The *Watchman of the South* declared that "the express law of God that 'whoso sheddeth man's blood, by man shall his blood be shed' stands unrepealed on the statute book of the only infallible Lawgiver." Whatever the other purposes of punishment, thundered the *Southern Presbyterian Review* in 1847, "the PRIMARY AND CHIEF END OF PUNISHMENT IS TO VINDICATE THE RIGHT," and the right could be vindicated only by an eye for an eye. The contest over the justice of capital punishment therefore raged "between atheism and theism,— between infidelity and inspiration,—between the Bible and the books of men,—between the wisdom of God and the wisdom of man."[47]

Christianity obviously meant something different to these Southern ministers from what it did to John Howard and American Quakers. Although the penitentiary depended upon religion as the primary agency of moral reform, Southern ministers perceived the institution as a threat to the rule of God's law. Southern evangelicalism put the individual at the heart of its concern. Religion should put people right with God, Southerners believed, not tamper with society. If society could be improved by saving two men from dueling, or by turning a husband away from the bottle, or by converting a slave to Christianity, so much the better. But organized attempts by religious people, much less the state, to disrupt the apparently ordained secular order won little enthusiasm from most evangelical Southerners. The Bible dealt specifically with punishment, and the Bible's punishment was swift, severe, and bloody. The Bible never mentioned a penitentiary.[48]

Advocates of the Southern penitentiary found themselves attacked not only by evangelicals who used the Old Testament as a benchmark, but also by worldly men who saw the penitentiary as an unnecessary intrusion in honorable conflict. As Governor Hugh McVay of Alabama complained in the 1830s, "a strange objection sometimes made to the penitentiary system is this: that the degradation of confinement in a penitentiary is too extreme to connect with offenses which honorable and high-minded men are liable in their frailty of human nature to commit. This objection comes, in general, from such as think it more high minded to decide their own quarrels with the Bowie knife and pistol, then to inculcate and practice respect to civil authority, and obedience to the laws." A correspondent to a Mobile newspaper urged the penitentiary precisely as an antidote to honor, "the spirit of revenge." The law should exist to "establish a confidence in the security of life and property," he urged, but "the dirks and pistols which attend us in the social circle—in the exercise of our daily avocations—and even in our solemn assemblies of devotion" reveal the law's failure. These scenes "speak in a language not to be misunderstood. They tell us in words of truth and power, that there is something wrong in our system." A "*change* is required," and that change must be the penitentiary.[49]

Most Southerners, it seems fair to say, did not oppose the penitentiary only because it contravened a consciously held allegiance to honor. But the same attitudes that perpetuated honor—distrust of the state in any of its forms and a conviction that directly aggrieved parties could best deal with their own problems—also undermined the penitentiary. The penitentiary seemed an undeniable agent of progress if one trusted an impersonal state to mete out

truly blind justice, and powerful men did trust such a state, for they
or men like themselves would control it. Other Southerners,
common men with no power other than their own votes, sought to
keep as much control as possible in their own hands and in the
hands of people whom they knew and could watch. They had no use
for a penitentiary and voted against it when they could. Nevertheless,
enough legislators sought to counterpoise the rationalizing power of
an impersonal state against a personalized local justice to create
penitentiary after penitentiary in the antebellum South. In this sense,
the penitentiary constituted an undemocratic institution.

But why, then, did South Carolina—generally recognized as the
least democratic state—not build a penitentiary? Support for the
institution surfaced there throughout the antebellum period,
enough support to convince one historian of "a general desire on the
part of the people" for a penitentiary. Editorials, letters, and
petitions urged the reform in the same rhetoric that appeared in
other states. The most visible penal reformer living in the South,
Francis Lieber, made his home in South Carolina. Lieber prepared
the English translation of Beaumont and Tocqueville's book on
American prisons and actively agitated for a penitentiary in his
adopted state. But Lieber met constant frustration, as did editor,
penitentiary proponent, and future governor Benjamin F. Perry.
Following the defeat in 1849 of yet another of the bills put forward
almost annually to establish a penitentiary in South Carolina, Perry
explained the failure of his state to join the rest of the nation in the
reform: "Our quarrel with the general government for the last
twenty years has absorbed all our thoughts and energies, until we are
about twenty years behind our sister States in everything else. . . . I
am surprised such a people should be in favor of Rail Roads—they
ought to stick to the old fashioned road wagon."[50]

South Carolina was the most conservative state in the Union
throughout the antebellum era. Following the Nullification Crisis of
1828–32, which preoccupied South Carolina in exactly the years
when so many other Southern states adopted penitentiaries, leaders
within South Carolina began to do what their counterparts in other
Southern states did not: define themselves in conscious opposition
to the values of "progress." South Carolina remained isolated from
the formal political democratization that swept the Jacksonian
South, an extremely conservative legislature appointed the
governor, and no two-party system battled over penal reform or
other issues.[51] It was not merely power that generated penitentiaries,

in other words, but power exercised through an ideology that found it necessary to rationalize and depersonalize power. South Carolina's leaders, like most Southerners, placed their faith in a profoundly localistic republicanism in which personality, honor, and precedent were more important than institutions. This faith did not call for a penitentiary. Southern leaders in other states, though, tried to mediate between locality and state, state and nation. These leaders were acutely aware of the changes in the rest of the Anglo-American world, and saw no reason why the republican South should not use the penitentiary to help maintain its free government. And the penitentiary became a Southern institution, however tenuous its base.

Once established, Southern penitentiaries took on a life of their own. Each Southern state experienced a complex history of penal innovation and stagnation, efficient and inefficient wardens, relative prosperity and poverty, fires, escapes, and legislative attack. Despite the roles played in each institution's history by particular individuals and luck, however, Southern penitentiaries followed a common path, albeit one strewn with obstacles.

As Beaumont and Tocqueville observed, in the penitentiary "the order of one day is that of the whole year." Southern prisons were no exception. At dawn a trumpet awakened each numbered convict; when the trumpet sounded again all doors opened at once, the prisoner stepped out and instantly shut his door behind him. Taking one step toward the central yard, each prisoner waited with his night and water buckets in his hands until ordered by the turnkey to empty them. Prisoners marched to their workbenches, where they labored silently, until signaled to march to breakfast, where they ate silently. The rest of the day's labor was broken only by two other brief meals, also in silence. The convicts worked from dawn to dark six days a week. On Sunday they might gather for a sermon and might get a chance to walk in the prison yard and chew the tobacco they had earned by their good behavior.[52]

Such discipline may have been the ideal, but prisoners continually subverted it—as they have in all prisons. Inmates at the Missouri penitentiary fashioned "dirk-knives" and were made to wear iron collars as punishment for fighting among themselves. Conversation, though forbidden, frequently punctuated the silence of the penitentiary. The Sabbath, designated a day of introspection and penitence by officials, served other purposes for the prisoners. After the mandatory sermon in the Maryland penitentiary, the prisoners' "songs of obscenity and mirth, or their curses and imprecations, resound from their gloomy walls, and the truth, which has been dispersed, is . . . like sparks on the ocean in a storm." Inmate arsonists perennially put the torch to Southern penitentiaries, and burned several to the ground. About forty of Mississippi's prisoners revolted in the state's model textile prison factory in 1860. Wielding loom-weights and other makeshift weapons, they attempted to knock a guard from his position on the prison wall. The guards opened fire, killing one convict and wounding six of the ten who reached the prison's outside gate. Fifty prisoners escaped from Missouri's penitentiary between February 1843 and November 1844; none was recaptured.[53]

The burden of reforming the character of the inmates fell upon the shoulders of underpaid chaplains, just as it did in virtually all penitentiaries in America and Europe. A chaplain appointed by the Tennessee legislature found that prisoners eagerly listened to the word of God, "hitherto to most of them a sealed book"; he baptized fifteen within the year. The Reverend Jesse Lee of Richmond preached to his state's convicts with even greater effect: "Prayer was attended to by them, in their rooms; and they were frequently engaged in singing psalms, hymns, and spiritual songs, as well as praying, until the whole circular building was made to resound with the high praises of God." Over thirty inmates professed conversion. In Mississippi, a chaplain pleaded with the legislature to remember that the criminal "should be viewed with an eye of compassion, and if we can reclaim him to virtue and to God, it is worth all the trouble and expense this may put us to." That expense was little enough: as Alabama's penitentiary inspectors disgustedly reported in 1852, "with the exception of 170 copies of small, badly printed Bibles, each copy costing when purchased about 20 cents, not a dime has ever been expended by authority of the Legislature in furnishing the miserable inmates of the Penitentiary with Knowledge or the means of reformation of any kind, either religiously or morally."[54]

Given such conditions, even chaplains did not long maintain their guarded optimism. The chaplain in Tennessee in 1858 could say that, unless dramatic changes were made, "the History of Penitentiaries forbids us to hope, that they will ever become schools of reform for the unfortunate, the ignorant and the vicious, their tendency being rather to render vice inveterate and crime contagious, by associating the depraved together in masses—the combustible element thus becoming more explosive by contact and compression." In Mississippi in 1860 a chaplain wrote despairingly, "I find that the men generally are more anxious concerning their release from confinement than their deliverance from the bondage of sin." The Virginia superintendant laconically remarked, "Divine service has been continued throughout the year, with about the usual effect upon the morals of the inmates." On the eve of the Civil War, the physician of the Kentucky penitentiary matter-of-factly noted that "there are now few men who believe a convict can be reformed."[55]

Such doubts developed partly because of the kinds of prisoners who soon filled the penitentiaries. Poor and alien white men constituted the majority of antebellum America's prisoners, North and South. The kinds of Southern white men who went to the penitentiary and the routes they followed to arrive there will be explored in the next two chapters. For now, however, it is important to see only that most of these prisoners were white and that virtually all black prisoners had been free men before they were incarcerated: slaves seldom appeared on the rolls of Southern prisons. Aside from the obvious financial considerations (which, after all, did not prevent the execution of valuable slaves who might have been put to work for the state), penitentiaries in a republican society simply were not for slaves. Slaves had no rights to respect, no civic virtue or character to restore, no freedom to abridge. As Thomas R. R. Cobb, an expert on the law of slavery, put it, the slave "can be reached only through his body." After 1818, only Louisiana consistently admitted slaves to its prison as an alternative to hanging.[56]

Although Southern penitentiaries had little to do with slaves, free blacks posed difficult problems for several of the institutions. The penitentiaries in the states of the lower South contained virtually no free black inmates; in the 1850s free blacks constituted only 1 percent of Alabama's and Mississippi's prison populations, and Georgia's penitentiary contained no blacks at all. Free blacks made up about 4 percent of Tennessee's prison population, about 8 percent of Kentucky's. But in the upper seaboard South a dramatically different picture emerges: over a third of Virginia's and over half of Maryland's inmates were free blacks.[57]

Such a condition caused distress among those responsible for these penitentiaries. "Although the free white persons usually confined to the penitentiary are for the most part from the lowest part of society," reported a Virginia committee in 1822, "yet the free

Negroes and mulattoes are a grade or so below them, and should not be associated with them." In the year after this pronouncement, Virginia lawmakers decided to embark upon an experiment: they would sell into slavery free blacks convicted of "serious" crimes. The law stayed in operation for four years, but was abandoned after it proved to be "more in conflict with public feeling and sentiment, than it is common for the acts of our Legislature to be." Nevertheless, forty-four free blacks were sold into slavery before Virginians decided that the law was "incompatible with every principle of morality and justice, and directly repugnant to the just, humane, and liberal policy of Virginia."[58]

For the three and a half decades of slavery that followed this brief experiment, Virginia and Maryland continued to wrestle with the problem of free blacks accused of breaking the law. Blacks' presence in the penitentiary seemed to destroy whatever reformatory effect the institution might exert on either race, prison officials felt, for it destroyed white men's feelings of pride while dangerously inflating that of the blacks. In 1849 Virginia's governor complained that "uniting black and white in one common association" in the penitentiary "can be productive of nothing else but mischief: it necessarily makes the negro insolent, and debases the white man: it is offensive to our habits and prejudices as well as to our feelings and policy, and ought to be discontinued." The eventual solution to the "problem," finally arrived at in 1858, was to lease free blacks to work outside the prison walls on canals, roads, and bridges.[59]

Perhaps not coincidentally, in the same year that Virginia retreated from the enslavement of free black criminals Governor Giles found something "so extraordinary in itself and so honorable to the white female population of this State" that he wanted it known "to the whole civilized world. It is, that for the last four years, but one white woman has been convicted of a Penitentiary offense." Virtually any Southern state in any year of the antebellum era could have made a similar boast; seldom could more than one or two women be found in a Southern penitentiary. When the inspectors of the Alabama penitentiary did find themselves confronted with a woman criminal, the officials sighed that they "had entertained the hope that there was not a female in Alabama, so destitute of virtue and honor as to commit an act sufficiently heinous as to justify the courts of the country committing one to the Penitentiary. But such seems not to be the good fortune of Alabama." The officers of the Mississippi penitentiary, relieved of the particularly "rude and ignominious" task of shaving the heads of female prisoners, received the understanding of legislators for their "natural and praiseworthy repugnance" to fulfill this rule of the prison.[60]

But despite the privilege of keeping their hair, women in Southern penitentiaries generally suffered more than their male counterparts. Since no cells had been built for them, women often languished in small, dirty, and unventilated buildings within the penitentiary walls. Not surprisingly, sexual abuse created the worst terror of their imprisonment. As a Georgia legislative committee delicately described the problem in 1845, "unless female convicts are placed in solitary confinement, there would be a class of persons soon springing not contemplated in any provisions made for the Institution, and under circumstances abhorrent to every feeling of humanity." Calling for reasonable facilities for women prisoners in Missouri in 1858, the governor argued that "the ends of justice do not certainly require that the weaker, who are often the victim of the sterner sex, and by them betrayed into the paths of vice and crime, shall thus be wholly sacrificed upon the altar of our penal code." But women convicts seemed too few and too depraved for anyone to concern himself with their plight. The best that officials could hope for was a pardon from the governor, and indeed women were often released early at the governor's command.[61]

They were not the only ones. Southern governors found themselves almost incessantly called upon to pardon inmates from the penitentiary or the gallows. Indeed, the largest part of their correspondence consists of requests for pardon. As Governor Herschel V. Johnson of Georgia wrote in the front of his "Pardon Docket" book in 1854, "The Executive is charged with no duty more embarrassing and delicate than that of deciding upon petitions for Pardon. In most cases, the application is sustained, not only by a long list of signers, but by the streaming tears of the heart broken wife or mother. To resist such appeals, requires a firmness of nerve, bordering upon stoicism." Later, in the notes Johnson recorded for each pardon, he reveals the agonies of indecision. There could be no doubt of one particular criminal's guilt, but "the tears of a grandmother . . . awaken my deep sorrow; if I dare pardon as a mere matter of mercy, it would afford me heartfelt pleasure to do so. But I must not. I must adhere to principles." In the next three years Governor Johnson received 213 petitions for pardon. He refused only 49 of them. Of those he granted, 52 merely released prisoners two or three days earlier than their sentence decreed in order to

restore the inmate's right to vote. Another 11 received pardons due
to their poor health, and 2 women were released because there was
no place for them in the penitentiary. The rest the governor
pardoned for a variety of reasons: insufficient evidence of their guilt,
good conduct while in prison, old age or extreme youth, or because
they came from good families and could be expected to reform.[62]

Petitioners asked governors to pardon because the inmate had
killed in the heat of passion, or under the influence of alcohol, or
under the influence of someone older or stronger. Southerners had
great respect for hot blood and human foibles, and expected their
governors to share that respect. But requests for pardon were
sometimes followed by petitions imploring the governor *not* to
pardon. One letter from Mississippi declared that a petition was
being signed by "boys, strangers and persons not resident of this
county and entirely ignorant of the facts." Another letter warned that
a "desperado" who had "committed several crimes of the most
inhuman character" was making an effort "to obtain his pardon and
people would fear not to sign his petition for fear of being killed by
him." Despite such pleas, governors generally listened to what
appeared to be community sentiment and pardoned most inmates
on whose behalf strong efforts were made. Besides, every prisoner
pardoned was one less prisoner the state had to feed. Such financial
concerns were never far from the minds of state officials where the
penitentiary was involved.[63]

Perhaps because so many of their constituents remained skeptical
about the penitentiary, legislators showed little patience when a
prison failed to pay its own way. Defenders of the institution argued
in vain that the penitentiary merely *appeared* expensive, that it
actually cost much less than the maintenance of criminals in each
county's antiquated jails. But, one reformer sarcastically noted, the
extra money spent to lock up criminals in local jails paid for "the
satisfaction of having a number of able bodied fellows wrapped up in
blankets and coiled down in the corners of dark, loathsome
dungeons, where they are deprived of all the means by which they
could benefit themselves, their families, or the community at large."
If housed in a penitentiary instead, these men could be kept hard at
work, helping to pay for their punishment and perhaps aiding the
state's treasury as well.[64]

A not inconsiderable amount of money might be made simply by
allowing paying visitors to see the convicts. In 1827, Virginia officials
complained of the number of visitors, who were not yet required to

pay: "The feelings of some of the convicts are harrowed up by being the objects of idle curiosity; to bear the sneers and frowns of thoughtless and giddy visitants; to hear their remarks, 'what is this,' or 'that man sent for.'" The superintendent of the prison pointed out that the Auburn penitentiary in New York had made $1,182.75 from admittance fees in an attempt to cut down the number of visitors, and thought Virginia might try this system, too. "Men, seeking irrational amusement in the misery of their fellow creatures, and those of wanton curiosity, ought to, and might be, excluded by fees," while visitors of noble motives would not mind paying. Twelve years later the Tennessee penitentiary considered "the propriety of exacting a moderate toll from all such visitors, and that [the money raised go to] the more indigent families of the convicts, or to such other charitable object as the wisdom and benevolence of the Legislature may prescribe."[65]

But the penitentiary offered greater financial opportunities than mere visitation fees. Whatever sway the Protestant work ethic may have exerted in the South in general, there is no question that regular labor was held up as a wholly beneficial—indeed, crucial—influence on Southern criminals. As in France and England, New York and Pennsylvania, work—rather than education or religion—lay at the heart of the penitentiary's day-to-day life. As a Georgia governor noted, "The habit of idleness and improper associations produce most of the offenses against society. It is therefore, that constant compulsory labor and entire seclusion from intercourse with others, is the most dreadful as well as the most effectual punishment."[66]

Lawmakers faced the quandary that penitentiaries could most easily and most profitably produce simple goods in steady demand, such as slave shoes, wagons, pails, bricks, and so on, but that such production undermined the livelihood of local free workers. Town and city workers fought bitterly against penitentiary labor. Although these workmen attacked the penitentiary in the familiar language of republicanism, their rhetoric often sounded far more like the equal rights demands of Northern workers—who also criticized the institution for decades and even rioted against its unjust competition—than like that of either cosmopolitan or localistic rural Southern republicans. "Is it right for a sovereign State to establish within her bounds a grand mechanical shop, that comes in *immediate* competition with the trades of its own citizens and subjects?" a letter from Alabama asked. "If it is, it is contrary to all rules of right and justice that we were ever taught; contrary to a genuine spirit of republicanism, and in opposition to the professed democratic doctrine, *the overthrow of all monopolies*." A Georgia newspaper conjured up an industrial nightmare for the individual artisan: the state was "carrying on through the aid of steam power and the labor of one hundred and fifty convicts, a vast amount of productive industry, which has inundated the country with its imperfect or worthless products and expelled from its vicinity, every mechanic who has attempted the competition." Worse, this monopoly was not obtained by "fair competition, but by taxing the people from ten to fifteen thousand dollars a year."[67]

Tennessee Governor Andrew Johnson, who began his adult life as a tailor and who retained his identification with artisans throughout his political career, waged war on the state penitentiary, which he sarcastically dubbed the *State Mechanic Institute*." According to Johnson, the admission standards to the Institute were high: the candidate must first commit a worthy crime and then obtain a certificate from a judge verifying that he had in fact accomplished the deed. As the lucky man began his ceremonial trip to the Institute, accompanied by no less a personage than the sheriff, all the spectators at the court house could observe "that the prisoner had done well in obtaining a traveling trip of pleasure and a money-making business for the sheriff and his escort, and he in the end to be made one of the mechanics of the country." Similarly, Georgia workers complained that their state penitentiary annually released "a corps of graduated villains, half skilled and too depraved, in most instances, to perform according to their ability, who will work at reduced prices." A public letter addressed to "Brother Mechanics of Georgia" implored all workmen to "determine our rights shall be respected as well as others', and that we will, regardless of party, cast our votes for no man who will not go for an entire change in the internal policy of the Penitentiary, and as speedily as possible abolish the present system entirely."[68]

Such demands compelled Southern lawmakers to experiment, sometimes successfully, with prison industry. Convicts in Georgia built 371 cars for the state-owned Western and Atlantic Railroad in the 1850s, clearing credits of over $85,000 for the penitentiary on the state's books. Mississippi logged an even more impressive record. After artisans demanded that Mississippi cease producing hand-crafted goods in its penitentiary, the state built a prison cotton factory in 1849. The enterprise grew throughout the next decade until it claimed 2,304 spindles, 24 cotton carding machines, 76 looms, and 4 mills. It marketed its goods in St. Louis, Mobile, and New Orleans, and produced a yearly profit of $20,000. The cotton bagging and coarse cloth manufactured in the Mississippi penitentiary, boasted the institution's inspectors, replaced that from the North for which planters had paid "an annual tribute of thousands of dollars." In 1851 Alabama legislators proclaimed their penitentiary a resource to help Southerners declare themselves "independent of all other sections, and particularly of that section that are waring [sic] upon our institutions." Because of the large steam engines within its walls, the Alabama penitentiary could easily become "one of the most extensive cotton factories . . . in the Southern country." In fact, some foresaw that penitentiary inmates might soon be put to mining iron ore and thus spur the South to industrial self-sufficiency; men with capital to invest would see the possibilities and major industry could begin in the region.[69]

But such rhetoric and the success of a few states are misleading. Most antebellum penitentiaries, North and South, seldom turned consistent profits and pleaded for appropriation after appropriation. Sickened at being forced to spend money on convicted felons, Virginia, Georgia, and Tennessee toyed with the idea of leasing their penitentiaries to businessmen in the late 1850s. Virginia compromised in 1858 by leasing only free black convicts to railroad and canal companies; the governor was so pleased with the results, however, he suggested extending it to white prisoners, too. Tennessee lawmakers rejected the lease, even though the state comptroller complained that the penitentiary "had been a vampire upon the public Treasury" since its inception—the institution cost the state an average of $15,000 a year throughout the antebellum era.[70]

In Georgia, the average annual cost was only $11,000, and as one newspaper put it, "This is after all, but a small sum for so large a State as Georgia to pay for the protection of her citizens from the vicious and depraved." Nevertheless, politicians seemed to love attacking the institution "in a pecuniary point of view," characterizing any favorable financial report as "shrouded in Egyptian darkness." In 1858, after no more orders for railroad cars appeared in Georgia, some legislators tried to move the penitentiary from the state capital in the small town of Milledgeville to Stone Mountain near Atlanta, where convicts could quarry rock. Unfortunately Georgians, still in the "log-cabin stage of civilization," did not use much stone, whereas with only ten years of labor at Stone Mountain,

Georgia's convicts could quarry "a sufficient quantity of material to
build the Pyramids of Egypt." One lawmaker facetiously suggested
that "the best use that could be made of the convicts would be to
take them to the Okefenokee Swamp, and let them drain it." A
Milledgeville paper later suggested that the penitentiary be burned
down, "and try what whipping, branding and hanging will do to
diminish crime in the State"—that is, if the inmates could not be
rented to some enterprising businessmen.[71]

The Georgia newspapers cited Alabama, Texas, and Kentucky as
examples of states which allowed a private citizen to incur the
financial risks and reap the financial rewards of the penitentiary, and
they might have added Missouri and Louisiana. Kentucky had leased
its penitentiary to a private businessman since 1828 and had not
suffered. In fact, the lessee, Joel Scott, appears to have been no worse
that most state-employed wardens, and national prison reform
societies thought well of him. The Missouri lessees, on the other
hand, worked the prisoners outside the prison walls under brutal
conditions and allowed many to escape. The inspectors of the
penitentiary admitted their doubt that a single convict left the
Missouri institution "without being a more abandoned man in his
moral feeling than when he entered prison." Texas, explicitly
copying Mississippi, built its penitentiary as a textile factory and
reaped large profits through leasing. Louisiana legislators invested
over $450,000 in a penitentiary between 1830 and 1844, and finally
decided they had spent enough. They leased the penitentiary.[72]

Alabama, after spending over $100,000 in the first four years of its
penitentiary, saw the institution burn down in 1844. After rebuilding
it, Alabama contracted the labor of its convicts, despite strong
opposition, but dictated that the warden retain control over and
responsibility for the inmates. In this regard it resembled many
Northern prisons, which allowed outside contractors to buy the
labor of the convicts within the penitentiary. After two years of
leasing, the Alabama penitentiary's board of inspectors bitterly
attacked the practice of "selling out so many human souls," and
absolved themselves from responsibility. They feared for the odium
and "many bitter reflections" cast upon Alabama for leasing its
convicts, a practice which undermined a fundamental principle of a
republican institution: the restoration of the prisoner's sense of
obligation to a just society. The lessee would naturally try to lengthen
the sentences of valuable workers by giving them bad reports; the
lessee would naturally spend as little and extract as much as possible.

Time-consuming reflection and moral teaching were out of the question. The result "holds up to view the relation which exists between master and slave in its plainest form."[73]

Georgia legislators decided against the lease because, as one newspaper explained, "it cannot be expected that the all pervading interest of self-interest would be less predominant in the Lessee than in others, and that it is not natural that he should sacrifice his own interests in experiments and projects for the moral reform of convicts." In an ironic foreshadowing of the tragic postbellum penal history of the South, a correspondent during the debate over the penitentiary in North Carolina warned that although "Yankee ingenuity" had discovered that the penitentiary could make crime pay to the state, that temptation must be avoided in the South: "The community should never derive benefit from crimes, because that makes it directly interested in their continuance and increase." In the absence of a penitentiary, North Carolina jurors often failed to convict the guilty, it was true, because the "conviction would impose a burthen upon the community, including themselves." But if a convicted felon could be shipped off to a distant penitentiary while an acquitted lawbreaker could remain in the community, the accused might well be convicted "upon too slight grounds—a more deplorable evil." Financial incentives would undermine justice by making crime pay to the state.[74]

Critics also charged that the penitentiary was a dangerously unrepublican institution because it hid the coercion of the state from its citizens. Jurors supposedly acquitted so frequently because they were too "fastidious" about the corporal punishment criminals received when no penitentiary waited to lock them up. But, North Carolina's Sylvanus asked, "what would the public think of the punishments *within* the penitentiary, were they not hidden from public gaze by high walls?" A Georgia legislator asked the same question: "which was the more barbarous, to whip at the whipping post, or to turn them over a barrel within the walls of the Penitentiary and paddle them?" A missionary imprisoned in the Missouri penitentiary in the 1840s for his aid to Indians in defiance of the law provided a more graphic description of the punishment that awaited inmates. "The guards for the most part were wicked, profane, dissolute men, and *these* were the men placed over others to *reform* them. . . . For trifles, and often for nothing, men were called up, and received ten, twenty, thirty, forty, fifty, one hundred, or more strokes, with the strap or paddle." The thick leather strap "did not break the skin, but bruised and mashed it till it turned black and blue"; every one of the holes bored in the paddle "would raise a blood-blister."[75]

The inspectors of the Alabama penitentiary reluctantly defended the punishments they found in use by the lessees: straitjackets, solitary confinement, bread and water, the gradual immersion of the head in ice-cold water, and, in extreme cases, the lash. "Immaterial how degraded a convict may be, how deep he may be imbued in crime, being placed under the lash is the most degrading of all imaginable positions." Some outsiders might oppose such physical punishment, the inspectors admitted, but the time when corporal punishment could be dispensed with "is as remote as the time promised in the Scriptures, when the 'Lion and the Lamb shall lie down together.'" But when that time of peace arrived, "we shall have no Penitentiaries, or if any, we can find none of the human race liable to be incarcerated in them." Punishment, until the millennium at least, "is indispensably necessary in every well regulated Penitentiary."[76]

Accounts of the barbarity within Southern prisons can be misleading if they suggest that Southern institutions were worse than most of their Northern counterparts, for in virtually every facet of their antebellum history the penitentiaries of North and South were far more similar than different. In 1850, for example, 5.8 percent of the nation's inmates died, with the highest death rates recorded in Ohio and at Sing Sing; the average Southern figure was 5.5 percent. In that same year, 7.6 percent of the national prison population received pardons, while 11 percent of Southern inmates went free ahead of schedule. Auburn and Ohio returned the highest profits to their states' treasuries of all American penitentiaries. Southerners did not stand alone in their lack of faith in reformation, or in their brutal physical punishment of recalcitrant inmates, or in the poor food given prisoners, or in their preoccupation with a financial return, or in the role political patronage played in prison administration, or in low appropriations for religious or educational reform, or in their willingness to let contractors or lessees assume real control of prisons. The major difference between penitentiaries in the South and the rest of America before the Civil War lay only in the ambitious dreams and rhetoric of Northern reformers. When, in the 1830s, Tocqueville asked the keeper of the blacksmith shop at New York's Utica prison, "Do you think there are many prisoners who mend their ways?" the official answered bluntly, "I am talking to you as a man who wants to know the truth. What the books say about the extent of reform is a fiction. I am certain no one here does." Tocqueville's subsequent research proved the New York official's convictions to be the rule in Northern prisons. The Northern public, too, despite the visibility and vitality of a wide range of reform organizations, apparently displayed little tolerance for criminals. Northerners as well as Southerners resisted the environmentalist conception of human nature reformers preached—at least when it came to crime. Most Americans, North and South, then as now, ultimately blamed criminals for their crimes and did not expect them to change their ways after a term in the state penitentiary.[77]

Northern and Southern governments built penitentiaries for the same reasons: legislators who shared the conscious and unconscious assumptions, hopes, and fears of republicanism wanted to abolish public physical punishment, segregate and confine criminals, and perhaps return a few to society without permanent damage. In the process, the law could be honed into a sharper and more precise instrument, and the cost of criminals' punishment could be reduced. By means of the penitentiary, the state government could exert a unifying, stabilizing influence throughout a diverse patchwork of unpredictable local governments. The penitentiary, historians too often forget, functioned, first and last, as an agent of the state, lived only because the state called it into existence. Reformers did not create penitentiaries; the institution spread so rapidly because obscure state legislators, with reasons and goals of their own, perceived in the institution a natural outgrowth of republicanism. That republicanism simultaneously generated, as Tocqueville saw, a proud freedom and a powerful undertow of coercion. The penitentiary explicitly embodied both.

In other places in the world where the penitentiary appeared, an emerging capitalist ideology fused with republicanism to make the institution seem less obtrusive than it did to many people in the South. Republicanism and capitalism reinforced each other's emphasis on internalized values, the transforming power of labor, and the necessity of order and regularity.[78] These economic and political ideologies fused with evangelical Protestantism to foster the ideal of dignity as well as the penitentiary. Surrounded by other reforming institutions, by early manufactories, and by a relatively strong state, the penitentiaries of the North and Europe did not stand out so starkly, did not call so much attention to the centralized power behind them as did the penitentiaries of the South. As a result, no

penitentiaries elsewhere in the world witnessed as much opposition
as Southern institutions confronted. The penitentiary could live on
republicanism alone, as it did in the South, but as a result its roots
were shallow, and its life destined to be short. The South was
American enough to build penitentiaries, but Southern enough to
remain skeptical of its own handiwork.

3

The City

As the Civil War loomed, John Reilly sat in the Georgia penitentiary. If he looked out his grated window he could see the high brick walls surrounding the grounds of the prison. If he looked out the front of his cell, he could see across the corridor into a cell exactly like his own: eight feet high, eight feet long, six and a half feet wide. John Reilly sat in his cell in the small town of Milledgeville, the state capital, because he had been sent there from Savannah, the largest city in the state. In its February term of 1861, Savannah's Chatham County Superior Court had convicted Reilly of a serious offense— "larceny from the house"—and had sentenced him to four years in the penitentiary.[1]

Reilly, like nine-tenths of the people convicted by the court, had committed his crime alone and had been arrested alone.[2] Most likely, he had been caught either because the victim of his crime had suspected Reilly and directed the Savannah police towards him, or because the police had happened upon Reilly during or soon after the commission of the offense; the police solved few undetected crimes. After Reilly's arrest, one of the city's four magistrate's courts had bound him over to the Superior Court, where all defendants accused of a state offense were tried. While he waited for the Superior Court to meet, Reilly languished in the Savannah City Jail. The jail, a Superior Court grand jury complained, was in terrible condition, so bad that it was "inhuman and demoralizing to those whose crimes or misfortunes bring them within its portals." There could be no excuse for such a building. "A jail is intended as a place for safe keeping. Punishment belongs to the Penitentiary. With wonderful economy the Jail of Chatham County answers for both."[3]

The great majority of the people with Reilly in jail the first night were marched before the Mayor's Court early the next morning and given a cursory hearing. Most received a fine for their drunkenness or disorderly conduct; some paid the fine and were released, others returned to the jail because they had no money. Reilly and others accused of serious crimes had to wait in the jail until the next session of the Superior Court, and the wait was often months. In the interim, Reilly saw a steady stream of sailors and laborers, blacks and whites, Irishmen and Southerners, men and women, pass through the damp and crowded jail. He shared quarters there with the insane, with vagrants, and with debtors.[4]

When the Chatham County Superior Court that heard Reilly's case finally met, its first business was to call the grand jury. It was the job of this body, composed of respectable property holders, to decide whether the state possessed sufficient cause to send John Reilly and the other accused men before a petit jury, which in turn would decide their guilt or innocence. In the 1850s the grand juries of the two sessions of court evaluated the cases of an average of seventy-four people each year. About thirty-one of these people were accused of a violent crime, another fourteen of a property offense, another nine of a crime against the public order (resisting an officer, malicious mischief, keeping a disorderly house, or carrying concealed weapons), another six of forgery or counterfeiting, and the other fourteen of a broad array of offenses: bigamy, trading with slaves, or gambling.[5] Although the numbers of defendants increased along with the population, the proportion of the different categories of crime had been roughly the same in Chatham County since at least the 1830s.[6]

The grand jury found sufficient cause to proceed—"true bills"— for slightly more than one-quarter of those brought before it in the 1850s. Most of those passed on to the petit jury were, like John Reilly, white men; of 234 defendants in the final antebellum decade, there were only 4 slaves and 4 white women.[7] Only 23 percent of the 98 defendants who appeared in the 1850 or 1860 census had been born in Georgia, while another 16 percent came from other Southern states. Thirteen percent had migrated from Northern states, and a full 47 percent had emigrated from Europe. The largest single group—31 percent—had been born, like John Reilly, in Ireland.[8] These were working men, often unskilled, in their twenties or thirties. John Reilly, at age 45, was older than 80 percent of those successfully indicted by the Chatham County Superior Court; but like most of them Reilly was flat broke when the census taker visited his room at a boarding house.[9]

Of the 814 people who went before the grand jury in the 1850s, those accused, like John Reilly, of a property crime stood the greatest chance of all defendants of being sent to the penitentiary. The percentage of thieves and burglars passed on to the petit jury for trial was higher than for any other offenses. The dictates of the legal code and the concerns of the jury ensured that property crime was dealt with more harshly than violence or disorder.[10]

The numbers embodied in John Reilly help to explain surprising patterns repeated in every Southern state. Although the foreign-born made up less than 3 percent of the free population in most antebellum Southern states in the 1850s, they represented anywhere between 8 and 37 percent of the prison populations of the Southern states.[11] Although more than nine out of ten white Southerners lived on farms, a large proportion of the region's prisoners came from cities.[12] Although fewer than one out of five people convicted of a crime in Southern courts were thieves or burglars, a far higher percentage of Southern penitentiary inmates—about half—were in prison for crimes against property.[13] The familiar antebellum South of plantation and farm, neighbor and kin, master and slave, looks quite different when viewed from over the region's penitentiary walls. From that vantage point the cities of the South look much larger than they do on any map.

The cities that contributed so many inmates to the state penitentiaries have always seemed out of place in the Old South—not unlike the penitentiaries themselves. Yet, the South spawned a number of vital cities, each with a unique personality. Charleston seems the most "Southern," the most languorous and exotic. But Richmond thrived as an industrial center; Memphis and Atlanta were young, bustling, and rough; New Orleans and Mobile mixed cosmopolitan allure and shrewed cotton trading. Savannah, with its long past and sudden prosperity in the late antebellum period, combined the plantation elegance of Charleston with the business hustle of Memphis. The civic leaders of these cities were Southern born and

bred, and the urban newspapers took decidedly sectional stands on
political issues. Slaves labored on docks and in factories. The cities
were unmistakably part of their region.[14]

As even the leaders of these cities recognized, though, the rural
South looked upon its urban centers with a mixture of fascination
and suspicion. The cities' large immigrant populations, the cities'
adoption of values and customs alien to the rural South, the cities'
frank and absorbing interest in trade—all set them apart from the
rural South. So did the large numbers of penitentiary inmates who
came from Southern cities. The city, even more than the rest of the
region, felt the conflicting pull of the South and the world, of unique
and universal. Neither force could overwhelm the other, and neither
force would loosen its grip. If we are to understand why so many
John Reillys followed the road from Southern city to Southern
penitentiary, we must understand the effect of both forces on the
urban South.

The fundamental fact about Southern cities is that they stood at
the juncture of the slave South and the international market
economy. Southern cities, whatever else they offered, rose and fell
according to their ability to link their hinterland with New York or
London. The forces of the market largely determined the physical
shape of the city, the number and kinds of people who lived there,
and the work they performed. And, to a degree not usually
appreciated, the market played a crucial role in shaping the crimes
committed and punished in cities. The interaction of market
economy, Southern culture, republican state, and urban setting
accounts for the preponderance of men such as John Reilly in
Southern penitentiaries. A case study of Savannah, the city that sent
Reilly to prison, can help define the role played by each of the
elements that made up the Southern city.

Savannah in the 1850s offers several advantages for such a study.
In the final antebellum decade Savannah exhibited a rate of
population growth, an overall size, a relative proportion of immigrants, and a ratio of penitentiary prisoners to population typical of
many Southern cities. Savannah was neither the newest nor the
oldest, the largest nor the smallest, the most nor least cosmopolitan,
the richest nor poorest of Southern cities. Savannah also preserved
valuable records of crime and punishment, as well as extensive
newspaper files and city documents. Most important, every important issue of crime and punishment that concerned cities in the
antebellum South surfaced in Savannah in the 1850s.[15]

In many ways, the Savannah of the final antebellum decade was, like most Southern cities of the period, a new city superimposed upon an old. James Oglethorpe established the first settlement in 1733 by carving a perfectly symmetrical pattern of streets and squares out of the virgin pine forests of the Georgia coast. But the town did not flourish, and as late as 1830 only 7,000 people lived in Savannah. In the 1840s, however, Georgia completed and expanded its Central Railroad system, and Savannah benefited immediately. "Take a stroll, reader, along our wharves," invited the Savannah *Republican* in 1854, "and notice our fine marine of 1 steamship, 15 ships, 16 barques, 5 brigs, 6 schooners, and many steamboats, and notice the bustle it is creating among sailors, stevedores, laborers, and others engaged in their various duties; clerks employed in receiving and shipping immense freights, and draymen loading and unloading their vehicles—all vigorously bending to work—and ask yourself if business has commenced." There could be no doubt that Savannah had become a thriving commercial center; by 1860 it was the third largest American cotton port, and its $18 million worth of exports in that year placed Savannah above Boston and San Francisco.[16]

The boom economy of the 1850s brought flush times to Southern cities, and Savannah residents with money to invest in railroad stock and mercantile interests did very well for themselves. But prosperity also brought an internal reordering of cities not always welcome to their more established citizens. For more than two decades before the completion of the Central Railroad, for example, Savannah had not added a single new ward to its area. But in the twenty years after the rail line began to bring cotton into the Georgia port, the number of wards nearly doubled. Not only did "splendid stores and tasteful dwellings rise with a rapidity heretofore unknown amongst us," but the city began to spread beyond its old rectangular confines. Building could not keep pace with the growth of Savannah's population, and rents more than doubled in the early 1850s as businesses and newcomers vied for city space. Savannah's population increased 45 percent in the final antebellum decade, and stood at over 22,000 in 1860. Two-thirds of the increase in the white population in the 1850s came from foreign-born immigrants and their children; by 1860 immigrants comprised half of Savannah's white population. The black population grew only modestly through the antebellum period, but still, at nearly 8,000 people, made up more than a third of the city's population in 1860. Despite its small size, Savannah, like many other Southern cities, contained as much ethnic diversity as the largest Northern metropolis.[17]

A relatively small number of families held a disproportionate share of all forms of wealth in Savannah, just as they did in the rest of urban America; in Savannah, about 6 percent of the population owned over 90 percent of the city's real estate. As in virtually all mid-nineteenth-century American cities, the wealthiest residents dominated the center of the Georgia city. Most of these wealthy families, the accompanying map of Savannah shows, clustered along several streets convenient to their businesses and professional offices. In an era before streetcars, proximity to one's work was of critical importance—especially in Savannah, a city notorious for its attractive but impractical sand streets.[18]

The wealthiest Savannah families lived in the center of town, too, because they sought neighbors with whom they could feel comfortable, but convenience and quiet comfort did not always go hand in

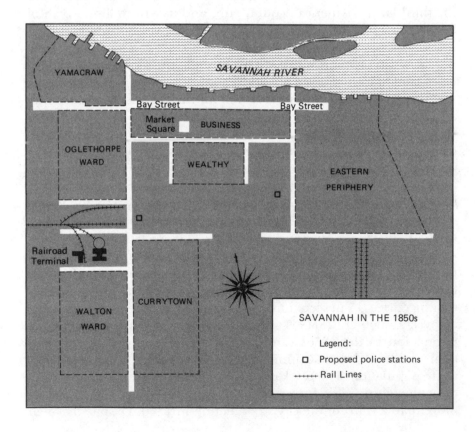

hand. In the late antebellum period, the central city came to seem congested, crowded with unwelcome faces and bodies. Only a few blocks from Savannah's most fashionable neighborhood lay Bay Street, where "most of the business in the city is transacted. No respectable families reside there. The buildings on this street are mostly stores, besides a few dwellings for colored people and sailors' boarding houses," Emily Burke, a visiting New England school-teacher explained. "This street is always so thronged by sailors, slaves and rowdies of all grades and color that it is not safe for ladies to walk there alone, and it is considered very disreputable for them to be seen there unaccompanied by a gentleman, even if several ladies are together." One Savannah resident vividly remembered a common city scene from his childhood in the 1850s: drunken sailors. "The most disgusting sight to me was to see these men in numbers lying in the squares nearest the waterfront in a state of insobriety—some too far gone to be noisy, others in a hilarious condition; all of them acting more like swine than human beings." Savannah's wealthiest people thus found themselves cut off from the riverside by the noisy work and unpleasant sport of laborers and sailors. In the center of town, as in every other section of Savannah, a large proportion of men were young single transients living in homes or boardinghouses.[19]

Whereas white males between the ages of twenty and thirty made up only 17 percent of Georgia's white population in 1860, in Savannah this able-bodied but troublemaking group made up over one-fourth of the white population. The city attracted these propertyless men from Ireland, the North, and the Southern countryside with the promise of good wages and good times. During the busy season in the fall, when the cotton flowed into Savannah from hundreds of miles away, men made respectable wages on Savannah's docks. The wages dried up during the lax season, but fun might still be had if one could find money for a bottle or for gambling stakes. Drunkenness, fighting, whoring, and gaming were part of the accommodations the commercial city had to offer.[20]

New recruits constantly replenished this aggregation of unattached young males. When young Daniel Baker, a devout orphan, left his rural home for Savannah early in the nineteenth century, he immediately felt the dangerous allure of the city. His employer put young Baker in a boardinghouse where no one "had any fear of God before his eyes," and all the young man's associates "were profane; and all desecrated the Sabbath. At first, I was very much shocked at these 'carryings on' and even ventured to reprove them, but gradually I began to look with less horror upon their conduct; and as 'attrition wears the solid rock,' in process of time, I began to some extent, to copy their example." Baker began by neglecting his prayers and strolling in the country during time he should have been in church on Sunday. Visits to beer gardens and raucous militia celebrations soon followed in the wake of these minor transgressions. Only the sudden death of a cardplaying companion, coinciding with Baker's own apparently providential brushes with a premature end, convinced him to buy a Bible surreptitiously and begin his return to religion. Had it not been for this turn of events, Baker might well have gone on to join the other young men who did a turn in the city's jail for disorderly conduct or who patronized the city's numerous prostitutes. As Savannah's mayor admitted, the city contained one prostitute for every thirty-nine men in 1859; the ratio in New York City was only one to every fifty-seven. Savannah's brothels flourished, not surprisingly, near the boardinghouses that sailors and laborers temporarily called home, and the boardinghouses in turn lay near the heart of town.[21]

Even so, C. G. Parsons, a Northern visitor, thought the downtown area of the city "exhibits unmistakable signs of enterprise, refinement, and wealth. Many of the dwelling houses are spacious and elegant, the stores are large and well filled. In the heart of the city every thing imparts to the view of the stranger an idea of comfort." But Parsons could not enjoy the bustle of downtown and the graciousness of the wealthy houses, for "in the suburbs, the low, dingy, dirty, squalid, cheerless negro huts, remind the Northern visitor of the fearful price paid by one class to support another." Many of the people who labored on Savannah's wharves, docks, and streets—people of both races—lived in the marshy outskirts of Savannah. The peripheral first and fourth districts housed 75 percent of the city's laborers (eight out of ten of whom were Irish) as well as the majority of the small free black population. Savannah's slaves comprised a highly visible part of the population in every part of town, but they too tended to cluster in the outskirts when given a chance to live on their own.[22]

As a result of these residential patterns, Savannah officials in the 1850s perceived three dangerous areas of town: the eastern periphery, the western periphery, and the market (see map). By 1855 the eastern part of Savannah contained "100 liquor vending shops, 26 sailor boarding houses, 5 large houses of ill fame, besides numerous small ones. It is the residence and resort of a large proportion of that floating and often lawless class, who seek employment here in the cool months, and who have no restraints of a local character or family ties to control them." The western parts of town—Yamacraw, Currytown, Oglethorpe Ward, and Walton Ward—seemed nearly as bad. Not only did they house a similar number of liquor shops, boardinghouses, and houses of prostitution, but the population was "very mixed, consisting of Americans, free negroes, and foreigners of all classes." Savannah's citizens should build two police stations, argued a city officer in 1855, one to serve as "a sort of barrier between the disturbers on the east, and the quieter population" in the center of town, and the other to be a "point of surveillance over all the western part of the city—such an arrangement must sooner or later be made, and the earlier the better." These two outposts could guard the respectable and propertied central city from the dangerous elements surrounding it.[23]

This dramatic portrayal of the city's geography is borne out by more objective evidence: most of the people successfully indicted for serious crimes in Chatham County who appeared in the 1860 census did in fact live on the periphery of Savannah; property crime and violent crime did surround and infiltrate the central area of Savannah. Thieves focused their efforts on the Market Square and on the three streets where most of the city's businesses operated: two-thirds of the property crimes reported in the Savannah *Morning News* in the 1850s occurred in those places.[24] As modern criminologists have discovered, the greatest number of crimes do not necessarily occur where property is most concentrated or where most criminals live, but in the borderline areas in between. In the ninteenth-century commercial city—unlike the more spatially segregated twentieth-century city—the greatest amount of valuable property necessarily lay extremely close to where most criminals lived. The entire commercial city constituted what would today be considered a high-risk area.[25]

Nevertheless, Southern civic leaders, as full of boosterism as any American businessmen, proclaimed their region a veritable paradise for the white workingman, free from the grinding poverty that beset the cities of the North. For skilled artisans this claim was true: wages were higher in the South than in the North. Further, just as republican defenders of slavery claimed, very few native-born Southern men could be found performing menial labor in Southern cities.[26] There can be no doubt, however, that the poverty-stricken, black and white, composed a visible portion of the population of every antebellum Southern city. The destitution of many of Savannah's lower-class white residents in the 1850s is "evident from the numerous cases of extreme poverty and occasional instances of outright starvation that were reported to the Board of Health." And such a fate was met not only by the ill or infirm. "There is every indication," antebellum Savannah's historian concludes, "that the lower-class white could not, in many instances, earn a satisfactory living during the 1850s. The average wage of the day laborer at the end of the decade was $1.25; boarding expenses took up about one-third of his weekly earnings. If he had a large family to support, which was very often the case, he was apt to find the burden intolerable." On the day the census taker polled the Savannah Poor House in 1860, ninety white men, thirteen women, and eight children had sought refuge there. Most had immigrated from Ireland a few years earlier. The situation in New Orleans was even worse; there the yards of "hundreds of old shanties, tottering with decay," contained stagnant cesspools, and whole families lived in single rooms. One observer argued that hardly a city in Europe "could show as many wretched destitute poor crowded together in the same place as that part of New Orleans."[27]

From the viewpoint of the propertied, the stable, and the familied, Savannah and other Southern cities were sometimes unpleasant places to live from the late 1830s through the 1850s. The cities' newfound prosperity brought too many rough, loud, and often drunken newcomers and transients, who crowded the most important streets and market area; too many destitute Irishmen—"niggers turned inside out," as the phrase went—fraternized with too many blacks enjoying the relative freedom of the city; too many prostitutes beckoned to sailors in "boardinghouses" too close to respectable neighborhoods. Savannah experienced this congestion, this sudden diversity, along with other cities, for every mid-nineteenth-century North American city reveals class and residential patterns similar to Savannah's. And Savannah, along with other Northern and Southern cities, created a new arm of the law to contain the disorder. It seems no accident that the modern American police began when the commercial city attained its greatest density and diversity, before the spatial segregation allowed by streetcars and the increasing order-liness of urban life bred by industrial discipline made at least part of the city seem a safe place to live. Between 1845 and the Civil War virtually all of the largest cities in the country established uniformed police forces, and included in this group were the Southern cities of Baltimore, New Orleans, Charleston, Richmond, and Savannah.[28]

Some of these cities had experience with "police" forces decades before their Northern counterparts adopted the idea from London. To guard the slaves in their midst, white residents of New Orleans formed a full-time force as early as 1809, and by 1822 Charleston could claim a guard of one hundred men. The police of both cities wore uniforms, carried guns and bayonets, trained, drilled, and walked a beat. A European visitor to Charleston in 1842 thought that city possessed "the best organized system of police that ever was devised." As soon as ten o'clock struck, all black people had to be off the streets, and "the city suddenly assumes the appearance of a great military garrison." Whatever their effectiveness, however, these early slave control forces were not composed of "policemen." By definition police, unlike urban slave patrols, do not rely on brute force alone for their authority. In a republican society the police exist only as extensions of the state, servants of the public will. The ideal of the police not merely as an armed force within a city but as a force that gains its power from the willing acquiescence and support of the city's citizens has often confronted a contradictory reality in America, but the ideal of the police, like that of the penitentiary, has remained constant since the time of its inception. For Savannah, that inception came in 1854, many years before most Northern cities of its size adopted a uniformed police.[29]

For decades prior to the creation of its police, Savannah, like other cities, relied on a part-time night watch of about one hundred men to protect the city's homes, businesses, and wharves. During the day fewer than ten men patrolled the city. These officers commanded little respect. One resident recalled the watch in later years, and could "scarcely keep from smiling when I refer to the officials appointed for the protection of the city." A letter to a local paper from "Merchant" called the night watch an object of "ridicule and contempt." "A 'watch' in Savannah! Capital joke," another paper sneered. But the deficiencies of the watch did not strike everyone as funny. A reporter walked through Savannah one Sunday in the winter of 1853 and saw "shops open and negroes in them, buying, selling, drinking, and talking." He also saw "a plenty of watchmen walking leisurely about," but they seemed unconcerned. "Where is the Marshal—where the Captain of the City Watch?" he wondered. "Will they not act before it is too late, and before public indignation breaks from its pent up bounds and overwhelms them in ruin?"[30]

In 1851, after a series of early-evening burglaries had been committed, the Savannah *Republican* concluded that the city was "infested by a set of bold adventurers, and *guarded*! by a set of sleepy watchmen." The night watch may well have been sleepy, for they worked all day as laborers and received only $25 a month for their nocturnal watchfulness. Mayor John Ward, with the unanimous support of the city council, sought to rectify this situation in June 1854, when he replaced half the watchmen with twenty mounted men. This change left fifty foot patrolmen to guard the downtown wards, while the mounted police patrolled the rest of the city. The new police also received the authority of uniforms, a recent innovation in America. Savannah's mounted police wore blue coats with silver buttons, gray pants, and a cap bearing a badge engraved with "M.P." The mayor and his new chief of police, Joseph Bryan, put the newly uniformed force on display in the streets of Savannah, and the *Republican* was duly impressed. "The Police have been brought to a state of great efficiency," observed the paper, "and their appearance on parade, yesterday, was such as to inspire the public with confidence and respect."[31]

Chief of Police Joseph Bryan was indeed a man the law-and-order forces of Savannah could respect. The orphaned son of a Georgia representative to Congress, Bryan had lived with John Randolph of Roanoke for four years and had then joined the United States Navy. After eighteen years in the service, Bryan came to Savannah in 1854 at the age of 42, "a dapper little man, wearing spectacles and a yachting hat, sharp and sudden in his movements," and with something of a fierce air about him. He made no secret of his nativism and seemed the perfect man—disciplined, ambitious, aggressive—to head a police force. Bryan organized his force around the familiar military model: under "Captain" Bryan were two lieutenants, four sergeants, and twenty privates. Captain Bryan, the *Republican* approvingly observed, "understands the importance of thorough discipline and rigid accountability among subordinates."[32]

Savannah's "respectable citizens and property holders," as one of their number characterized them, claimed responsibility for the creation of the new police force. The men who governed Savannah in the 1850s were, like their counterparts all over America, wealthy men of middle age, merchants or professionals, born in the places they governed. These men sought to impose their own values and concerns on the city through the local government they controlled; they felt they had the greatest stake in the town's prosperity, and they worked assiduously for Savannah's welfare—or what they perceived as its welfare. In their opinion, that welfare depended upon a police force.[33]

From the very beginning, however, the members of the new force had trouble defining their position and making their authority felt throughout the city. The only precedents for the police in a republican society, after all, were the ineffectual watch, the standing army, and the slave patrols—none of which offered a positive example. The police had to find some way to combine unobtrusiveness with effectiveness. Savannah's police, like most early forces, tended to veer from one extreme to another. It seemed impossible for the police to satisfy any segment of the community. The Savannah merchants engaged in the shipping trade made sure the new police force understood that its first task was to prevent the keepers of "boardinghouses" from spiriting sailors away from their ships in port and duping them into spending their sea pay on high-priced liquor, food, and prostitutes. Such practices made captains reluctant to bring their ships to Savannah and hurt legitimate merchants who dealt with the sailors in port. The police largely succeeded in the suppression of this "river piracy"; "those connected with the shipping interest" as well as "all who desire to preserve the good name of our city and port" were pleased. But not for long. When bales of cotton disappeared from Savannah's wharves, "Merchant" called the police to task: "They have stopped the stealing of sailors from our ships—and why not this? One inflicts as deep an injury on the business and character of our city and people as the other." And yet when the police tried to enforce city ordinances with some strictness, the outcry from the same quarter came just as swiftly. "A *merchant*," complained a Savannah businessman, "who has a few bales of Cotton left in the street for a moment while he is receiving it, is fined, 10, 20, and $30, while the *vagabond* who resists an officer or is guilty of disorderly conduct, is fined only 2 or $4. Is this right?"[34]

"Vagabonds," unfortunately, did not write letters to newspapers, so we do not know much about their perception of the new police. They may well have been annoyed, though, when the police tried to enforce a "Sunday Ordinance" which closed all grog shops—"the gateways to prison or the gallows"—on the Sabbath. The response from the immigrant proprietors of these small shops came just as quickly and vehemently as it had from wealthy merchants. When a barroom owner received a fine for violating the ordinance on the evidence of a policeman who "peeped through a key hole and saw a light in Mr. Southcott's premises, and heard what he thought was the rattling of glasses," a "Mr. W." was outraged. It turned out that Mr. Southcott's wife had given birth to a child that Sunday, and the proud father was merely celebrating with a few friends. Mr. W. thought it strange that a policeman with such acute hearing could not "hear the drilling or breaking of a lock on a safe, or the forceful entry of a store on a public street. Perhaps it is accounted for by the fact that the burglar, when convicted, gets a jail sentence, while the violator of an ordinance is subject to a fine, of which the [policeman] gets half." This monetary incentive to create "crime" by selectively enforcing minor ordinances had already been noted by "A Looker On, in Savannah," who thought it obvious that "persons will rarely prevent the commission of that, the detection of which, if committed, is largely beneficial to themselves."[35]

Many of the problems of Savannah's police seemed a result of the patrolmen's class background. An effective force, Savannah Mayor Edward Anderson advised the mayor of Charleston, must be drawn from "a better class of men" than were currently serving in Savannah's foot police, for "the laboring man mingling among his fellows by day, cannot assume the authority to govern them by night. He is one of them in spite of himself. He cannot serve two masters." Anderson suggested that higher pay would encourage an esprit de corps "which would induce the very best class of mechanics and others to take service" for a longer period of time. Anderson sought to create a "pride of position" and "moral force"; Anderson wished, in other words, to create a more impersonal and efficient tool of the republican state.[36]

Like the penitentiary, the new invention of a police force promised to deter crime as well as punish it. Like the penitentiary, too, the uniformed, disciplined police could make the state appear simultaneously more just, less arbitrary, and stronger. And just as the penitentiary could infiltrate the criminal's personality, so too could the police penetrate into the criminal society outside the prison. As Chief Joseph Bryan explained when detailing his plan to build two police stations to watch over the evil parts of Savannah, "An examination of most cities, will show that there are particular localities, where the dissipated and the vicious congregate, and that these haunts are not easily changed; and yet more, that they may in a great measure be confined within certain limits." By keeping the "dissipated and the vicious" in one place and by locating the police station nearby, "a great police point is gained in making the policemen familiar with the features of all criminals." The police could actually infiltrate more deeply into criminal society because of the working-class backgrounds of most officers. In Savannah, Bryan believed, the officers' "habitual presence" in the working-class neighborhoods where they lived "has done much to check disorder." Savannah's police, in theory at least, could introduce the surveillance of the modern prison into the city. As with the penitentiary, the messy job of enforcing the criminal law could be sanitized for the public: the close proximity of police headquarters to criminals' neighborhoods, Bryan observed, would avoid exposing law-abiding people to "the nuisance (often shocking) in publicly conducting prisoners from the Guard Barracks to the Jail."[37]

Bryan's goals were those of most police administrators in the nineteenth century, and on paper they sound as if the small city of Savannah, like London, Paris, and New York, was coming under tighter and tighter police control. But reformers' intentions are not necessarily reformers' results; the police force, like the penitentiary, met strong resistance, both for its inefficiency and for its corruption of power. As even the city council admitted, the system by which police and informers received half of the fines they generated, while a "stimulus to increased vigilance," also held out a "temptation to men of weak principles to a tyrannical abuse of the power which is thus placed in their hands." Although the Savannah police contained many good men, "human nature is weak," and it was inevitable that some men would "succumb to the power of the almighty dollar." Nothing could more quickly undermine a republican state than paid spies.[38]

Discontent with the Savannah police, again as with the penitentiary, took its most tangible form in the political arena. Resistance began as soon as the new force made its presence felt in 1854. After noting with approval the increased business of the Mayor's Court in that year, the *Republican* warned that "the public will not be surprised that a disposition is manifested in certain quarters, to bring forward a candidate for Mayor next fall, who will restore the inefficient police organization." Six months later, the opposition to the force had gained momentum, and the *Republican* asked in disbelief, "Do the people desire to see the bar-rooms thrown open, and the Sabbath desecrated? Are they tired of the security they now enjoy both in person and in property, and do they wish to see the present Police force disbanded and the inefficient system of olden times substituted?" Apparently so, for the city's immigrant shopkeepers did support a Democratic ticket opposed to the new police reforms, and conflict over the police continued to define the major issue in virtually every annual municipal election in Savannah between 1854 and the Civil War. The nativist "Americans" and the propertied "conservative element" championed the extension of police reform, but feared that "the keepers of two hundred rum-holes in the city, the pirates who infest the river, and the heterogeneous mass . . . whose interests lie in a loose administration of the law, would compel them to relax the rein."[39]

The fears of the "conservative element" were well founded, for the "heterogeneous mass" did indeed resist the newly efficient police force of Savannah. The urban poor did not oppose the police in principle—as did rural dwellers who opposed the penitentiary—but they did oppose the control of the force by their political adversaries. The wealthy were not the only city people who wanted to live in a safe place, after all, and the police, if "properly" administered, seemed to offer security to the law-abiding residents of Savannah's more disorderly districts. But in cities so divided between classes and ethnic groups as those of mid-nineteenth-century America, conflict was bound to arise over the control of the police. There is no understanding the evolution of America's police without understanding the role of politics in their history.

Savannah's police, like all those of the nineteenth century, served as important cogs in political machines, whoever ran them. Police forces could absorb large numbers of untrained but politically loyal working-class men, could help ensure that certain people voted, and could strictly enforce the law against political enemies while looking the other way for political friends. Policemen, unlike the penitentiary, did not stand by as passive and helpless objects of manipulation, but played a major role in the politics which determined their future. As an unsuccessful reform candidate for Savannah's mayoralty sighed, "When I saw the city guard come up in solid phalanx and observed the whole Police of the city evidently organized and at work for electioneering, I knew the die was cast." Attempts to "professionalize" the police often reflected efforts by politically outnumbered elites to put control in the hands of "disinterested" city administrators—not local politicians. The merchants of Savannah had selected Joseph Bryan as captain of their new police precisely because "he appreciates too fully the wants of the community and the responsibilities of his position to allow the City

Watch . . . to be converted into a corps of electioneering spoils-seekers and toads."[40]

The new "conservative" police immediately clashed with the other arms of government controlled by Savannah's Democratic majority. Democratic councilmen frequently overruled the Know-Nothing mayor's decisions on appeals from the Police Court. Mayor and council wrangled over appointments and dismissals, and Chief Bryan became disgusted with his lack of control over the force. In 1856, after only two years of the new police, the Democrats regained the mayoralty of Savannah, and the discontent surrounding the police chief—now a lame duck Know-Nothing within a Democratic administration—immediately burst into the open. On the very night of the election, in fact, a large band of Democrats paraded noisily through Savannah, serenading the homes of the mayor-elect and several new aldermen. "When the procession passed in front of Captain Bryan's house," reported the next morning's newspaper, "a glass bottle was thrown from one of the windows which felled one of the men of the party, and then another. Now satisfied of the truth that they were assailed, indignation took the place of surprise and stones were thrown into the house—a pistol was discharged from the house and then a discharge of stones and weapons from the crowd." A few weeks later, Chief Bryan resigned, declaring that the city administration appointed "imbecile party fools" while he could not "save a worthy officer from the fang of party venom."[41]

Such conflicts were replayed for decades in cities throughout America. The police always occupied a difficult position in an American society that was simultaneously diverse and republican—two characteristics some Americans feared could not coexist. Unlike London, where the police assumed the authority of a massive and powerful national state, the decentralized American police have been forced—often unsuccessfully—to create their own authority. In contrast to England, "the constable here is regarded less as the embodiment of the law than as the instrument of a meddling, despotic Executive," Englishman James Stirling commented after viewing the New Orleans police. "In no city of the Union have I seen any appearance of an efficient, well-organized body of police. Any stray policeman you may encounter seems a poor, isolated, dispirited creature, half-ashamed of himself and his office, and utterly inefficient for any public good."[42]

Perhaps because American police were invested with so little of the authority of the state, they often turned to violence—and often suffered violence at the hands of criminals and rioters. In the days before call boxes and patrol cars, individual and isolated policemen often ran considerable risk trying to arrest a belligerent drunk, not to mention a dangerous criminal. For example, in Savannah in 1860, after another conservative mayor had instituted new police reforms designed to make the force as effective as it had been in the days of Joseph Bryan, "A Citizen" complained, "What is Savannah coming to? It takes about a half dozen policemen to convey one poor drunk to the Barracks; everyone must show his authority by striking the poor fellow with his club." Savannah's newspaper and residents alternated between deploring the cruelty of their police forces and berating the policemen for their ineffectuality. Americans, as Tocqueville observed, wanted to have both freedom and uniformity, liberty and homogeneity. Therein lay the dilemma of the American police, whose task it was to impose public uniformity in an increasingly diverse republican city.[43]

Police imposed that uniformity by creating "crime" out of the much more ambiguous materials of "disorder" and "nuisance." Since police initiative exerted so much of an impact on the apparent number of relatively trivial crimes, statistics based on minor offenses reveal as much about police behavior as they do about the amount of crime actually committed. More serious crimes, however, are less subject to such distortion. Although many serious crimes remain undiscovered and unpunished, as a general rule the more serious the kind of crime, the more reliable its records. Police rarely invent a robbery or murder; tangible evidence proves that someone—though not necessarily the person prosecuted—committed the crime. The Chatham County Superior Court processed the most serious crimes detected in Savannah, and the indictments made by the grand jury in the final antebellum decade reveal the relative ineffectiveness of the creation of the Savannah police: the years following that much-vaunted event in 1854 witnessed no marked increase in indictments for any serious crime.

The configuration of prosecuted crimes in the 1850s, in fact, did not differ significantly from those prosecuted in the sample years of the 1830s and 1840s. Violent crimes predominated throughout the antebellum era, but property crimes constituted the second largest category of cases before the Superior Court. Indeed, the vast majority of the theft and burglary prosecuted in the antebellum South originated in the region's cities. As *DeBow's Review* warned, cities held a dangerous contradiction that spawned theft and burglary: they "draw together the dissolute and idle from all quarters. It is there, too, that the wealth and enterprise of a country is concentrated." Or, in the more colorful language of a "Hard-Shell Baptist" preacher from Louisiana, the city was "the mother of harlots and hard lots, whar corn is wuth six bits a bushel one day and nary a red the nex . . . and gamblers, thieves, and pickpockets goes skiting about the streets like weasels in a barnyard."[44] Opportunities for theft multiplied in the prosperous cities of the Cotton South in the 1850s; and the same prosperity attracted poor working people from the North and Europe as well as from Southern farms. The merchants conducting their booming businesses on the wharves and docks of the South could use these people in times and places where slaves were unavailable or too expensive, and in good years only relatively few of these white laborers were forced to the poorhouse by accident, drink, or luck. But in bad years significant numbers of the poor decided to steal, and some of them were caught.

The Chatham County Superior Court prosecuted more people for property crimes in 1858 and 1860 than in any other years in the decade. The numbers are too small and subject to too many distorting forces to prove anything about real increases in crime. Yet Figures 3.1 and 3.2 show that the incarceration rates of Northern and Southern penitentiaries reveal a pattern strikingly similar to one another and to that of Savannah: a dramatic rise in the late 1850s. The Southern cities of Vicksburg, Memphis, Nashville, and Louisville sent many more people to their state penitentiaries in 1858 and 1859 than in any other years in the 1850s.[45] Arrest patterns for cities as diverse as Boston, Detroit, Indianapolis, and New York also point to an increase in property crime late in the decade.[46] The United States, North and South, shared a common experience of a crime wave on the eve of the Civil War. That wave was triggered by a depression in the market economy that bound the two regions together.

The North and South had not always followed a parallel path of prison commitments. Figures 3.1 and 3.2 show that at least some Northern states witnessed an earlier increase of incarceration in the 1830s and 1840s which the South had experienced to a significantly smaller degree. The major depression of the late thirties and early fourties left little mark on the imprisonment rates of the South due to the nature of the Southern economy, Southern transportation, and the Southern state. Most poorer white farmers in the region took little part in the market economy throughout the antebellum era: "Panics, financial pressures, and the like are unknown amongst

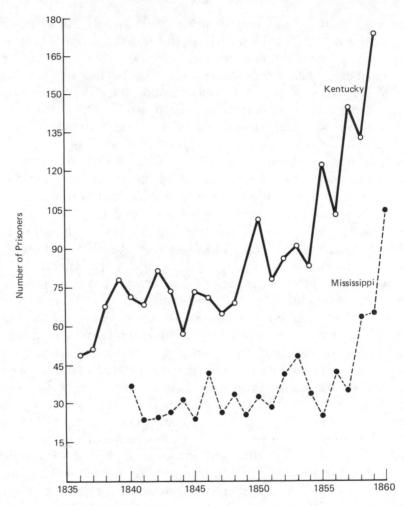

Figure 3.1. Prisoners Received in Two Southern States

them," Daniel R. Hundley wrote in 1860, "and about the only crisis of which they know any thing, is when a poor fellow is called upon to 'shuffle off this mortal coil.' Money, in truth, is almost a perfectly unknown commodity in their midst, and nearly all of their trafficking is carried on by means of barter alone."[47] Such people, especially before railroads had penetrated much of the South, would have been little affected by a depression.

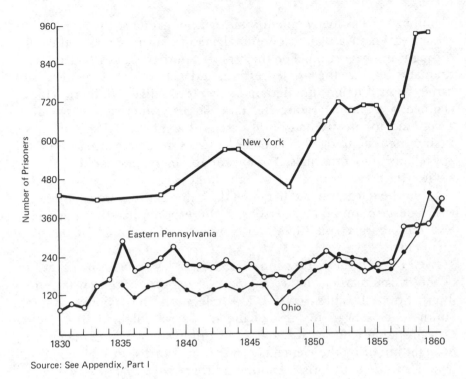

Source: See Appendix, Part I

Figure 3.2. Prisoners Received in Three Northern States

During the depression of the 1830s, too, law enforcement in the sparsely settled South was weak. As Mississippian William Sparks remembered, following the panic of 1837 "there was no restraining influence on the conduct of men, save only the law, and, for the want of efficient administration, this was almost powerless. . . . Society was a chaos, and . . . take care of yourself the rule." If a rural constable did happen to apprehend a thief in the South of the 1830s, the expense and difficulty of transporting him overland by wagon or horse to one of the new penitentiaries in the state capitals may well have made it seem more reasonable to punish him in the county. There may have been a "crime wave" in the South in the late 1830s, but penitentiary records cannot tell us much about it.[48]

By the time the depression of 1857 arrived, however, the South had experienced deep changes, all of which tied the South more firmly and more intricately to the international market economy. The South doubled its railroad mileage in the 1850s, giving the region in 1860 as many miles of railroad per capita as the North and fueling, as in Savannah, economic development in towns and cities throughout the region. For their part, Southern cities had grown dramatically since the last depression, and a large part of the increase came from foreign immigration. By 1857, five Southern cities claimed a position among the nine largest American ports, and accounted for nearly half of all domestic exports. Telegraph lines bound the region together and exerted an immediate impact on the apprehension of criminals. As a Savannah newspaper noted in 1853, "A few days ago, a number of light fingered gentry arrived in this city, but the telegraph had heralded their departure from Charleston with a description of their persons, and no sooner had they put their feet on Georgia soil, than our vigilant officers made their acquaintance."[49]

Even though the depression of 1857 was less severe than that of twenty years earlier, it acted upon a region more sensitive to international business cycles. The telegraph that connected the South so closely to the rest of the world was blamed by a New Orleans paper as "the cause of more trouble and pressure than were brought about by the elements of weather, storms, or real financial troubles in distant ports." Another editor agreed that "every one at all capable of thinking" could see "the intimate connection in business every portion of the country has with every other portion. The throbs of the heart are not more certainly felt at the extremities of the human system than are the pulses of trade and commerce." Thus when a financial panic struck New York in October of 1857, "almost in the twinkling of an eye, with the suddenness of an earthquake, and unexpectedly as a stroke of lightning from a cloudless sky, cotton was struck down, and became almost unsalable in the Southern market." Even businessmen were stunned by the capriciousness of the market economy: "No war, no pestilence, or famine; no interference of the government; no obstruction in commerce; no 'dissolution of the Union'; no heavy adverse balance of trade;—none of these. In broad daylight and in fair weather, the blast came, in obedience to its own laws of existence and motion."[50] Great suffering struck Northern cities in the winter of 1857–58. New York saw 100,000 of its workers unemployed; 20,000 of them lost their jobs within a terrible two-week period. Workmen marched in New York's streets with signs declaring "Hunger is a Sharp Thorn."[51]

The depression affected Southern cities as well, although economic historians stress the immunity of the slave South from the crisis of 1857. The panic began in August, and by September Southern cities began to feel its effects. Businesses failed at a dizzying rate in Baltimore, and more than 5,000 families, over 18,000 people, were officially classified as "poor." In Richmond, most tobacco factories had closed by the beginning of October. The Richmond papers admitted that destitution "was stalking working-class neighborhoods and that many laborers, particularly free blacks thrown out of work at the tobacco factories, were turning to petty crime to survive." Only slaves seemed untouched by the panic: the First African Church of Richmond gathered a small donation to aid the city's Irish poor in 1857.[52]

Savannah managed to avoid the worst of the panic when the city's bankers and merchants agreed to suspend bank payments to prevent the flow of specie to the North. A prominent merchant confided that "without help from the Banks it was impossible not to break. . . . The Bank helped and we stood." But although no major firm in Savannah broke, many bent. "The week now under review," glumly concluded the Savannah market report for October 15, "has been the gloomiest, in a commercial point of view, which has ever passed over our city. No sacrifice was great enough to force the sales of Cotton, the utter impossibility of getting money to pay for it has prevented a single transaction." This inactivity seemed especially ominous at a time of the year when the usual scene in Savannah was one in which the city's residents "are tumbling over boxes and barrels, lying in front of stores and warehouses; clerks are running into each other at the corners, with their bills of lading and marking pots in hand." By October 23, Savannah's cotton shipments had fallen 82 percent below the previous year's level; by the end of 1857, Southern ports had received 381,894 fewer bales of cotton for shipment than in 1856. It required many hands and strong backs to move nearly 400,000 bales of cotton, and in 1857 those hands and backs were not needed. Even in the best of times, Savannah's white workingmen had complained that they could not make ends meet; the effect of the virtual cessation of business in the winter of 1857 on that fourth of Savannah's free population who possessed absolutely no property, absolutely no money to tide them over for even a few weeks, can only be imagined. The city's press ignored their plight.[53]

In December of 1857 several besieged storekeepers in Savannah "determined to put no further reliance in the police, but will have a clerk sleep in their stores, armed for any emergency." This step followed a warning to the Savannah police "to keep a sharp lookout, as Savannah seems to be infested with a set of persons who live by thieving." A later issue of the *Republican* cautioned residents to beware of "a class of people, who live by their wits," driven to the South from the North by the depression. Savannah was not the only Southern city to complain of invasion by drifting criminals. As early as the depression of the 1830s and 1840s Southerners perceived the liabilities of their increased connection with the rest of the nation and the world. A Mississippi legislative committee argued in 1836 that the Mississippi River "has become the great thoroughfare of vice and crime, as well as of wealth and enterprise. Villains of every description, out-laws from other states, refugees from justice, thieves, robbers and banditti of all sorts, are continually floating upon its current, and collect in the towns and villages upon its banks, like drifting wood in its eddies." The legislators called for a special court to handle the criminal business of counties bordering the river, a court which could benefit the isolated portions of the state by serving as "a sort of frontier guard, a barrier against the inroads of vice, a levee against the overflow of crime." By the late 1850s such a strategy would not have worked, for railroads had by then pene- trated parts of the South hundreds of miles from a river. Georgia state officials complained in 1839, when railroads were still a novelty, that "the number of prisoners are greatly increased by the transient population that collects about our commercial cities and Rail Road operations." Southerners claimed that their region's agricultural wealth was not of the ephemeral, "fictitious" sort which disappeared in the North during depressions; Southerners wanted to believe that any criminals in their region must have come from somewhere else. But the South did not import all its thieves; the city and the crisis in the international market economy had joined to create them within the region itself.[54]

Although prosperity returned in 1858 and 1859, no one could be sure when the next business crisis would strike. It came much earlier than most expected. In October 1860 Savannah's paper reported that "an idea has taken general possession of the public mind, that we are to have season of great financial trouble the coming winter and spring." The paper suggested that people "control expenses, lop off luxuries." By November, the *Republican* lamented that "the stringency in money matters which now characterizes our commercial community, was not exceeded by the incidents of the panic of 1857." A Savannah resident confided to his son that all was not well in the city: "The banks are all curtailing their business and the merchants are hard up for money. So that we all have to be economical in our expenditures, for fear that *ere long* we will not have the wherewithal to purchase the *necessities of life*." "Already we have been treated to a foretaste of pecuniary ruin," wrote another Savannah citizen late in the year. "Even the impending shadow of disunion has been sufficient to disturb the business of the country from our extreme North to the Gulf and from the Atlantic to the Pacific. . . . Confidence is deserting the most hopeful of our citizens." In 1860 indictments for property crime in the Superior Court of Chatham County reached their highest level of the preceding decade.[55]

For some cities, the entire period from 1854 to 1860 constituted a prolonged period of economic trouble—trouble reflected in the rise in penitentiary commitments from 1855 on, North and South. The crisis of 1857 "was only the most acute phase of a broader pattern of depression, one so severe as to invite comparison with its unforgotten predecessor, the depression of 1837–43." As early as the winter of 1854–55, one historian has discovered, "business stagnated, unemployment increased greatly, and there was considerable distress and popular unrest, especially in New York City." In 1855 the editor of the Savannah *Republican* claimed that in New York, Philadelphia, Boston, and Baltimore alone "there is probably more suffering growing out of poverty, and more crime committed than in the slave States." As proof, he proudly observed, slaves from the South could be found contributing "from their abundance to the relief of the hungry and the naked" in the North. "The poor we have with us," the editor admitted, "but they are not reduced to a level with the brutes that perish."[56] In March 1859 an Alexandria, Virginia, newspaper sadly observed that "an unusual stringency in monetary affairs, a great falling off in trade, and a general stagnation in business, all conspire to cast an unwonted gloom over our whole community." In May 1860 a Baltimore journal observed that the crisis of three years earlier had left its mark "in the shape of unemployment or unremunerated labor, an unhealthy accumulation of capital in some quarters, and a sad deficiency in others, . . . and general symptoms of poverty."[57]

Poverty alone does not explain crime, not even theft. The context of poverty provides the key, and the context of the crime waves of the late 1850s was the commercial city—with just as much stress on

the word "commercial" as on "city." The panics hit Southern cities
not because they were cities but because the market economy had
established dominance there. The market largely determined who
came to Savannah and where they lived after they arrived. The
young, the unattached, the male, the immigrant came to Savannah
in order to find work, and they lived in dilapidated boardinghouses
because those were the only places they could afford. But there was
more than this to connect cities and property crime.

Although Daniel R. Hundley was deeply conservative and believed that "we are as near perfection now in our own social
organization, as we need ever expect to be," the Panic of 1857
stunned him, so much so that he wrote a pamphlet, *Work and Bread*,
on its effects. "In prosperous times it is very true that competition is
the life of trade; but when times are anything else than prosperous,
the converse of the proposition is equally true," he pointed out.
When the demand for labor fell dramatically, as it did in the winter
of 1857, it "cannot be laid on the shelf until there arises a demand
for it." Instead, laborers immediately began to settle for lower and
lower wages to get work. "Self-preservation on the part of the laborer
prompts him to such a course, while self-interest on the part of the
capitalist leads him to encourage the former in his suicidal policy."
The result was that in 1857 "we have gaunt famine stalking through
the homes of the poor, and beggarly want knocking at every laboring
man's door." Commercial capitalism defined the relationship
between most people in cities: as Maurice Dobb explained, commercial capitalism was "not simply a system of production for the
market . . . but a system under which labour power had itself
became a commodity and was bought and sold on the market like
any other object of exchange."[58] The historian can never uncover the
individual factors of personality, opportunity, and chance that led
some people to break the law. What we do know is that only those
forced to sell their labor were forced to make the choice between
hunger and theft. Such were the costs of commerce.

Despite the importance of property crime in Southern cities,
however, despite the convergence between North and South in 1857,
the fact remains that the majority of people brought before the
Chatham County Superior Court were there because of their
violence. This is particularly striking because most nineteenth-
century cities—outside the South, at least—experienced considerably higher levels of property crime than of violent crime. In fact,
historians of France, England, Germany, and the northern United

States have discovered that cities have until relatively recently recorded fewer crimes of violence per capita than the countryside. Michael Hindus has discovered, too, that while antebellum Charleston, like Savannah, experienced more violent crime than property crime, Boston exhibited the opposite pattern.[59] Southern cities, which shared so much with their Northern counterparts—spatial organization, white class structure, immigration, policing, and response to financial crisis—still harbored a markedly different configuration of crime, one marked by a higher percentage of violence. Southern urban dwellers admitted that violence flourished about them. "Within the last four years there have been at least eight or nine murders or manslaughters (and the manslaughters in some cases were nothing but murders)," reported a letter to the *Republican* in 1854. "And thus far, of all these cases, there has not been a single conviction for murder."[60]

Fights and duels of honor continually erupted in antebellum Savannah. In the 1850s alone, the city jailer challenged the city judge, a constable and a policeman engaged in a "rencontre," and two men dueled at church. Dueling had been so rampant earlier in the antebellum era that in 1827 leading citizens, in much the same spirit that made the 1820s such a decade of penal reform, banded together to form the Anti-Duelling Society of Savannah. For a few years the group managed to calm the fires of ritualized violence, but when the society disbanded in 1837, dueling broke out with renewed force. A Savannah "gentleman of the old school" argued, however, that the duels which so disgusted the reformers actually controlled more dangerous and unpredictable currents of violence: "The fatalities are recalled, but it is not remembered that had it not been for the code the participants in many duels, in the first heat of anger, might, in all probability would, have resorted to weapons without the intervening endeavors of friends to pacify."[61]

Northern and English visitors believed the heavy drinking of young, rich, idle urban Southerners bred violence among the elite. C. G. Parsons, with some exaggeration, complained that "the most prolific source of the drunkenness, licentiousness, and crime, which abound in the South, is in the idleness of the slaveholding class. . . . The theater, the billiard table, the drinking saloon, the horse race, the cock fight, are but so many ways devised to banish *ennui*, and prevent life from being a burden." Writing in the early 1840s, James Silk Buckingham thought "the habits of drinking," to which he ascribed many Southern murders, were "more openly practiced and encouraged in the cities of the South than at the North." In the drinking establishments of the elite, institutions given such exalted names as the "Alhambra" or the "Rialto," wealthy young men spent many hours, "and there is hardly a night passes by without furnishing occasion for a duel or a murder at some subsequent time." Joseph Holt Ingraham noted in 1835 that when numbers of "high-spirited young men" congregated, "a code of honour, woven of the finest texture and of the most sensitive materials, will naturally be established." To such a delicate fabric of honor, Ingraham thought, could be traced "the numerous *affaires d'honneur* which have occurred in the south during the last twenty years."[62]

The patterns in Chatham County's Superior Court show that while the wealthy, not surprisingly, virtually never experienced prose- cution for property crime, several appeared before the court for crimes of violence. When the usual prerogatives of class are added to the usual Southern avoidance of legal redress for violence, even these small numbers are surprising. After all, as one Savannah merchant observed when yet another duel between "two young bloods" of good family went unmentioned in the newspapers and unpunished by the courts, laws in Savannah resembled "cobwebs made to catch poor flies but thro' which respectable wasps break with impunity.' " Criminologists have shown that today people of all class levels steal, through various means, while violence rarely occurs outside the lower class.[63] In antebellum Savannah, however, violence erupted on all class levels. Of all the occupational groups in antebellum Savannah, only the very poorest—the unskilled workers—were convicted for property offenses more frequently than personal offenses. Clerks and grocers as well as sailors, carpenters, and blacksmiths engaged in violent crimes serious enough to make their way to the Superior Court.[64]

There is no way to know how many more hundreds of barroom fights and riverside brawls than appeared in the court docket went unpunished in the 1850s. We do know, however, that their numbers were swollen by the Irish immigrants, who contributed their own violent ways to Southern cities. The Irish who gathered in Southern ports soon became famous for their fighting, alone and en masse. A Savannah resident remembered that by the time of the Civil War the largely Irish "people of the laboring class took residence in the eastern section of the city and their children . . . were great fighters." The Irish brought strong traditions of violence with them from the

Old World, traditions which led to fights in Northern as well as Southern cities. The Irish in the American South adapted quickly to Southern improvements in weaponry, however. As a visitor to Savannah from New York commented in 1851, the Irish "were the grand movers in all disturbances. The green horns or 'Country crakers,' suffered when they got among the Hibernians. . . . This all appeared to me very natural," except that the Irish had picked up Southern customs: "here, Bowie Knives, Revolvers, and Clubs were used, and with us fists only."[65]

Despite the disruptions caused by such infusions of immigrants' violence, the long-run effect of cities throughout the Western world has apparently been to reduce violence, as tightly controlled patterns of behavior gradually assumed sway throughout most class levels and ethnic groups. Mere urban growth, mere population density and diversity, were not responsible for the emergence of this new behavior. Rather, changes associated with the rise of industrial capitalism—work discipline, time schedules, early and prolonged schooling, and greater spatial segregation—appear to have been the crucial factors. Indeed, the commercial city, as opposed to the later industrial city, may well have been among the most violent of places, as people with essentially rural values and habits came into frequent forced contact. It depended, of course, on what rural values migrants to the city brought with them, and the values of Southerners who ventured into the city bred considerably more violence than those of their Northern counterparts. Because antebellum Southern cities remained almost exclusively commercial centers with little large-scale manufacturing, because the values and habits native Southerners adhered to included honor and its violence, and because the non-Southerners who came to Southern cities were the young, unattached males most prone to violence in any culture, antebellum Southern cities seem to have bred as much violence as contemporaries believed.[66]

Despite the highly visible violence among whites, and despite the waves of theft in the late 1850s, most of the people in Savannah's miserable damp jail were slaves left there for "safekeeping" when masters could not watch them.[67] A visitor to a Southern jail from the Boston Prison Discipline Society could hardly believe his eyes: "I saw these slaves working, and freely conversing with the most corrupt and abandoned characters, who had lately come from the brothel and State Prison." Fredrika Bremer contrasted the faces of the white female prisoners in the New Orleans jail—faces full of "violent and evil passion"—with a group of black women who "looked so good and quiet," especially two young girls who appeared particularly innocent. Bremer asked, "with no small degree of astonishment, 'Why are these here? What crimes have they committed?' 'They have committed no offense whatever,'" was the reply; their master had gone bankrupt. But, Bremer's guide assured her, the young black girls would have to stay in the jail "at furthest, two or three weeks—quite a short time." Upon hearing this, "One of the young negro girls smiled, half sadly, half bitterly, 'Two weeks!' said she; 'we have already been here two years!' "[68]

Urban slaveowners used the city's penal apparatus not only for the safe storage of their human property, but also to punish their slaves for wrongdoings. Emily Burke saw Savannah slaves dragged to the city's public whipping place, where the slave "receives as many lashes from the knotted thong as his master chooses to order from the man who takes his place there every morning for this purpose and is recompensed for his labor. It was easy enough to know when the hour of flagellation in the jail had arrived, from the dreadful groans and shrieks that poured forth from the iron grated windows of that dark and gloomy abode of wretchedness and cruelty." One rural slaveowner told his overseer to send a troublesome slave to the Savannah jail and invoked the language of the penitentiary: "give him prison discipline, and by all means solitary confinement for three weeks," and then before leaving the jail have the keeper "jog his memory again."[69]

The public punishment of slaves and free blacks by city authorities was a common sight in the urban South. A Richmond newspaper laconically described a city court's business: "There was nothing of moment before 'His Honor' yesterday. An average amount of niggerdom was ordered to be thrashed . . . for violations of the police regulations and city ordinances of so slight a character that it is hardly worthwhile publishing them in a newspaper." As this quotation suggests, most white Southerners simply did not perceive whipping to be a particularly cruel or even harsh punishment for blacks. A Savannah newspaper even congratulated the community that a slave sentenced to receive thirty-nine lashes three days in a row for stealing $400 and a gold watch was better off than he would have been in the North. "Had Robert committed a similar larceny in a free state, he would have been sent to the penitentiary at hard labor for four or five years."[70]

Masters have always complained of their servants' misbehavior, but such concerns took on a new dimension in the late antebellum Southern city. "From Jan'y to Decr," a Savannah planter fretted, "many owners cannot tell where their servants are, or what they are doing." Other masters admitted their inability to keep an eye on their slaves, largely because Savannah slaves—like those in every other Southern city—were often permitted to hire their own time and to live away from their masters. Rice mills employed hundreds of slaves and free blacks in Savannah, offering the allure of good wages for owners of slaves willing to let their slaves work outside their immediate control. Other whites, short of help, often hired a slave without concern for badges or permits. White children and friendly nonslaveholders furnished passes to slaves upon request. One slaveowner, fed up with such disorder, sent a slave to his family plantation outside of Savannah rather than let the slave stay alone in the city for a week: "I am afraid to let George run at large in the city, while we are away, as he most assuredly will do,—it being almost an impossibility to prevent the contraction of idle, vagrant habits especially by young servants in this place."[71]

The proportion of blacks in Savannah's central city steadily declined as slaves moved to the outskirts of town, to the physical discomfort but relative freedom of the "heterogeneous mass." Even those slaves who stayed in the center of town lived in alleys out of sight of prying white eyes; nearly 60 percent of the slaves in Savannah lived away from the immediate control of their masters. When whites and blacks met on Savannah's better streets they often met as strangers. Whites did not like what they saw: "There is a carelessness, a disrespect, and '*devil may care*' sort of independence, an absence of wholesome restraint, a neglect of common propriety and courtesy of manner, which is becoming almost intolerable." Just as with white immigrants, most conflict between blacks and police resulted from "misbehavior" in public places, although the range of behavior permitted to blacks was much narrower than that permitted whites.[72]

Urban blacks were constantly harassed by sporadically enforced but demeaning local ordinances. Of the 103 blacks brought before the Mayor's Court in the first half of 1859, 35 had been arrested for disorderly conduct, fighting, gambling, or drunkenness—just like their white counterparts. But 41 slaves had been picked up for failure to wear their required badge, and 13 others had been arrested for "unlawful assembly," it being forbidden for more than seven blacks to gather without white supervision for any purpose other than religious worship.[73]

While whites expressed little fear of assault from blacks, they did constantly agitate against what they saw as a dangerous cycle of black drunkenness and black theft. Richard Arnold, a prominent physician and mayor of Savannah, explained the problem to a friend in 1850. Immigrant shopkeepers, he observed, often dealt with blacks. One group of these "adopted citizens," he said, traded with industrious country slaves who cultivated gardens in their spare time, but "as there are some rascals in every race and class of men, some negroes prefer abstracting from their master's Cotton Houses or Rice Barns, enough wherewithal to satisfy their extra want. These little shops afford an ever ready market where the demand is always equal to the supply. The equivalent given whether for cash or in barter is generally liquor. These men often acquire large fortunes." Whites seemed the real culprits, for without whites blacks could not sell their stolen goods and could not buy liquor. "Our black population are duped by unprincipled white men," complained the Savannah *Republican*, "and seduced into the commission of thefts and robberies, and corrupted perhaps, by bartering stolen goods for ardent spirits."[74]

Richard Wade argues in his classic account of urban slavery that the problems of slave control and disorder troubled whites to such an extent that slavery was in effect driven out of the city in the late antebellum era. Subsequent statistical research has challenged this argument by showing that urban slavery was a viable institution and that only the high cotton and slave prices of the 1850s pulled slaves out of the cities.[75] Both interpretations contain an element of truth. Slave misbehavior did not mean that slavery could not survive in cities, any more than the crime and disorder of the foreign-born meant that immigrants and cities were fundamentally incompatible. Yet it is easy to see how the persistent complaints of slave disorder in the late antebellum urban South led a historian who based his argument on newspapers and ordinances to believe that slavery and cities made a poor mixture, that slavery and the compact, congested, yet impersonal commercial city of midcentury were not meant for each other. Slave disorder, like white disorder, may well have seemed to be increasing in the 1840s and 1850s as the market economy transformed the city. Urban slavery and Southern city life in general had been less threatening to whites before the conjunction of railroads and steamships combined to fuel the growth of Southern cities, before slaves in growing cities lived in places their masters feared or did not wish to go, before whites found themselves confronted with the "insolence" of strange slaves in increasingly congested public places, before the dangers of slavery were magnified by the presence of immigrants who fraternized with slaves and free blacks.

Southern cities experiencing unprecedented prosperity attracted people from Ireland, the North, and the Southern countryside in the 1840s and 1850s. The market economy that created that prosperity brought sudden destitution and theft in the late 1850s, however, and indirectly fueled a heightened perception of public disorder by throwing diverse classes, races, and ethnic groups into forced contact. The commercial city of the South also attracted large numbers of young men whose thirst for excitement and sensitivity to insult sparked fights, brawls, and homicides, and Southern cities witnessed relatively large amounts of violence. Partly as a result of all these disruptions and tensions, Southern cities, along with their Northern counterparts, created police forces to watch over the new businesses and the boundaries between neighborhoods. In all these ways, the cities of the slave South stood within their region as isolated monuments to the dangers of commercial capitalism.

4

The Black Belt
and the Upcountry

Court week had "long been anticipated by many" people in Greene County, Georgia, in the fall of 1859. The event, observed the editor of the local newspaper, "brought with it sorrows to some, and joy to others, while it crowded together men of dissimilar habits, professions and pursuits." The ritual had put on display the best and worst aspects of Greene County and of humankind in general: "while justice has been meted out on the principles of truth, wisdom exhibited, many of the lowest passions of the human heart have been elicited from their lurking places." The county became conscious of itself during court week, judged itself, defined itself.[1]

The true drama of rural crime and punishment, so avidly observed by nineteenth-century Southerners, can best be captured on a small stage. This chapter focuses on two rural counties in Georgia, Greene and Whitfield, to see how crime and punishment were woven into the community life of the slave South. These two counties appear economically and demographically typical of the two major cultural and economic subregions of the South; their court records survive intact to the present; both counties sustained a newspaper for several crucial decades; and they shared a legal system with each other and with Savannah. An understanding of these two Georgia counties will allow us to glimpse the differences and similarities of crime and punishment between plantation counties and upcountry counties, old counties and new counties. As the comparison of Greene and Whitfield shows, even slightly different

106

societies create and punish different kinds and amounts of crime, and the histories of crime in counties in Mississippi or South Carolina or Kentucky differ from each other and from those in Georgia. But despite significant, if subtle, differences within the South, there can be little doubt that the South as a region shared a common experience with crime in the nineteenth century, an experience distinct from that of the rest of the United States. As a later commentator on violent crimes remarked, offenses throughout the region "vary only in minute detail. They are all cut from the same cloth and the outgrowth of the same peculiar civilization."[2] The heart of that civilization lay in the Southern countryside.

Although separated by fewer than 200 miles of Georgia countryside, antebellum Greene and Whitfield counties would seem to have had little in common. Greene lay in wealthy middle Georgia, a fertile and well-watered region of red soil and rolling hills, "the one not rising many feet above the other, generally with beautiful slopes, and scarcely at any place with so much abruptness as to forbid cultivation."[3] Slaves made up two-thirds of Greene's population in 1860, and one of them, "Grandma" Lawrence, remembered the texture of life in Greene County before the Civil War: "This sho wuz a busy place, lots of houses on bofe sides uv de river, six mule wagon trains going to Greensboro every day, carrying cloth an bringin' back cotton goods, and mail for all dis country. De white folks all had carriages, buggies, saddle horses, and lots uv niggers to look after um."[4] Crepe myrtle and jasmine adorned plantations christened "Dover," "Oak Grove," and "Jefferson Hall." One plantation owner, Dr. Thomas Poullain, owned 278 slaves; his mansion boasted twenty-two rooms and a two-story brick kitchen, and was filled with European china, silver, and furniture. In the 1850s twenty-two families in Greene County owned fifty or more slaves each. The total value of slaves in Greene in 1860 was over $5 million, the seventh largest total in the state.[5]

On the other hand, half the white taxpayers of Greene County owned no slaves at all in the final antebellum decade. During the 1850s Greene and other counties throughout the Georgia black belt witnessed a widening gulf between slaveholders and nonslaveholders as slave prices increased beyond the range of the average farmer. For at least thirty years before the Civil War the white population of Greene gradually decreased while the black population gradually grew. The number of farms in Greene decreased from 512 in 1850 to only 412 in 1860. Some slaveless farmers went to the southwest, to

Alabama and Mississippi, while others moved to north Georgia, where the Cherokees had finally been driven out.[6]

Whitfield County was formed in 1852 in the mountains of north Georgia. The editor of the *North Georgia Citizen*, recalling his first visit to the area in the spring of 1847, described it as a "wild country with trackless forests, only here and there a small clearing and a log house. . . . Everything looked dreary enough to us as we stepped from the train and clambered into a miserable looking dugout called the stagecoach for Dalton. . . . We stood it out for four mortal hours over the worst road we had ever traveled before or since. . . . It was growing dark when we hauled up in front of a small double-log building, over the door of which was rudely printed in struggling letters 'Cross Plains Hotel.' " A far cry, indeed, from the mansions, academies, and impressive churches of "old Greene."[7]

While in the 1850s the great wealth produced by Greene's 8,000 slaves benefited a white population of 5,000, slaves made up only one-sixth of Whitfield's population of 10,000. And while nearly 40 percent of the few who did hold slaves in Whitfield owned only one or two bondsmen, nearly one-third of Greene's slaveowners owned between ten and thirty slaves. As might be expected, too, farm land was worth considerably more in Greene than in hilly and undeveloped Whitfield. Wealthy men in both counties controlled resources far greater than their numbers would warrant, but on a different scale: a fifth of the farms in Greene were over 500 acres, while in Whitfield only a few people owned farms that large.[8]

Railroad stations dominated the villages that served as the seats for the two counties; the trains pulling out of Greensboro in 1860 hauled 10,000 bales of cotton, the trains leaving Dalton carried virtually no cotton but nearly 50,000 bushels of wheat instead. The coming of the railroad in the 1830s had changed Greene County dramatically. Gwynn Allison, a cousin of Andrew Jackson, opposed the road crossing his land and drove surveyors off at gunpoint. Tried for contempt of court, Allison chose to go to jail for a brief period rather than relent; he later refused to accept the money arbitrators judged to be his due for the railroad right of way. The railroad came in any case, of course, and Greene prospered. Several cotton mills, run with slave labor and Northern supervisors, operated in the county from the 1830s through the 1850s. Fifteen years after the railroad came to Greene County it came to Whitfield, transforming Dalton in the process. "From a population of two or three hundred the place in less than one year thereafter numbered all of fifteen hundred inhabitants—a rapid growth for a southern town in those days." The vast majority of people in the area remained farmers, but the railroad nevertheless exerted its influence on rural families as "the wagon trade, for a radius of over fifty miles, grew to be enormous in a few months." Entire trains "of hogs and cattle driven over the highways from East Tennessee were loaded and shipped from Dalton. . . . At times grain was piled to the ceiling of the old depot, and all the platforms were filled, clogging the railroad to capacity."[9]

The small nonslaveholding farmers who sold their produce or livestock in Greensboro and Dalton were obviously engaged in a market economy. Unlike urban workers, however, farmers did not depend on daily or weekly wages for food and shelter. Currency remained scarce, barter was common. Even the poorest family could hunt, raise a garden, and keep a few hogs in the woods. The fluctuations of the world economy thus had little impact on crime and punishment in the rural slave South. Thefts rarely appeared in the court records.[10]

As a comparison of Greene and Whitfield reveals, the rural South was marked by great internal variation before the Civil War. Political differences reflected fundamental demographic and economic differences within the South: the Whigs dominated Greene and the rest of wealthy middle Georgia, while Whitfield and the rest of poorer north Georgia voted strongly Democratic. In many ways, the black belt and upcountry were different societies, with different economies, politics, and histories. Yet whatever their differences, rural Georgia counties were tied together by a shared criminal justice system.[11]

The usual procedure within this system was for a victim of violence or theft to initiate a case by swearing out a complaint before a neighborhood justice of the peace, who in turn would issue a warrant for the arrest of the accused party. The county sheriff then brought the accused before the magistrate for a preliminary hearing, after which the magistrate could either dismiss the case or, if he found sufficient cause, bind the accused over to the Superior Court for a hearing by the grand jury. Other cases, gambling and selling liquor without a license in particular, were initiated by the grand jury itself, which kept a vigilant eye upon the community. After the grand jury had indicted a defendant, a petit jury would determine his guilt or innocence. Clearly, such a system of criminal justice offered many avenues of escape. Surprisingly, although citizens levied many charges against the Southern machinery of justice, few complained that crime escaped undetected and untried. Victims, magistrates, and sheriffs in rural counties usually had a pretty good idea who had committed a particular crime and usually knew where to find the person suspected if he remained in the county.[12]

To contain violators of its laws, Greene maintained a jail commensurate with the county's wealth and age: a forbidding two-story stone dungeon, built in 1807 after a runaway slave burned down a previous structure. The walls of the dungeon stood two feet thick, its small windows covered only by closely spaced bars. A trapdoor in the floor of the second of the two stories facilitated hangings. The ominous building stood, and still stands, in the center of Greensboro, right behind the white-colonnaded court house on Main Street.[13] Whitfield County, on the other hand, built its jail of wood in 1854 for $189.50. The grand jury complained five years later that the timbers of the jail were "almost entirely rotten, so much so that Prisoners cannot be kept there with any degree of safety. . . . We find the jail needs repairing in places almost too tedious to mention." Repairs were not made and the jail remained nearly useless. The Whitfield jail fit Joseph G. Baldwin's description of certain jails in the early Southwest: "It was a matter of free election for the culprit in a desperate case, whether he would remain in jail or not, and it is astonishing how few exercised their privilege in favor of staying."[14]

Greene County's court, like its jail, was less vulnerable to escape than Whitfield's. There had been a Superior Court in Greene County since 1767; the court's first judge was George Walton, a signer of the Declaration of Independence. Eleven of the thirty-eight grand juries that met from 1827 to 1847 in Greene reported "with much satisfaction" that "so much good order has prevailed" in the county that they could find nothing of which to complain. The Greene Superior Court was an exceedingly stable institution; one man, Vincent Sanford, served as its clerk from 1829 until his death in 1859. In 1860 the local *Planter's Weekly* scoffed at those who were willing to pay good tax dollars for extra police for the hamlet of Greensboro: better to leave "the protection of the property of its citizens and the securing of their peace and quiet . . . to the Grand Jury of Greene, who have become notoriously strict in bringing all offenders to punishment."[15]

Whitfield could make no such boast. While nearly a third of the defendants who came before the Greene County court went on to be tried by a petit jury—a higher percentage than in Savannah—fewer than one-tenth of the accused met the same fate in Whitfield. And of those defendants who reached the petit jury in Greene, nearly 75 percent—again, greater than Savannah's 63 percent—were found guilty; in Whitfield only 50 percent were convicted. Many cases before the Whitfield court simply disappeared altogether; some of those cases were settled out of court, while in others the defendants or witnesses left the county. Although a relatively larger percentage of the defendants in both rural counties appeared in the 1850 or 1860 census than did those of urban Chatham County, even the oldest plantation counties witnessed high levels of geographic mobility in the late antebellum era—and criminals apparently moved about as frequently as other Southerners. Only about half the defendants in Greene and Whitfield were recorded in the two censuses. Grand jurors, in fact, may well have indicted a larger number than they otherwise would have, knowing that a considerable proportion of the troublemakers—especially the landless—would leave the county rather than remain and clog the overtaxed judicial system.[16]

Rural counties, like urban counties, treated property offenders much more harshly than those accused of violence. Despite the relative paucity of defendants accused of any kind of property crime in either Whitfield or Greene, the majority of men sent to the Georgia penitentiary from those counties had committed an offense against property. Of the ten defendants Whitfield sentenced to the penitentiary in the 1850s, only one served a term for a crime of violence—stabbing; the others were sentenced to various terms for larceny or burglary. Greene, with its smaller white population, sent only three men to the Georgia penitentiary—Wiley Morris, a bricklayer originally from South Carolina, convicted of larceny; George Mackey, the enigmatic figure of a mattress maker from New York living in Greene (perhaps a factory supervisor?), also convicted of larceny; and Josiah Janall, about whom we know nothing except that he murdered a man. Savannah sent forty-seven men to prison in the fifties: thirty-four for larceny or forgery, eight for various crimes of violence, and the other seven for a broad range of offenses.[17]

Unlike Savannah, though, rural places virtually never used a jail sentence as a punishment. Fines, usually for ten dollars or less plus costs (which, depending on the case, might exceed the fine), were the most frequent penalty imposed by all levels of courts. This was not necessarily a sign of leniency. In the antebellum South ten dollars

was a not inconsiderable amount of cash for a small farmer to raise.
Fines, too, generated revenue for the county, while people sitting in
jail had to be fed—often for a long time. As a resident of a mountain
county remembered, "Back when I was growing up if you done a
pretty dirty crime, a dirty deed, you went to jail and stayed in there
from fall to spring, or spring to fall, till your trial. You stayed in there
six months because they just had court every six months. Back then
nobody would go your bond. People didn't have the money to put
up a cash bond and they sure wouldn't sign over their farm for a
bond."[18]

Defendants in jail had to wait until the circuit followed by the
Superior Court judge brought him to the county court house. The
judge was usually accompanied by a lawyer or two and the state's
solicitor general, or prosecutor. These officials confronted a knot of
cases that had accumulated over the preceding six months. As many
cases as possible had to be tried in the one or two weeks allotted to
the meeting of the Superior Court. The haste and confusion that
necessarily grew out of such a system did not foster careful
construction of the state's cases. The prosecutor also faced difficulties because often he did not live in the county. As one prosecutor
in Kentucky told his legislature, "I have, on many occasions, gone to
a Court when I had never seen a witness on behalf of the
Commonwealth." Often, within five minutes of handing the indictment to the sheriff, the prosecutor complained, "we were selecting a
jury to try that case . . . ; never having had a history of the case given
me by any one, when there were able counsel defending the
criminal, which is always the case—especially if he has money to
back him." The prosecutor took his pay from any fines the state
received as a result of his efforts. Not surprisingly, few established
lawyers aspired to the position of prosecutor, and as a result the state
seldom presented as strong a case as did lawyers for well-heeled
clients. Even relatively poor long-time residents of the community
enjoyed an advantage in court over a prosecutor who came to town
only twice a year.[19]

Disinterested jurors were also hard to find in rural counties. In
Greene County in 1860, for example, the white population consisted
of fewer than 800 families, with a few more than 1,000 men over
twenty years of age among them. Kin ties, no doubt, bound a good
number of these families together. Since the grand jury alone
demanded twenty-four men at two terms of court each year, and
several panels of petit jurors might be called from the tax rolls each

term, the necessarily personal scale of antebellum Southern justice can easily be imagined. Grand jurymen served because "their superior intelligence, wealth, and purity of character" set them apart, and only a relatively few men in each county fit this description— however broadly it might be interpreted. Of the twenty-four grand jurors of the March term of the Greene County Superior Court in 1853, for example, twenty-three could be located in the tax digests for that year or in the 1850 census. Only one of the men owned no property; all but seven were slaveholders, with an average of fifteen slaves each among them. The average worth of all grand jurors was over $9,000, while the average for the white males of the county in 1860 was only $3,957. The Whitfield grand jurors of the April term of 1854 were worth about half as much as their plantation county counterparts—$4,727—but nevertheless about $1,800 more than the average citizen in the county.[20]

If grand jurors were relatively wealthy men, petit jurors were not. Twenty-four Greene County petit jurors in 1853 were worth about half as much as the grand jurors who served at the same term of court; in Whitfield, petit jurors' wealth was even below the average for the county's citizens in 1860. Just as significant, perhaps, nine of the twenty-four petit jurors in Greene and ten of the twenty-four in Whitfield could not be located in either the tax digests or the census. Throughout the South people complained that sheriffs and court clerks merely rounded up anyone they could get their hands on when it came time for court, and hardworking farmers did not want to squander hours or days in the jury box. When in 1858 a Georgia newspaper counseled state legislators to abolish the penitentiary in favor of whipping, branding, and hanging, the paper made one revealing stipulation: "provided honest and intelligent men sit upon criminal cases, and not vagabonds, as is too often the case now." A critic in Kentucky charged that the "miserable wretches" who hung around courthouses in the hopes of picking up money for liquor by serving on juries returned acquittals "in defiance of the most positive proof." Others charged that it was all too easy to influence a jury; as a Mississippi paper claimed in 1854, "even the bloodiest murderer has no fears of the Penitentiary, *provided* he has either money or friends."[21]

This leniency seems generally to have been the rule in cases of violence, but there were exceptions. In 1852 Pinckney Tuggle came before the Greene County Superior Court as a defendant. The scene must have caused some conversation around the Greene County courthouse, for Tuggle was a relatively wealthy man. When he appeared in court, Tuggle was 35 years old, headed a family of six children, owned land worth $5,000, and possessed $8,000 of additional property, including his slaves. Pinckney Tuggle stood accused of a crime of honor: assaulting a man who had made an "indecent proposition" to Tuggle's sister. Apparently the evidence was strong that Tuggle had indeed attacked the man, for he was indicted and found guilty of assault. The court levied a relatively stiff fine of $25, but two years later Pinckney Tuggle was selected from among the county's most respectable men to sit on a grand jury himself. Such was the ambiguity of the relationship between honor and the courts in the rural antebelleum South.[22]

The violence of pride could flare up, too, in a center of learning which brought students to Greene from surrounding counties. In 1859 the "incumbent of the Male Academy" in Greene, a Mr. Briscoe, whipped a fifteen-year-old boy named Adams for "incorrigible idleness." After the correction had been administered, Adams, boiling with indignation, slowly returned to his seat and opened a nearby window. Then he drew a pistol, shot at but missed Mr. Briscoe, and escaped through the window.[23]

One story of violence in Greene passed down through the decades and could still be heard in the county in the mid–twentieth century. An early representative to the Georgia legislature from Greene, Jonas Fauche, voted for the Yazoo land deal and found himself publicly condemned by a resident of Greensboro for his action. Fauche felt obliged to challenge his detractor, who felt obliged to accept. They met at Love Spring to fight their duel. Both Fauche and his opponent fired, but only Fauche's bullet found its mark. His opponent fell to the ground, mortally wounded. In later years, residents of Greensboro frequently saw Fauche, then an old man, visit the gravesite where his opponent was buried. When someone asked him whether he suffered from a guilty conscience, Fauche replied, "I killed him, it is true. I do not weep that I did wrong, for I did not. I weep that so brave a man and so noble an opponent was forced to die. That is all."[24]

This was the stuff of which Southern myths were made, but reality was seldom so exalted. The entry in the diary of an antebellum lawyer traveling on circuit probably came closer to capturing the general temper of violence in the rural South. "The State Docket has been disposed of today. No case of importance has been tried. Almost or quite every one were A. & B. [assault and battery] and invariably they were brought on by intoxicating drinks."[25] A Greene County newspaper recounted, with fitting humor, the trouble caused young Whitfield County by alcohol-induced violence. A family moving from north Georgia in 1855 stopped near "an old, long established rum shop" in the upper part of Whitfield "where they always keep a plenty of old ball face. Some of their friends and relatives accompanied them as far as the grocery. All stopped and commenced drinking at a rapid rate, and in a short time the largest part of the crowd was drunk." Drinking soon led to fighting between different factions of the family. First, "two old men" launched into a wrestling match, but two young male cousins ran their elders "from the battle ground . . . and commenced fighting each other." A sister of one of the combatants tried to stop the fight, but her brother's opponent threatened to kill her with an axe. At this point, another brother stepped forward to fend off the blow, but to no avail: both he and his sister received deep gashes from the axe. When the newspaper printed its report two weeks later, all the parties were thought to be recovering, and all were "still at liberty."[26] Despite the failure of the sheriffs and courts to arrest and punish these particular people, the records still show that courts in both Greene and Whitfield prosecuted more crimes of violence than anything else. Crimes of violence predominated in the black belt and the hills, just as they predominated in the city and the country, the Upper South and Lower South, old counties and new counties. In the 1850s alone, Greene County prosecuted thirteen murders and Whitfield eleven—dramatic figures for communities of such small size. But murders were only the tip of the iceberg.

In 1854 in Whitfield, for example, a year when two men accused of murder came before the court, a whole array of lesser violent crimes was prosecuted—violent crimes that might easily, given a gun or a few more drinks, have also become murders. Eighteen victims of assault and battery took their cases to the Superior Court in 1854, as did six victims of stabbing with intent to kill, and five victims of assault. In the 1850s, in fact, ninety-one men stood accused of assault and battery in Whitfield, twenty-nine of assault, twenty-two of assault with intent to kill. Further, these incidents of violence did not always merely pit one individual against another. In 1852, thirty-five Whitfield men were prosecuted by the Whitfield court for "riot," which occurred in Georgia law "if any two or more persons, either with or without a common cause or quarrel, do an unlawful act of violence, or any other act in a violent and tumultuous manner."

Such violent riots—more likely, drunken brawls or fights, such as the family spree described above—broke out in Whitfield County in 1854 (thirteen defendants), 1856 (nineteen defendants), 1858 (thirteen defendants), and 1860 (twenty-nine defendants).[27] Life in Greene County, as might be expected, was not nearly as rough-and-tumble as in young Whitfield, but still recorded its share of the full array of violent crimes. In the 1850s, thirty-four white men were accused of assault and battery, three more of assault with intent to kill, two for shooting with intent to kill. And while no defendants appeared for rioting in Greene, eleven were indicted for "affray": "the fighting of two or more persons in some public place, to the terror of the citizens, and disturbance of the public tranquility." Two counties in Virginia show a virtually identical pattern: the mountain county, Shenandoah, recorded more assaults and stabbings than Louisa, the plantation county, but both experienced more violent crimes than any other kind between the 1820s and the Civil War.[28]

Rural "criminals," unlike their urban counterparts, did not come primarily from the ranks of the poorest whites. While only 12 percent of Savannah's Superior Court defendants who appeared in the 1850 or 1860 census owned any personal property, two-thirds of Greene's and Whitfield's did so—a proportion similar to the number of property-holding citizens in each county as a whole.[29] And rural criminals were not the outsiders they were in cities, primarily because very few immigrants lived in most of the rural South. No one born outside of the United States committed a crime in Greene and only three did so in Whitfield, despite the fact that a sizable community of German-born people lived in a part of Whitfield in 1860. In fact, people born in the South itself made up 94 percent of Greene's defendants and 85 percent of Whitfield's.[30] Further, married men accounted for nine out of ten of Whitfield's defendants and seven out of ten of Greene's, while only half of Chatham County's defendants in the census had wives.[31]

It is easy to exaggerate, however, the unity and sense of community engendered by the homogeneity of rural counties. There is little doubt that, as *DeBow's Review* claimed in 1855, many offenses in rural areas were "passed over for charity or a hope of reformation" because "more kindness, and fellow feeling" characterized rural than urban counties, whereas in the city, "the smallest offense must be punished, without inquiring into the motives which led, or perhaps drove, the offender to commit it." But there was another side to rural "fellow feeling": coercion could be more direct, more effectual in the country than in the city, for in the country "the man of bad character is known, marked, and watched." As Kai Erikson has argued, a community may "need" deviants to clarify what is normal and good; if not enough serious criminals surface, then those in charge of punishing offenders—in this case, the grand jury—will look a bit harder to find someone who is not living up to community standards.[32] Although this pattern was probably not conscious, its effects seem apparent in the court records of the rural counties, where the majority of nonviolent crimes involved liquor, gambling, and sexual misconduct. Savannah officials reserved such matters for the police court—if they bothered to pursue them at all.[33]

Unlike Savannah, too, any sudden increases in the trial rates of Greene and Whitfield had little to do with the market economy and much to do with campaigns against some moral crime. In 1859, for example, the Whitfield grand jury warned that gambling was rampant in the county, and "by men of whom better things and better examples should be expected, and we do trust that while we sit as Grand Jurors to ferret out crime, that those in higher power will *punish to the last letter of the law those whom we present.*" They were as good as their word: thirty men were indicted that year for playing "Seven Up" and other card games. And in Greene the court indicted nineteen men for gaming in 1857.[34] Indictments for these crimes virtually always resulted from such crusades; in some years no one would be prosecuted for gambling, but suddenly in others anywhere from twelve to thirty gamblers might find themselves before the courts of Greene and Whitfield.

Many nineteenth-century Southerners, whether they drank alcoholic beverages or not, would have agreed with the Whitfield grand jury when it declared after a particularly busy criminal session in 1852 that "nine tenths of the cases have been the result of the intemperate use of ardent spirits." Despite the South's association with mint juleps and moonshine, influential people in the region attacked the abuse of alcohol with a startling vehemence. At the same time that the penitentiary movement gathered steam in the South, local temperance societies sprang up throughout the region, and churches increasingly adopted temperance throughout the antebellum era. The only newspaper in Greene County for several years in the 1850s was the Penfield *Temperance-Banner*, official organ of the Georgia Sons of Temperance. The paper constantly preached the values of family, prudence, and religion and attacked alcohol and the violence that so often accompanied it in virtually every issue.

Because the Georgia legislature licensed grog shops, the *Temperance-Banner* denounced the state for its role in perpetuating drunkenness—and the violence that followed in its wake. After two drunken murders in nearby Gilmer County in 1854, the paper traced the genealogy of the bloodshed:

1. The Legislature granted the License.
2. The License set up the grogshop.
3. The grogshop made the parties drunk.
4. The being drunk made the men commit murder.
5. The committing murder will cause the men to be hanged.

If the murderer happened to be "a man of wealth and with wealthy and respectable connexions," however, the legislature was likely to compound its offense by pardoning the murderers; if, on the other hand, the drunken murderer "be a poor dog, they let him die the dog's death. And this is the end of the boasted liberty of the poor man. He must have equal liberty with rich men to drink; but he can't buy a pardon for the crimes committed in his drunkenness."[35]

The *Temperance-Banner* launched its attack in the language of liberty, of republicanism, because opponents of temperance defended the drinking of alcohol as a political right. Temperance advocates, however, saw themselves as "enlightened" republicans who wanted to use stronger laws to guarantee society's freedom from the violence and the social waste of drunkenness. The temperance debate turned around the same issues, in other words, that defined the debate on the penitentiary: individual and community autonomy versus legislation for a larger and somewhat abstract social good. Primitive Baptists, in the same spirit of biblical literalness with which other Christians in the South defended capital punishment, defended liquor: "God gave the spirit in the fruit of the grain, and the ability to extract and decoct it, and then to drink"—thus "it is sinful to oppose the full use of God's rich mercies!" These churches even excommunicated members who joined temperance societies. Such groups were obviously the exception in the South, however, where evangelical Christians increasingly adopted not merely temperance but total abstinence as their official policy.[36]

Not everyone in the South appreciated the attempts of these Christian men to enforce their values through temperance societies, earnest sermons, and determined efforts, when on jury duty, to prosecute drinking and gambling. The people who cared little for the church and gamed, drank, and fought left few records other than their names in court minutes. We can suppose that after a particularly dark night of the soul or after much pleading by beloved family members some "criminals" became good Christians. It can also be assumed that others who gambled and drank considered church members of both sexes to be meddling old hens and had their fun with little or no guilt. Rural Southern communities saw themselves divided not only by class lines—by who owned how much land and how many slaves—but also by religion. And divisions between those who believed that their eternal salvation depended upon "Christian living" and those who did not often proved difficult to bridge.

In the late eighteenth century, religious and class lines had tended to coincide: more of the poor adhered to evangelical Christianity than did planters. Evangelicals, in fact, consciously defined themselves in opposition to the hedonistic display of wealthy Southerners. The battle between those who had adopted the values of the English gentry and those who defined themselves above all as Christians erupted in 1800 in Greene County. A jury lashed out at two justices who allowed "profane swearing, drinking, fidling [*sic*], and dancing at the time and place of holding their courts"; at the same time, the jury denounced gambling, cardplaying, and, especially, the "custom of leading and parading stud horses in the main street of Greenesborough on public occasions . . . and the profane and indelicate practice of showing stud horses on the Sabbath day at places of public worship." The Baptist Church of Greene County strongly disapproved of such behavior: "Charges of immoral and un-Christian conduct will be brought against Brother K——. He is charged with aiding and abetting in the un-Godly practice of horseracing, in that, he allowed visiting horse owners to quarter their horses on his land." Only the wealthy had the means to indulge in these kinds of "immoral conduct."[37]

As the nineteenth century progressed, class and religious lines ceased to coincide so neatly. Southern evangelicalism, once the preserve of the lower classes and the estranged, changed, as Donald Mathews has observed, from a "relatively volatile, alienated, defiant, and charismatic movement" to one whose "symbols, style of self-control, and rules of social decorum became dominant in the social system." Many in the planter class slowly changed from the rigid haughty patriarchalism of the early eighteenth century into Christian family men, their attitudes toward wives and children guided as much by sentiment and feeling as by unilateral decrees. Devout slaveholders saw the world in a different way than did hedonistic agnostic slaveholders; they respected poor Christian men in a way eighteenth-century planters could not and would not. Similarly, when the wealthy came to abide by the same values that bound the poor, the poor necessarily felt less resentment and social distance between themselves and the rich.[38]

But while class and religious lines became blurred in the mid-nineteenth-century South, the conflict between churchgoers and the more worldly did not. As in the eighteenth century, conflict often surfaced during public occasions. When in 1850, after years of labor, workers finished the long railroad tunnel in Whitfield County which completed the line from Atlanta to Chattanooga, a huge celebration ensued. Champagne, brandy, port, Madeira, and scuppernong wine flowed in abundance. But the religious residents of the community "disapproved bitterly of the bringing into the picture the bottles of intoxicating drinks. They were a religious community, and the ministers for months and months preached against the use of strong drink." Instead of wine, the religious people of Whitfield brought a bottle of water from the River Jordan with which to anoint the tunnel.[39]

Churches had been built in the area that became Whitfield as early as 1847, when "Indians were still roaming the forests." Methodists, Baptists, and Presbyterians joined together to build a log chapel for all to use. By 1851, each denomination had gathered enough strength and money to erect its own church. But when the Reverend J. P. Anthony came to Whitfield as a young Methodist minister in 1853, he "was discouraged by the two local preachers who lived in the town, who assured me that there was no use in trying to run a protracted meeting there; that it had been tried often without result; that it would be a waste of time and strength, etc. I found, too, that most of the membership held the same views." Anthony, undaunted, "began our series of protracted meetings, holding prayer meetings in the day and preaching at night. We ran for some weeks without decided results, but at length the Spirit triumphed. The meeting continued for NINETY-SIX consecutive nights." As a result, the Methodist Church of Dalton added 115 new members.[40]

While Christians struggled to establish new churches in the wilderness of Whitfield, every small neighborhood in Greene had long maintained its own congregation and building. These churches, more than any other institution, provided the center of gravity for Southern public life. People who never set foot inside Greene's impressive courthouse—and a few who did—spent hours every week in church. Churches offered the only place where men and women, whites and blacks, children and adults, rich and poor gathered together—although they did not gather in equality. In one of Greene's larger churches men entered through one door, women and children through another. They sat on different sides of the church as well, the men's side equipped with sand-filled spit boxes for tobacco chewers. Slaves, also divided by gender, sat in the rear of the church. The preachings of these churches provided the standard by which all these Southerners, despite the obvious divisions among them, judged their lives and the lives of others.

Christian morality was not merely a tool used by humorless prudes against irresponsible hedonists in the Superior Court; evangelical Christianity's demanding discipline maintained the community of the God-fearing in the face of temptation. A revealing glimpse of the moral life of these people, of the central temptations and renunciations of the South, appears in the records of the churches. At every monthly conference of the church, the first order of business was to ask, "Are all members present in fellowship and love?" Any member with a grievance against another member remained standing to express his or her concern. The church formed a committee to look into the matter; when the committee made its report the church decided whether to exonerate or reprimand the offenders or, the ultimate punishment, exclude them from member-ship.[41]

In Greene County, as in counties throughout the South, drunken-ness, swearing, quarreling, adultery, and dancing constituted the major transgressions tried before church congregations. One tor-mented man requested that the Bethesda Baptist Church erase his name from the church book: "The dead member should be cut off in order that it might not be offensive and an encumbrance to the living body." Another man, who had committed adultery, confessed his sins and threw himself upon the mercy of the church. "Dear Brethren," he wrote, "it is with pain and grief that I confess that I have grossly violated the law of Christ. . . . I am sorry for my sin but I shall submit without a murmur to any actions the Church may take." He was excluded from fellowship. A native of a mountain com-munity in Virginia remembered the impact of being unchurched:

"To be excluded from the only group that was really meeting and had any influence in the community was right much of a jolt to anyone."[42]

As Frederick Law Olmsted perceived, Southerners, even religious Southerners, seemed adverse to moderation: "Their amusements must be exciting, their festivities are exhausting, as if they were trials of muscular agility and wind and bottom; if they engage in politics, it is as if they were in a battle." Southern religion, too, was "a matter of excitement—of spasms and experiences—of fights with Apollyon and wrestling with Jehovah—of maddening despair, and of ecstatic hope and triumph. . . . " Southerners, more than dignified Northern Protestants of the antebellum period, seemed to find it necessary to impose a rigid and painful discipline upon themselves; they did not seem to rest easily with their godliness. The same distrust of human institutions and human nature that led evangelical ministers to oppose the penitentiary and the state in general also caused them to question themselves. The diaries of Southern women are filled with constant lamentations over the state of their souls, and church minutes are filled with the efforts of Christians to keep themselves separate from the world of assertiveness, pride, and drinking that surrounded them. Southern evangelicals seemed only to be holding the dike until the Kingdom of God arrived, when "Jails and Court Houses dilapidated by time will not be repaired, or perhaps be fitted up for places of worship. The meaning of such words as stocks, pillory, penitentiary and gallows will be forgotten."[43]

Although the sternly enforced moral code of the churches supported the secular legal order, Christians as well as other Southerners perceived the state as only a necessary evil. The deacons of the Penfield Church in Greene warned its members against resorting to the courts in ill will without trying Christian understanding first: "It is evident that if a person engages in a law suit with a desire to trample upon his opponent or to rejoice in his defeat, he is violating the Spirit of the Gospel." The deacons admitted that Christians might sometimes find themselves forced to use the secular law, but warned that the courts should not be resorted to for anything other than "legal formality." Other churches in the South made a rule against "going to law" before taking "Gospel steps."[44]

In effect, the church served as a "state" to govern the lives of church members who took no recourse to the secular state. As a writer in the *Methodist Quarterly Review* observed in 1855, "The pulpit is cheaper than the prison; the Church and the Sabbath school less costly than the police and the standing army that would otherwise be needed to prevent the lawless passions of one class in society from bursting out against another." Or, as a Presbyterian journal put it, "To the end of time there will be Murderers, till then there will be Adulterers, and Fornicators, and Thieves and Liars. But God has given His church the power of discipline, requiring her to expel all such from her bosom." The power was exercised with some frequency. In Greene County, for example, records for three churches show that thirty-eight church members were excommunicated between 1830 and 1860. As in the secular courts, men were disciplined far more often than women. Two Baptist churches in Greene in the 1850s listed a total of 177 white male church members, out of which 17 were excommunicated; of 238 white female members, though, only 4 were excluded from membership. The secular world offered greater temptations, greater rewards, to men than women, while the church reinforced the values of self-abnegation held up as the ideal for Christian daughters, wives, and mothers. To many Southern men, piety seemed fine for women and slaves but too confining for a truly masculine personality.[45]

And yet the church exercised an influence even on men who never came within its walls. The entire community felt the effects of religion, not only in the rural court, in business dealings, in matrimony, and in public affairs, but also when a large revival agitated a community—as one did in Whitfield in 1853 and in Greene in 1859. Unfortunately for the pious, this relatively infrequent social event could not help but attract people little devoted to religion. "There were a great many people there," reported Greene County's local newspaper in 1859, "some went, no doubt, to hear the preaching, while others went to see and to be seen, the latter class being greatly in the majority." One of those apparently less interested in the services, Charles Copelan, attempted to enter the revival tent while drunk. Wesley A. Carlton sought to prevent Copelan from disturbing the services and twice asked him to leave. When Copelan put his hand into his pocket, "as if to take out a knife or pistol," Carlton hit the drunk man over the head with a chair. The resulting wound was "severe, but not dangerous." Three people, not including Copelan, went before the Greene County Superior Court during its next term for disrupting a religious congregation.[46]

Apparently Greene County's black community was marked by the same moral divisions as separated the county's white people, for another altercation also disrupted the 1859 revival. "As is usual at

camp-meetings a large number of negroes were allowed to congregate," complained the *Weekly Gazette*, and "several of them repaired
to the woods, a short distance off, to play cards, drink, or do some
other mischief, when they fell out, got to fighting and the stabbing of
two of the number was the result." But despite the "mischief" of
some, blacks formed an active part of the congregations of all the
churches in Greene County. The black members had "their own
stewards and deacons and elders of their own race who ministered to
them separately." One man, Cyrus, preached to his fellow slaves in
the grove at the Bethesda Baptist Church; after Cyrus chose a topic
for his sermon, his master located the appropriate scripture and read
it to the slave to use as his text. The black officers of the churches
kept as close a watch on black members as white deacons did on
whites. In 1856 a church appointed a committee of three slaves—
Caesar, Shadrach, and Charles—to investigate rumors of "bad
character" concerning three other slaves. In another instance, one
male and two female black church members were excommunicated
for adultery, despite the fact that slave marriage had no basis in
secular law. Christian slaves, no less than Christian whites, lived by
rigid discipline and hated "to be up before the church and
excommunicated, more than aught else in the world," thought Mary
Boykin Chesnut. One slave woman even hanged herself after she had
been expelled from her church.[47]

Although blacks as well as whites received discipline in Greene's
churches for intoxication, sexual offenses, and lying, theft constituted the major infraction for which slaves appeared before the
church—while whites, not surprisingly, were almost never accused
of this offense. In 1850, Brother Peek of the Bethesda Baptist Church
charged his servant Patsy with theft; the next conference "took up the
case of Sister Patsy" and excluded her from membership. Tom,
another slave and a member of another church in Greene, "stated to
the church that he *did take* a small portion of syrup from his master at
the mill when they first commenced making—merely took a little to
eat—was sorry that he had *even* done that and wished the church to
forgive him." It did, after the pastor cautioned Tom against a
repetition of the offense. But black church members often denied
that taking food was theft at all, claiming that "they had merely taken
what was justly theirs."[48]

In 1856, the same Cyrus whom whites trusted enough to preach
to his fellow slaves, "having gotten himself into a difficulty came
forward to the church and acknowledged being guilty . . . of eating

meat which he had reason to believe was stolen. He stated that he was sorry for it, and asked the forgiveness of his offended brethren." Normally, the white church leaders might have been willing to look the other way for such a devout member as Cyrus, "but the Church being aware that the boy who stole the meat was a *runaway* and had been harbored on the plantation to Brother Cyrus's knowledge at least three days before he made it known," the church felt compelled to censure the slave. He was forbidden to preach, and not until two years later was his right to minister to his fellow slaves restored. Slaves such as Cyrus, no matter how devoted to Christianity, necessarily found their faith in conflict with their secular life. The institutional church, despite the spiritual equality with whites it offered, often held out only a dry crust to black members. "We went to the white folks' church," remembered one ex-slave, "so we sit in the back on the floor." When a slave in that church felt redemption, he or she made a profession of faith to the white minister, who would "ask our miss and master what they thought about it and if they could see any change. They would get up and say: 'I notice she don't steal and I notice she don't lie as much and I notice she works better.' Then they let us join. We served our mistress and master in slavery time and not God."[49]

Other ex-slaves made the same complaint. White ministers would preach only " 'Don't steal your master's turkey. Don't steal your master's chickens. Don't steal your master's hawgs. Don't steal your master's meat. Do whatsomeever your master tells you to do.' Same old thing all the time." Regardless of what masters believed, such admonitions apparently convinced few slaves. As one Georgia ex-slave remembered, when the white preacher came to the quarters, "all he ever said was: 'It's a sin to steal; don't steal Master's and Mist'ess' chickens and hogs;' and such lak. How could anybody be converted on that kind of preachin'?" And "sides it never helped none to listen to dat sort of preachin' 'cause de stealin' kept goin' right on every night." Indeed, on the Thornton plantation in Greene County, as on plantations throughout the South, "Everything on the plantation was locked—corn crib, wheat house, carpentry tools, gears and saddles, closets and trunks, and even the attic. The smokehouses were built of brick or stone, with thick walls, heavy doors, and barred windows to keep the slaves away from the meat."[50]

Historians agree that slaves stole, but do not agree on the exact meaning of that theft. Some see theft as rebellious resistance, others as the product of necessity, others as guilt-inducing lapses of the slaves' own Christian morality. Slave theft, of course, was all these things, but analysts have tended to interpret slave testimony concerning theft out of context, thus imposing a false simplicity and uniformity upon a complex phenomenon. Slaves resorted to theft in some places and times more than others, and defended or rationalized it in different ways.

The most unambiguous defense of theft came from those who had run away; hungry runaways did not hesitate, reported one ex-slave, "to knock anybody's pig in the head." Slaves who escaped from the South and wrote accounts of their ordeal portrayed theft as a heroic, revolutionary attack on the system of bondage. Frederick Douglass's protagonist in *The Heroic Slave* told a sympathetic white Northerner that "in contempt of their conventionalities, I did not scruple to take bread where I could get it." The fictional white man responded, "And just there you were right. . . . I once had doubts on this point myself, but a conversation with Gerrit Smith . . . put an end to all my doubts on this point." And Josiah Henson glorified appropriation of white property in the highest terms: "No *white* knight, rescuing white fair ones from cruel oppression, ever felt the throbbing of a chivalrous heart more intensely than I, a *black* knight, did, in running down a chicken in an out-of-the-way place to hide till dark, and then carry it to some poor overworked black fair one, to whom it was at once food, luxury, and medicine. . . . I felt good, moral, heroic." Henson's conscience, he proclaimed, did not "reproach me for it," for such theft was "all the chivalry of which my circumstances and conditions in life admitted."[51]

Slaves who neither ran away nor wrote books also defended theft wholeheartedly. "I don't think I done wrong," remarked one ex-slave who admitted stealing chickens, "cause the place was full of 'em. We sho' earned what we et." A black minister, the Reverend W. B. Allen, said he knew of a few slaves beaten to death for "taking things (the Whites called it 'stealing')." A slave song portrayed theft as something of a necessary challenge:

> I'll eat when I'se hongry,
> An' I'll drink when I'se dry;
> An' if de whitefolks don't kill me,
> I'll live till I die.

In my liddle log cabin,
Ever since I'se been born;
Dere hain't been no nothin'
'Cept dat hard salt parch corn.

But I know whar's a henhouse,
An' de tucky he charve;
An' if ole Masser don't kill me,
I cain't never starve.

Several slave tales portray bondsmen winning their freedom through successful wagers with their masters that they can steal the clothes off the white man's very back.[52]

Several visitors from outside the South commented that slaves saw no wrong in theft from the master. Olmsted argued that "the agrarian notion has become a fixed point of the negro system of ethics: that the result of labour belongs of right to the labourer, and on this ground, even the religious feel justified in using 'massa's' property for their own temporal benefit. This they term 'taking,' and it is never admitted to be a reproach to a man among them that he is charged with it, though 'stealing,' or taking from another than their master, and particularly from one another, is so." An Irish visitor proclaimed, "On becoming more intimate with the general character of the Africans, I like it better: I find they steal, cheat, and hate their masters; and if they were to do otherwise I should think them unworthy of liberty—they justly consider whatever they take to be but a portion of their own." One ex-slave completely turned the tables on whites: "Dey talks a heap 'bout de niggers stealin'. Well, you know what was de fust stealin' done? Hit was in Africky, when de white folks stole de niggers jes' like you'd go get a drove a' hosses and sell 'em."[53]

Other ex-slaves admitted they stole, but showed little pride in the fact. One ex-slave explained, "See old Marse and Missus give us such little rations led her slaves to stealin'. . . . We knowd hit was de wrong thing to do but hunger will make you do a lot of things." Charles Grandy of Virginia said that white preachers warned against theft from masters: " 'Cose we knowed it was wrong to steal, but de niggers had to steal to git sompin' to eat. I know I did." Others seemed angry that they had to steal, and blamed the whites: "White fo'ks allus talkin' 'bout nigger roguish, nigger roguish, an ef it hadn't been fo' dem, nigger wouldn't know nothin' 'bout stealin. . . . Chile, nigger had to steal, an I know ma mommer didn't tell no lie, fo' she was a good woman." Lunsford Lane, a slave who escaped from North Carolina, fumed that "it makes my blood chill to think of, confined to the plantation, with not enough of food and that little of the coarsest kind, to satisfy the gnawings of hunger—compelled oftentimes, to hie away in the night-time, when worn down with work, and *steal*, (if it be stealing). . . . " Arthur Greene made a similar charge. "All you hear now is 'bout de nigger stealin' from dese here po' white devils. De whole cause of stealin' and crime [in the twentieth century] is cause dey fo'ced the niggers to do hit in dem back days. Now hits er following 'em."[54]

For some ex-slaves, there was simply no ambiguity at all. "De Lawd say, 'Dey shall not steal.' . . . Fuddermore, in de 'pistle ob de 'postle, Isiah, he say, 'Be a clean vessel ob de Lawd God.' " Another ex-slave showed pride in his father, for "In slavery days dey was allus whippin' us niggers 'bout stealin'. Massa jus' didn't give us nuff to eat. Dey said my daddy was de only slave he had who wouldn't steal, he'd go hungry first." Fanny Kemble told the story of a slave family one of whose members had been demoted from cook to field hand for stealing a ham. The brother of the reprimanded slave told Kemble that " 'this action had brought disgrace upon the family.' Does not that sound," Kemble asked, "very like the very best sort of free pride, the pride of character, the honourable pride of honesty, integrity, and fidelity?"[55]

Even though slave narratives from the twentieth century probably exaggerated the guilt ex-slaves felt over past thefts, it is obvious that slaves held no single or simple attitude about stealing. Aside from differences in temperament, upbringing, and opportunities, slaves may have been more willing to steal at certain times in their lives than at others. In most cultures, young people are much more prone to theft and other crimes than are older people. Although it cannot be proven, perhaps slave crime followed a similar pattern: young slaves may have seen theft as a challenge and act of rebelliousness, and felt no guilt at all as they enjoyed stolen food. Young fathers and mothers may have stolen periodically; they could and did defend theft to themselves and their children as absolutely justifiable. But the responsibility young adults felt for each other and for their children, and the harsher punishment inflicted on adults caught stealing, may have prevented them from taking advantage of all the opportunities for theft they encountered. On the other hand, slave theft may have been so commonplace partly because so many slaves were young: in the 1850s nearly three-quarters of all slaves were less than 30 years old. Conversely, the elderly seldom commit crimes in any society, and it should not be surprising that elderly ex-slaves were ambivalent about theft in interviews during the 1930s.[56]

The process of reasoning described by Frederick Douglass offers a glimpse into the evolution of a slave's ideas about theft. "So wretchedly starved were we," he remembered, "that we were compelled to live at the expense of our neighbors, or to steal from the home larder. This was a hard thing to do, but after much reflection I reasoned myself into the conviction that there was no other way to do, and that after all there was no wrong in it." Douglass, in other words, did not steal without considering the morality of the act. Young slaves had doubtless been taught by their masters from an early age that it was wrong to steal from them, and it seems unlikely that many slave parents, knowing the likely penalty, encouraged their children to steal. A hungry stomach had to confront a conscience. "To be sure," Douglass continued, "this was stealing, according to the law and gospel I heard from the pulpit, but I had begun to attach less importance to what dropped from that quarter on such points." Young slaves soon learned that much their master told them was self-serving; they could soon see that there was not one absolute truth.[57]

From this understanding grew another, as the young Douglass saw. "It was not always convenient to steal from master, and the same reason why I might innocently steal from him did not seem to justify me in stealing from others. . . . It was necessary that the right to steal from others should be established." A philosophy of rebellion grew out of Douglass's rationalization of theft from all whites. "I am," thought the young Douglass, "not only the slave of Master Thomas, but I am the slave of society at large. Society at large has bound itself, in form and in fact, to assist Master Thomas in robbing me of my rightful liberty, and of the just reward of my labor. . . . The morality of free society could have no application to slave society."[58]

Theft does not usually lead to this realization, which can be seen not only as caste consciousness but also as class consciousness. Even in slavery, where there existed such a convenient and convincing justification for stealing, many slaves apparently did not steal. Slaves who had decided, unlike Frederick Douglass, to combat slavery from within its seemingly unbreakable confines by a total devotion to the Christianity taught in the Bible had, in Eugene Genovese's words, "mixed feelings" and experienced "some degradation" when they saw theft in their midst. This is evidence both of humankind's capacity for righteousness in the face of adversity and of the force of a hegemonic morality—the ability of a dominant group to convince oppressed groups than one standard of morality should apply to all, even though that standard serves the needs of the powerful. Slavery is the most naked example of class exploitation, and slaves' tensions over theft are those, albeit in an extreme form, that underlie any society in which one class suffers at the hands of another. As in slavery, only a few in any society make the leap from justifying theft to justifying, as Douglass did, revolution. The great majority of poor thieves, slave and free, do not create an alternative system of values—they merely explain away, or "neutralize," the existing one. And while such neutralization may balm the thief's conscience, it leaves the oppression that created the conditions for theft untouched and unchallenged.[59]

Whites, of course, did not present a united front against black theft; there is much evidence that slaves and whites often worked in criminal collusion. Such cooperation across racial lines enjoyed a long tradition. In colonial South Carolina a brisk "underground economy" developed in which slaves provided and whites bought a wide range of stolen property. In the nineteenth century, too, slaveowners frequently complained that poor whites trafficked with slaves. "Liquor is no respecter of persons or color," observed Daniel R. Hundley. "Hence the Southern slaves always contrive, either by hook or by crook, to carry on their nefarious but secret traffic, often exchanging a whole porker, worth from five to ten dollars, for a single bottle of rum, worth intrinsically perhaps not more than fifty cents." But because the state had virtually nothing to do with slaves, the white men at the other end of this trade actually risked greater danger than the slave: "the porker costs the darkey only the trouble of killing and cleaning it, and the [white] midnight purchaser runs the risk of the penitentiary every time he closes such a bargain." Nevertheless, propertied whites worried about blacks' role in this exchange. Not only did slaves have to steal to procure something to trade, but the association of black and white on terms of such equality eroded racial boundaries. "Whenever two criminals have the same terrible secret to keep," warned Hundley, "there is sure to spring up a sympathy betwixt them; hence, there is a real sympathy between the slaves and the groggery keepers, and this is why the latter are sometimes abolitionists."[60]

Moreover, as a Greene grand jury warned, liquor was "ruinous alike to the health and morals of this class of our community, and detrimental to the best interests of their owners by impairing their value and general usefulness." The *Temperance-Banner* of Greene protested in vain that "with due respect to all parties concerned, we must remark, for the life of us, we could not account for the fact, or see the reason of the thing, in the Legislature taking so much care of the life, morals, and usefulness of the black population, in the stringent enactments against furnishing them with spiritous liquors, and not one word in regard to the white man." The jurors suggested that the fee for a liquor license be raised to $500; the class bias of such a step is obvious, and so is the fear it betrayed. "What is it these fellows say practically—perhaps in words—to the negroes whom they furnish with bad whiskey?" asked Greene's *Weekly Gazette* in 1859. "This, 'your master is a tyrant who abridges your rights when he forbids you to drink at my bar.' "[61]

But the cross-racial sympathy engendered by what might be called the "gray market" should not be exaggerated; for valuable stolen property, slaves received only "poisonous liquors—chiefly the worst whiskey, much watered and made stupefying by an infusion of tobacco." And violence frequently erupted between blacks and whites in such settings. A judge of the North Carolina Supreme Court described the slaveowners' perception of these conflicts: "These offenses are usually committed by men of dissolute habits, hanging loose upon society, who, being repelled from association with well disposed citizens, take refuge in the company of colored persons and slaves, whom they deprave by their example, embolden by their familiarity, and then beat, under the expectation that a slave dare not resent a blow from a white man." This expectation was often wrong: the surviving records of slave crime reveal that whites other than owners and overseers were the most frequent victims of slave violence. When lower-class whites and blacks associated outside the institutional boundaries of slavery, both sides played with fire. When a white and a slave mixed in the temporary familiarity, even equality, of a shared bottle or card game, either person might easily perceive an affront, intended or not.[62]

Although whites considered most blacks to be thieves and knew that some blacks had killed whites, whites did not generally consider slaves violent people. The feelings of a Southern physician who often traveled alone at night seem to have been widely shared: "in a solitary place, the sudden appearance of a white man generally excited some apprehension with regard to personal safety, but the sight of a black man was always cheering, and made him feel safe. Husbands and fathers felt secure on leaving home for several days, even where their houses are surrounded by negro cabins and the dwellings of the whites are much scattered." Similarly, U. B. Phillips's claim that whites "learned of crimes by individual negroes with considerable equanimity" seems essentially correct. Although slave-owners locked up their smokehouses and corn cribs, they did not lock their houses or bedroom doors. One slaveholder thought slaves "are more generally good-tempered than other people—they are kind to each other." And the Reverend Charles Colcock Jones, a master not indiscriminate in his praise for slaves, was forced to conclude that "with truth it may be said, there are fewer personal injuries, and manslaughters, and murders among the Negroes in the South, than among the same amount of population in any part of the United States; or, perhaps, in the world." At the time of emancipation white Southerners did not believe that slaves, by Southern standards, were particularly violent. But that was because they believed that slavery "tamed" the naturally bestial black. As George Fredrickson has argued, Southern whites felt that as a slave the black man "was lovable, but as a freedman he would be a monster"; or as a slaveholder put it, "the negro must, from necessity, be the slave of man or the slave of Satan."[63] Such stereotypes did not bode well for the future.

Slave violence was by no means as rare as white Southerners wanted to believe. For example, six slaves—including two women— were tried for murder in Greene County in the decade before the Civil War. In one case, William F. Luckie was preparing to punish one of his slaves, who had been hiding in the woods of Greene County for several months and had just been caught, when suddenly, reported the *Weekly Gazette*, "the negro grasped him and taking a knife from his hand, stabbed him, we understand, in fifteen different places, killing him in a very few minutes." Violence of slave against master frequently began during such scenes of punishment, or after a sudden or humiliating change in an established though tacit balance of power between slave and master. Violence erupted when a young son of a master used his authority too strongly, when a detested overseer tried to rule exclusively by coercion, when a usually lenient master or mistress asserted authority in an arbitrary or cruel way, when a widowed master or mistress remarried and the new partner pushed too hard too soon. In other words, violence erupted when slaves believed their fragile traditional rights had been infringed upon in an inexcusable way.[64]

Blacks, of course, also killed each other, though there is no way to know how often, since courts often overlooked such matters. Daniel R. Hundley's description of the violence of slave against slave conveys the same bewilderment that Northerners and foreign visitors experienced when confronting the violence of white Southerners: "And it is utterly confounding for what trivial causes they will take the life of a fellow-slave. Sometimes it is simply a dispute about a game of cards or marbles; sometimes the being supplanted by a rival in the confidence of the master or overseer is the exciting cause; but much more frequently jealousy leads to the fatal deeds." Perhaps slaves were as sensitive to insult from each other as were their masters and other white men. One ex-slave, Henry Bland, told of fighting another slave who had pulled a pistol at a "frolic" at Bland's home plantation; his master had told Bland always to fight back when anyone struck him, whether the person was white or black. Indeed, if the master "heard of his not fighting back a whipping would be in store for him." Not many masters encouraged black violence against whites, but apparently blacks in slavery did not hesitate to fight each other when the occasion warranted. Much of this violence remained hidden from white view, however, and blacks were generally perceived as a gentle people by whites who knew them.[65]

The punishment of slaves by masters was as varied as human nature. The slave narratives tell of tolerant masters, but they also tell of a slaveowner who forced a slave thief to eat a raw chicken, of a master who "made de overseer tie dat dead Nigger to de one what kilt him, and de killer had to drag de corpse 'round 'til he died too," and of the shame of a young black woman who refused to submit sexually to her young master and so was whipped, naked, in the courthouse square. Some masters hated to inflict punishment, but another "just whupped them because he could." Masters hesitated to punish respected slaves who could foment resistance among other slaves, but hastened to make examples of troublemakers. Unfortunately for the master's consistency, however, these two kinds of slaves were not mutually exclusive. Every plantation contained a complex social world, and masters whipped indiscriminately at the risk of throwing that world into chaos.[66]

Most rural masters had little choice, unlike their urban counter-parts, except to punish their slaves without the help of the state. But the state did punish slaves for crimes committed off the plantation. As with urban whites, the less formal magistrate's courts dealt most harshly with suspects, handing out sentences of thirty-nine lashes to slaves for relatively minor offenses with little compunction and little deliberation. The Superior Courts, though, handled the trials of slaves accused of more serious offenses with close attention to procedural rules; in fact, wherever scholars have looked they have found that slaves were convicted no more frequently than whites in Superior and state Supreme Courts. Greene County's court found slaves guilty in exactly the same proportion as white defendants: three out of four. Further, the written law of slavery became less harsh as the antebellum era progressed and slavery became a stronger and more firmly entrenched institution. In general, too, the newer states in the southwest placed the greatest emphasis on procedural fairness for slaves.[67]

It must be recognized, however, that the law acted as a shield for blacks only in a very limited sense. It was true that blacks accused of major offenses could expect procedural fairness; once slaves entered the higher levels of the judicial machinery, in particular, they were treated much like whites. When masters resorted to the courts to punish their slaves and saw to it that at least the forms of justice were followed, they strengthened their sense of moral legitimacy. When, for example, the Reverend Charles Colcock Jones accused one of his female slaves, Lucy, of killing her newborn baby, he took her before a local court. The magistrate sentenced the slave to eight days' imprisonment and ninety lashes—the lightest possible punish-ment for the crime. Although, Jones wrote his son, he decided not to prosecute two accessories, Mose and Katy, "for the sake of impres-sion, the constable by my discretion gave them a few stripes over their jackets. And so the matter ended. The trial was conducted with fairness, deliberation, and gravity." Jones drew out the moral of the story: "if owners would more frequently refer criminal acts of their servants to the decision of the courts, they would aid in establishing correct public sentiment among themselves in relation to different kinds of crimes committed by the Negroes, give better support to their own authority, and restrain the vices of the Negroes them-selves." The reverend's son, a lawyer (and future mayor of Savan-nah), concurred: "The effect upon Mose and Katy is probably better than it would have been had actual punishment been inflicted. The power of the law is brought to bear, they made to realize the fact of a misdemeanor committed and a new element of mercy and forebearance impressed upon them."[68]

A fair legal system may have helped convince slaveholders that they were just, but slaves saw too much evidence to the contrary to place much faith in the law. As one slave put it when told by Olmsted that the law required masters to give their slaves meat, "Oh, but some of 'em don't mind Law, if he does say so, massa. Law never here; don't know anything about him." The law, it seems, protected slaves when they were on the highly visible stage of the courtroom, but did little to protect slaves from their masters when both were out of the spotlight. Few masters were punished by the courts for cruelty to their slaves, although mistreatment of slaves by men other than the master or overseer did receive punishment; eight white men came before the Greene Superior Court in the 1850s for "beating, whipping, or wounding a slave." Four of them were found guilty and received fines. Slaveholders thus exercised two kinds of power through the law. By adhering to a highly formalistic system of justice for serious slave criminals, slaveholders helped legitimize their class rule, at least in their own eyes; by preserving their personal control over day-to-day life on the plantation, slaveholders prevented the law from insulating slaves from their master's will. The slaves had to provide that insulation themselves.[69] As Frederick Douglass commented, the plantation was "a little nation of its own, having its own language, its own rules, regulations and custom. The law and institutions of the state, apparently touch it nowhere. The troubles arising here, are not settled by the civil power of the state. The overseer is generally accuser, judge, jury, advocate and executioner. The criminal is always dumb." White Southerners were pleased with the efficiency and cheapness of this system: "On our estates we dispose with the whole machinery of public police and public courts of justice," bragged J.D.B. DeBow. "Thus we try, decide, and execute the sentence of *thousands of cases*, which, in other countries would go into the courts." Southerners believed this system was evidence of a healthy society, and gloated when the North had to wrestle with criminal blacks. A North Carolina newspaper observed in 1845 that New York's Sing Sing prison contained 195 black inmates, and commented, "Here we see the degraded and melancholy condition to which the free blacks of New York are reduced. . . . North Carolina contains more than two hundred and fifty thousand slaves and free persons of color, and yet we doubt whether, out of all these, as many as 195 are convicted of crimes in one year. Such facts speak for themselves." Except, of course, that "the facts" did not say that North Carolina's courts had little to do with slaves and that the state contained no penitentiary to confine slaves if courts did convict them.[70]

When Southern courts did find slave criminals guilty, their punishment necessarily focused on the body. A slave named Scott convicted for the murder of another slave in Greene County in 1851, for example, received thirty-nine lashes at five different times— "severely but not barbarously inflicted"—and was branded with an *M* on his right cheek. Greene County saw three slaves hanged in the 1850s, all for murder. A young girl described the hanging of a slave in a county neighboring Greene: "By ten Oclock a great many people thronged the streets, and clustered around the old weather beaten jail. Our little company had become quite a respectable crowd before we reached the Public Square where we drove slowly through the immense mass of living beings. . . . The high and low the rich and poor the free and the bond alike pressing forward to the gallows their desires of seeing the law enforced and crime meet its own reward."[71]

When whites hanged slaves, they used the ritual to impress upon the blacks in attendance the folly of violence against whites. And whites made sure most blacks were in attendance. Some two to three thousand people, including slaveholder and diarist John Horrey Dent, heard a slave in Alabama exhort his fellow bondsmen from the scaffold: "Dabney's last confession was, that, disobedience had brot him to the gallows, and advised his colored brethren to take warning by his case and be obedient." Dabney and the other slave guilty of the same offense then knelt in secret prayer, while the sheriff lowered caps over their heads, adjusted the ropes around their necks, and made the ropes secure to the beam. When the sheriff cut the rope with a hatchet "they were launched into another world. . . . The whole was conducted in a very solemn and proper manner."[72]

The parts people played, both large and small, in all the dramas of crime and punishment in the rural slave South were simple and well-rehearsed. In black belt and upcountry, many white men drank hard, gambled, and fought—and sometimes went to court and paid a fine for their offenses. An unlucky few were caught stealing a horse or money—and almost certainly went to the penitentiary. And there were those, too, who assaulted a friend over cards in a drunken fury or more soberly murdered an enemy over an insult. Some of these violent men, thanks to circumstances or their connections, went free; less fortunate men received a small fine, while others were loaded on a train for the state penitentiary. Very few went to the gallows.

Justice was personal and concrete in the slave South, for whites and for blacks. Twice a year respectable citizens, wealthier and perhaps more upright than the usual run of rural white men, performed jury duty; they surveyed the moral condition of the county, chided its shortcomings, and periodically brought gamblers, liquor vendors, and fornicators to mild justice. They dismissed most cases brought before them, though, and other cases disappeared of their own accord when offenders or witnesses left the county. Petit jurors, men of more diverse economic background than grand jurors and certainly of less visible stature in the county, judged the relatively few offenders sent before them with neither great leniency nor great harshness. Most convicted people left the courthouse a bit poorer after paying a fine, but had to spend no time in the ramshackle jail. Other people who might have eventually met trouble because of their drunkenness or fighting were disciplined by their church instead. Cases of theft by blacks that would otherwise have filled court dockets never went beyond the bounds of the plantation.

Southerners such as George Fitzhugh looked at the effect of these interlocking institutions and proclaimed that "at the slaveholding South all is peace, quiet, plenty and contentment. . . . We have but few in our jails, and fewer in our poor houses."[73] Southerners who made these claims were not lying—but neither were they acknowledging the hidden costs of the antebellum order. As long as slavery held the vast majority of the region's poor under rigid control, the South could afford a weak state, could afford to leave most white men alone, could afford to treat even accused criminals with leniency. But what would happen if the unimaginable came to pass, if slavery should come to a sudden end, if the white South had to pay the price for the peace and security purchased by its centuries of slavery?

PART TWO

5

War and Reconstruction

On the eve of the Civil War the South presented a complicated, even paradoxical picture of crime and punishment. An archaic culture of honor bred violence among all classes of white men, yet one of the most "modern" institutions—the penitentiary—functioned throughout the South, so that the state exercised centralized, if tenuous, control of its most serious convicted criminals. Southern cities had become in many ways indistinguishable from their Northern counterparts, prosperous but vulnerable to the juxtaposition of divergent classes and ethnic groups as well as to the whims of the international market. The internal life of the plantations producing for that same market, however, showed no signs of change or weakness. Slaves remained under firm control, although they did engage in widespread theft. In general, crime did not present a topic of great worry in the Old South. Cities remained small, the state remained weak; most white people had come to expect some violence in their communities and accepted slave theft as one of the unavoidable and rather minor costs of the system. Rural courts spent as much time and energy dealing with liquor and gambling offenses as with serious crime. Southerners believed that crime was far more characteristic of the North than of their own ordered agrarian society.

The Civil War brought overwhelming change to this society so distrustful of change. The walls of slavery, walls that had given structure to the entire South, slowly crumbled. For a while after the

141

war nothing took their place. Whites and blacks fended for themselves throughout the South, while the federal government and local vigilante groups vied for power. Soon, local governments expanded their reach to include the freedmen, and as a result the state became fundamentally altered in the South. Simultaneously, the international market economy engulfed individuals and large portions of the region that had remained untouched by the market before the war. Neither the state nor the market exercised total control over their respective spheres, however, and pure physical coercion by individuals and vigilantes remained a crucial element of Southern "crime" control, political conflict, and economic relationships. By the end of Reconstruction a new configuration of crime and punishment had emerged in the South, a hybrid that was to endure for generations to come.

I

Every community in the South experienced its own war, its own trajectory of hope and despair. Greene County's war had more in common with the experiences of other black belt counties throughout the South than it did with Whitfield's; Whitfield's war resembled that of mountain areas in Tennessee, Virginia, North Carolina, and Alabama; Savannah's war bore striking similarities to that of other towns and cities throughout the South. Every kind of Southern community saw its wartime history punctuated by distinct kinds of crime and punishment.

A group of outraged citizens assembled at the courthouse in Greensboro as soon as the news of Abraham Lincoln's election reached Greene County. The court building, the *Planters' Weekly* reported, "was crowded to its utmost capacity, and it is believed that so large a meeting has never before been held in the County." The election of Abraham Lincoln, the meeting resolved, had "taken place on grounds prejudiced to the interests and honor of the Southern portion of the Confederacy, making it necessary for the people of the South to vindicate their rights and their position before the world." The meeting did not rush headlong into calling for secession, and the lengthy resolutions it passed soberly weighed expediency against principle. Greene's leading citizens foresaw that secession would throw their world into greater chaos than they could ever suffer within the Union. The Union, too, was precious for its own sake and should not be tossed aside casually: "the monarchies of Europe have ever looked with a jealous eye upon the Republican Institutions of

America," read the resolutions, "and are even now predicting their downfall." Every means of settling the conflict between North and South should be tried, but should such efforts fail, "which may heaven avert, we believe that the people of the Southern States should secede from the American Union, peaceably if they can, forcibly if they must." Of all the men gathered in Greene's courthouse, only five or six voted against the resolutions. Within a week, Greensboro saw vigilant citizens form into groups of "Minute Men," as they called themselves, to protect what they perceived to be their republican freedom. The band soon recruited "numbers very creditable to the noble spirit of Southern Independence." All three of Greene's delegates to the state secession convention two months later voted for immediate disunion.[1]

Savannah, too, ultimately endorsed secession, apparently with "wild enthusiasm," and its delegates unanimously lent their voices to the chorus calling for Southern independence. But Savannah had faced discord in reaching this decision that Greene had not; the city's diversity of population bred diversity of opinion when civil war threatened. Recognizing the danger of dissent and without waiting for their officials to act, citizens held a public meeting in Savannah and created a Vigilance Committee in 1859, before Lincoln's election, "to detect and expose such persons as may be suspected of entertaining or uttering sentiments hostile to slavery" and to "use the most expedient means to secure their immediate removal." A special meeting of the city council declared its "decided disapprobation" when, a few months later, "certain individuals in the community . . . inflicted violent punishment upon persons in this city, without due authority of law." Not surprisingly, those Savannah residents who opposed secession generally kept their opinions to themselves for the time being; unionists met openly elsewhere in Georgia but not in Savannah. The city's foreign-born and Northern-born who expressed unionist sympathies would not receive the same toleration respected native Southerners might enjoy. When push came to shove, the Southernness of the Southern city triumphed. Dissent from outsiders would not be tolerated.[2]

In Whitfield County, on the other hand, people opposed to secession made their feelings known. As in upcountry counties throughout the region, small farmers harbored deep reservations about fighting a war to protect what some considered to be the interests of distant planters. Whereas all of Greene's and Savannah's delegates to the secession convention supported immediate disunion, two of Whitfield's three delegates opposed an immediate break. The republicanism of the small farmer, as the earlier debates over the penitentiary revealed, focused loyalty on the local community, not on the state. The individual rights of white men, not states' rights, were their primary concern. Fortunately for the Confederacy, however, many in the upcountry became convinced after the fall of Fort Sumter that the "tyrannical" North threatened the liberty of all Southerners, not just that of the wealthy. As the Whitfield grand jury of May 1861 declared, the federal government had become "converted into an engine of injustice and oppression" which had let "loose the dogs of war upon us. In this our hour of trial, it behooves us as patriots all standing as sentinels upon the watch-tower of liberty, to guard well the Citadel." In the midst of this rousing call to valiant republicans, however, a tone of worry crept in: the grand jury warned good Confederates to "see that no enemies approach from without, and that no traitors are ensconced within." The Whitfield grand jury assured itself that all citizens of the county would be loyal to the South, but they recommended that "home guards should be organized . . . to keep a vigilant eye upon all."[3]

While these admonitions revealed the potential divisions within the new Confederate nation, whatever its form, the black belt enthusiastically armed itself for war. Two-thirds of the adult white men in Greene County joined the rebel army. Most of them enlisted immediately after secession, and the draft law of 1862 touched Greene lightly. As Greene's men prepared to go off to war, the county's residents gathered at a ceremony. Laura Alfriend, a beautiful girl of fourteen, stood behind a curtain on a stage as a symbol of the emerging Southern nation. The curtains rose to reveal Laura dressed in flowing robes, the new Confederate flag draped from her arm. Suddenly the flame of the candle footlights ignited her dress and "the horrified audience saw the flames flare up and envelop her, saw the Confederate flag burn in her outstretched hand." The political allegory of Laura Alfriend's death proved to be truer and more terrible than anyone in Greene could have imagined in the heady days of 1861.[4]

As the months passed and war raged in Virginia, Tennessee, and Mississippi, poverty and unequal sacrifices on the Georgia home front began to reveal conflicts that had remained hidden in antebellum Southern society, and to create new ones as well. As early as June of 1861, "A Citizen and A Soldier" wrote a stern letter to Greene's *Planters' Weekly* in which he declared: "This is emphatically the People's war, and the people must sustain it or perish." In the county's efforts to raise money for indigent soldiers and their families, "the very men who have not contributed are frequently men of wealth, having lands and negroes, and wives and daughters to defend. The very women who grumble when requested to make soldiers' clothing are the wives of rich men! Thank God such men are few, and such women are fewer. Yet such exist; I know it and it makes my heart burn." In Whitfield County the grand jury complained of the "continued circulation amongst our citizens of abolition and incendiary News Papers, and Pamphlets, published by our enemies."[5]

In Savannah, some people of Northern and foreign birth left the city soon after the the war began. Many of these people, a letter to the *News* complained, had been merchants: "three dry goods men, two shoe establishments, two jewellers, one cotton press man, several cotton merchants, one *artist*, and many others besides." After the Confederacy began drafting soldiers in 1862, several hundred of the foreign-born of the working class—most of them Irish—signed oaths swearing that they had never intended to declare citizenship, and thus made themselves ineligible for the draft. A newspaper in Georgia's capital observed these desertions from the Southern cause and contemptuously declared, "There is a vast deal of traitorous material in Savannah." The fault lines in Southern society previously hidden by republicanism and prosperity—fault lines of class, subregion, and ethnicity—began to tremble and widen as the war shook the continent.[6]

Soon the market economy entered a period of crisis as well. As early as the spring of 1862, a visitor to Savannah discovered that "a strange, mysterious, weird quietude reigns perpetually. Stagnation and paralysis obstruct the channels where business briskly flowed. Indeed the whole town—everything—*seems* to have *halted*, in the precise attitude of one who . . . is listening all agog for some unidentified announcement to be made." A Savannah merchant wrote to his daughter in New York that "Business has played out in Savannah and if possible is getting worse every day. . . . Two-thirds of the business houses have closed." The city spent nearly $23,000 in 1862 alone to feed the poor and keep them warm. Several private charitable groups organized to help the destitute.[7]

The poor in other Southern cities suffered even more than those in Savannah, and a wave of provision riots, often led by soldiers' wives, swept through the urban South in 1863. In Richmond the rioters, according to one observer, were "dressed in all sorts of odd rigs; armed with hatchets, knives, axes,—anything they could lay their hands on." The governor of Virginia tried to calm them: "They hooted at him. Then Jeff Davis made a speech; they hooted at him too; they didn't want speeches, they said; they wanted bread. Then they begun to plunder the stores." Riots broke out in small towns such as Salisbury and High Point, North Carolina; in major ports such as Mobile; and in cities throughout Georgia: Augusta, Macon, Atlanta, Columbus. These Southern cities spawned riots for the same reasons they had spawned most of the region's recorded crime against property before the war: they attracted large numbers of people who depended on the market economy for their subsistence, and they forced widely varying classes and ethnic groups into close quarters. With rail lines closed and with a Union blockade strangling the South, anything other than a purely local market ceased to exist. Food became increasingly scarce. Inflation ran rampant; many kinds of commodities virtually disappeared. The rich, however, seemed as immune from suffering in wartime as they had in the fifties, and the poor bitterly resented the failure of the wealthy to join in the common sacrifice. Large-scale though sporadic revolt was temporarily the result of the poor's hunger and resentment.[8]

The war brought desperate poverty, too, to rural areas that had escaped the worst of antebellum financial panics. Unfortunately for the Confederacy, military strategy dictated that the ravages of war fall with special vengeance upon the upcountry, the very part of the South whose allegiance to the new Confederate state was most tenuous. The Southern army, strapped for supplies, often "impressed" whatever it needed from local farmers. The "army waggons and parts of command of cavalry of our army is taking our produce our horses cattle sheep and hogs and very seldom pay anything when they do it," John W. Cains of Whitfield complained to Governor Joseph E. Brown in 1863. "They go into the cornfields and load their wagons and goes off and dont let a person know anything about it." As Confederate Secretary of War James Seddon admitted, impressment was "a harsh, unequal, and odious mode of supply." But the armies had to eat, and the poor farmers of the upcountry had to feed the soldiers—voluntarily or involuntarily.[9]

Just as hardship engendered by the market economy had triggered theft in Southern cities in 1857, so did the hardship of war trigger widespread theft on the Southern home front after 1861. Whitfield's Superior Court, which had prosecuted few thieves before the war, saw 106 people come before the grand jury for theft between 1861 and 1865—and no court records have survived from 1864. Gangs of deserters roamed the upcountry late in the war, stealing whatever they wanted, especially from the homes of the wealthy. Some of the accused thieves in Whitfield's records may well have belonged to such bands, for many defendants were prosecuted in groups; before the war, most thieves had been prosecuted individually. In the country as in the city, the Civil War saw group action emerge alongside isolated theft.[10]

Throughout the Confederacy, planters in localities disrupted by the war complained that "the lower classes . . . are engaged in rob[b]ing and stealing every thing that comes in their way, and that people of property suffer more from these wretches than from the Yankees." As a Georgia overseer described matters, "Times is hard here and worse is coming for if the yanks dont get here our own people is getting so mean that I see no chance to live among them for they can nearly steal the chew tobacco out a man's mouth and him not know it." Wealthy people in the rural South worried that class tensions might flare into open rebellion if the hunger and privation of the poor persisted. The divisions that had always lain beneath the surface of Southern republicanism threatened to break into the open, destroying the fiction of white equality. Mass desertion, bread riots, and widespread theft testified to discontent and increasing desperation.[11]

Meanwhile, the war itself came closer and closer to Georgia. Union forces finally fought their way through Tennessee to the "Empire State of the South" in 1864, and it soon became clear that they planned to enter Georgia through Whitfield. The county knew what to expect from the invaders, for it had seen evidence of the war's terrors months before Federal forces pushed into Georgia. During the battles in nearby Chattanooga in late 1863, carloads of wounded had been shipped to Dalton. Wounded soldiers filled every church and house in the small town; "the ladies of Dalton gave up for bandages every linen table cloth, and every sheet they possessed." When word came that the Confederate army had lost Missionary Ridge and was falling back to Dalton, "the whole town was hushed in gloom and despair. Some gathered together what household goods they could pack and ship, closed up their homes, and refugeed to South Georgia and Alabama." Those who remained in Dalton in the winter of 1863–64 saw 50,000 Confederates camped out in the country surrounding the town; thousands of campfires lit up the snow-covered hills at night. The winter was unusually cold for Georgia, and the ragged and freezing army foraged for food among farms that had little left to offer.[12]

To make matters even more troublesome in Whitfield, prostitutes flocked to the winter encampment in Dalton. One officer in the Army of Tennessee wrote that "complaints are daily made to me of the number of lewd women in this town, and on the outskirts of the army. They are said to be impregnating this whole command, and the Commissariat has been frequently robbed, with a view of supporting these disreputable characters." General Johnston, fearing the effects of these "lewd women," ordered Whitfield searched; all females unable to prove their "respectability" and honest means of support were to be shipped away from the soldiers. If a prostitute returned, she was to be locked up and given only bread and water.[13]

With the spring of 1864 the fighting began again in Whitfield; theft and prostitution slowed as two huge armies moved into combat. General William T. Sherman had spent the winter in Chattanooga with 90,000 men—almost twice as many as the Confederate force in Dalton—and now he began to move south toward Atlanta. Battles thundered in the hills of Whitfield throughout the summer as the Union army ground its way southward through the county. By September, despite resistance by the Confederates south of Dalton, Sherman occupied Atlanta. A small Northern force remained in Dalton, and the town saw scattered fighting for the rest of the war.[14]

After provisioning themselves in Atlanta, Sherman's troops burned vital portions of the important rail center, cut their lines to the north, and set out 60,000 strong on a march to the sea. The Union forces followed the railroad, the instrument of the market economy, the link between the wealthy cotton-producing counties and the commercial cities on the coast. Fortunately for Greene, Sherman's forces passed on a railroad to the south of the county. Even so, "bands of foraging soldiers came through here for nearly a week, carrying off much of the livestock and provisions still in the county." The Union soldiers met no resistance as they walked through Greene, and several slaves took advantage of the soldiers' presence to leave the county. Like their counterparts throughout the South, Greene's slaves apparently kept a low profile until the right opportunity to seize their freedom appeared. Whether still on the plantation or following the Union army, slaves, like hungry whites, stole with relative impunity during the war. One "Old Planter" complained, "There is no police, no watch, no guards to arrest them. . . . The usual safeguards of locks, houses, fences, are as nothing." When masters abandoned their houses, slaves who remained behind sometimes carried off everything of value; others, later glorified in Southern legend, protected the whites' property from foragers of both races.[15]

Slaves in Savannah, like slaves throughout the South, took advantage of wartime laxity to steal food and take freedom wherever they found it. As the war dragged on, blacks made up a higher and higher percentage of those before the Mayor's Court. By 1864 over half of those arrested by Savannah's police were black; before the war it had been only 16 percent. The increase was largely relative, however, for the court records reveal no "crime wave" perpetrated by either race; despite complaints of lawlessness, police in wartime Savannah had less strength than their antebellum predecessors and could do little to maintain the strict public order of the 1850s. One letter to the *News* in 1864 urged the city police, "(if we have any)," to do something about "uproarious" blacks who had been gathering on the streets for months. Other whites claimed it "almost impossible to walk the streets without meeting some negro with a segar stuck in his mouth, puffing its smoke in the faces of persons passing." Savannah's whites made the same discovery whites made everywhere in the South: the obedience of slaves had not been as willing, as "natural," as it had appeared. Without the strength of the state, and without the constant vigilance of united whites, the intricate fabric of racial etiquette began to unravel almost immediately.[16]

Appomattox was an anticlimax for much of the South; the war had already ended hundreds of times throughout the Confederacy as the inexorable march of the Union army divided the South into smaller and smaller pieces. For Greene County, the formal end of the war actually brought renewed hardship. As the defeated Confederate troops straggled home, hundreds of men on their way to farms and families in south Georgia passed through Greene. One night, over 1,600 exhausted and hungry ex-soldiers camped near the Bethesda Baptist Church. "Though much of the county's food supplies had been carried away, eaten, or stolen," Arthur Raper has written, "the bottoms of the flour barrels were scraped again, and the corn cribs hidden away in the pine thickets were opened. At the command of the officers, the farm stock was driven away to a safe place so no Southern solidier on foot would be tempted to take a mule or horse." While these scenes were being enacted in Greene, the county's own surviving soldiers were walking home through other depleted communities. But of the 600 men the county had sent to war, 200 would never return; 200 more had been crippled or wounded.[17]

The most far-reaching change in the history of crime and punishment in the nineteenth-century South—the state's assumption of control over blacks from their ex-masters—was halting and tenuous. The transition began the moment a master told his slaves they were free. Alfred Parrott, a young slave in Greene County, heard a version of the speech reluctantly delivered throughout the slave South in 1865. "You all is just as free as I is," the Reverend Hardy C. Peek told his slaves. "You ain't obliged to call me old Mahster no more. You can call me Mister Peek, if you want to. You just go now and catch your mules. I'll give you a third of all you make." The mules had to wait. The Reverend Peek's slaves, along with the other slaves in Greene, would celebrate their freedom first. "Shouting, laughing, singing, crying, the men, women, and children made for the big road, joined passing slaves from other plantations. Hundreds of them gathered on the road, walked along together." They stopped as darkness approached and listened to Joe Peek, an elderly slave, who preached the first sermon of his life on that night. Some ex-slaves embarked on journeys to find lost families, others came from outside the county to be reunited with their spouses and children in Greene. Whites shook their heads, worried and waited to see what the following days, months, and years would bring.[18]

Not dramatic battles, but quiet and increasingly desperate poverty constituted the central experience of most people on the home front. The war came in small ways as well as large: word that scarce corn had been stolen from the crib as well as bad news from the front, a bitter quarrel with one's richer or poorer neighbor as well as with the distant Yankees, an emotionally charged parting of master and slave as well as accounts of Appomattox. The war exerted a drastic change in Southern life, but many of the surface things remained the same. One knew the same people, black and white. People held on to the religion, political creed, and culture that had always sustained them, even as the basis of the government and the economy shifted beneath their feet. The South in 1865 was a society without a center, a sense of control, a sense of direction. All certainties had been destroyed.

II

In the five years following the end of the Civil War two groups—one a bureaucratic agency of the federal government and the other a vigilante organization of rural white Southerners—tried to impose their vision of order upon the South. The Freedmen's Bureau and the Ku Klux Klan wrestled not only for power, but also for differing ideals of justice. These organizations faded away within a few turbulent years, but the South long bore their imprints.

Southern whites tried to salvage as much of the antebellum order as they could and waited to see what change would be forced upon them. The legislatures of Mississippi and South Carolina met in the fall of 1865 and enacted their notorious "Black Codes," laws which reserved corporal punishment for blacks and which defined "vagrancy" in such a broad and ambiguous way as to perpetuate de facto slavery. Although many Northern states themselves severely circumscribed blacks' legal rights, the defiant new laws of the South seemed to announce that the white South had not repented, had not changed despite the sacrifice of over 300,000 Northern men. The reaction to the Black Codes was swift in the newspapers of the North and in the halls of Congress, and Southern lawmakers soon recognized that blatant discrimination recorded in legal codes for all to see was unnecessary and unwise. Laws could be devised that, although officially color-blind, could still effectively control the freedmen. These new statutes made no mention of race, but instead greatly enlarged the discretionary power of local judges and juries. County courts could now choose lengths and types of punishment from a much broader range than had been available in the antebellum era. The possible punishments for vagrancy, rape, arson, and burglary— crimes whites considered peculiarly "black"—widened considerably in the first years after the war. Although legislators in Georgia in the winter of 1865–66 declared, with an eye on the North, that "persons of color . . . shall not be subjected to any other or different punishment, pain or penalty for the commission of any act or offense, than such as are prescribed for white persons, committing like acts or offenses," they denied blacks the right to vote and to serve on juries.[19]

Freedmen and their Northern defenders understood that equal justice could never be theirs with such limited legal rights. "To be sure, sah, we wants to vote," commented one ex-slave, "but, sah, de great matter is to git into de witness-box." "The kind and fatherly protection of the law in all its majesty," a Northerner living in the

South pronounced, "should be the heavenly aegis, placed before all classes." A strong faith in an impersonal legalism became a bulwark of Congressional Reconstruction and took tangible form in the shape of the Freedmen's Bureau. The Bureau distributed food and clothing to the destitute and aided black schools in the South, but its most dramatic function was to interpose the power of the national state between ex-slaves and ex-masters. The Bureau sought to make the state an active guarantor of legal equality. Bureau agents insisted, in turn, that blacks abide by the same standards of self-control and contract that motivated free labor in the North. The freedmen, armed with legal rights, would have to struggle for their bread just as Northern workers did.[20]

To protect blacks' legal rights, the Bureau maintained courts in the South from 1865 to 1868 to adjudicate minor civil and criminal cases involving the freedmen. The courts varied in composition from state to state, but usually the local Freedmen's Bureau agent acted alone. The head of the Freedmen's Bureau in Georgia, General Davis Tillson, found that he had too few military officers to administer the courts, and so he decided that civilian magistrates might serve as subagents in their localities. Such a decision helped mollify Georgia whites resentful of military officers in their counties, but the weaknesses of a system based on the judgment of Southern whites drew the wrath of the freedpeople. A convention of ex-slaves in Georgia in 1866 declared that "the rebel civil agents treated them in such a manner that their case is worse than if the Bureau had no Agents at all." Such an agent might actually buttress the status quo by clothing injustice in the mantle of formal justice. A great deal depended on the character and conscience of individual agents.[21]

Although the convention of Georgia's freedmen explicity excluded Whitfield's agent from their blanket denunciation, some white Unionists in the mountain county regarded him as a traitor. One white woman, "a poor widow," wrote to the general of the Third Military District in 1867 to complain that the Freedmen's Bureau agent in Dalton, Captain Ralph Finney, "will not issue Rations to me as he does the other destitute of the County. His wife has told me that he was a Rebel and pretended Unionism to keep his Situation under the Government. He is also a minister and I have heard him pray for the overthrow of the Government and Success of the Confederacy." Although the Freedmen's Bureau had been created to dispense evenhanded justice, "if there is a lease against a union man by a Rebel in the Courts in this County the Rebel will always get the Judgment in his favor. I can't live unless Something is done for me. I have always been a union woman." A Unionist doctor in Dalton charged that Finney had been led astray by ex-Confederates and "the influence of *spirits*." The doctor did not place the full blame on the Bureau agent, who "makes a good Officer" and had the respect of all, but warned that "these Rebels are very sharp and they wire work it very well." All in all, despite these complaints the Bureau's representative in Dalton received relatively little criticism from the people of the upcountry and enjoyed a relatively calm tour of duty.[22]

The same, however, could not be said for his counterpart in Greene County. The white minority in the plantation county made it known early on that it intended to remain in control, Freedmen's Bureau or not. The mayor of Greensboro "seized arms in possession of the freedpeople" in early 1866, and only relinquished them when forced to do so by General Tillson. But the ex-rebels did not pose the only problems for the agent in Greensboro, Jonathon T. Dawson. Dawson complained in February 1866 that when he first appeared in Greene "everything was in the greatest confusion as regards the freedpeople." After "a good of deal of trouble" Dawson got matters under control, only to learn that one of the county's delegates to the Freedmen's Convention had returned and preached a sermon in which he told his audience they were entitled to back pay from January 1, 1863—the day of the Emancipation Proclamation. This announcement "had the effect of producing considerable dissatisfaction among them." Some stopped work and demanded immediate payment from their ex-masters. Agent Dawson finally managed to persuade them to return to the fields, but no sooner had he dealt with this crisis than the state superintendent of education visited Greene and reportedly told the freedpeople that they "had a right to break their contracts if they saw fit to do so." The effect of the speech, Dawson lamented, was "beyond description" and led to the virtual abandonment of many plantations. The Bureau agent could not decide what course of action to take regarding the freedmen, for "it would be at the risk of his life for him to attempt to compel them to abide by their contracts." He requested that "some prudent man be sent up to arrange matters, or that he be relieved of his appointment." W. B. Moore soon came to replace Dawson.[23]

The new agent had little better luck than his predecessor in calming the racial fires in Greene County. Within a year six of the county's blacks signed a petition calling for Agent Moore's replacement because his laxness had allowed frauds to be perpetrated against the freedmen. Another petition pleaded for the release of Clara Harris, a freedwoman convicted by a civil court of stealing nine dollars and locked in the Greene County jail for thirty days. "She has a young child sick about five months old, and three others to support by Her own labor; prejudice existed in her case, which is well known to every one; we ask as Friends to give Her justice." The petitioners believed that the woman had been treated more harshly than she deserved because she "told Her Lawyer that she would get better justice if she had a Yankee Lawyer." The petition was signed with the marks of thirty-two freedmen, "Mbs. [Members] of U.S.A." The head officer of the Georgia military district ordered an "immediate and thorough investigation" by W. B. Moore. Given the complaints other freedmen had lodged against Moore only a few weeks earlier, however, this order obviously offered little hope to Greene County's ex-slaves. The Freedmen's Bureau in the rural South was only as strong and fair as its thinly scattered and isolated agents. No matter how courageous and conscientious some of those men might be, the weakness inherent in their situation often led them to follow the path of least resistance between freedmen's expectations and planters' demands.[24]

In Savannah, perhaps even more than in the Georgia countryside, the path of least resistance for the agents seemed to veer in the direction whites wished. In January of 1866 the Freedmen's Court in the city punished blacks by working them on chain gangs; provost marshals punished the typical convicted freedman by tying him "by his thumbs on tiptoe, or shaving off one-half of his head, or putting him in a barrel with armholes and labeled: 'I am a thief.' " Other ex-slaves found themselves arrested for "shouting at a religious colored meeting." In March of 1866 Abraham Winfield and ten other blacks petitioned the head of Georgia's Freedmen's Bureau "to be relieved from outrages practised upon them by the Freedmen's Court and the civil authorities of the place." The judge of the court, they complained, was "wholly ignorant of the law, and very unjust towards the freedpeople"; in fact, "the condition of the freedpeople is worse than slavery itself." One agent supposedly ordered several blacks arrested "for speaking disrespectfully to a white man" and then put them on a chain gang. Such harsh punishment was not inflicted upon whites, the petition charged, and those freedmen put to work in the streets "have been U.S. soldiers and cannot long endure such treatment." The Savannah freedmen requested a court of appeals to hear their grievances. The officer in charge of the Bureau in Georgia assured the head of the Freedman's Bureau, General O. O. Howard, that an investigation into the matter showed the charges to be "without any real foundation," the product of "instigation" by a black carpetbagger from Massachusetts.[25]

It seems clear that while the Freedmen's Bureau performed crucial services for the ex-slaves throughout the South—providing food and clothing to the destitute, supporting schools, furnishing blacks at least some leverage in disputes over contracts with plantation owners—crime and violence against the freedmen remained largely impervious to the Bureau's efforts to stop them. News of violence against ex-slaves committed in remote communities might never reach the ears of agents, and other crimes the Bureau learned of only long after the fact. Of the fifteen "outrages" committed against freedmen in Greene County in the first eleven months of 1868, in only one case was there a conviction in the civil courts of the county, and in that case the assailants as well as the victim were black. Even when Bureau courts did hear active cases, their jurisdiction was severely limited and, as local studies have shown, their judgment was shaped by local power and prejudice. The Freedmen's Bureau, in other words, was a well-intentioned experiment that exerted only a temporary and limited influence on the fundamental patterns of postwar Southern crime and punishment.[26]

Internal weakness accounted for only part of the Bureau's ineffectuality. Counterpoised to the legalistic bureaucracy of this short-lived agency of the federal government was what the Greensboro *Herald* called "the Organic Law of the Land": white supremacy in all its forms. "The great problem of the destiny of the negro upon this continent," proclaimed the paper, "can never be solved by the strong arm of the law." White Southerners had always circumscribed the sphere of the written and institutionalized law—even when that law was made and enforced by white Southerners for white Southerners. Once the law became, in their eyes, an instrument of outside oppression, many whites found little reason to respect its dictates. Localistic republicanism easily justified vigilante resistance to "tyranny," and honor as well as greed and fear dictated that ex-slaves and whites of little standing would not control Southern localities unchallenged.[27]

In December 1868 the agent of the Freedmen's Bureau in Greensboro told the county's Superior Court "of the existence of an organized band of Ku Klux in the County." The Greene County grand jury testified that "we have made diligent inquiry and can learn nothing to satisfy us of the existence of such a band." But a person reading the Greensboro *Herald* nine months earlier would have seen evidence that the Klan was, at the least, a source of fascination for whites in the vicinity. An alluring advertisement read: "K____K____K____. Our friends, J. C. Palmer & Co., has recently renovated their old store house and have opened a choice selection of Confectionaries, consisting partly of Kakes, Kandies, and Koaconuts. Their clerk Bob McWherter, will take pleasure in explaining to the curious the meaning of the above letters. Give him a call." And only three months before the grand jury disclaimed any knowledge of the Klan, the *Herald* carried a public notice that Greensboro would host "a game of Base Ball" between a local team and the "Ku-Klub of Covington, Ga. . . . All lovers of amusement, and especially the fair sex of your city are solicited to be present and witness the game"; the paper of the following week noted that "the 'fair' of our city were out in full force." Yet the Greene grand jury could find no evidence of the Ku Klux Klan in the area, though the jurors did make the ambiguous pledge to "hold themselves in readiness to do all in our power to put down everything like lawlessness that may come to our knowledge."[28]

Abram Colby, a black man elected by Greene's black majority to serve in the Georgia state legislature in 1868 and 1870, gave graphic testimony of the Klan's existence in the county. Colby, the mulatto son and slave of a Connecticut-born master in Greene County, was freed when his father died. One of the county's few free blacks in the antebellum era, Colby had worked as a barber. After the war, he became active in the Republican party and ran a small farm two miles outside of Greensboro. In the fall of 1869, after serving a term in the Georgia House of Representatives, Colby and his family were awakened one night by a gang of sixty-five disguised men. The band broke down the door of Colby's house and dragged him through the woods, where they took turns whipping him with revolver belts. Colby recognized several of his tormenters by their voices, boots, and horses. Some of them were "the first-class men in our town. One is a lawyer, one a doctor, and some are farmers; but among them some are not worth the bread they eat." If these men were not the Ku Klux Klan, Colby argued, "then there are not any."[29]

Such vigilante groups had killed several black men in Greene County, Abram Colby charged, and "there is no use talking about whipping; they whip them whenever they want to, in my county."

Only military control by the federal government, Colby believed, could give blacks a chance. When asked which judges he felt he could trust, Colby bitterly responded, "I do not know one that I think would give us any rights at all, who has been on the bench." All the freedmen wanted was to be left alone to work and have something left to show for their labor. "There never has been known in my county any instance where a colored man has attacked a white man. They are just as obedient and humble now as when they were slaves, and in many cases more so, I think." Influential white men in Greene County wanted to make sure blacks stayed that way. A white teacher of a school for blacks in Greene had been whipped and driven out of the county by disguised men, supposedly for walking down a Greensboro street with a black woman on his arm.[30]

But blacks in Greene were not as supine as Colby related—indeed, as Colby's own bravery attested. The freedmen often chose to fight fire with fire, vigilante justice with vigilante justice. In 1867 a white man killed a black man during a fight at "Robinson's Southern Show Circus and Menagerie" in Greensboro. "A large crowd of negroes rushed up and seized Curry, and were using him very roughly, and it is unknown what they would have done had it not been for the timely interposition of our brave and fearless Marshal," reported the *Herald.* "While the prisoner was being conveyed to jail, the negroes followed in large gangs clamoring for his life. Some two hundred formed in front of the Court House armed with pistols, clubs, etc. and threatened to wrest the prisoner from the hands of the officers and put into execution the Lynch law," but they were persuaded to desist. "From the demonstrations made and the language used by the colored population," the newspaper warned, "we think it high time that some precautionary measures should be adopted by the citizens."[31]

Despite these threats, blacks still retaliated when provoked. Hearing the news of the murder of a black man by his white employer in Greene County in 1867, about forty neighboring blacks "organized themselves into a regular armed company" and marched on the white man's house. "They surrounded the house and, with horrid oaths and vows of vengeance, commenced an indiscriminate fire on the premises, in which Mr. Marchman was severely wounded." The blacks made no effort at concealment and were arrested. "It really seems that the negroes are determined to follow the advice of their Carpet-bag friends from the land of the Puritans," the *Herald* warned, "until it will bring on a war of the races *in earnest.*

Let the war commence, and in three months time, not a vestige of the African race will be found in the South."[32]

Bloody threats alternated with sentimental pleas to the blacks. "We white people wish to say a few things to you black people who were once our slaves. We wish to say that we are still your friends," began an "Address of the White People of Greene Co. Ga. to the Colored People of the same county." "It is to our interest to be friendly with you for we expect to live with you always. . . . You cannot get away from us, and we cannot get [away] from you. We form but one community. We are like one family. . . . We were boys together, we were raised together." The speaker implored the blacks to vote in the coming state election with the "little slips of paper" their ex-masters gave them, not the ones the Yankees held out. But the election returns showed 1,632 votes, virtually all blacks', cast for the Republican candidate for governor, while the Democratic candidate received only 808 votes. Between that election in April and the one for president in November, many counties in the old plantation region surrounding Greene saw Republican majorities melt away—largely as the result of violence and intimidation. But Greene's blacks still managed to hold on to a slight majority. In fact, it was not until 1874, four years after the state as a whole had been "redeemed," that whites in Greene County reasserted their political dominance.[33]

In the wake of that 1874 election the Greensboro *Herald* congratulated the county's blacks for finally voting with "a white man's mind." But, it turned out, blacks had been prevented from voting their own mind by the failure of a white notary public to open the polls in a heavily black district. Three hundred enraged black voters took over the neighborhood, "making divers threats, and incendiary speeches, the ruling spirit being a negro by name of Montgomery Shepard." A white posse went out to arrest the leaders for "riot," and one of the whites was wounded. A fire broke out in the gin house belonging to the Democratic candidate. Six of the black leaders were captured and convicted by the county court. Montgomery Shepard received a sentence of twelve months on the chain gang and a $500 fine. Less than a month later, the *Herald* reported that Shepard had been killed on the chain gang, supposedly while trying to escape. The paper concluded its report on Shepard's death with a dark admonition: "All right, set 'em up again."[34]

Greene and the surrounding counties in Georgia's upper cotton belt probably experienced more racial conflict and more evidence of vigilante violence than any other part of Georgia—and Georgia experienced more than most Southern states. It is significant, though, that other areas of the state where blacks were in the majority witnessed considerably less bloodshed than did Greene and its neighbors. In the rice-growing region of Georgia's coast, where blacks heavily outnumbered whites and where strong black leaders won huge followings, whites maintained little hope of regaining power by force. Racial tension smoldered but did not break into open conflagration. In the rich southwestern part of the state where the Union army had not penetrated, on the other hand, native whites remained firmly in control. No Republican leaders of either race emerged, and Democrats held uncontested sway. Relative economic prosperity for both races helped calm passions and conflict.[35]

In the older plantation counties such as Greene, however, people of both races could see power within their grasp. The relative poverty of the increasingly infertile upper black belt, which bore the brunt, too, of hungry armies, created an atmosphere of desperation. Both sides feared that power lost now might be lost forever. The Freedmen's Bureau stood as a weak barrier between scared and angry men of both races. The Ku Klux Klan served as a symbol of white determination, solidarity, and contempt for blacks; it also revealed white fear. Blacks had no organization such as the Klan, but they did band together when the white authorities did not obey the law. In Greene County, at least, the freedmen were not cowed. The Klan was indirect testimony to black assertion and autonomy in the old plantation regions, not to black powerlessness.[36]

The other major locus of Klan activity in Georgia cannot be explained by such a model. Blacks in counties such as Whitfield in the mountainous northwestern corner of the state offered whites no political challenge and little economic competition or resistance. And yet the whites of the area were notorious for their brutality toward blacks. The usual explanation for their hatred is that, as historian Mildred Thompson wrote early in the twentieth century, "emancipation removed the most important barrier between the poor whites and the negroes, and when the two classes were given political equality, the poor white, with neither economic nor political advantage, had no source of superiority except his race." There must be something to this: those with the least to lose are often the most tenacious in the defense of what little they do possess. In the upcountry, too, blacks were such a minority that they could be harassed in a way that might not be safe in a black belt county. Honor reigned with as much volatility among the whites of the hills as among their low-country brethren, and most Klan violence in the upcountry flared up after breaches of racial etiquette, real or imagined. In a county neighboring Whitfield, a mulatto received a whipping after he "greeted a white woman insolently—'How d'ye, Sis.' "[37]

In the mountains, as in areas throughout the South, white men abused blacks for pure economic gain and used the Klan as an ally in their exploitation. The major reported incident of organized violence in Whitfield County in the Reconstruction era turned on just such an incident. James Nance, a respected white Democrat from Whitfield, received a visit from a threatening band of disguised men one night in 1871. Several weeks earlier Nance had happened upon a freedman chained to an outhouse on some land where Posey Sebastian, a white neighbor of Nance, was cutting timber for the railroad. The black man told Nance that Sebastian had held him against his will for three weeks—chained during the night and forced to work under the lash during the day. "He was all cut and smashed with hickories," Nance testified. "I went to a neighbor's house, and asked some of them to go with me with the intention of liberating the negro; but the men told me that they would not go into it, for they were afraid of the Sebastians; that it ought to be done, but they were afraid they would get into trouble if they did it." The next Sunday someone found the black man dead in a river, a railroad clamp around his neck.[38]

Nance was taken before the coroner's jury and he told what he had seen the week before. The jury ruled that the freedman had been killed by Posey Sebastian. Authorities were unable to apprehend the murderer, however, for he would appear in his neighborhood only "once a week or so, and stay a day and a night, and that was all that the people would see of him." The five Sebastian brothers, "all large, stout, young men," constituted a force to be reckoned with in Whitfield; the "kindly disposed and decent community" agreed that Posey Sebastian should pay for his crime, but everyone except Nance was afraid to antagonize the family. Several Sundays after the murder, Sebastian suddenly appeared in church, "where all of his associates and acquaintances were. There was not a man there, young or old," Nance said, "who would speak to him or who would sit with him, but his brothers." Yet the murderer still remained free. The bailiff and the judge were willing to prosecute, but they could not catch Sebastian. The justice of the peace in the district where the suspect lived was William Sebastian, Posey's older brother, so the culprit's arrest by local officials seemed unlikely. Even if a citizens' posse did arrest Posey Sebastian and take him the eleven miles to the Dalton jail, Nance felt sure, "his friends would take him out of jail." The machinery of the law, in other words, had no more weight in postbellum Whitfield than in antebellum Whitfield; most citizens willingly abided by the law, but those who did not and possessed sufficient strength and connections had little to fear. Such was to be the case in Whitfield throughout the nineteenth century.[39]

Indeed, the most significant fact about upcountry mob violence was neither its appearance during the years of Reconstruction nor its preoccupation with blacks. Rather, the Ku Klux Klan formed only a relatively brief episode in a long history of postwar group violence in the Southern mountains—much of it inflicted by whites upon whites. During the war, bands of deserters and bandits roamed the mountains. After Reconstruction, as we will see, the upcountry nourished vigilante groups for decades, groups that feuded, that fought over moonshining, that persecuted Mormons, that enforced "morality" upon their neighbors. The Ku Klux Klan reflected a tradition of extralegal retribution in the mountains; the Klan's birth did not initiate that tradition nor did the Klan's disappearance terminate it. Honor, kinship, isolation, localistic republicanism, and poverty—along with hatred for blacks—fed group violence in the Southern hills for generations.[40]

The night ride of the Klan stood as the archetypal form of violence in the rural South during Reconstruction, but the Southern city witnessed a different form of mob violence. Race riots erupted as early as 1865 in Charleston and Norfolk, recorded their highest fatalities in 1866 in Memphis and New Orleans, and continued to erupt in cities throughout the South for years after the Civil War. Race riots, long a feature of Northern cities, were new to the South. Many changes conspired to create an environment conducive to riots. Antebellum legal restraints on blacks—badges, passes, laws against black meetings and black migration—disappeared in the burgeoning cities of the immediate postwar period, and whites were concerned. Simultaneously, widespread destitution put tremendous strains on financially strapped cities as well as on the poor; thefts were common and denunciations of vagrancy even more so. Union soldiers far from home after a long war taunted blacks and yet infuriated native whites by their mere presence. Immigrant whites resented the competition of hungry blacks for jobs and housing. Police, often unreconstructed Southerners, exerted their authority with little tact and much force. To whites, blacks on street corners appeared lazy and insolent; to blacks, whites appeared belligerent and uncharitable.[41]

Given this volatile atmosphere, the boundaries between crime and revolt, between an isolated fight and a large-scale insurrection, became blurred. A spark thrown off in a conflict between two people could ignite a conflagration involving hundreds. Neither whites nor blacks were willing to see a member of their race bested by a member of the other: "in collisons between whites and blacks the friends of the respective parties think themselves bound to interfere, *not to stop the fight*, but to help out their comrade."[42]

Clashes between black troops and white police broke out on Savannah's streets in 1865 and 1866, but the largest riots did not take place until three years after the end of the war. Conflict between the races in the city, as in the countryside, heated up when whites saw political power within their grasp and as blacks realized that whites would stop at nothing to regain that power. Many Savannah blacks found the radical urgings of Aaron A. Bradley, a flamboyant black leader, more and more attractive as postwar dreams began to fade. To whites of both parties Bradley was an oily demagogue convicted of seduction and disbarred in New York before coming south; to blacks he was a charismatic leader who had no fear of whites. In April of 1868 the Ku Klux Klan posted warnings to black voters not to vote Republican. The Republican Loyal League and Aaron A. Bradley responded in kind: a handbill passed from one black hand to another on the streets of Savannah warning the Klan "and all BADMEN of the city of Savannah" that violence would be met by violence. Blacks carried their defiance to the polls as well: the Republican candidate for governor won by nearly 1,700 notes.[43]

By the time the election for president approached seven months later, however, white intimidation had begun to take its toll. Many blacks decided the risk of violence at the polls was too great. Nevertheless, at four o'clock on the morning of the election in Savannah several hundred blacks gathered at the polls to vote before work. At seven o'clock, just as the polls opened, a large group of white railroad laborers appeared and ordered the black voters to get out of the way so that the railroad men could vote and get back to their jobs. The blacks waiting in line refused to step aside, and eight policemen appeared to move the blacks by force. Shooting broke out; two black men died, two white policemen died, and several on both sides suffered serious wounds. Despite this black resistance, white intimidation triumphed in the Savannah election. The Democrats, who had lost so heavily only six months earlier, won by 2,300 votes in November 1868. As a matter of fact, Democrats won throughout Georgia; the people of both parties realized that after the next state election in 1870 the Democrats would dominate both houses of the state legislature and Reconstruction would be over in Georgia.[44]

The Ku Klux Klan played a crucial role in bringing about the restoration of white Southern control. Although the defenders of the Klan obviously approved of this political function, the Klan's proponents insisted on portraying the organization primarily as an opponent of black crime and lawlessness. As one member of the Georgia Klan described the organization in 1868, it was "a police, rather than a military force, an underground and nocturnal constabulary, detective, interclusive, interceptive, repressive, preventive—in the main—punitive only now and then." When the Klan did act to secure patently political ends, as it did against Abram Colby in Greene County, Klan members persisted in justifying their actions as crime-fighting tactics. As federal officer George S. Hoyt testified before the Ku Klux Committee, he had questioned both blacks and whites in Greene County and "heard some people allege that there was a feeling against Colby for living with a near relative of his, I think his daughter, as his wife. . . . I also heard other people, white men, say that there was nothing against Colby except his politics." Further, the white schoolteacher in Greene who was whipped ostensibly suffered his punishment for publicly escorting a black woman, not for teaching a school for blacks.[45]

The Northern Republican press and Congress portrayed all Klan violence as political violence, but a sympathetic Northern visitor to the South argued that Klansmen only sought to create "one feeling of terror as a counterpoise to another"—the terror of vigilantism as a counterpoise to the terror of black theft and black violence. White Southerners did not fear so much that the federal government might confiscate their land, thought the visitor, as they feared "the smaller but more present dangers of life and property, virtue and honor, arising from the social anarchy around them." A Democratic state senator from an area near Savannah also argued that the Ku Klux Klan was not nearly as novel and as political as it appeared to outsiders. "My idea of these organizations is this: When gin-houses are burned, or when a man loses his horse, when these things happen in a neighborhood frequently, and it is thought that certain persons in the vicinity are the guilty parties, some men gather together to punish the supposed offenders in some way or other. It is in pursuance of the old plan, which has been followed for years back, of enforcing order by what they call 'regulators' or 'lynch law.' " But, asked a member of the investigating committee, could not the courts handle horse thieves and other offenders? "There is no difficulty, of course, where the offenders are known and legal proof can be obtained; but sometimes a community may be satisfied that a person is guilty of an offense when there is no positive legal proof." In that case, "young men" take the problem "in hand on the spur of the moment" "for the purpose of having such depredations stopped. . . . I have thought a great many of these reported outrages originated in that way." Indeed, what was called the Ku Klux Klan was largely autonomous, *ad hoc* groups that joined together temporarily to "right" local "wrongs." White vigilantes, whatever they called themselves, believed their night rides enforced law and order, that their vigilantism filled the vacuum left by the conflicting claims of weak civil courts and weak Freedmen's Bureau courts. In the eyes of most white Southerners, the Klan assumed the temporary and unfortunate—but ultimately necessary and justifiable—job of protecting life and property in the face of chaos.[46]

The leaders and agents of Congressional Reconstruction believed that only their program could guarantee true republicanism, true democracy; they believed that only the unprecedented state intervention they sponsored could counterbalance the forces of vigilantism and racial rule in the South. But white Southerners claimed without hypocrisy that Reconstruction violated their republican ideals. The Southern republican ideology presupposed citizens of independence and equality, while whites deemed blacks neither; that ideology, too, valued local autonomy above all else, and black political equality had been imposed on the South from outside. Conservative whites denounced Reconstruction as much for its alien control of the South as for its purely racial aspects; hatred and vituperation were directed at carpetbaggers of both races, while Southern black leaders met with mere condescending contempt for their role as "puppets" and "tools." The Freedmen's Bureau, which seems so passive and benign today, symbolized for the South the long arm of a hypocritical minority in Congress, stirring up social disorder and bloodshed in the South while leaving the North's peace

and unquestioned white rule untouched.) The fascination of generations of Southerners (and Northerners) with the "corruption" of the
"radicals" echoes the deepest republican fears of decay and anarchy,
of the usurpation of power from those whose education and wealth
qualified them to wield power. Chaos, early republican thinkers had
warned, would be the inevitable result when people who had no
property and no stake in society—whatever their color—ruled over
those who did.[47]

III

The conscious efforts of black Republicans, Northern radicals, and
Southern conservatives were only part of the story of Southern crime
and punishment in the 1860s and 1870s. The subtle and obvious
coercions of an expanding market economy and state came to
dominate the picture as the Freedmen's Bureau and the Ku Klux
Klan faded away. Poorer white farmers found themselves in new
positions of dependency, blacks found that the planters now had
faceless but powerful new allies. The map of Southern crime and
punishment was being redrawn before people's eyes.

Four years after the war Middle Georgia was still "dull and
dilapidated," a citizen of Greene sadly observed, while the upcountry, with its white labor, seemed to be thriving. "And why is
this? We answer: It is the unreliable and uncontrollable character of
our labor in the first instance, their vagrancy and thievishness; and in
the next place, a want of concert of action on the part of the land
owners, in forming and carrying out a wise and uniform system of
plantation discipline. At present, there is no uniformity in regard to
the hours of labor or price of labor—hence there is no certainty of
labor. A sort of grab game is the order of the day." The problem, in
other words, was that the black belt South had become a society in
which labor had become free. The plantation owner now had to
compete for the services of black wage laborers.[48]

Ex-masters had no experience with the covert coercion of the
marketplace. They had little faith in the power of internalized
discipline among their black workforce, little faith in contracts with
ex-slaves. Only overt coercion would work, planters believed, and
the Black Codes, tough vagrancy laws, and the Ku Klux Klan
supplied that coercion) In Greene County, twenty-one blacks came
before the County Court for vagrancy in 1866; most of them
received a whipping of thirty-nine lashes. Despite these attempts to
perpetuate the brute force that had been the heart of slavery,

however, free labor had come to the South. No amount of whipping could change that fact.[49]

The complete transformation from slavery to free labor would take decades, lifetimes, to unfold. Unfortunately for all concerned, however, one basic change took place almost immediately. Long before Southern workers enjoyed the prosperity and relative self-determination that free labor had the capacity to bestow, they felt the pain and liability of their freedom. No longer were the rural Southern poor insulated in their poverty from the effects of the international market economy. The world demand for cotton, the price of food and clothing, and the level of interest rates mattered to freedmen in a way that they had not mattered to slaves. Freedmen might be sharecroppers, might see money only rarely, but their material well-being had nevertheless become at least partially dependent on forces outside local control. The local control that did exist often compounded the unpredictability: illiterate slaves could never be sure they were not being cheated by the landowner or merchant who dispensed their supplies and sold their cotton. If freedmen did suspect they were being cheated and if they were willing to risk being picked up for vagrancy or suffering violence at the hands of the Klan, they could pack up in the night and move to another county. But there was nowhere to hide from the declining price of cotton. When a cotton crop earned less than ex-slaves had expected because Egyptian cotton had prospered the previous year, the desperation and destitution that followed in Greene County were just as real as if someone had stolen part of the crop out of the field.[50]

Ex-slaves were not the only ones in the South to become tied to the national and world economy in a new way after the Civil War. Whites with small farms began to grow cotton in the early postwar years. Cotton prices were high in 1865 and 1866, and the crop seemed easy enough to grow, and so many white farmers in the South sacrificed part of their self-sufficiency to raise cotton in order to get back on their feet after years of war. They borrowed money to put in the crop and to feed their families in the meantime. Yet the price of cotton declined in the world market for whites just as it did for blacks; farmers of both races went ever deeper into debt. A growing number of merchants demanded repayment from an ever-growing number of indebted farmers. "More and more it was the time-merchants instead of the landowners who advanced supplies to the tenants and sharecroppers," Greene County's historian has written. "To meet these cash demands on farm operation the whole countryside was planted in cotton. . . . By the middle of the 1870s there were at least a dozen time-merchants operating in the county, half of them in Greensboro." These merchants did well for themselves with high interest rates and foreclosures. The wealthiest merchant, Charles A. Davis, erected an impressive brick home in 1875; subscribers to the Greensboro *Herald* could read of merchant Davis's new staircases, chandeliers, and mantlepieces.[51]

In the upcountry as well as the black belt merchants emerged as a new force and farmers slid into dependence. "It is bad policy—yea, ruinous policy—when the farmer has to come to town and buy his flower [*sic*] and meat. And yet this is just what some of our farmers are doing," sadly observed Whitfield's *North Georgia Citizen*. "We have a splendid country—the lands are rich enough and the seasons propitious enough for our farmers to raise more than their own supplies, and until they do this the thread-bare cry of 'hard times' will continue to be heard." Yet the farmers could get cash to pay off their debts only by growing a cash crop, and so they repeated the cycle again the next year—and again failed to pay off their debts. If they failed enough times, the merchant might foreclose and the worst possible fate of a farmer would follow: his land would pass out of his family's hands. Apparently this happened with some frequency in Greene and Whitfield, for the proportion of whites in the two counties who owned no land, the only source of independence and standing in a rural society, jumped dramatically between 1860 and 1870: from 33 percent to 53 percent in Greene, and from 60 percent to 71 percent in Whitfield. Greene's and Whitfield's black population was more dependent than white farmers upon others for wages and credit, for virtually no black man in either county owned the land he farmed in 1870.[52]

This vulnerability of Southern farmers of both races to the swings of the national and international market descended upon the South with astonishing speed. Economic historian Gavin Wright has observed that the changes involved with the emergence of a market economy "represent the kind of long-run developments normally associated with the slow pressure of populations against land, with basic legal, institutional, and attitudinal changes evolving over decades and centuries. In the South, it happened overnight, historically speaking." The abrupt transition of Southern farmers from self-sufficiency to dependence on external events and forces meant, as one contemporary observed, that they lost their "immunity to financial crisis" and could no longer remain "relatively unscathed by the collapse of prices." In 1883, in the shadow of the prolonged economic crisis of the previous decade, an editorial entitled "The Crop Lien Full of Evil" charged that "larceny and State convicts are the annual fruits of this system"; the merchant's thirst for high profits meant that the laborer must "steal or suffer."[53]

To Greene and Whitfield, the 1870s saw things go from bad to worse. The Greensboro *Herald* worried in January of 1875 that vagrancy, "confined to no locality, race or color . . . stalks all over the land unhindered. The rural districts are full, the towns and cities are flooded with it." This unemployed mass "is populating poor houses, filling prisons, and cursing the land." The paper warned later in 1875 that a "heavy increase" in state convicts could be anticipated for the coming fall because "jails are full all over the State." Greene's Superior Court, which had prosecuted virtually no vagrants since the years immediately following the war, tried nineteen people for the offense in 1875. And the consequences of hardship did not end in 1875. Three years later the *Herald* commented that 1878 had "been a bad year for farmers"; and again "many of 'Cuffee's' class have been improving on the provisions of Providence by *borrowing* from their prosperous neighbors *unbeknownst* to them. Cases of larceny here are as common as divorce cases in Chicago."[54]

The situation in Whitfield seemed equally bad. "Business of all kinds is at a stand still," lamented the *North Georgia Citizen* in June 1874, "and greenbacks—well, we are minus that article, and judging from the number of dolorous complaints we hear, we presume everybody else is in the same fix." Several Dalton businesses went bankrupt in 1874 and 1875, but the farmers were hardest hit; by early 1875 the "country wagons come grinding along through the mud with a dull sound that breaks dully upon our dull ears. . . . An old farmer follows, his lugubrious looks giving evidence that cotton is down." John Horrey Dent, a planter in a neighboring upcountry county, wrote in his diary in 1876 that he expected even more theft than before, for "as the negroes have neither meat nor money—they will break into places where it is." Eight months later, Dent's black neighbors had become "ragged and poor, poorer than they have been since their freedom hence they must steal for a living."[55]

Whitfield, on the railroad between Chattanooga and Atlanta, found that many people looking for work dropped off in Dalton to try their luck—and to beg when they failed. The rail line brought not only the opportunities of the market economy but also the people whom the market economy could not use. In November 1874 the editor of the Whitfield newspaper noted that "many able-bodied looking men, asking for work or bread, have infested Dalton of late." By 1875 the problem was even worse; the newspaper admitted that "little beggars and big beggars, white and black, literally swarm on Mondays. . . . On this day importunities for work or money are frequent, and at one's home there is a perfect raid upon the flour and meal barrels, the lard can, the coffee, tea, sugar, meat, everything. . . . Oh, for a round million of dollars just to erect industrial schools and alms houses in our county."[56]

Just when the lamentations over the hard times in the local papers reached their peak in Greene and Whitfield, between 1875 and 1879, so did the number of people indicted for theft and burglary in the counties' Superior Courts. No longer were white men who had assaulted other white men the most common defendants before the Greene County court; now black men who had stolen a farm animal, food, or cotton from the fields made up the majority of the courts' business. Violent whites still predominated in Whitfield's court, but after the war the proportion of thefts and burglaries increased fourfold. In Greene County the proportion of property crime increased ninefold. As Figure 5.1 reveals, the general pattern of penitentiary convictions throughout the entire South reflected this same dramatic increase in the 1870s. The prison populations of the region did not display a steady path of growth after the war. Rather, after an initial surge, the number of people sent to prison throughout the South remained stable and then actually declined before the early and mid-1870s, when prison populations throughout the region again soared.[57]

Governor James M. Smith assured the citizens of Georgia in 1872 that "this marked increase in the number of convicts is not due to any augmentation of crime in the South, but is believed to be the result entirely of a more rigid and proper enforcement of the laws." In 1875 Tennessee Governor John C. Brown echoed his Georgia counterpart: "The large increase in the number of inmates is to be attributed in no sense to an increase of crime. It is solely the result of a more efficient administration of the criminal law, aided by an improved and more healthy state of public sentiment." It was no accident that black incarceration peaked before and after radical Reconstruction, when native whites exercised virtually unchecked power and restored "efficiency" to the courts. The number of all prosecuted crimes increased substantially after Greene County's

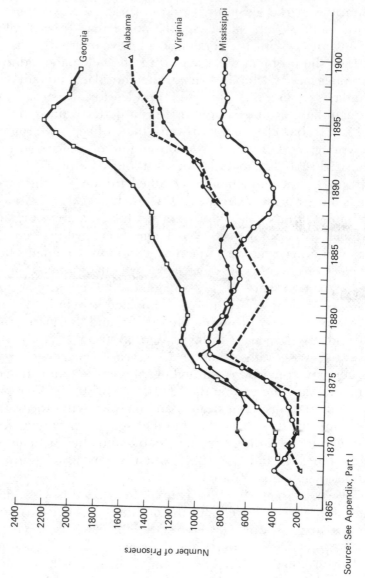

Figure 5.1. Black Prison Populations in Four Southern States

Source: See Appendix, Part I

delayed "redemption" in 1874. But "the more rigid and proper enforcement of the laws" in the South cannot explain the fact that the rate of growth in the prison population of the North reveals a contour virtually identical with that of black prison populations in the South throughout the second half of the nineteenth century—

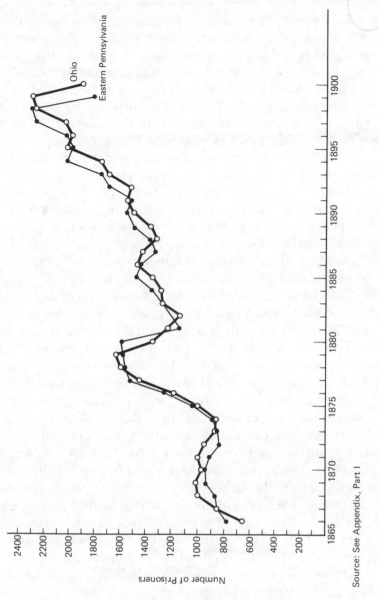

Figure 5.2. Prison Populations in Two Northern States

including the years of Reconstruction (see Figure 5.2). As in the 1850s, sharp upswings in prison populations followed in the wake of national economic depressions, but in the 1870s rural areas in the South contributed to the increase in a way they had not before the war.[58]

Despite the increases in theft in Greene and Whitfield in the mid-1870s, postwar urban Chatham County prosecuted an even higher percentage of thieves and burglars than did rural counties—just as it had before the war. In the 1850s, property crimes made up 19 percent of all cases prosecuted in the Chatham Superior Court, but by the late 1860s and 1870s that proportion had jumped to 35 percent. The reasons were not hard to find. Emancipation created a large pool of underemployed and unemployed blacks, who came to cities such as Savannah for work, pleasure, and the education of their children. Chatham County's black population increased from 15,532 in 1860 to 24,518 in 1870 while the number of whites changed hardly at all. The poverty and hunger of many of these newcomers created a sort of permanent depression in parts of the city. The outlying districts where Savannah's black antebellum population had tended to concentrate also proved the only housing for most postbellum black migrants, and the city, like cities throughout the South, became encircled by a band of destitution. In 1867, 3,000 of Savannah's 30,000 people depended "for subsistence on the city and county treasury, on charity, thievery and prostitution." As in every other city in the United States, blacks in Savannah received the most menial and lowest-paying jobs and stood the greatest danger of losing the positions they won. Five years after the war, nine out of ten blacks in Savannah owned nothing.[59]

Unskilled work might be available to those able to move quickly up and down the coast, but seasonally unemployed men with families could not migrate to other jobs. In many instances, the Savannah *News* reported, "children are suffering for the common necessaries of life, the father being out of employment, and the mother trying to keep the life of her family by odd jobs of washing and sewing." When the Panic of 1873 struck Savannah, not surprisingly, the condition of the poor deteriorated even further and, as in the antebellum city and postbellum countryside, court records reflected the deterioration. Black property crime prosecutions and penitentiary sentences nearly doubled in Chatham County between 1872 and 1875, and declined after the initial shock of the panic had passed. The city's economy and courts seem to have felt the impact of the panic more quickly than those of rural areas and to have recovered from it more quickly as well. But no one knew when another panic might strike. The postbellum city, still based on commerce rather than manufacturing, still the home of thousands of poverty-stricken people whose only subsistence came from providing whatever unskilled labor might be needed from one day to the next, found itself even more vulnerable to economic crises during the Gilded Age than during the antebellum period.[60]

The numbers of people prosecuted for any kind of crime, of course, reflect the workings of the criminal justice machinery as well as the workings of the market economy, the "demand" for criminals as well as their "supply." In postbellum Savannah, that machinery had changed little from its antebellum predecessor; the police force created in 1854 seemed more than sufficient to keep matters under control. Whereas the antebellum Savannah police had been a great source of divisiveness and political turmoil, however, the white community could find little but praise for the postbellum force. A common enemy, after all, united the city's whites behind the police; as Mayor Edward C. Anderson proclaimed in 1866, "In the changed circumstances that surround us, with a vagabond freed element in our midst, and constantly pouring into the city, together with the influx of 'roughs' coming by every steamer, it is a matter of necessity to keep up at any cost an efficient Police Force for our protection." When Mayor Anderson ended his tenure three years later, the police force staged a significant ceremony: they presented the Mayor a silver service engraved with an inscription from "The Boys in Gray," drank a glass of wine, and sang "Dixie." An ex-Confederate officer, General R. H. Anderson, served as chief of police from 1865 until his death in 1888—a far cry from the antebellum pattern, when the chief changed with every political administration.[61]

The force General Anderson presided over, observed a visitor in 1875, resembled "a military organization, clothed in Confederate gray, subject to strict discipline, armed with rifles, revolvers and sabres. . . . It is one of the prides of the city." The visitor noted parenthetically one reason for the good order of Savannah: "The negroes no longer have any voice whatever in political matters, and are not represented in the City Government." Republican administrations in other Southern cities sometimes hired black policemen, but within a few years Savannah's pattern of white police supported by white citizens had become the rule in the urban South.[62]

"We have a police who will manage anybody," ex-mayor Anderson told the Congressional Ku Klux Klan committee in 1871. There was no reason or toleration for the Klan in Savannah, Anderson claimed, because "our police force is in thorough order and discipline, and very vigilant. The men are all well paid." But the investigating committee, more than likely aware of the ninety-two-page petition Savannah freedmen had submitted in 1868 attacking Mayor Anderson's administration of justice, wondered if there was not "any difficulty in administering the laws in your courts?" "None in the world," Anderson assured them. A skeptical investigator asked, "Can justice be administered there, regardless of race, color, previous condition, or politics? *Answer*: Beyond peradventure."[63]

An observant visitor to Savannah would have seen evidence to the contrary. "In the Mayor's Court they have two Bibles—white people swear on one, and negroes on the other," Savannah's black *Tribune* caustically commented. "We are told that equal justice is meted out to all. Ah, ha! is that so?" "This is a new offense to me," remarked a Chatham County Superior Court judge in 1866 when confronted with several freedmen arrested for "improper conduct." "What is improper conduct? Surely not anything that the mayor might think improper. If this be so then what might be a crime under one mayor would not be a crime under another." But judges had limited power. A. W. Stone, a United States official and Savannah resident, testified in 1869, "The condition of things in Savannah for the past year has been what I call bad, so far as security to person and property is concerned. So far as the Judges of the Superior Court are concerned, I think they administer justice impartially . . . but I cannot say as much for the juries. I think their verdicts are more or less governed by prejudice." Savannah's *Tribune* put the point in stronger terms: the black paper indignantly attacked those men "who unblushingly assert that justice is fully accorded the colored people of Georgia, when it is known that a malignant prejudice excludes them from the jury box." In fact, charged a letter from a black "Tax-Payer" in 1876, "There is not a single instance on record where a Colored juror has served upon any jury in this city or County."[64]

The pattern of monoracial law enforcement that was to prevail in the urban South far into the next century, in other words, was established almost immediately after the war in Savannah. Many other Southern cities where the key component of control, the police, had not been in place before the Civil War quickly established such forces during the Reconstruction era. Richmond, Memphis, Augusta, Nashville, and Atlanta adopted uniformed police in the decade following the war. These cities had clear models to follow, and soon one Southern police force differed little from another. Throughout the South, blacks felt themselves persecuted by the entire machinery of government, and the police stood as the most visible and galling element of that state.[65]

White officials in the rural South had no antebellum models to follow, no form of police to adopt. If they looked to the past for guidance they found only two unworkable extremes: slavery, and the lax law enforcement that had been the rule for antebellum whites. In the changed circumstances of Reconstruction, neither would do. Ready or not, the state had to be expanded. In rural districts before the war, after all, "a negro thief received thirty-nine lashes from the overseer, and there an end," observed a Northern traveler. But after the war the punishment of the same black thief necessarily became much more complicated: "a constable catches him, a prison holds him for a trial, a grand jury indicts him, a judge sentences him if he is guilty, and thereupon a penitentiary receives him just as it does his white brother-in-law." At the same time, in other words, that contracts, wage labor, merchants, and the new sensitivity to the turns of the world market transformed Southern agriculture and society in the decade after the Civil War, so did the sudden expansion of the state's responsibility for blacks reorient rural justice.[66]

The *North Georgia Citizen* made little effort to obscure the feelings of the whites who witnessed and conducted this transformation. "In nine cases out of ten" where black defendants were involved, the paper reported in 1875, "these odorous essences of 'Civil Rights' are guilty of the crime with which they are charged, and we are glad to see our leading lawyers refusing to 'fatigue public attention' and help increase the county taxes by representing them." Such were the freely expressed attitudes of whites throughout the region, a climate of contempt which led Tennessee blacks "most emphatically" to denounce "the continued, persistent and unlawful manner in which they are tried, condemned, hanged, and enslaved, by individuals who have been taught from cradle to the jury box, that the negro is naturally inferior to them." And as a white man from North Carolina pointed out, "You must have niggers in the jury-box, too, or nigger evidence will not be believed. I don't think you could find twelve men in the whole State who would attach any weight to the testimony of ninety-nine niggers in a hundred."[67]

Whites considered black attempts to participate in legal proceedings to be ludicrous. In 1867 the Greensboro *Herald* reprinted a story from a Kentucky newspaper of an event that supposedly occurred in Reconstruction Texas. A black jury, assembled from the cotton fields to hear a case, returned to the courtroom to render the verdict. The foreman "squared himself before the court, displaying the paper with great pomposity, and then delivered himself to his Honor: 'See here, Mr. Court, we's been down to dat are room, and we hunts in every crack in every corner, up the chimney, and under de floor, and can't find any thing that looks like a wordick." Whites used such stories to convince themselves that even respectable Christian black men who exercised great responsibilities on plantations and in large families should always be excluded from juries—juries where whites of dubious background and judgment were allowed to preside.[68]

Black lawyers, not surprisingly, were few and far between in the rural South, and skilled white lawyers could find little time for impoverished blacks accused of larceny. Although during the antebellum years slaves accused of felonies had been guaranteed the right to counsel in most states, freedmen did not enjoy this right. All too often, a solitary and illiterate black man came before a white judge and jury already convinced of his guilt. For generations, black defendants experienced the desperation expressed in a blues song:

> White folks and nigger in great Co't house
> Like Cat down Celler wit' no-hole mouse.

Blacks in Greene County called the courthouse on Greensboro's Main Street the "white folks' court"; the ex-slaves observed the court's actions from a distant balcony or the Jim Crow corner. About eight out of ten blacks before the Greene Superior Court were found guilty, while the same court convicted only six out of ten whites. Urban Chatham County recorded almost precisely the same ratios. The conviction rates for both races were lower in Whitfield County, but the same pattern of unequal justice emerged: seven out of ten blacks received guilty verdicts, but closer to four out of ten whites were convicted.[69]

People accused of property crime stood a greater chance of a conviction than those accused of other kinds of crimes and blacks and property crime were virtually synonymous in Southern courts from Reconstruction on. As a white South Carolinian explained in 1877, "Whenever larceny, burglary, arson and similar crimes are committed in the South, no one is suspected save negroes." Whitfield's *North Georgia Citizen* defined an honest freedman as one "who wouldn't take anything that didn't belong to him if the owner was watching." The paper suggested, "If the white people of the South find that the negro continues to steal all they raise, they may possibly conclude to raise troops and see whether the negroes will steal them." "The truth is," a white Northerner who tried to establish a farm in the South admitted, "that with all our vigilance, the niggers will steal, and we may congratulate ourselves if they do not get the Lion's share." Apparently some of the freedpeople carried into the postwar era a definition of theft that could justify "taking" what they needed, and grinding poverty created great need for most blacks.[70]

Blacks arrested for larceny filled Greene County's ancient stone jail, still the "very strongest as well as the most *gloomy* structure" in Georgia. The county's semiannual Superior Court met so infrequently that a steadily mounting number of "prisoners lie in jail and almost rot before it is possible to bring them to trial, and at a heavy expense to the taxpayers." Largely in an attempt to rid the jail of such burdens, urban and rural counties throughout the South's black belt turned to a new form of punishment: the county chain gang. Confronting a great many new black prisoners, in 1866 the Georgia legislature passed a series of laws designed to transfer the punishment of more criminals from the penitentiary to the county level. The counties could either work the convicts on public roads or hire them out to private contractors. Other Southern states did the same.[71]

From the point of view of officers in financially strapped counties, such plans made a great deal of sense. Not only would jails empty, but county roads could be maintained as criminal blacks suffered in public. "We are pleased to see a number of stalwart freedmen at work on the streets of our city," commented the Greensboro *Herald* in 1869. "This is right." The Savannah *News* did complain in 1866 that "passerby have dirt thrown upon them intentionally" by members of the city's new chain gang, "and the ears of ladies who may be passing are greeted with the most indecent language," but these were minor inconveniences; the institution endured throughout the rest of the century with little opposition from whites. The Greene County paper argued that hard labor was not a harsh punishment for black convicts. "Every one conversant with negro character," the *Herald* commented, "must know that so long as he is clothed and fed, it matters but little with him whether he works as a hired laborer in a field in Greene county, or as a convict in Washington county, except, that in the latter case his freedom is slightly abridged."[72]

The birth of the chain gang changed the punishment of crime from a heavy expense for the county to a source of public revenue, and as a result the entire criminal justice system became reoriented. Before the war a county stood to lose money by prosecuting a minor criminal, but after the adoption of the chain gang all the incentives ran in the other direction. A black chain gang could solve two major problems of poor rural counties, crowded jails and troublesome, even impassable roads. Once a county hired guards and bought equipment for the chain gang, officials may well have felt some pressure to provide labor sufficient to justify the overhead. Crime, to a certain extent, became an asset to the county. Even a misdemeanor could be turned to economic advantage: "a defendant, convicted of a misdemeanor, may be, and frequently is, sentenced to ten days hard labor for his crime, and to three, six or eight months, for costs," observed Alabama legislators. "In such cases, his poverty seems to be punished more severely than his offense against the law." Or as a black New Orleans newspaper put it, "three days for the stealing, and eighty-seven for being colored."[73]

Poor defendants could escape the county chain gang only by finding a white sponsor to testify in the defendant's behalf or to pay the fine if the defendant were found guilty. More than a few white planters were willing to do just this, for the transformation in the Southern economy forced employers to scrounge and compete for laborers, even in the courthouse. The Greensboro *Herald* noted unhappily in 1875 that many of the county's white men attended court for such reasons: "There are so many violations of the law, especially the criminal part of it, that nearly half the people become involved, either as prosecutors or defendants. One party seems to be interested in trying to punish the guilty and protect society, the other is interested to keep his labor and save his crop, law or no law."[74]

But whites were not the only parties interested in the ancient ritual of court week. "There are enough negroes in attendance on our Superior Court this week, to pick out all the cotton in Greene county in one week; and what business they've got here, nobody knows," complained the *Herald*. "They crowd in the Court room by the hundreds, and understand about as much of the proceedings there as a man in the moon." Perhaps some of the arcane legal terminology did not make sense to those hundreds of blacks so attentive to the court, but there can be little doubt that they found more meaning in the unfair proceedings than Greene County's whites would have liked to admit.[75]

A speaker at a postwar black convention in Raleigh articulated the feelings of black courtroom audiences throughout the South: "If they makes a white man pay five dollars for doing something today, and makes a nigger pay ten dollars for doing that thing tomorrow, don't I know that ain't justice?" Referring to the familiar embodiment of justice—a blindfolded woman holding scales—the black speaker concluded, "When a white man and a nigger gets into the scales, don't I know the nigger is always mighty light? don't we all see it? Ain't it so at your court-house, Mr. President?" It was no accident, a black commentator later argued, that Southern blacks "came to view the law as something to be feared and evaded but not necessarily to be respected." Even when interested whites secured the acquittal of a guilty black or paid his fine with few questions asked, black respect for the law was only further eroded. Blacks who knew that their white sponsor would pay their fine often became "nuisances to the respectable Negroes of the communities. They often give much trouble at the churches and other public gatherings, with the boast that 'captain so and so will stand to me in anything.' "[76]

The preoccupation of white courts with black wrongdoing led them to ignore white transgressions that would have drawn their attention before the war. "It is not so much that the negro fails to get justice before the Courts in the trial of the specific indictments against him," a black man analyzing Southern justice several decades later claimed, "but too often it is that the native white man *escapes it*." In Greene and Whitfield, as well as in Savannah, the conviction rate for whites, whatever their offense, declined substantially from ante-bellum levels. Whitfield County, which displayed the lowest conviction rate of the three counties before as well as after the war, ran an extremely casual court. The editor of the *North Georgia Citizen* laconically described a session in 1873: "the first case in which there was an announcement other than 'no arrest,' 'recognizance forfeited,' defendant 'dead' or 'gone to Texas,' was that of the State vs. Robt. Hill, charged with the offense of stabbing—verdict 'Not Guilty.' " As this report makes clear, many defendants simply left the county—posted "leg bail"—rather than face the court. The *North Georgia Citizen* applauded such departures and suggested in 1874 that the laws should be enforced so strictly that "offenders would invariably 'emigrate' or plead guilty, thereby relieving the State of their presence, or prevent the cost to the county of a tedious trial. The county is frequently taxed $100 or more to dispose of a misdemeanor, wherein the culprit, if found guilty, cannot be fined more than $25." As Figure 5.3 shows, the proportion of whites relative to population sent to prison actually declined throughout the rest of the nineteenth century in the South. Of those whites who did manage to get indicted by the Superior Courts of Greene,

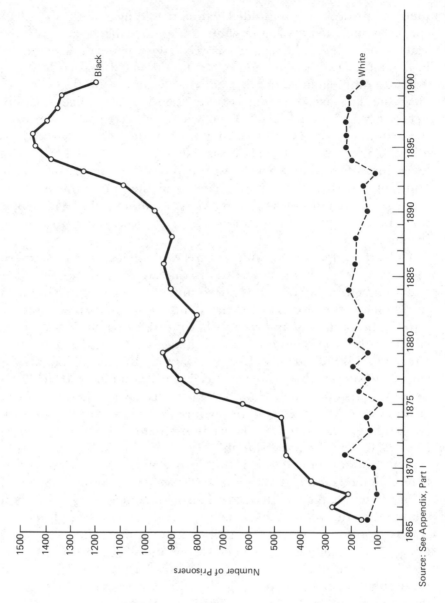

Figure 5.3. Average Prison Population in Tennessee, Virginia, Alabama, Mississippi, and Georgia

Whitfield, and Chatham, the majority had been accused of a crime of violence. It was rare in the rural areas, in fact, for a white to be accused of anything else.[77]

The great concern with the serious crimes of violence and property in the Reconstruction era deflected attention from the crimes of morality, liquor, and gambling that elicited so much vigilance from the antebellum courts of Greene and Whitfield. Such a decline did not mean that Southerners no longer worried about such things as liquor drinking, gambling, and sexual transgressions; rather it reflected the courts' preoccupation with more urgent matters. Courts met so infrequently that the number of crimes they could handle was severely limited, and black thefts and white assaults received first attention.[78]

Even if grand juries did not enjoy the opportunity they had had before the war of scouring the county for wrongdoers, however, many Southerners of both races still denounced "crimes" of morality and still found the church the greatest source of their strength. The churches maintained their role as police and courts of first resort throughout the nineteenth century. The Penfield Baptist Church in Greene denounced dancing in 1866 because "it is the duty of Churches to define clearly their views on questions of disorder at all times, and especially after periods of great political convulsions (like the late war) which naturally tend to efface the lines of distinction between the Church and the world, and to beget a conformity to practices and amusements not sanctioned by the word of God." Four years later, even as political battles raged in Greene County, the White Plains Baptist Church still worried about dancing: "some professed Christians seem to doubt whether it be criminal, while others boldly justify it." The Church, however, had no doubt: "the Dance of modern society is *expressly* prohibited in the word of God, being there called 'rioting' . . . and classed with 'drunkenness,' 'fornication,' and abominable idolatries."[79]

The fellowship and discipline of the church could still bring together blacks and whites during the difficult years of the late 1860s. Two years after the end of the war "Brother Ned formerly the property of Col. Sutton was charged with adultery" in Greene County's Bethesda Baptist Church. A committee found him guilty and excluded him. Nine months later when he expressed the wish to "talk with the Church in regard to being restored," the church agreed and subsequently readmitted him to fellowship.[80]

Despite continued respect between black and white Christians, distance increasingly grew between the "good people" of both races in the postwar South. Blacks sought the freedom of their own churches with their own ministers, and white churches even assisted in the establishment of separate churches for their black members. Blacks placed their new churches at the center of their communities. Black congregations disciplined their own members, helped their poor and elderly, ministered to one another. But whites were not always enthusiastic about the new black institutions. No longer, whites realized, could they exert moral control through the church. Parodies of black religious meetings soon became commonplace in Southern newspapers. In 1873 Whitfield's *North Georgia Citizen* ran a notice of a revival under the caption "Bad News": "we are fearful our accustomed morning dish of fried chicken will disappear with the opening of that *black* camp meeting." The Greensboro paper made a similar joke in 1877, but by 1879 the humor had disappeared: "We have noticed closely for several years and have invariably found it to be a fact, that the meanest negroes in the country are those who are members of the churches; and, as a general thing, the more devout and officious they are, the more closely they need watching." The Dalton paper lamented, "The negroes, as a race, are to be pitied. Everywhere at the South the same idle, lazy, shiftless, lawless habits characterize them, and the result is they fill our jails and penitentiaries. Only at the recent term of our Superior Court a half dozen or more of this worthless population were tried, convicted and sentenced to the penitentiary and chain gang. . . . They have their schools and their houses of worship, but it does seem that instead of being benefited by these civilizing influences, they are daily made worse."[81]

Such contempt and hatred rose easily to the surface of Southern society in the aftermath of the Civil War. Few people have been so buffeted by chaos and change as the blacks and whites of the South in the twenty years between 1860 and 1880. The suffering of those twenty years, as inevitable as it may have been, left a bitter legacy—a legacy more damaging in its effect on crime and punishment, perhaps, than on any other facet of Southern society. Looking back from the perspective of 1904, W.E.B. DuBois admitted that "there can be no doubt that crime among Negroes has sensibly increased in the last thirty years, and that there has appeared in the slums of great cities a distinct criminal class among the blacks." Black criminality did not merely grow inexorably out of black depravity, ignorance, and destitution, DuBois wanted to make clear. Black lawbreaking was the result of a distinct historical process in which whites had made crucial and disastrous decisions. After the war the freed-people's offenses "were those of laziness, carelessness, and impulse, rather than of malignity or ungoverned viciousness. Such mis-demeanors needed discriminating treatment, firm but reformatory, with no hint of injustice, and full proof of guilt." Instead, Southern justice "erred on the white side by undue leniency and the practical immunity of red-handed criminals, and erred on the black side by undue severity, injustice, and lack of discrimination." The result was that "Negroes came to look upon courts as instruments of injustice and oppression, and upon those convicted in them as martyrs and victims." DuBois believed that when blacks committed more serious crimes in later years "the greatest deterrent to crime, the public opinion of one's own social caste, was lost, and the criminal was looked upon as crucified rather than hanged."[82]

This lament echoed through the New South for generations, a lament of a society, once bound together by slavery, witnessing rampant fragmentation. The South's fragmentation began with secession, as whites suddenly saw their differences exposed. Classes, ethnic groups, and subregions found themselves at odds with their neighbors. The privation of war heightened the South's internal divisions, and mass theft, bread riots, and armed resistance were the results. The Civil War set the South adrift. Slaves and slaveowners confronted each other in a new light. Southerners of all classes and races became unsure of themselves and of each other.

When the Civil War destroyed slavery, it destroyed the basic structure that gave shape to the South. Slavery had sealed off vast numbers of people from the state and the market economy, and when the walls of slavery fell nothing stood ready to replace them. Neither slavery nor true free labor could prevail, neither the master nor the state exercised the control they wished. The Freedmen's Bureau tried to supply a rudimentary state and the framework for the beginning of free labor, but its efforts were temporary and soon overwhelmed. The Ku Klux Klan spasmodically enforced the "organic law of the land," and tried to reassert the racial control whites had enjoyed with slavery, but the Klan's brutal and clan-destine power subsided as white Southerners found more certain and less volatile forms of racial domination.

Slowly and haltingly, new institutions grew up. Ex-masters and ex-slaves settled on forms of labor and payment that contained enough control to mollify the planter and enough freedom to help mollify the laborer. For the freedman the control remained galling, and his freedom came at the price of subjection to the relentless pressures of the international market. Black farmers as well as white ones found new masters in liens and mortgages. Masters no longer felt bound by duty and investment to supply food to hungry blacks, and white farmers sacrificed their abilty to feed themselves in order to grow cotton. Theft, already a problem, increased dramatically in country as well as city when the South suffered its first debilitating postwar depression in the 1870s.

The most dramatic battles during Reconstruction were fought over the control of the state. Radicals in Congress sought to guarantee republicanism by enfranchising the disenfranchised; the conservative white South sought to guarantee republicanism by restoring "home rule." The latter triumphed, and the criminal courts soon reflected the reassertion of local white control. In urban as well as rural areas, white officers arrested, prosecuted, and sentenced blacks accused of minor theft while neglecting white malefactors. Black property crime, fueled by widespread destitution and the special effort expended by white courts, suddenly superseded white violent crime in the court records. Whites made little attempt to disguise the injustice in their courts. Thousands of black people served long terms on chain gangs for petty theft and misdemeanors in the 1860s and 1870s. Thousands more went to the convict lease system, the most visible product of a society caught between the worst of the past and the worst of the future.

6

The Convict Lease System

Scarlett O'Hara decided to use convicts in her New South saw mill. Fed up with the demands of the "free darkies" to be paid every day, Scarlett wanted convicts. She could get them "for next to nothing and feed them dirt cheap." To the good people of Atlanta, including her husband, this was "the very worst of all the wild schemes Scarlett had ever suggested, worse even than her notion of building a saloon." It required Scarlett's "tears and supplications and promises" to persuade Ashley Wilkes, the embodiment of all that was good in the Old South, to exploit unfortunate criminals. Scarlett got her convicts, and her mill soon doubled its production.[1]

Convict labor, like Scarlett O'Hara, has become a symbol, even a cliché of the New South. The convict lease system is often perceived as merely a bald attempt by whites to resurrect slavery in a disguised form. But it was much more than this, an institution that reflected fundamental changes as well as continuities in the postwar South. The convict lease system emerged because Southern governments, still wedded to the antebellum innovation of centralized state penal institutions, suddenly found themselves responsible for millions of black people untouched by the state only a few years earlier. Convict labor also developed as an adjunct of a nascent industrial capitalism short of capital and labor. Once established, the South's network of convict labor became a force of its own in the region, shaping local justice, labor relations, and politics. The most lasting effect of the convict lease system was the role it played as the symbol, to blacks

185

and whites alike, of the white South's injustice and inhumanity. The Ku Klux Klan or urban mobs might be explained away as local and temporary disturbances in otherwise benevolent race relations, but the death and suffering in the convict lease system went on for decades with the approbation of the South's "leading men." As a result, that system played a central role in the history of crime and punishment in the postwar South.

For half a century following the Civil War, convict camps could be seen scattered over the Southern landscape. Thousands of Southern men and women, most of them black, passed years of their lives in the convict lease system, deep in mines or waist-high in swamps during the day, in wet clothes and filthy shacks during the night. Men with capital, from the North as well as the South, bought these years of convicts' lives. The largest mining and railroad companies in the region as well as small-time businessmen scrambled to win the leases. The crumbling antebellum penitentiaries, granite monuments of another social order, became mere outposts of the huge and amorphous new system of convict labor. Only a few white men convicted of murder, a few black men too sick to remain profitable at the work site, and a few women of both races remained in the dilapidated penitentiaries. Wardens had little to do; the state had become superfluous in the punishment and reclamation of its criminals.

One by one, Southern penitentiaries had fallen apart during the Civil War. Mississippi sent its state prisoners to Alabama for safekeeping; Louisiana shipped its inmates to a city workhouse. When Union troops came to Arkansas in 1863 they found the penitentiary empty, the prisoners dispersed. Occupied Tennessee hired out its prisoners to the United States government. As Sherman's troops approached Georgia's capital, the governor freed most of the inmates in return for their promise to help remove state property and then fight for the Confederacy. The freed prisoners, who felt little devotion to the Southern cause, deserted at the first chance. Sherman's army burned the Georgia penitentiary, which had served the Confederacy as a gun factory. Not long after, the prisoners in the Virginia penitentiary, seizing the opportunity offered when the last Confederate forces pulled out of Richmond, "broke up and made instruments of escape out of their own iron bedsteads, set fire to the building . . . ransacked the place, taking everything valuable they could find, including some 7,000 pairs of shoes, and let themselves loose on the community."[2]

In 1865 the ruined Georgia penitentiary held only four inmates. Governor Joseph E. Brown surveyed the scene and estimated the cost of repairs at $1 million Confederate currency. The wisest course of action, the chief executive thought, would be to abolish the penitentiary system entirely and do what opponents of the institution had been advocating for over fifty years: restore whipping, branding, hanging, and county jails to their rightful place at the heart of the Southern criminal justice system. Some Georgia legislators agreed with Governor Brown, and a newspaper in the state's capital city urged state leaders to "Hang, hang quick" as a response to the widespread postwar lawlessness. The principal keeper of the state penitentiary found himself without any money to feed the prisoners and sold part of the manufacturing equipment to buy food.[3]

The Georgia legislature, revealing the ambivalence and indecision with which Southern lawmakers confronted the crisis of the penitentiary immediately after the war, criticized the penitentiary and yet refused to abolish it. "The friends of the Penitentiary system are not able to point to many instances of reformation in those who have been convicts in Georgia," a majority in the General Assembly admitted in early 1866, yet they would not abandon hope that the institution might actually be made to work if only it were organized as it should be. The legislators offered a vision of a penitentiary unchanged since the 1820s: "by the erection of separate buildings, with properly constructed cells, thorough classification of offenders, the prevention of all intercourse of such separate classes with each other, and the judicious employment of many of the means of reformation which are used in the best conducted prisons," many inmates might emerge "better men and more obedient to law than they were when first imprisoned."[4]

At the same time that Georgia officials debated the future of their penitentiary, other legislators and governors in the region wrestled with the same problems. As the difficult months of 1865 and 1866 passed, the costs of maintaining dilapidated penitentiaries mounted steadily and the number of prisoners began to increase rapidly. A future warden of the Mississippi penitentiary, A. Philips, made a thorough study of the increasingly desperate situation. "Emancipating the negroes will require a system of penitentiaries," he reported. "The one in Jackson was nearly full, when the courts had but little to do with the negroes, how will it be now?" Philips suggested a tour of Northern penitentiaries to gather ideas, but certain problems would persist no matter what sort of institution

Mississippi built. An enlarged manufacturing prison of the sort the state had maintained before the war threatened the honest "working white men." "Labour concentrated and well directed at a cost of 20 or 25 cents a day, and aided by machinery with capital to back it, will break down any common shop, no matter how much industry or ingenuity the owner may display." Despite these obstacles, Philips concluded, Mississippi should rebuild its penitentiary; he could think of no other reasonable alternative.[5]

The officials charged with creating a new penal system for the South naturally looked to the past for their model. In the first year after Appomattox, legislators throughout the South made plans to resurrect bigger and better penitentiaries on the foundations of the old. The conversion of the penitentiary to the convict lease system, like the transformation of slave labor to free labor and the expansion of the state's jurisdiction to include blacks, did not proceed as automatically as it has sometimes seemed in retrospect. The convict lease system, not unlike the penitentiary which preceded it before the war, developed haltingly and unevenly throughout the region. Officials of different political persuasions refused to give up on the penitentiary. Despite a hostile legislature and a desperate economic situation in the Georgia penitentiary in 1866, for example, provisional Governor Jenkins took steps to rebuild the penitentiary that made the institution more comfortable and potentially more productive than ever before in its tumultuous history. To abandon the penitentiary would be to abandon the criminal, warned another Georgia official, for it would "destroy the heart, deprave the mind and make men engines of destruction of man—set him against laws, against moral government and God." The directors of the Tennessee penitentiary invoked the language of paternalism to explain the institution's duty: "the relation of the State to its citizens being that of a parent to a child, and however wayward and reckless the latter, the responsibility cannot be gotten rid of, but must be met with firmness and truest philanthropy."[6]

The penitentiary had become a Southern institution; the Southern criminal justice system depended upon the centralized penitentiary as the major form of punishment for serious crime. If state institutions were to be abolished, the entire criminal code of each state would have to be revised to return the task of punishing felons to the counties. Despite the deep reservations many antebellum Southerners had about the penitentiary, the institution had established a tradition in the region, had developed its own inertia. In fact, the two states that had not built a penitentiary in the antebellum era, the Carolinas, made sustained attempts to establish penitentiaries after the Civil War. The very first postwar General Assembly in South Carolina provided for a penitentiary, something no prewar assembly had been able to do. Benjamin F. Perry, an ardent advocate of the penitentiary in South Carolina since the 1840s, used his position as provisional governor to urge this action. The Radicals who followed in power spent nearly half a million dollars planning, locating, and erecting the institution between 1867 and 1876. North Carolina, too, made continued and expensive efforts to build a penitentiary. Explicitly drawing upon Northern models and talent, the Reconstruction government of North Carolina planned and began construction of a large structure. The Democrats who followed in power continued the work and even expanded the plan to include a thousand cells. The institution was so elaborate that it took years to build, and in the interim the number of convicts grew so rapidly that legislators felt compelled to use them on railroads to help defray expenses.[7]

Throughout the South, as in North Carolina, widespread poverty during the immediate postwar years took its toll on state finances and simultaneously led to ever-increasing prosecutions; the number of defendants who received penitentiary sentences soon outstripped even ambitious attempts by state officials to build penitentiaries. Many Southern states turned to the lease as a temporary expedient. In 1866 Mississippi's military governor offered a large planter $18,000 dollars a year to defray his expenses during an unprecedented attempt to work convict labor outside the prison walls. In 1867 Arkansas's governor proposed a temporary subsidized lease of two years to buy time while the legislature planned a better system. Virginia loaned its convicts to work on state-related railroads until a shoe contractor offered better terms for their labor inside the prison. Georgia's military governor leased 100 convicts to work on a railroad in 1868, and several other railroad leases soon followed. Despite these efforts to cut costs, it was not until the next year that Georgia managed to spend less than $20,000 per year on its convicts—far more than the state had spent during the antebellum era. In Alabama, too, convicts were leased from 1866 until 1872 without profit. The South, in other words, more or less stumbled into the lease, seeking a way to avoid large expenditures while hoping a truly satisfactory plan would emerge.[8]

Even those who called for the lease did so in cautious language that betrayed doubt. "It is true, this will, to some extent, be an experiment," a Mississippi legislative committee admitted in 1866 when it suggested leasing, but "as all new plans do not fail, and many experiments are successful, let us hope that the Legislature, in its combined wisdom, may be able to relieve our State of this vampire, which is, and has been from its creation, continually sapping our Treasury, and drawing from those who, by honest toil, must replenish its coffers by their hard earnings, the result of industry and frugality." Another Mississippi official looked at the flood of prisoners coming into the penitentiary in the wake of the panic of the 1870s and offered a warning to the board of inspectors: "It is hardly necessary for me to say to your honorable board that the system of leasing out convicts had to be resorted to from absolute necessity; and while I have nothing to urge in its favor, outside of its being a necessity, I must reiterate my former objections to it, and all the evils following in its trail."[9]

Presidential Reconstruction, Congressional Reconstruction, and Redemption passed without any obvious watershed in the South's penal system, without any one group bearing sole responsibility for inaugurating the convict lease system. Every party that exercised power in the postwar South shared responsibility for the lease's birth and survival. No group—black or white, Republican or Democrat— consistently opposed the lease once it gained power, though they all criticized each other's handling of the problem. The provisional governments that assumed control immediately after the war in Mississippi and Alabama initiated the lease in those states, and the Republicans who followed them did not abolish it. In South Carolina in 1872 black Republicans played a major role in inaugurating the lease, but then two years later helped bring it to an end. In Louisiana, twenty-four out of twenty-five black representatives and all four black senators were instrumental in passing a lease law in 1870; black votes were also crucial in renewing the lease fifteen years later. Regardless of race, both Louisiana Democrats and Louisiana Republicans crossed party lines to vote for or against the lease in later years. Despite the provisional government of Georgia's ambitious rebuilding of the penitentiary, the Republicans who followed leased the state's convicts. The Radicals in Tennessee were also responsible for first removing the convicts from the walls of the penitentiary. The Democrats who presided over the South from the end of Reconstruction through the end of the century did not invent the lease, but they reaped most of the financial benefits—and moral castigation—the lease generated.[10]

The same forces impinged on every political group in the South and led them to tolerate, if not endorse, the convict lease system. Demands for governmental frugality, the necessity of avoiding competition between convict and free labor, political pressures for party unity, white unwillingness to support criminal blacks in apparent idleness, and the usual disregard of the law-abiding for the welfare of the criminal remained constant throughout the postwar years. Within fifteen years after the war, all the ex-Confederate states allowed businessmen to submit bids for the labor of the state's felons.

The labor that convicts performed varied from year to year and from place to place. In the late 1860s and early 1870s there was cautious experimentation with convict labor; leases ran for relatively short periods and convicts worked primarily as agricultural and railroad laborers. Railroad work on a larger scale dominated the penal labor of virtually every state throughout the 1870s. In the 1880s and 1890s convict labor became increasingly concentrated in mining, especially in the states leasing the largest number of convicts: Alabama, Georgia, Florida, and Tennessee.[11]

The evolution of the convict lease system traces the contours of the evolving Southern economy in general. The early leases were inaugurated in a period of political and economic uncertainty, and neither the capitalist nor the state had a clear sense of the true value or utility of convict labor. To planters used to managing slaves, the bound labor of convicts must have seemed a welcome opportunity to return to accustomed ways, to a control of every facet of the worker's life impossible even in slavery. The lease system was part of a continuum of forced labor in the New South, a continuum that ran from the monopolistic company store, to the coercions of share-cropping, to peonage, to the complete subjugation of convict labor. Obviously, the roots of such forced labor reached into slavery, not only for the work force itself but also for the habits of thought that encouraged employers to turn so readily to such heavy-handed means of securing labor.[12]

As Harold Woodman has observed, however, the "desire for a dependent, easily controlled, docile, and cheap labor force burns as fiercely in the heart of a thoroughly bourgeois factory owner as it does in the heart of a plantation owner."[13] The convict lease system was not simply slavery reincarnated, and ex-slaveowners were not the only employers interested in convict labor. The lease system must be viewed in relation to the new demands of the postbellum South and not merely as the inertia of the antebellum South. The convict lease system, along with the other variations of forced labor, bridged the chasm between an agricultural slave economy and a society in the earliest states of capitalist industrial development. On railroads and then in mines, the convict lease system served as the entering wedge, as the only labor force capitalists investing in the South knew they could count on to penetrate dangerous swamps and to work in deadly primitive mines. Convict labor depended upon both the heritage of slavery and the allure of industrial capitalism.

Many parts of the postwar South suffered from a severe labor shortage, and planters and railroad builders found themselves in competition for scarce workers. The postwar South had no pool of displaced male agricultural laborers of the sort that fed indus- trialization in England and Europe. For decades, the new factories of the South would be dominated by women and children—but women and children could not be used in many of the South's more profitable and dangerous new industries. New Yorker Charles K. Dutton, head of a turpentine and naval stores company, leased Florida's convicts because "turpentine culture was exhausting work, and it was difficult to obtain enough labor for the proper cultivation of any great number of trees. Natives of Florida's piney woods would quickly abandon the work when any other type of livelihood became available." Phosphate mining was little better, and as one historian put it, the discovery of phosphate in Florida had "the same effect on convict leasing as the invention of the cotton gin had had on slavery." Colonel Arthur Colyar used convict labor in his Tennessee coal mines because, he said, he could not find 300 free men willing to work in the mines.[14]

Railroad building presented the same problems of labor short- ages; the South's antebellum rail network, in fact, had been built largely by companies using slaves instead of scarce, expensive, and unreliable free white labor. The postbellum railroads, therefore, seemed a natural place for convicts to labor. The railroads needed rebuilding, state governments had often invested heavily in the lines, the roads seemed to serve the entire state economy, and railroad laborers were unorganized and powerless. The work was back- breaking and took workers into the most remote and most dangerous reaches of the South. In the mid-1870s, for example, Tennessee leased its convicts to the Cincinnati Southern Railroad.

Other contractors on the line had managed to entice some Italians, Irishmen, blacks, and perhaps even Chinese to labor in the mountain wilderness. These free laborers, not surprisingly, drank freely of the local moonshine whiskey sold in the log taverns that sprang up along the route, and fights broke out between gangs of workers. Employers discovered their free labor force was frequently decimated by desertions and injuries. But the convicts working on the railroad could not get whiskey, could not run away, could not brawl. They were guarded by young white men who practiced target shooting in their spare time; the convicts slackened their labor at the risk of a whipping or worse.[15] Owners of a railroad in Mississippi also turned to convict labor. When they could not persuade contractors of free laborers to build through the Canay Swamps, they subleased convicts for $1.75 per day. As a legislative committee discovered, the convicts "were placed in the swamp in water ranging to their knees, and in almost nude state they spaded caney and rooty ground, their bare feet chained together by chains that fretted the flesh. They were compelled to attend to the calls of nature in line as they stood day in and day out, their thirst compelling them to drink the water in which they were compelled to deposit their excrement." Eighteen convicts nearly died, and had to be transported through Vicksburg hidden in a wagon.[16]

The lease system was tailor-made for capitalists concerned only with making money fast.[17] Labor costs were fixed and low, problems of labor uncertainty were reduced to the vanishing point, lucrative jobs could be undertaken that others would not risk, convicts could be driven at a pace free workers would not tolerate. In many camps throughout the New South era, guards awakened convict workers at 4:30 in the morning and had them at work within thirty minutes. The convicts received forty minutes for dinner, and "then worked until after sundown, and as long as it is light enough for a guard to see how to shoot. They are worked every day, rain or shine, cold or wet." One report claimed that Mississippi's convicts "do 30 percent more work than free laborers, being worked long, hard, and steadily." The benefits of a captive workforce took on greater luster, too, when compared to the scene in the North in 1877, as the warden of the Alabama penitentiary pointed out: "considering the depression in business throughout the country, the frightful upheavings of labor against capital of some of our sister States, its consequent injury and derangement of the general business of the country, we have cause to congratulate ourselves as to our financial success."[18]

Convict labor, not unlike slavery, insulated the lessee from "frightful upheavings of labor" and labor shortages. But as in slavery, laborers had to be supported during slack times; and convicts, unlike slaves, could not be sold. "Epidemics may prevail," a Tennessee official pointed out in 1867, "contagion may spread death and devastation all over the country—debtors may become insolvent, and cause the prison to sustain heavy losses—the labor market may be dull, and no remunerative employment be found for the convicts—but the State is indemnified against all these, and if any loss is sustained, it must be borne by the lessees, and not by the state." Similarly, if the lease decreed that the lessee must accept all hands in the prison, many of the advantages of convict labor disappeared. "Now, every convict, old or young, skilled or unpracticed, clumsy, indolent, or vicious, is at once turned over, at forty-three cents per day, and it is the lessee's business, to provide work profitable or otherwise, without regard to the character, condition, or competency of the laborer." Increasingly, lessees accepted only able-bodied men from the state, but another problem with convict labor persisted despite this winnowing. A visitor to a Tennessee coal-mining camp discovered that "some of those in charge spoke with great contempt of the value of this class of convict labor, and said that they grudged paying the twenty-five dollars for the recapture of such lazy loafers." Not unlike slaves, convicts resisted. Some loaded the bottoms of their coal wagons with stones to fill their quota. Others did not even bother resorting to such subterfuge: although a mandatory whipping followed "any shirking of the task, the men will sometimes lounge away the day and at its close take the punishment, rather than do the work."[19]

Inefficiency and fixed costs in times of depression no doubt hurt the lessee's profits, but apparently most convict labor paid handsomely. Some of the largest mining companies and shrewdest entrepreneurs in the South avidly sought and used convict labor for decades. As early as 1872 a competitor of the Tennessee Coal, Iron, and Railroad Company charged that convict labor gave that company a $70,000 annual advantage over mines that depended on free labor. The convict lease system, argued a Northern member of the American Iron and Steel Association, was the major reason the South could produce such cheap iron. Southern industrialists did not deny the charge. In fact, one entrepreneur who worked convicts in Alabama and Tennessee mines recalled that in the 1870s "a strong effort was at that time being made to develop the iron and coal interests of our states; it was a practical impossibility to get our native free people, either white or black, their training having been principally of an agricultural tendency, to work in the mines, rendering it necessary to send abroad for miners, and even then the demand could not be supplied." But then the firm acquired convicts, and the effects were immediate and wide-reaching: "this made possible the rapid development of the wonderful natural resources of the two states, and gave an impetus to the manufacturing interests of the entire South which could not otherwise have been possible, for at least many years."[20]

As businessmen and officeholders jostled for and haggled over the lease widespread corruption grew up around the system. First Republicans and then Democrats accepted bribes from prospective lessees to vote the right way or exercise their influence. As the Southern minister Atticus Haygood explained, the lease system simply offered too great an opportunity for corruption for many officials to resist: "While legislators are men, and money is money, the convict lease system will corrupt legislation." The Southern convict lease system was politically transparent; every change of political fortune brought a new division of the spoils. Every prison official in every Southern state, "from the superintendent of the penitentiary down to the merest guard that stands sentry over a county chaingang, is a politician, and holds his office because he is a politician."[21]

The convict lease system became a sort of mutual aid society for the new breed of capitalists and politicians of the white Democratic regimes of the New South, and often the same man played the roles of both entrepreneur and officeholder. Although Joseph Emerson Brown had called for the abolition of a centralized penitentiary when he was governor of Georgia in 1865, he made a fortune leasing convicts when he was senator in the 1880s. Jeremiah W. South, lessee of Kentucky convicts from 1869 to his death in 1880, supposedly exercised greater power over Kentucky's government than any other official, controlling a third of the legislators "as absolutely as he controlled the convicts." A political dynasty sprang from convict labor in Alabama, where John H. Bankhead ruled. In 1883 a retired Alabama official wrote to an influential Democratic editor expressing his dismay at Bankhead's blatant manipulation of the legislature. "How can the Governor fail to cause proceedings to be instituted at once against him—The party cannot carry such a scoundrel as this report makes him. Are we all thieves? . . . There

will be a heavy reckoning at the ballot box one of these days. . . . "
The recipient of this letter wrote to another party member: "The
penitentiary ring is well organized, capable, unscrupulous, and
rotten through and through and through. . . . The ring have shaped,
moulded, framed the legislation of the session just closed. . . . I am
heartsick and sore."[22]

Because prison officials so often had something to hide, their
reports, whether written during Reconstruction or Redemption,
were models of obfuscation and officialese. Reports in Alabama give
glowing accounts of the "good order" of the convict camps, yet a
mere glance at the statistical tables accompanying these reports
shows that up to 40 percent of the prisoners were dying. When
investigators uncovered horrible conditions, officials self-righteously
refuted the charges. "The one whipped," they intoned, "burning
under the sting of the lash, and provoked to feelings of revenge, is
hardly competent to fully judge and describe the punishment."[23]
Fragmentary and missing reports were not so much mistakes as they
were part of a built-in incompetency, a purposeful confusion. Even
today, the air of smoky-room politics hangs about the documents of
the convict lease system.

Most Southern state governments were happy just to break even in
their dealings with lessees during the early postwar years, just to be
rid of the penitentiary's relentless drain upon the state treasury. They
were quick to up the ante, however, when they realized convicts
could command great prices. By 1886 the mining states of Alabama
and Tennessee enjoyed the most profitable systems; convicts there
brought in around $100,000 to each state annually—about one-
tenth of the states' total revenue. Georgia, Mississippi, Arkansas,
North Carolina, and Kentucky made the lesser but still respectable
sums of between $25,000 and $50,000 each per year. Nationally, all
prisons which did not use the lease system earned only 32 percent of
their total expenses, while those who did take advantage of the
demand for convict labor outside the prison walls earned 267
percent. In comparison with manufacturing enterprises within the
penitentiaries of the North, the profitability of the lease system was
real and sustained. Substantially lower overhead, more profitable
products, longer hours, and the more brutal exploitation made
possible by a disregard for the prisoner's health and welfare
generated considerable short-term profits for the state as well as for
the businessmen lucky enough and callous enough to lease
convicts.[24]

Exposés of the convict lease system appeared with increasing frequency in newspapers, state documents, Northern publications, and proceedings from national prison associations, but the convicts themselves remained faceless and nameless. They emerged only as victims of torture or as mulelike workers on railroads and levees— mainly because the racial composition of the Southern prison population had changed radically overnight. Before the Civil War, virtually all the prisoners had been white; now about nine out of ten were black. Before the Civil War, white immigrants made up a disproportionate share of the prison populations; after the war, these immigrants almost disappeared. Before the Civil War, rural counties sent few people to the penitentiary; in the postbellum era, black belt counties became major suppliers of the state penal apparatus.

Greene, Whitefield, and Chatham counties, along with hundreds of their counterparts throughout the South, saw these changes at first hand. The population size and racial composition of Greene and Whitfield in the 1860s and 1870s were almost identical to their antebellum figures. Yet in the 1850s Greene had sent only 3 men to the state penitentiary and Whitfield had sent only 10. Between 1866 and 1879, however, Greene's courts sentenced 54 people to the Georgia convict lease system, 47 of them black. Whitfield sent 21 to the lease system, 13 of whom were blacks. Greene County's Superior Court, in fact, sentenced 23 black men to prison for three years or longer, but only indicted 48 white men for any kind of crime, serious or minor, in the fourteen-year period.

As in the antebellum years, postwar Southern cities accounted for a disproportionate share of their states' prison inmates. Savannah sent three times as many convicts to the railroads and mines as its population alone would led us to expect, a pattern amplified by the fact that 76 percent of the blacks convicted in the Chatham Superior Court received prison sentences.[25] Despite such numbers, the domination of postwar Southern prison populations by cities registered a decline from antebellum levels because rural areas contributed so many more prisoners than they had previously. A decline in the prosecution of white immigrants in the city also made urban areas stand out less in the penitentiary records than before emancipation. In Chatham County in the 1850s, 47 percent of the defendants before the Superior Court who also appeared in the manuscript census had been born abroad, but in the 1870s only 6.5 percent of the white defendants were of foreign birth. White immigrants steered clear of the postwar South; hundreds of thousands of freedmen seemed to offer too much competition and the South offered too few opportunities for poor white men. The fall in immigrant prosecution and incarceration may well have owed something, too, to the preoccupation of police and courts with blacks. Even the Irish, after all, were white.[26]

Whatever his ethnicity, any Southern white man of wealth stood little danger of finding himself in a convict camp. As an Alabama prison official aptly noted, middle- and upper-class white men either "do not commit crime, or else they are safely insulated from the penitentiary by greenbacks or other penal non-conductors." Accordingly, the occupations of white prisoners in the postbellum South closely resembled those of the antebellum era: a few farmers, shoemakers, sailors, and blacksmiths mixed with a host of unskilled laborers and an incongruous and solitary schoolteacher or merchant.[27]

Virtually all the blacks were labeled "laborers," and the architects of the convict lease system never intended that black and white should mix. As early as 1866 planners decreed it "not only important—but vital" that the races be kept separate in any penal institution in "the new order of things"; "under no circumstances [should we] recognize social equality between the two races, not even with felons." Because relatively few whites went to the penitentiary, and since these few had been convicted of serious crimes and were thus often ineligible to leave the walls of the dilapidated central penitentiaries, some segregation was possible. The white criminals who managed to filter through the South's criminal justice system and into the lease were considered the lowest of their race, though, and racial lines blurred in the convict lease camps. As a contemporary commenting on the equal treatment of the races observed, "Death and the penitentiary are great levelers." Even the conventional racial epithets were confused in the lease system: "In the recent legislative investigation of the convict lease system a witness would frequently speak of a convict as a 'nigger,' when it was found he meant a white man."[28]

Commentators were appalled at the lowering of the color barrier within the system. A Southerner told the National Prison Congress in 1886 that whites should not be imprisoned with blacks: "It is akin to the torture anciently practised of tieing [*sic*] a murderer to the dead body of his victim limb to limb, from head to foot, until the decaying corpse brought death to the living." The governor of Tennessee revealed much in his observation about white inmates sentenced for "the lower grades of homicide . . . , who are otherwise respectable and highly esteemed, and have a high sense of honor": "It is unjust to compel such men to a daily association with thieves, robbers, and assassins." It was wrong, in other words, to imprison together white murderers and a black who had stolen a pig—it was unjust to the whites. The Southern ideal of honor here reveals its full measure.[29]

Perhaps the most startling characteristic of the postwar prison population of the South was its youth: anywhere from two-thirds to over three-fourths of the convicts working and dying in the convict lease system were in their twenties or younger. Despite the fact that the Southern population as a whole registered a higher median age after the war than before, the postbellum South's convicts were substantially younger than their antebellum predecessors and their postbellum Northern counterparts. "Very few Georgians realize how large a proportion of the criminals in the penitentiary are juveniles," observed the Savannah *Morning News* in 1893. Over a third of those convicts were under 20 years old. "There are 80 who are below the age of 15, 40 below the age of 14, 27 below the age of 13, 15 below the age of 12, 2 below the age of 11, and one who is only 10 years old."[30]

"As it now is," sadly commented the Greensboro *Herald*, "if a boy ten, twelve or even fifteen years of age, commits a crime, he is either turned loose by Courts and Juries on account of his youth, from sympathy; or he is convicted and sent to the Chaingang among the most hardened criminals." The postwar South apparently saw "a large number of boys who are without proper parental control, and many of them without parents—boys, we might say, who have to look out for their own living. . . . Hundreds of them in our State are ragged waifs, harmless, fatherless, motherless, with never a kind word spoken to them. They feel like the world is against them as they wander shivering in the winter's wind, and stand hungry even when the birds are singing their summer song." Urban dwellers in particular confronted the haunting image of youngsters, as a Tennessee legislative committee portrayed them, "at every corner and in every alley—at the doors of saloons and the theatre, at our depots and wharves—here their faces greet you with features pinched, by their necessities, into expressions of premature shrewdness, bordering on villainy." From this *"teeming crop"* of youths came "the large majority, if not all the thieves, forgers, burglars, robbers, and murderers, who fill our penitentiaries."[31]

We can only imagine the horrors an adolescent boy felt when he found himself "thrown in the cells at night, on Sundays and holidays, with hardened and habitual criminals of the most dangerous class." Many first offenders did not belong to what the nineteenth century called the "criminal class," and these youths were "disheartened and degraded by the association" in the lease camps; others, who "have an inclination towards a life of crime . . . look upon the expert criminal as a hero, prize his acquaintance as an honor, and seek to be as great a criminal as their companion." One investigating committee found Tennessee's branch prisons "hell holes of rage, cruelty, despair, and vice"; homosexual assaults on young boys were common and "Gal boys" were in great demand.[32]

Sexual abuse was not reserved for adolescent boys: the women in the lease system suffered constantly from the threat and reality of such assault. The principal keeper of Georgia's prison system reported in 1874 that "we have on hand about 25 female convicts, one of the number white, apportioned promiscuously to the several lessees, and employed as cooks, washer-women, and at other light work in and about the prison quarters. They have separate lock-ups at night, and with strict orders to keep them apart from the males. Still, the guard and trustees come in contact with them, and the result is there are children born in the penitentiary." Three years later, a legislative committee found "in some of the camps men and women chained together and occupying the same sleeping bunks. The result is that there are now in the Penitentiary 25 bastard children, ranging from 3 months to 5 years of age, and many of the women are now far advanced in pregnancy." Women were not always victims; in Kentucky's prison "it was a common occurrence for the men and women to loosen the boards in the fence that separated them so that the women might slip into the men's prison. Although iron bars remained between the men and the women, they succeeded in having sexual intercourse." Women—virtually all of them black—made up about 7 percent of the South's postwar prison population; this proportion differed little from the national average but showed a sevenfold increase from the antebellum era in the South, when almost no women went to prison.[33]

One convict captured the essence of life in the lease system, no matter what one's race, age, or gender: "This place is nine kinds of hell. Am suffering death every day here." Mortality rates ranged widely, but at its worst the convict lease was lethal. In 1870, 41 percent of Alabama's 180 convicts died, and the preceding two years had seen death rates of 18 and 17 percent. In Mississippi in the 1880s the proportion who died was nine times that of typical Northern prisons. But for a cruel subterfuge, a convict reported, the death rates of Southern prisons would have been even higher: "Did you know of the scores of broken down men who have been pardoned and sent to their homes to die it would make your very heart bleed."[34]

The lease was something less (and something more) than a total institution. Escapes were amazingly frequent; in the mid-1870s in Georgia, for example, more than 523 convicts, nearly half the total number of prisoners then incarcerated, had escaped. "Nearly the whole Penitentiary is managed by hirelings," explained Georgia's principal keeper in 1878, "selected generally for the ability to drive with severity, rather than to hold securely." The lessees themselves could usually be found "in some other portion of the State, applying their time and talents to other vocations." Order was extremely tenuous and punishment was dealt out with a certain sense of desperation. At the Rising Fawn Mines in Georgia, when the "whipping boss"—the only man legally authorized to punish the men—was stabbed by a convict, other prisoners used the occasion to test the limits of their captivity. The ensuing riot ended only after guards killed a prisoner. Lessees were afraid of their convicts. One warned the legislature that attempts to reform the lease had been heard of by the prisoners, and they were becoming restless and insubordinate. If would-be reformers continued "to sow the wind, it will not be many years before they will reap the whirlwind." Even a convict noted the lack of discipline and control: "The discipline of the prison is boasted of[.] Great God what a satire on the word, Discipline when there is Gamboling and vice of every description carried on through the entire prison[.] [W]ould to God you could visit this prison . . . and see the dire confusion that reigns rampant."[35]

The same laxness that bred disorder, however, could also breed a sort of inmate subculture. Traditional amusements helped fill convicts' free time. "Some pray, some sing, women all cook ginger-cakes, men play chuck-luck, seven-up, poker, eucher, wrestle, play leap-frog, and all kinds of amusements, such as patting and dancing." Religion, too, constituted a major element of convict subculture. Black men, some of whom were preachers before their imprisonment and some who felt compelled to preach only after their ordeal had begun, rose up in lieu of or in addition to the occasional white minister who visited the camps. Some white guards distrusted this religiosity, just as whites had always feared the unifying effects of black religion:

> *Q:* Do you, or do you not believe, yourself, that prayer, piety, and preaching is necessary and becoming to persons in the conditions of those convicts?
>
> *A:* I do not. I always double the guard when they begin to pray, etc.

This perception of religion reveals the difference between the lease system and the antebellum penitentiary, where officials relied upon religion as the engine of reform.[36]

As in the antebellum penitentiary, however, work dominated convict life. Inmates were able, not unlike slaves, to infuse forced labor with their own needs and pride. One convict in Alabama bragged of his work: "Never whipped for not getting task. I was one of the best coal cutters here when I came out of mine. Am now running the rope on outside; this takes a responsible man." A Tennessee convict argued that it was not work in general he and the 600 inmates for whom he spoke resented, it was the lack of fairness. "If the prison was conducted in accordance with the rules laid down for its Government not a murmur would be heard from any of us. . . . There is but few men who desire to shirk their duty and none are afraid to work provided they received sufficient food."[37]

Black convicts fused their culture with their experience in the lease system to create a distinctive folk art that has survived to the present: the convict work song. These songs revolve around the themes and images of confinement and release, and thus serve as metaphors for much of the black experience. One song reveals the tension at the heart of any slavelike relationship, be it in slavery or in a penitentiary: the boss needs the labor of the worker, but the worker does not share that need.

> The captain holler hurry
> I'm going to take my time.
> Say's he's making money
> And trying to make time.
> Says he can lose his job
> But I can't lose mine.

The lease was terrible, but in an archaic way; the bosses were content to punish the body and let the mind think what it would.[38]

The warden of the Alabama penitentiary, although generally opposed to leasing, admitted that nine-tenths of the convicts were "greatly preferring the plantation, sawmill, coal or iron mines, than to remain in the walls of the penitentiary." In fact, officials sometimes complained that such outdoor work did not offer punishment enough for blacks. It was not merely that convicts enjoyed doing work with which they were familiar and which helped pass the time, but the convict camps were often more comfortable than the alternatives. All the Southern penitentiaries in states where most convicts were leased were mere shells of buildings, depositories for the old, the sick, and the most dangerous. Although Virginia maintained a manufacturing penitentiary which seemed to set it off from other Southern states, a governor complained in 1898 that 1,300 convicts had been crowded into the state's ancient penitentiary designed to hold only 300 inmates. The convicts were "almost as thick as cattle in a railroad car . . . and in summer pant for breath when locked up for the night." The cells in the Tennessee penitentiary, observed a report from the State Board of Health, provided "less air space to the individual than the cubic contents of a good-sized grave."[39]

The vast majority of prisoners, however, were not within prison walls but in far-flung camps. A diary of a dedicated prison camp inspector in Alabama, R. H. Dawson, reveals details of their situation invisible in official reports. The diary attests, above all, to the amorphousness of the lease. Even as tireless a worker as Dawson could not keep the scattered camps under control; he would note that he had done some good at one camp, only to sigh at the next one: "Found things very bad—Cells so low that a man cannot stand upright—No hospital—No privy—No shoes—Bad clothes—and very little to eat." Conditions in the camps constantly fluctuated with the seasons, with fortune, with the mood of the bosses. A camp would sometimes have "plenty of food" and at other times starve the convicts with rations that weighed only one-fourth of an ounce. Sometimes, too, even the convict lease contained islands of decency. In Dawson's diary, where there would be no need to varnish the facts, he characterized one such place: "Entirely satisfied with the treatment—well, plenty of good food—Comfortable lodgings—Negroes satisfied—No complaint."[40]

About half the prisoners in the lease system had been sentenced for theft or burglary, often of petty amounts. The social costs of punishing such minor crimes with such harsh punishment were obvious. "The husband and father, the only support of a wife and children, charged with the larcency of some article of property of small value, perhaps necessary for his family, is arrested, torn from his family, and placed in prison," Tennessee Governor Alvin Hawkins noted in 1883. "His wife and children are the real sufferers. Perhaps houseless and homeless, and without any means of support, they are driven forth as outcasts, dependent upon the cold charities of the world."[41]

The wives of prisoners worked frantically for the release of their husbands. Black women visited local white men of influence and asked for their aid. The wife of Mississippi prisoner Van Massar pleaded with the governor: "he Dide note stel the monay the men will sine a paper. . . . I have 4 littal chrildren and . . . I have ben to white men and thea all say if you can do any thinge with hit thea will send you a paper to sho that he clair of stel this monay please Sair let mee know if you can helpe mee." A woman in Alabama wrote: "Dear husban i want you to tel me . . . the amounte of money that it will take to git you out and i can git it fer thair was a man tolde me that he would help me." In another letter she promised their potential benefactor that "i and him wil work for you until you air pade if it is a live time please mr. smith do al you can fer me and if work wil pay you i will take a sarvints place the reste of my life . . . i would giv my life fer him if it would take him out." Another wife, one without influential friends, appealed directly to the governor: "I call upon you in the Name of God to Pardon my Husban. my 3 childrin are very sick . . . and I see nothing but Starvation and death before Us we have no one to look to for assistance and if you will let him out so that he can provide for his helpless Babes that are sick and crying For bred." Even if starvation did not threaten, the separation and uncertainty alone could be nearly unbearable. A white woman wrote from Michigan to the Tennessee penitentiary: "Dear husband i sit down to write to you again. . . . you said you would be at home last month and i looked for you all the month and you did not come . . . and o how bad i do feal it seams as if i shal go crazy, o i want to see you so much."[42]

Letters and petitions for pardon from the convicts themselves also give glimpses into the more obscure corners of Southern society. Although there was little official pretense that the convict lease system actually reformed its prisoners, several inmates declared themselves, in fact, reformed. Phillip Hopkins, a black man working in coal mines for the state of Tennessee, wrote a letter that would gratify even the most idealistic penal reformer: "dear Sir I fell it my duty to inform you of my reformation yes Sir I have searched the issue and termination of vice and Crime and am Satisfied they lead to ruin and disgrace and perdition. and I have resolved . . . to travel the road of honor and industry and practice Christianity." Another inmate made a more pragmatic argument. "I have been imprisoned very near three years . . . and I ask of your Excellency that if I am not a reformed man by this time I will not be in three more years." Apparently, chaplains (and perhaps guilty consciences) did not work without effect in the convict camps and dilapidated prisons. Wilson Jordon, "Col'd," told Governor John Brown of Tennessee that "God has for gave me I know I hope you will." W. D. Highlander, a white man, felt an equally close communion with the deity. "Dear Mother," he wrote, "do you remember the old hymn that says:

> And prisons would palaces prove,
> If Jesus would dwell with me there.

Well my little cell, narrow as it seems, is a grand palace tonight, because Jesus, that Dear Friend is here even now."[43]

Not all the petitions for pardon, however, appealed to such high principles. A petition to Governor Brown of Tennessee in 1872 asked that a prisoner be released because the man he killed was "known to this Community as a most exceedingly bad and dangerous man, and a notorious scoundrel and thief. He was the terror of his neighbors, and his 'taking off' was regretted by not one of the good and respectable citizens who knew him." The simplest, though perhaps not the most effective, plea came from one Gideon Barnes in Tennessee. Barnes thought he should be pardoned because the Governor had "pardoned some worse."[44]

A surprising and revealing "genre" of petitions for pardon were those from whites in behalf of blacks. A number of distinct themes recur in these letters. Several petitioners argued that freedmen should not be punished because they did not, indeed could not, understand the full meaning of the laws. The most theoretical letter came from Joseph A. Smith of Mississippi, who defended an ex-slave sentenced for adultery. "I believe it is a sound maxim in moral ethics, that the moral quality of every act should be judged by the interest of the party to the act," Smith wrote. "If this be true can a temporary deflexion from the law carry with it much moral, or legal guilt, when the party deflecting in the very nature of things could not know the consequences of the act committed?"[45]

Theft, too, could sometimes be excused in freedmen. T. F. Scott wrote from West Point, Mississippi, that an ex-slave was "no doubt guilty of killing a hog valued above $25." But "he is an uneducated Negro that never knew how great a crime he had committed— Wilson Boykin, 'FMC' is an old man and generally considered a good Negro. . . . I have known Wilson B. a long while and believe him to be much better than many, who have their liberty." This petition, like many others, came from an ex-master, and more than one revealed very real paternalistic feelings of master toward slave. "There is one of my old servants in the State Penitentiary," a planter wrote to Governor Brownlow of Tennessee. "A boy about seventeen years old. Put in for stealing a horse. his term is ten years he has been in now about one year. I raised the boy in my House as a Dining room servant and I know it could not have been *his* fault, stealing the horse. His father and mother are both with me and they are very old. . . . I am willing to pay myself Five hundred Dollars to the man that he stole the horse from if I can get him out to restore him to his father and mother." An Alabama minister asked that a freedman who had once been his grandfather's slave be pardoned "because of the many tender recollections of the past and present sympathy with and appreciation of 'Uncle Cain and Aunt Kate.' "[46]

Intertwined with the benevolence of paternalism, though, was the desire for control, and at least one ex-slaveowner used the state's penal institution to discipline and then "forgive" an ex-slave. Lucinda Banks was sent to the Tennessee penitentiary for six years for stealing "some twenty dollars worth of Tobacco"; the prosecutor was her ex-owner. After Banks had served two years, her ex-owner requested that she be pardoned because "before the war she was an old family servant of our family, and was raised in the family, and was always a good, obedient, and efficient Servant Girl. . . . I cherish no malice against her. . . . I would now like to see her pardoned and released from Prison." The pardon was granted the next day.[47]

Not all the whites who defended blacks were old or new masters. In 1869 a group of citizens in Mississippi asked that four black men be pardoned who had already served a year for stealing a cow; the signers varied in class from those who could sign only an X to the judge and mayor. A letter written in a bad scrawl to the governor of Tennessee asked "to be heard as an humble citizen who desires simply to cail your attention to a negro who was incarcerated in the penitentiary for three years for an accusation of stealing a pocket knife. . . . The negro is nothing to me in any respect. . . . How is it right? . . . but he is only a negro."[48]

The best that concerned citizens felt they could win from the lease was humane treatment; the ideal of reform had long since died with the penitentiary. An articulate inmate captured the situation with wry humor in a plea for pardon: "I have been in this Institution a long time, and if the present system was reformatory I ought to be a second Beecher—as it is not, I candidly confess that I am as selfish and wicked as the 'rest of the world.' " As in the antebellum period, the entire burden of reform fell on the shoulders of the chaplains. Some of these men showed little devotion to their difficult task, as this laconic inspectors' report testifies: "The moral tone of the convicts here is as high as could be expected under the circumstances, though we regret our inability to refer your Excellency to any report of the Chaplain, that officer having failed up to this time to render any."[49]

Other chaplains, however, were outraged by their circumscribed role in the lease: "If the ultimate aim of a penitentiary is gained in swelling the treasury, possibly—or in inducing a slavish fear of the law, then we confess we are interlopers." A counterpart in another state fumed that "the faithful, earnest Chaplain will find duty, duty, duty enough to tax all the brain and talents God has given him; and yet he is met by men, professed Christians, and even ministers, with this inquiry: *What good are you doing with all your labors?*" He answered this question with conviction. "Inmates of the penitentiary are men like other men"; they could be saved. The ministers' protests and affirmations, however, were cries in the wilderness. The ideal of moral regeneration, always tenuous even in the best penitentiary, was seldom even mentioned in connection with the convict lease system.[50]

The convict lease, however, did claim "reform" of another sort; it supposedly taught blacks how to work. The ideal of work, the centuries-old panacea for deviancy, grew luxuriantly in the post-bellum South. One advocate of prison labor traced the lineage of his recommendation of work as the solution to crime to the beginning of mankind. "When our first parents fell, and were turned out of paradise, the Almighty put man to work, and as a rule, those who have best obeyed this injunction, have been the best people, and if Eve had been busy sewing fig leaves, it is probable that she would not have had time to enter into that fatal conversation with the

Devil." Another defender of convict labor invoked, with no intended irony, John Howard, the central figure in the birth of the penitentiary: "It was a maxim with Howard, 'Make men diligent, and they will be honest.' " And according to a British traveler in the region, the lease system won a reputation for turning out good workers: "I have heard it said by reliable men that they employ no man so readily as one who has come out of the chain gangs, because he has there learnt discipline." Black convicts may have learned discipline, but few white Southerners claimed any deeper "reformation" of the race they dominated.[51]

White Southerners doubted black reformation not because they considered criminal blacks hopelessly evil, but because whites realized the convict lease system itself was useless as a way to convince blacks they owed a debt to society. The theoretical justification of the penitentiary had been built around the ideal of consensus as the cement between males in a republican state. To maintain that consensus, the moral order that supported the penitentiary had to be recognized as the only morality which deserved allegiance. Justice had to appear fair, equitable, certain. The convict lease system undermined that sense of justice. The convict lease system made a mockery of any pretensions white leaders made to paternalism or noblesse oblige, and in the process actually eroded their power. Healthy ruling classes do not rule by overt violence but by a system of values accepted throughout society. These values support the status quo. There is a sense that the dominant class remains the dominant class because it deserves to be, because it best embodies and protects the values everyone believes to be just. For that sense of justice to be maintained, deviants must receive "fair" treatment. As C. Vann Woodward argues, "The convict lease system did greater violence to the moral authority of the Redeemers than did anything else. For it was upon the tradition of paternalism that the Redeemer regimes claimed authority to settle the race problem and 'deal with the Negro.' "[52]

This erosion of the Redeemers' moral authority, the true price for whites of the convict lease system, was recognized by some white Southerners as early as 1871. One proponent of a more just penal system argued that a young criminal "who has just touched upon the outermost circle of the maelstrom of crime" and for his minor transgression was suddenly thrown into the "vortex" of the convict lease, was certain to reject the justice of the society that sent him there. "He feels that vindictiveness only governed in his conviction, and all the reformatory effects of punishment are utterly lost on him." Even a warden could recognize the effect of the system he presided over: "The first lesson taught is, that the State cares nothing for the criminal nor his well being, that the only interest felt in him is as to how much money the State and contractor can jointly realize from his labor." The self-appointed spokesman for Tennessee's convicts, "Louisiana Tiger," put the matter well: "How in the name of heaven is a man going to respect the law when he sees the laws for his government *Daily and hourly violated*[?]"[53]

One white argued that black convicts passing through the lease system "came back hating law, despising the restraints of law, enemies of society, the enemies of the white people with hatred and malignity in their hearts. Determined to have revenge for what they call unjust punishment of their crimes." Another white cautioned that "the desire for vengeance," not a contrite realization of past mistakes, was uppermost in the convict's mind. And the prison social order mirrored that of society at large; when violence was the only means of maintaining control—as it was in the lease—there was no chance of inculcating the desired values. "Every time it becomes necessary to punish a convict, his reformation is thereby retarded."[54]

Surprisingly, given everything else said against the ex-slaves, whites mouthed almost no rhetoric about the inherent nonreformability of blacks. For one thing, whites had long believed and preached that white civilization was slowly improving the black race; to argue that blacks were basically evil would contradict much of the rationalization that whites used to justify their continued domination of blacks. An Alabama chaplain scoffed at those who would argue otherwise: "Some metaphilosopher will say the convicts are nearly all negroes, and that a negro cannot be reformed. This is false. For they can be educated mentally, morally and religiously." Blacks may not have been considered inherently evil, but whites did recognize that many blacks rejected white pretensions to moral authority. Such observations appeared with startling frequency. "A convict whose term of service has expired stands as high in the estimation of the colored masses as if no charge of crime had ever been preferred against him," wrote a Georgia prison official in 1876. "Indeed, in some instances, he is lionized by his race, who seem unable or unwilling to discover the clear distinction between unwarranted persecution and the just enforcement of the just penalties."[55] "There is no loss of caste on account of their incarcera-

tion," another official complained to the National Prison Congress
ten years later; "on the contrary, it rather contributes to social
distinction, and ex-convicts, posing as heroes and martyrs, are met
by their friends with formal receptions, with music, with prayer and
with shouting." Prominent Southern penal officials argued before
Northern audiences that "the Negro regards it as no disgrace to be
sent to the penitentiary. He never cares to conceal the fact that he has
been there. How we are going to reform that race we do not yet
know." A colleague agreed: "People at the North know very little
what we have to encounter. It is almost impossible to reach the
Negro by means applied to the white convicts. We waste time in
trying to make a Negro think he needs reformation." "Nearly all our
convicts are negroes, and in most cases they go back to the
neighborhood whence they came from, and to farming generally,"
the secretary of North Carolina's Board of Public Charities wrote in
1894. "Confinement in the penitentiary has very little effect upon
their social status. Indeed, a preacher may be imprisoned for such
crimes as stealing, forgery, burglary, etc., and be received by
attentive hearers. It is possibly," the officer concluded in a flash of
insight, "viewed as persecution by the white man."[56]

Several commentators noted that younger blacks in particular
disdained white expectations of black behavior. "I am told,"
reported one traveler, "that the people most often convicted and
sent to the chain-gang are the undisciplined young negroes who have
grown up since the days of slavery." As early as 1875, the warden of
the Georgia penitentiary had already come to view the present
generation through the pleasant haze of slavery. "We seldom get an
old 'Cuffee' from the rural districts, who was trained, in ante-bellum
days, to gain his bread by the sweat of his brow; but the
augmentation is made by colored preachers, teachers, and politicians, and during the last twelve months, the very large number of
negro boys, from 10 to 15 years of age." Not only had the young
"criminals" missed the formative process of slavery, but their world
also offered novel temptations. "New desires, too, new passions and
new ambitions have been created by freedom," intoned another
official, "but no adequate power has been supplied for the legitimate
gratification of these new desires."[57]

The "colored preachers, teachers, and politicians" of the South,
whether or not they were overrepresented in the convict population,
as whites charged, spread the word of the convict lease system's evil
among black audiences who could not read of its cruelties them-

selves. "Our colored population from whose ranks unfortunately the bulk of the convicts are recruited are very fond of catching at every report of so called cruelty," complained a Florida official. "A reasonable amount of severity to reduce a prisoner to obedience is exaggerated into a charge of brutality and the story goes forth from mouth to mouth with increasing magnitude until the whole race is aflame. We have heard the negro orator depict the 'inhuman outrage' inflicted on 'the poor colored prisoner' and witnessed the effects of such allegations on the credulous and prejudiced blacks in shouts and groans and maledictions against the State authorities who are held responsible for the imaginary wrongs." All blacks, not only those prosecuted by the courts, knew of the inhumane treatment countenanced by white governments.[58]

No articulate, self-conscious black ideology celebrated criminals, but a vast and ever-increasing store of knowledge of white injustice and white hypocrisy did exist among blacks. There was also the subtle moral economy of black folklife, in which Christianity merged with an accumulated store of techniques for survival. These included strategies for the deception of the white man and for the appropriation of what black hands had produced. There were tensions between Christianity and these techniques, and leaders of the black community did not elevate theft into a positive good. All blacks recognized the injustice of their treatment at the hands of the white authorities, however, and something like a reservoir of toleration existed for those of the black community who sought to tip the scales of justice by means defined by whites as criminal. It is for this reason that those surviving a term in the convict lease were met "with music, with prayer and with shouting" upon their release.

Whites by no means presented a united front in defense of the convict lease system. Far more white Southerners, in fact, risked public indifference and scorn by attacking powerful lessees and state officials than ever agitated for an antebellum penitentiary. Denunciations of the lease system came from aggrieved workers in competition with convict labor, residents of communities where lessees established camps, cynical politicians of opposition parties, and people of conscience who opposed the lease because it offended their sense of justice.

Labor launched some of the best-organized and most effective opposition to the lease. Free workers, especially miners, recognized that convict labor was keeping them from earning a living wage. "Mine owners," read one report, "say they could not work at a profit

without the lowering effect in wages of convict-labor competition."
One of the very largest mine owners in the South elaborated: "I
rather think that convict labor competing with free labor is
advantageous to the mine owner. If all were free miners they could
combine and strike, and thereby put up the price of coal, but where
convict labor exists the mine owner can sell coal cheaper." In other
words, convicts aided not only the firms who leased them, but all
mine owners in the region—and in the process hurt all free mine
workers as well. A conservative newspaper in Alabama remarked that
"employers of convicts pay so little for their labor that it makes it
next to impossible for those who give work to free labor to compete
with them in any line of business. As a result, the price paid for labor
is based upon the price paid convicts." The report of a federal
Industrial Commission on Prison Labor in 1900 deplored the fact,
but argued that "as the shipment of 1 or 2 per cent of the gold of the
country disturbs the money market, so, the underselling in any
industry by manufacturers employing convict labor, materially
affects the entire market as to the price of the products of that
industry."[59]

The precise impact of convict labor in the South is impossible to
measure; the convict lease system was too scattered and shifting, the
statistical indexes too ambiguous. The judgment of an 1886 report
seems essentially correct, however: "the competition arising from
the employment of convicts, so far as the whole country is
concerned, would not of itself constitute a question worthy of serious
consideration. The products of the prisons were then but fifty-four
one-hundreths of 1 per cent of the total mechanical products of the
country." But workers, manufacturers, and state officials agreed that
these facts "do not invalidate the claim that locally and in certain
industries the competition may be serious and of such proportions
as to claim the most earnest attention." Convict labor took on an
exaggerated importance in the South more because of its context
than its mere size—which was nevertheless considerable: in 1890
alone over 27,000 convicts performed some kind of labor in the
South. Because the region had so few industries, because those
industries were concentrated in relatively small areas, because the
products of those industries, especially coal, were so crucial to the
growth of the Southern economy, and because Southern labor was
relatively unorganized, convict labor could in fact disrupt the wage
scale and working conditions of entire Southern industries. The New
South depended heavily on extractive enterprises such as mining

and turpentine production, and such grueling and life-threatening work tended to attract lessees of convict labor. When the railroad cars of convicts arrived in a community to take over this work, free workers and their families quickly felt the painful effects.[60]

Whitfield County's newspaper complained in 1893 that "free labor is absolutely driven out" of North Georgia by Senator Joseph E. Brown's convict labor. "No wonder so many go west, or that there is so little immigration to us. Where there is now only a convict pen and guard houses at these mines, if they were worked by free labor, there would be a thriving mining village of 1500 or 2000 inhabitants, scattering money profusely and giving a market to the farmer. It also keeps capital from coming in and developing other mines and other enterprises, for how can they compete with the favored few who have the convicts at $11.00 per year?" Letters from Alabama to the *National Labor Tribune* portrayed convict labor as a perversion of republican government. In language reminiscent of Andrew Johnson's 1857 attack on Tennessee's penitentiary as a "State Mechanics Institute," an Alabama miner sarcastically told other workers that "you see it is something to be an American citizen after all. . . . If you don't like common labor or farming you can go to the State warden of the prison and get a suit of striped clothes and be appointed a coal miner, provided the judge and grand jury are favorable." Six months later, conditions had not improved: "Labor in the mines is very dull at present, except for convicts, and they get all they can do and about as much as two common men can do." Alabama, Georgia, and Tennessee each employed hundreds of convicts in the mines, and "the Democratic politicians have begun to shoot and kill each other in order to get the spoils of their thieving legislation."[61]

In the eyes of free workers, lessees and mine owners added insult to injury when they employed miners who had learned the job while they were convicts. One report estimated that more than half the black coal miners in the Birmingham coal district learned their trade as convicts. "The fact of their having been convicts did not militate against them with their employers, and but to a slight extent, if at all, with their associates of their own race." Many of the ex-convicts in Tracy County, Tennessee, brought in their families and established their own community; local whites burned the former prisoners' cabins and schoolhouses to force them to leave.[62]

Petitions and citizens' meetings throughout the region protested convict labor, but to little effect. Birmingham, the center of Southern industrialization, was also the center of opposition to the lease system. Workers founded an Anti-Convict League there in 1885; it charged that mine owners were using convicts to keep wages at subsistence level, dissolve worker organization, and make Birmingham "the dumping ground for crime . . . the Botany Bay of the Commonwealth." In Georgia in 1884, free miners threatened violence at the Rising Fawn Mines when its owner, Senator Joseph E. Brown, abruptly posted notices at the iron works telling free workers they "would be relieved from employment and their places supplied by the convicts. To this brief and peremptory notification the free laborers have taken bitter exception and are in a state of excited discontent," the Greensboro *Herald* reported. Some of the workers threatened resistance by force, both because they resented losing their jobs to felons and because the sudden loss of work would subject "themselves and their families to enforced idleness and hardship at a very critical season of the year." But Senator Brown warned workers that "any turbulence or interference with the safety and proper custody of the convicts would involve them in a serious conflict with the State authorities." Brown faced trouble from another quarter, however, for the convicts themselves soon rebelled, declaring themselves "ready to die, and would as soon be dead as to live in torture." The governor responded by sending militia and artillery to the mines. The principal keeper of the convicts could not decide which strategy would be more effective—to kill three or four of the leaders or to starve the group as a whole into submission. The governor thought starvation preferable, and quelled the uprising in two days by withholding food.[63]

Advocates of free labor as well as convict labor constructed elaborate arguments for their positions. The inspectors of the Tennessee penitentiary offered seven points of "sound political economy," showing that the protests of free workers were unfounded. The crucial argument was that "society is benefited by the production of the greatest possible amount of values, so that if prisoners are to cease working, society must be content to be poorer." "Convicts worked in the mine appear to compete with free labor," admitted a statement from Alabama, "but as a matter of fact it is beneficial to free labor, as it prevents strikes, keeps the free miners employed and insures the running of the industries of the State that use coal. . . . Hence, the employment of convicts in the coal mines is of the greatest benefit to the free labor of the State." Such abstractions were of little solace to starving miners. One of the miners offered a different analysis of the effects of convict labor. Computing the number of tons of coal mined by convicts and how much free workers would have been paid for the same work, he figured that in Alabama in 1894 alone over half a million dollars did not become "circulating medium." This money could have fed miners, enriched local merchants, and developed the state; instead, the money "has gone into the pockets of three or four vaults, one of the State, next the two mining corporation[s]."[64]

After twenty years of suffering at the hands of the convict lease system, and twenty years of ineffectual efforts to halt convict labor, miners in Tennessee and Alabama revolted. The revolt was triggered in 1891 when an advance force of convicts tore down the homes of the free workers at Tennessee mines and built a stockade to contain the convicts expected to arrive by rail within two weeks. The homeless and infuriated miners marched to the stockades and, without firing a shot, loaded convicts and their keepers on a train to Knoxville. The governor of Tennessee, John P Buchanan, sided with the mine owners and the convicts were sent back to the mines accompanied by three companies of militia. The miners managed to repeat their bloodless revolt of a few days earlier and sent another trainload of convicts and guards out of the mines. The governor agreed, after much resistance, to call a special session of the general assembly. The Tennessee legislature, with Populists in a position of power, did nothing to help the miners. After months of fruitless negotiating, the miners, armed and starving, set free all 500 of the convicts at the mines of three companies. Other miners adopted the same strategy on an even larger scale the following year in middle Tennessee: again they burned stockades and railroaded convicts out of the area. Although state officials replaced the convicts, the price to the state had become too high; the legislature abolished the convict lease system in Tennessee in 1895.[65]

These fights against convict labor played a crucial role in the history of Southern organized labor. In the midst of the Tennessee revolt, Colonel Arthur S. Colyar, general counsel to the coal company and Democratic leader of the state, commented that "for some years after we began the convict labor system, we found that we were right in calculating that free laborers would be loath to enter upon strikes when they saw that the company was amply provided with convict labor." But at the same time, it was the highly visible, flagrantly unfair, and notoriously corrupt system that united fiercely independent miners for the first time. Between 1881 and 1900 coal miners launched twenty-two recorded strikes against convict labor.[66]

The convict lease also served to unite miners with other members of their community and with miners from other places. In Anderson County, Tennessee, members of "all classes and professions" came to the support of the miners against the coal-mining company and the state. Groups throughout the state passed resolutions supporting the miners and sent them aid. When the Tennessee miners decided to move against the stockade of convicts, other miners came all the way from Kentucky "on foot, on mules, and on trains" to help in the fight. In Alabama, black and white miners fought the lease side by side, carrying banners that read: "We, the Colored Miners of Alabama, Stand with Our White Brothers." In Tennessee, the funeral for a black miner killed in the protest against convict labor was attended by several thousand white allies. A large number of the militiamen sent to quell the miners were also in sympathy with their supposed foes. Many of the militia members sought leaves of absence during the struggle and others threatened desertion. Miners, for their part, brought the militiamen food and invited them into their homes. After the confrontation, the miners voted their ostensible opponents "excellent fellows," and when a soldier asked rhetorically, "What's the matter with the miners?" the militia replied in unison, "They are all right."[67]

Middle-class reformers in the South, while sympathetic to the free workers, were more concerned about the general improvement of the prisoners' lot, whatever work the convicts performed. Julia Tutwiler of Alabama, Rebecca Latimer Felton of Georgia, and George Washington Cable of Louisiana were the most visible opponents of the system. Tutwiler became known as the "angel of the stockades" as she traveled to Alabama's remote convict camps to minister to the inmates. She tried to persuade the state legislature in the mid-1880s to separate inmates by age, offense, and prior records. But the most she could do was to persuade the vice-president of the Tennessee Coal, Iron, and Railroad Company that it would be good business to allow her to establish a school at the mines where the company worked convicts. Felton and Cable, for their part, publicized the evils of the lease and created large stirs with their disclosures. Cable's passionate attack on the system received national attention and threw the South on the defensive.[68]

Reformers found themselves patronized by "practical" men of affairs. The penitentiary inspectors of Alabama, for example, dismissed Julia Tutwiler: "She is actuated by the noblest motives and most sincere desire to benefit the convicts; but unfortunately a woman's heart is too pure and kind to fully understand the most of the convicts." When reformers did succeed in forcing the formation of a legislative investigative committee that actually performed its intended function, the effort could backfire, as a scene from the Texas penitentiary illustrates. A guard with a whip stood over a black man who had complained. The guard taunted the prisoner: "You G—— d—— son of a b——. Looking for a committee are you? Those d——d educated sons of b—— can't run it over me." Still, some of the strongest condemnations of the convict lease system came from outraged government officials in the leasing states themselves. The mortality figures of Tennessee's lease system in 1884—a death rate of 148 per thousand—caused humanity to stand "aghast, and our boasted civilization must hide her face in shame," read a report of the State Board of Health. "They are our own published records, made by ourselves, for ourselves. The once proud State of Tennessee, chivalrous and public-spirited, stands to-day before the world a self-convicted murderer. Her own sons and daughters are her victims." A chaplain of Alabama's lease system must have caused some discomfort among legislators when he declared, "This neglect of, and cruelty to convicts may go on for a time yet, but sooner or later curses of the Almighty God will be showered down upon the proud commonwealth. Unless the present system is changed, the Judge of all the earth will see that retributive justice is meted in due season to the State of Alabama." The penal system stood as "one of the grandest farces, and one of the most sublime humbugs that human intelligence could possibly imagine. The whole of the present regime is a palpable falsehood, the State Penitentiary is itself a lie." Most of the testimony and criticism generated by the lease, in fact, appears in official state documents. Southern governments were never complacent about the lease; they could not afford to be.[69]

Newspapers, such as those published in Greene, Whitfield, and Savannah, that defended virtually every other facet of life in the New South gradually turned against the convict lease system. In the heated days of the 1870s, when racial animosity ran high and Democrats had only recently regained power, the rural papers defended the lease—sometimes with fervor. A letter to the Greensboro *Herald* in 1879 looked back upon antebellum history and scorned the penitentiary as a vain Southern attempt to copy the North. The institution had been a mistake, a misdirected effort "made reputable by a large class of educated and humane men, whose tastes and judgments were gathered from speculative treatises rather than from criminal records and practical reform." The penitentiary ran contrary to the laws of Moses, common sense, and the best interests of the South. Punishment should demand "blood for blood," and an "occasional hanging clears the atmosphere of crime as lightning purifies the summer sky. . . . This shutting a man up to reform him amounts to a farce." In 1881 Whitfield County's *North Georgia Citizen* unleashed a blistering attack on all critics of the lease system: "Not only have one-horse ambitious politicians in the State, who wanted office, condemned the system for the purpose of furthering their political aspirations; but the North—that country where the goose hangs high and everything is as pure as was Paradise before old Mother Eve ate the apple—has seen fit to condemn the system in unmeasured terms, characterizing it as a relic of barbarism. Now, we do not care a brass farthing what the opinions of the saintly (!) North may be upon this or any other subject."[70]

By 1881, however, the tide of public opinion had already begun to turn against the lease. Residents of Greene County, whose Superior Court sent so many convicts to the state penal system, read that a recent report on the convict lease system by a special committee of the legislature was "so full of horrors that it would furnish material for a thousand bloody shirt speeches." Although lobbyists had succeeded in convincing legislators to keep the lease, the *Herald*'s correspondent charged that the lease system was "already a reproach to us in the eyes of the nation and the Georgian who sees his state pointed out with the finger of scorn on this account may blush in silence for he can find no words with which to justify her or even palliate her dishonor." As a result, as early as 1881 "there is all over the State a feeling strong and strengthening against the continuance of a system remarkable only for its imperfections and its cruelties." Five years later, even a Whitfield County newspaper admitted that the time when "the condition of things rendered an apology for such a system" had passed; "the controversy of the matter at each succeeding legislature indicates its final abolition."[71]

Just as a reading of antebellum newspapers would suggest, erroneously, that "public opinion" in the South favored penitentiaries, so might the newspapers of the New South give a misleading picture of popular attitudes toward the convict lease system. No state governments ever held referenda on the convict lease, but if they did, argued one defender of the lease system, no more than a quarter of the electorate would vote to abolish the system. Given the distinctly draconian attitudes white Southerners expressed in favor of public hangings, lynchings, and chain gangs, this claim may well be true. In any case, Southerners could not stand to hear their penal practices denounced by Northerners.[72]

Even people who worked for the system's reform resented the North's criticism. "When a stately mansion is burned to the ground and the owner thereof is doing all in his power to rebuild his home," remarked one Southern delegate to a national prison convention, "it ill becomes him, who was, in part, responsible for its destruction, to stand by and deride his efforts and to criticize the style of architecture he has adopted." In a letter to George Washington Cable, the best-known critic of the convict lease, a Southerner confided, "I have had men admit that the convict lease system was an evil—and yet condemn your efforts to abolish it as an attack upon the section you once claimed as your own." Southern defensiveness led men to defend, well into the 1890s, an indefensible institution. Not unlike their antebellum slaveholding predecessors, apologists for the lease rationalized a "necessary evil" into a "positive good."[73]

Forgetting or repudiating their own antebellum penal history, defenders of the lease attacked the more subtle yet equally powerful coercion inherent in the Auburn-style penitentiary still dominant in the North. The lack of discipline in the convict lease, so often deplored, was transfigured into a virtue. "We have not yet reached that point in refined cruelty," a Southerner bragged, "where the convict is kept in a solitary cell and not allowed to raise his eyes from his work or to speak to anyone but his keeper, until his mind, from constant communion with its own thoughts, is liable to become a wreck." In the lease, conversation was common, and even singing rang through the mines. "A happy contrast this," another philosopher of punishment rhapsodized, "with some prisons where convicts are struck dumb, and wear the shackles on their very eyelids; denied the last privilege of manhood, the privilege of looking up! Could punishment be more crushing? Could degradation be deeper?" Just as some defenders of slavery had been insightful critics of the hidden coercions of capitalism, so did defenders of the lease perceive the deep but less tangible cruelty of the penitentiary.[74]

Defenders of the lease before national prison associations did find, however, a sympathetic audience among the adherents of the hardening "scientific" racial attitudes of the late nineteenth century.

In the context of speeches by Northerners filled with references to recently "discovered" linkages between crime, race, and heredity, the old-fashioned racism of Southern speakers fell on sympathetic ears. A Tennessee physician would not apologize for the lease: "We have difficulties at the South which you at the North have not. We must not be held to too strict an accountability. We have a large alien population, an inferior race." Another Southern doctor asserted that one "fact beyond dispute" had to be kept in mind at all times: "as a race, the negro is physically and mentally inferior." No one at the national congress argued with the "fact." One woman thought that black convicts died with such frequency in the mines because "the blood of educated people can resist a great deal more than the blood of the uneducated classes." Another Southerner unblushingly asserted that "to the ignorant negro, brought to manhood during the days of slavery, a term in the penitentiary was without question the best lesson he could obtain in citizenship."[75]

The Northern delegates to the national prison congresses of the late nineteenth century did not exude the confidence of their antebellum predecessors. The penitentiaries of the North, after all, had suffered their own decades of decline and scandal. "One string is harped upon *ad nauseum*—money, money, money," complained one reader of American prison reports in the Gilded Age. "The directors of a bank or a railroad could hardly be more anxious for large dividends than these gentlemen are for good round incomes from the labor of their prisoners. Where one word is spoken for reformation, hundreds are spoken for revenue." The Pennsylvania penitentiary, which had built its worldwide reputation on strict isolation, began to pile prisoners into shared cells. Some reformers expressed interest in a new system of prison discipline from Ireland based on incentives for early release, but few Northern penitentiaries adopted the method. Legislators in Ohio remained unimpressed with this "mere theory," and invoked language used by their Southern contemporaries: most criminals, despite all the programs officials implemented for their reformation, left prison "as hardened and as dangerous to the State as they were when they were sentenced." Others charged that "party politics, and, even worse, party cliques or rings, have too long controlled the appointments and consequently the management of the Ohio Penitentiary." In 1883 Republican state officials supposedly joined with contractors to defraud the state.[76]

Despite a great concern with finances, and despite long work days, advanced machinery, and sometimes brutal punishment, very few Northern penitentiaries managed to pay their own way. Northern labor unions continued their increasingly successful crusades against the contract system in which state prisons produced for the market. Prisons in the North and the South searched for an alternative way to keep convicts at work without undermining the livelihoods of workmen outside the prison walls. These efforts led Northern prisons to adopt the public account system, in which prison labor only produced goods other state agencies could use. Most of the Southern states followed another path when they finally abandoned the convict lease system.[77]

Although some states in the South—Virginia, Texas, Tennessee, Kentucky, and Missouri—had long used manufacturing prisons in addition to the lease system, as late as 1890 the majority of Southern convicts still passed their sentences in convict camps run by absentee businessmen. In 1890 Mississippi's constitutional convention decreed that such a system would end when the current lease expired in 1894; the convicts were to be worked on a state-owned farm instead. The nineties saw a gradual shift toward the compromise of such state farms, as Southern legislatures began to separate women, youths, and the ill from the prisoners in the camps and dilapidated prisons. These vulnerable convicts had been particularly brutalized (and unprofitable) in railroad and mining camps, but on the farms they could perform healthful labor, help pay their way, stay out of competition with free labor, and avoid contamination from more hardened criminals. The Carolinas had used this plan for part of their prisoners in the 1880s, and in the 1890s Alabama, Virginia, and Georgia adopted the state farm plan as a way to ameliorate what most observers considered the worst features of the lease system.[78]

Despite these changes, and despite attacks from Greenbackers and Populists throughout the South, only two Southern states besides Mississippi completely abolished the lease before the end of the nineteenth century. Tennessee, reeling from the rebellion of free miners against the lease, abandoned the system in 1895. Louisiana saw a breakdown in the lessee's political control lead to the termination of the system there. In general, the Southern convict lease system ended the way it began—uncertainly, ambiguously. A federal commission found that in 1898 nine states still leased convicts, "but in almost every case the objectionable features of the system had been eradicated, as far as possible, by stringent laws, rules, and inspections; and in all but two of the states (Florida and Lousiana) the convicts were also worked under other systems in connection with the lease system."[79]

(The introduction of centralized state-operated prison farms and the imposition of stricter controls over the lessees seemed important victories at the time. Death rates declined and conditions improved, but many of the evils of the lease remained. Not until the first two decades of the twentieth century did the South finally dismantle the lease system. By 1920 only Alabama had failed to pass a law ending the control of state convicts by anyone other than the state. To the eyes of the world, however, the replacements for the convict lease system seemed virtually indistinguishable from their beleaguered predecessor. Southern states did not erect new penitentiaries, but instead worked their convicts on chain gangs on public roads or on huge state-owned prison farms. Dedicated individuals continued to agitate for juvenile reformatories and gradually they were established, along with prison schools, libraries, and commutation laws. But the image of black convicts in striped uniforms laboring under the gaze of armed white guards has endured as one of the most telling symbols of the American South.[89]

The New South was no less an anomaly, no less an unstable mixture of contradictory elements, than the Old South had been. The convict lease system grew out of the unique hybrid of a republican past and undisguised minority rule, of the South's history of slavery and nascent capitalism. Had the Old South not built state penitentiaries, after all, the New South would have had little reason to erect centralized state-sanctioned convict lease systems. Had the abolition of slavery not opened the New South to the promise of industrial development, capitalists would not have sought convict labor to build new railroads and dig new coal mines. Convict labor helped forge crucial parts of a new industrial economy and thus make the South more like the North, but at the same time the lease system testified to the South's separate and tragic destiny. The flagrant racial injustice of the lease system, whites admitted, bred crime among alienated young blacks as it helped destroy any bonds of trust and mutual obligation that survived between the races. From every perspective, even that of prominent Southern whites, the convict camps were incontrovertible evidence of the New South's moral failure.

7

The Crisis of the New South

After the turmoil and bloodshed of the 1860s and 1870s, the South settled into relative calm in the early 1880s. Commitments to the convict lease system, prosecutions in the Superior Courts of Greene, Whitfield, and Chatham counties, arrest rates for homicide in Southern cities, political violence, and race riots reached the lowest levels registered in the South between Reconstruction and World War I. Within a few years, however, a new crisis of crime and violence wracked the South. In the late 1880s and early 1890s lynching threw the black belt into heightened fear and chaos; feuding and the vigilante violence called whitecapping terrorized parts of the upcountry. These years of crisis cast the fears of the New South into sharp relief as the region stood on the threshold of a new century.

I

The fundamental patterns of institutionalized Southern justice and injustice established during the 1860s changed little for generations. Southern blacks in 1900 no less than in 1870 found themselves singled out for arrest, indictment, conviction, hanging, and long sentences to the chain gang or convict lease system. The punishment for whites remained as lenient as ever. One reason justice changed so little was that the machinery of the police and courts rested in the hands of a few white men, their offices secure in the absence of a vital two-party political system. "Dutch" English of Greene County, for example, held the position of sheriff from 1866 to 1896 with the exception of only seven scattered years. The judge of the Greene County Court, W. M. Weaver, received his appointment in 1877 (after serving as mayor of Greensboro between 1871 and 1877) and presided over the court until 1897. The same pattern appeared in the upcountry. "The appointed officers under the democrats seem to go in families," a Whitfield resident charged in 1893, "and generally the families that have been at the public teat ever since the war."[1]

Even the grand jury, the key agency in ferreting out crime in rural counties, drew upon a small pool of men. In Greene County between 1890 and 1900, for example, only 307 men filled the 630 openings for grand jurors, and only 174 different surnames appeared among those 307 men. A mere eleven families accounted for 125 jurors, or almost 20 percent of the decade's total, and 25 men appeared in the jury box four times or more. These men steered Greene County's criminal justice system of the 1890s down the same path it had followed since the war. Black property crime constituted their primary concern, but they could move strongly against gambling and liquor when things seemed to get out of hand. A steady stream of men accused of assault and murder also came before the familiar faces of the Greene grand jurors. Their counterparts in Whitfield indicted people for the same sort of criminal actions, but, as always, violent crime continued to account for a larger portion of prosecuted crime in the mountains than in the black belt.[2]

Savannah saw little more change in its patterns of formal justice than did rural areas. When General R. H. Anderson, Savannah's chief of police, died in 1888, he had served twenty-two uninterrupted years—ever since the chaotic days of 1866. The oldest officer on Savannah's force died while on his beat in 1893 at the age of 84; he had served since 1850, before Savannah's police had even been outfitted in uniforms under the vigilant eye of its first chief, the nativist Joseph Bryan. The number of police in Savannah failed to grow in proportion to the city's population between 1880 and 1900, but the force did keep pace with the times by adopting the "Gamewell police telegraph system" in 1891, and in 1893 tested a new method of identifying criminals by the "accurate measurement of given portions of the human frame." Despite these imposing-sounding innovations, though, Savannah's police officers, like their counterparts throughout the South, spent the greater portion of their time "arresting a drunken man now and then who becomes violent or in carrying to the barracks a lot of quarreling and fighting black people." Southern cities maintained the smallest police forces per capita in the nation in the 1890s; they arrested slightly more people per capita than their Midwestern counterparts but considerably fewer than Northeastern police. Police forces throughout the United States continued to bear a striking resemblance to one another, just as they had since their inception.[3]

Southern justice did maintain its unique institutions, however; chain gangs, prominently displayed on city streets as well as country roads, endured as central and highly visible features of the Southern criminal justice machinery far into the twentieth century. Rural counties often leased their convicts, while cities usually maintained them for labor on public roads and property. Through all the decades of their existence the chain gangs remained time bombs, dangerous to the criminal and the public alike. Treatment of the gangs fluctuated between being too lax and too brutal. As early as 1881 Greene County's grand jury had warned that the county's leased convicts enjoyed too much liberty, allowed to "do about as hired laborers would." Only a week later, word arrived that a white guard had beaten a black convict to death at a state camp. "There can be no doubt that abuses of this kind often occur in our present convict system," the Greensboro *Herald* charged. "We do not advocate any easy berth for convicted felons. . . . But they have rights which should be respected, be they white or colored; and all those who treat them brutally should be prosecuted as vigorously and punished as severely as they would be if their inhuman treatment was inflicted upon the freest citizen of the land."[4]

Convict labor posed dangers for guards and society as well as convicts. In May 1881 Greene County convicts were at work on the farm of their lessee, Judge W. H. McWhorter. Two of the black convicts, Jim Allen and Joe Harris, aged 21 and 18 respectively, were hoeing cotton when Harris "pretended that he was no hand at hoeing." The guard, a 27-year-old white man named George Langston, became annoyed at Harris's awkwardness and laid down his gun to demonstrate how to use the hoe. As soon as Langston picked up the hoe the other convict grabbed the gun and shot the guard in the back of the head, killing him instantly. The two convicts fled with the shotgun and the guard dogs. The *Herald* urged the governor to post a reward for the convicts' capture, and the state offered $150. "Here is an opportunity for some one to make some money," the newspaper beckoned. "The colored people, perhaps, have a better opportunity to apprehend Jim than others. More

money could be made by his arrest than could be cleared by an
ordinary laborer in 12 months." Two weeks later Harris was caught
in Athens, returned to Greene, and hanged after the next term of
court.[5]

Scenes of violence occurred throughout the South's vast but
amorphous web of county convict camps. As a study of Alabama's
county penal system observed in 1886, the failure of local officials to
keep records of those leased out meant that many convicts simply
"disappeared as completely as if the earth had opened and
swallowed them. The very fact of their existence has been forgotten,
except for the few at the humble home, who still wait and look in
vain for him who does not come." Counties followed different
practices; in some, felons were "hired out" to relatives or friends and
served their term "under no restraint whatsoever," while in others
many men guilty of the slightest misdemeanors labored in coal
mines where "they are fortunate if they are as well treated as the
incendiary or the assassin who are State convicts." By 1890, the death
rate of Alabama's leased county convicts had become twice as high as
that of the notorious state convict lease system. The boundary
between the two systems often became indistinguishable.[6]

The fact that Chatham County, like other urban counties in the
South, did not lease its considerable number of convicts but instead
employed them for the municipality offered little relief to the
convicts. During one month in 1893, for example, 138 black men, 25
black boys, 26 black women, 9 white men, and 2 white women
worked from dawn to dark building a canal for the county, many of
the convicts up to their knees in "muddy and slimy ditches." This
labor force did not display great diligence or efficiency, for many
were "physical wrecks, who have sunk so low that they are
incapacitated for labor." On the other hand, they only cost the
county about forty cents each per day, no more than it would have
cost to keep them idle and in jail. The chain gang exacted other
costs, though: between 1887 and 1894 fifty-two convicts escaped
from Chatham convict camps, and half of them were never
recaptured. One young white man who had been caught stealing a
hat from a sleeping patron of a barroom tried to kill himself by
slashing his throat with "an old piece of iron barrel hoop" after three
days on the gang. A young German immigrant who spoke no English
was arrested for vagrancy and put to work in the ditches, where he
developed ulcerous sores under his shackles. The sores became so
serious he had to be hospitalized. Chain gang officials complained

that the sores would not have appeared had the immigrant followed the example of his more experienced fellow convicts and worn his shackles over his pants legs.[7]

Blacks suffered at least as much as these young white men, but mistreatment of blacks did not receive the same attention in the white press, even though Savannah's black newspaper, the *Tribune*, recorded one instance after another of brutality on the chain gang "inflicted under the guise of so-called law." Little better could be expected, the paper warned, "so long as the very lowest order and scum of white men" reigned over the camps. In despair, the *Tribune* lamented that "the vengeance of a just God will sooner or later frown down upon this barbarous system, and bring contempt upon its authors." The chain gang, like the convict lease system and the thousand other indignities inflicted upon blacks, drove a wedge between the races, bred fear among whites, undermined the authority of the law, and fed the growing crisis of the South.[8]

Even privileged white Southerners began to express concern about the inefficiency, brutality, and partiality of their criminal justice system. Class played far too large a role, bitterly complained the Greensboro *Herald and Journal* in 1895: "Nobody but a simpleton believes that ancient fiction that one man's life and liberty are as highly esteemed by the law as another's; and that one man, without reference to the lining of his pockets, has the same chance before the law as his neighbor who may be able to fee lawyers." While the wealthy could delay cases indefinitely and then escape without punishment, "the poor wretch, white and black, is promptly forced to trial, ready or not ready, and as promptly convicted and punished. Such inequalities in the enforcement of our criminal laws have destroyed public confidence in the integrity and impartiality of our courts."[9]

Others criticized the Southern courts for treating every defendant with excessive leniency. In 1887 the Dalton *Argus* unleashed an equally angry denunciation of Southern justice: "Between a farce of jury system, the emotional character of our people, and the almost irresistible influence to which a Governor is subjected [to pardon], followed by a penitentiary system that only rates the character of its subjects by the money they can earn, if the devil has not broke loose in Georgia, there is certainly a smooth way paved for his coming." Savannah's *Morning News* made the same scathing charge: "With sophomoric judges, Demosthenian lawyers, and juries well sprink-led with cranks, or worse, the criminal has a good chance of escaping even conviction. If he should be so unlucky as to lack the advantages referred to, he falls back upon the pardoning power." Judges, the Savannah paper charged on another occasion, were too "easy going," too "anxious to accommodate members of the bar whose influence they may desire to secure reappointment, or who are ever ready to shirk work by putting off cases on very slight pretexts." Equally despicable were the "professional jurymen who hang about the court house or in some other place where they may be conveniently found when wanted. These jurymen are in the business for what money there is in it for them."[10]

In an 1893 case in Chatham county, the district attorney tried to convict two prominent citizens, father and son, for murder. The prosecutor pleaded with the jury for hours. "It would be a sad commentary," he warned, "that because a man happens to be rich and influential in his community he can kill a lowly person simply because he happened to trespass upon his land over an imaginary line. If that is law I advise everybody to shake the dust of Georgia from their feet and seek homes in other states. If that is law," he charged in a revealing choice of metaphor, "I would prefer to go away from Georgia to the deep recesses of Africa where civilization is unknown and men are eaten by cannibals." The jury remained deadlocked for several hours, but then acquitted the wealthy men. Once again, the lesson of the court's inequality had been driven home and made public.[11]

Savannah's black newspaper never expressed surprise at the injustice of the courts. The *Tribune*, like other black papers in the South, prominently displayed accounts and denunciations of white brutality, corruption, and hypocrisy in virtually every issue. The black editors realized that charges of black criminality stood as a major bulwark of white supremacy by buttressing white claims to superiority and eroding black self-respect. "Some of our white exchanges are always very eager to bloat about the large amount of crime committed by the colored people," the *Tribune* commented in 1893. But "if the crimes committed by the whites were recorded and they punished accordingly, they would doubly offset that of the colored people." Virginia's Richmond *Planet* worded its rebuttal more strongly: "All of the hog, sheep, cow and chicken stealing by the dishonest members of [our] race since the world began will not begin to equal one hundreth part of the amount of money which has been stolen by members of the white race, who lay claim to all of the intelligence, religion and learning."[12]

The entire criminal justice system—from the police, to the jury, to the judge, to the chain gang, to the convict lease system—came under attack from blacks. The white police and blacks seemed locked in constant battle. "Nearly every day we can hear of some brutality exhibited toward our people by the policemen," Savannah's *Tribune* charged. "Their actions are becoming too frequent and uncalled for; a halt must be made." The paper even used the occasional instance of impartial justice to good effect. "Wonders never cease," exclaimed the *Tribune* in 1894 when a Chatham County jury actually convicted and sentenced a white man to the chain gang for stealing a pair of trousers from a black man. "It is the first such incident to happen in this city to our knowledge." "It is being in the midst of such scenes as these," sighed the Richmond *Planet* at the end of another story of white injustice, "that cause the anguish of the heart and nerve us at times to write as though our pen had been dipped in vitriol, the paper upon which we write soaked in blood." But things will not always be so, for a "reaction must follow, retribution will come and woe be it to those who have been forward in venting their spleen and exercising their prejudice upon those whom they have for the time being in their power."[13]

From the viewpoint of urban whites, too, the two races were becoming dangerously estranged, self-consciously in opposition over the very definition of crime. In 1888 a riot began in the predominantly black Yamacraw District of Savannah when a white policeman shot and killed an escaping black suspect. Two officers were severely beaten by "a mob of several hundred Negroes armed with clubs and rocks hooting and yelling 'kill him.' " Several blacks served long penitentiary terms for their part in the row. Cities across the South witnessed versions of this conflict. The chief of police in Atlanta cautioned in 1883 that "this thing is becoming too common. Almost every day something of the kind occurs. The negroes, whenever an arrest is made in an 'out of the way' part of the city, try every way to obstruct the officers." The editor of the Atlanta paper invoked the imagery of martyrdom, a recurring theme in descriptions of black attitudes toward black criminals: "The moment that a negro steals, robs, or commits some other crime, his person seems to become sacred in the eyes of his race, and he is harbored, protected and deified." Although the paper had earlier claimed that the "better class of colored people" supported the police, Atlanta's black newspaper, the *Weekly Defiance*, condemned the police in virulent terms. "We have lived in Atlanta twenty-seven years, and we have heard the lash resounding from the cabins of the slaves, poured on by their masters, but we have never seen a meaner set of low down cut throats, scrapes and murderers than the city of Atlanta has to protect the peace." Upper South black newspapers made similar charges. "The police-officers of Richmond have generally been regarded with a distrust bordering on hatred by the colored people of this community," the Virginia city's black paper commented, and "this feeling was reciprocated with compound interest by the officers."[14]

Blacks in the countryside apparently shared this anger and distrust of white justice. According to Philip A. Bruce, in the 1880s blacks in plantation counties tended to become "very much aroused if one negro is slain by another, under aggravated circumstances, and they condemn the murderer with as much severity as the white people." There existed "no public opinion among them, however, that uncompromisingly reprobates an individual of their own color who is guilty of a violation of the law, however gross, from which white people alone suffer." In fact, "a curious freemasonry . . . voluntarily and passionately sustained" by all blacks in the community, united them "in a conspiracy to protect the criminal, by throwing his pursuers off the scent." Blacks did not merely protect the criminal, Bruce claimed, they revered him. "No political felon in a conquered country, whose boldness has endeared him to the hearts of his people, but exposed him to imprisonment at the hands of alien authorities, was ever silently and surreptitiously befriended with more ardor than such a burglar or incendiary thus out of the pale of the law, who throws himself upon the good offices of his race." White Southerners became convinced that the black community celebrated criminals, made heroes, martyrs, champions of those who dared injure whites. The injustice of Southern courts and the convict lease system, whites increasingly admitted, alienated blacks, made them see the law as white law.[15]

Bruce observed that, ironically, "the negro is not disposed to have affrays with members of the other race, his natural peaceableness being increased in his association with white men by that restraining spirit of subserviency to them which still lingers in his heart. This is disclosed in the fact that it is very rare that he seeks to kill a white man by an open and direct assault." Whether the result of "subserviency" or not, evidence from Savannah and studies of homicide from the early twentieth century (and ever since) show the same pattern: most homicides in the South involved a black assailant and a black victim. The second most frequent type of killing pitted white assailant against white victim, and the third largest category involved white assailant and black victim. Black violence against whites was not a common occurrence.[16]

The lack of black violence against whites did not result only from the ingrained fear Bruce thought he perceived. As a white Southerner explained in 1882, "The murderer and murdered are regularly of the same race and the same social class. Castes and classes are well defined: they mingle without associating, and only exceptionally come into collision with each other." Violence in the postbellum South, as in the antebellum South, usually developed among social equals. Historian Howard Rabinowitz has found that "the great proportion of violent crimes by Negroes were indeed committed against other Negroes, including repeated cases of gambling altercations, barroom brawls, and domestic fights." Court, prison, and arrest records suggest the same pattern, despite a well-known tendency of white police to ignore black violence against blacks. Southern police, one officer related, recognized three classes of homicide: "If a nigger kills a white man, that's murder. If a white man kills a nigger, that's justifiable homicide. If a nigger kills another nigger, that's one less nigger."[17]

Such black violence remained hidden from the eyes of most whites, but sometimes readers of the South's white newspapers would catch a glimpse of a new sort of black character: the "desperado" or "bad nigger." In 1893 a 19-year-old mulatto named Samuel Thorpe was playing "skin," a popular game of chance, with Charles Brinson in a black Savannah barroom. Brinson lost fifty cents, but refused to pay Thorpe, who "got mad, quit the game, stepped out into the yard and fired into the room, hitting Brinson in the stomach. Then he pulled his hat over his eyes, and ran into the street through the house, flourishing his pistol and yelling, 'The kid is in town, by ____.' " Thorpe, the paper's reporter discovered, "has been a sort of dime novel hero, calling himself 'Sammy the Kid,' and carrying a big revolver around to intimidate anybody who might question his method of gambling."

A white jury convicted Thorpe of murder after only fifteen minutes of deliberation and the judge sentenced him to be hanged. When asked if he had anything to say, "Thorpe's lips quivered, tears welled up in his eyes, and in a choking voice he answered: 'I am a colored man and there is no use for me to say anything.' " The judge studied Thorpe's face for a moment, then quietly replied, "I have

listened carefully to every particle of evidence in the case, and I
consider the verdict a satisfactory one. . . . The laws of Georgia are
not revengeful. . . . I regret to notice that members of your race
commit so many atrocious crimes, particularly among the younger
class, some of which seem to be extremely vicious and hard-
hearted." The verdict did not reflect upon blacks as a whole, the
judge was careful to point out, for the race "has many noble men
and women who are exemplars in living upright, honest lives,
respecting the laws and striving hard to educate and rear their
children so they may become useful citizens." But many whites
would remember the exploits of "Sammy the Kid" rather than the
judge's praise of the black majority.[18]

Another black man grabbed headlines in Savannah the very next
year. The Savannah *Morning News* received a letter from Abe Smalls,
a black accused of killing a white policeman. Smalls, the object of an
intensive search, thumbed his nose at the white police. The outlaw
was in the vicinity of Chatham County, he claimed, "and will stay
here until i get good and ready to go, and when i go i will go on the
train." He had plenty of food, a place to stay, $432, and a "good
Winchester." "I have a friend in the city I would like to see, but it is
not so handy to see her because if i come thair i may be compel to
kill one of those Brave and Cool headed offercers." Smalls boasted,
in the paper's paraphrase, that "he don't care when he dies, just so
he is not taken alive and that he is game enough to die with his boots
on." Smalls planned to come to Savannah again, and if anyone tried
to capture him he vowed to sell his life "as dear as diamonds."[19]

Partly because of such scenes, black violence came to figure largely
in black lore and white stereotypes in the late nineteenth-century
South. The "bad nigger" became a stock character in the region's
imagination and its reality. Historian Lawrence Levine has written
that "from the late nineteenth century black lore was filled with tales,
toasts, and songs of hard, merciless toughs and killers confronting
and generally vanquishing their adversaries without hesitation and
without remorse." These bandits, unlike their counterparts in white
lore, were not "sanitized"; they did not steal from the rich and give
to the poor. They killed blacks as easily and unhesitatingly as they
killed whites, unfaithful women as well as insulting men, innocent as
well as guilty. The bandits of black lore "never really tried to change
anything. They were pure force, pure vengeance; explosions of fury
and futility. They were not given any socially redeeming character-

istics simply because in them there was no hope of social redemption."[20]

Such bad men ridiculed the piety that lay at the heart of so much black culture. As one folk song went,

> I'm so bad, I don't ever want to be good, uh, huh;
> I'm going to be devil and I wouldn't go to heaven, uh, huh,
> No I wouldn't go to heaven if I could.

The blues, another form of black lore coming into being in these decades, often celebrated such men. As Greil Marcus observes, "Blues grew out of the need to live in the brutal world that stood ready in ambush the moment one walked out of the church. Unlike gospel, blues was not a music of transcendence; its equivalent to God's Grace was sex and love." Bad men sneered at accommodation in any form, sneered at any restrictions on their lives in a world built on restrictions. Such a stance was dangerous indeed, both to the bad man himself and to the black community in which he lived. In the tales and songs of black lore, the bandit frequently died a violent death after wreaking violence himself.[21]

Whites often remarked, with a mixture of dismay and forced laughter, on the black propensity for violence against blacks. "In nearly every community in this State men and even boys think no more of carrying a pistol than a pen-knife. This is especially true of negroes and it is an exception when you find in the country a boy who has not in his possession some kind of firearm," the Greensboro *Herald and Journal* complained in 1890. "This he carries upon all occasions and most especially when a ball, frolic or entertainment is on hand. And being ready to fight it is not astonishing that they use the pistol on the slightest provocation." Other reports from the South agreed. Blacks fought, Philip A. Bruce averred, because of "the vehement passions aroused by heated disputes as to proprietorship in women." Such arguments, black men believed, could only be "settled by a resort to violence as desperate as it is impetuous; in the struggle no quarter is expected or allowed, and it is only terminated by the hasty retirement or the complete disablement of one of the parties." William Alexander Percy noted several decades later that while whites did not really know how to relax and have fun, "Negro convocations, legal or otherwise, are always enjoyable affairs right down to the first pistol shot."[22]

Such violence was not mere random pathology, sociologists living as participant observers in black communities of the early twentieth century discovered, but constituted a "tradition." Accounts of Southern black violence have a familiar ring about them, for they sound much like honor-related violence among whites. The prosecutor in a Georgia black belt county told Arthur Raper that black bloodshed frequently began at gatherings where drinking increased sensitivity to insult: "In the hilarity some Negro will say something of little consequence, but there will be a show of guns and razors and knives." According to John Dollard, "The caste culture of lower-class Negroes does not offer a mold for the type of character in which aggressive expression is controlled to the degree required by the dominant patterns of American civilization"; in other words, in black culture, as in much Southern white culture, aggression faced outward, not inward. Honor, not dignity, shaped character and bred violence. Black homicide rates far outstripped suicide rates, while for Northern whites the pattern was just the opposite. Southern whites displayed a pattern midway between that of Southern blacks and Northern whites.[23]

Just as the antebellum Southern aristocracy believed itself to be above the law and thus adjudicated conflicts by using the means of honor, so did postwar black Southerners know themselves to be *outside* the law—whether they wanted to be or not. H. C. Brearley argued that "the exclusive control of the administration of criminal justice by the whites resulted in a distrust for 'the white folks' law' that directly increases the amount of homicide, both among the Negroes themselves and between the races. In some Negro groups it is not quite honorable to appeal to the courts for redress of an affront that seriously affects one's status in the community." Social control in the black community, one sociologist thought, "is related only vaguely to law. The courts are outside the scheme of life. . . . Instead of providing security as the arbitrator of personal differences, the courts are an institution to be feared, a medium through which justice is to be secured only by recourse to some individual white protector." Violence often seemed the only choice; whites had long ago destroyed blacks' faith in the law.[24]

The cleavage between honor and legality widened over time; honor that originally grew in the vacuum of justice soon acquired a force of its own that actively repelled the dictates of the written, abstract law. Manhood came to be equated with the extralegal defense of one's honor, a manhood made manifest in control of one's woman and in unquestioning respect from one's peers. The contempt antebellum whites felt for those who were so weak they had to go to the law for redress was amplified in the postbellum black community, for the law there represented not only an outside force, but the force of the oppressors. Black honor thus fed upon itself and upon white injustice. Ironically, honor may have been even more lethal in the postwar black community than among antebellum whites. Poverty and degradation often raise the stakes of honor. A wealthy man could afford to ignore the opinions of all but the few he considered his equals, but a poor man had to worry about the opinions of a vastly larger group of peers.

Black honor and black violence were usually contained within the black community, for retribution, legal and illegal, almost inevitably fell upon any black man who dared fight a white man with any standing at all in the white community. "I have seen whites who, actuated by religion or cowardice, were more passive under insult from other whites than Southerners are wont to be," wrote a white South Carolinian in 1877. "But let a colored person insult them, and their nature seemed wholly altered. To swallow an insult from a negro would be perpetual infamy. Accordingly, the whites do not think it wrong to shoot, stab, or knock down negroes on slight provocation." "The truth is," explained a Tennessean, "a white man can't take impudence from 'em. It may be a long ways removed from what you or I would think impudence, but these passionate men call it that, and pitch in." When black gestures signaled flagrant contempt, many white Southern men literally knew no way to react other than with violence. If a black man insulted a white man and the white did not strike back immediately, he had, in his own eyes and in the eyes of his peers, no honor left to lose.[25]

Blacks responded in a variety of ways to this situation. As Richard Wright later explained, blacks "could accept the role created for them by the whites and perpetually resolve the resulting conflicts through the hope and emotional catharsis of Negro religion; they could repress their dislike of Jim Crow social relations while striving for a middle way of respectability, becoming—consciously or unconsciously—the accomplices of the whites in oppressing their brothers; or they could reject the situation, adopt a criminal attitude, and carry on an unceasing psychological scrimmage with the whites, which often flared forth into physical violence." Whites in the late 1880s and early 1890s thought that more and more blacks had adopted the "criminal attitude," that they sneered at white pretensions, contemptuously challenged white authority, assaulted white honor.[26]

"It is not often we find among the colored people of to-day," the Greensboro *Herald and Journal* commented, in a common observation by whites in the 1890s, "the genuine conservative feeling of respect and humble obedience to patriotism as we are apt to portray in the old slave time darkey. Just a few of them survive, and I very often wonder what will become of this new-born race when the old ones are gone. Only a few of the scions that sucker up from the old stumps can afford to raise their hats to a white lady, and very seldom does a white man even get a handle to the first end of his name." In an 1893 article in a national magazine, Charles H. Smith lamented that "both males and females have become lazy and insolent. They have ceased to show proper respect to the white people, and they will not work for them, so long as they can avoid it. The alienation is going on, widening, deepening and intensifying. The white man is losing his sympathy and the negro his feeling of dependence."[27]

Blacks agreed that the chasm between the two races grew larger with every year. An 1889 article in the *Fisk Herald* argued that the rising tide of mass violence against blacks by whites could be traced to the "younger whites who are even more hostile and bitter than the older ones" and to "the younger Negroes [who] are ignorant of the so-called instinctive fear of their fathers . . . [and are] prone to brood in bitterness and suppressed rage over their wrongs, [and] are more sensitive to injustice and quick to resent." Both W.E.B. DuBois and Booker T. Washington remarked on the dangerous and increasing alienation between the "best" people of the two races. "The negro loafer, drunkard and gambler can be seen without social contact" with whites, Washington noted, but "the higher life cannot be seen without social contact." DuBois observed that "the best of the whites and the best of the Negroes almost never live in anything like close proximity. It thus happens that in nearly every Southern town and city, both whites and blacks see commonly the worst of each other. This is a vast change from the situation in the past, when, through the close contact of master and house-servant in the patriarchal big house, one found the best of both races in close contact and sympathy, while at the same time the squalor and dull round of toil among the field-hands was removed from the sight and hearing of the family." Such physical isolation alone was enough to lead whites to exaggerate black "degeneracy." "One can easily see how a person who saw slavery thus from his father's parlors, and sees freedom on the streets of a great city, fails to grasp or comprehend the whole of the new picture."[28]

Late nineteenth-century observers of Southern race relations almost ritualistically evoked the memory of "loyal" and peaceful slaves during the Civil War and even during Reconstruction as evidence of the dramatic change for the worse among the newer generations. "Throughout all these terrible years, and throughout the whole vast extent of the South, there never was committed by a Negro a single murder or a single crime that could properly be called an outrage," Clifton R. Breckenridge of Arkansas claimed in 1900. Even though Reconstruction brought "race rivalry, race interference, active race contact . . . what did we witness? Few of the older Negroes were led into positively evil ways; but the younger generation, with the docility of the race, were largely perverted. Occasional outbreaks occurred. But, in the main, in a country practically without law, there was necessity for life, and the more shocking forms of crime were rare." Things had deteriorated dramatically in the short span between Reconstruction and the early 1890s, whites believed. "Most of the men who were masters and most who were slaves are dead," sadly commented Walter Hines Page in 1893. The "somewhat new race-clash which is different from the old political race-clash [of Reconstruction], brings for the first time a grave social danger. Whatever race conflicts might come, it had generally been taken for granted that we should be spared this one. For this kind of crime may light all the inflammable material in the race-relation." This "new race-clash," this new "kind of crime" Page so feared was the crime that haunted so many other white Southerners in the late 1880s and early 1890s: the rape of white women by black men.[29]

The phobia seemed to emerge rather suddenly in these decades. Indeed, Ida Wells-Barnett, a black campaigner against lynching, pointed out that "during the period of alleged 'insurrection,' and alarming 'race riots' " of earlier years, "it never occurred to the white man, that his wife and children were in danger of assault."[30] All the more reason to worry, whites responded. Writers in the North and South, in small newspapers and in national magazines, in black publications and white, tried to explain why lynching suddenly reached epidemic proportions in the early 1890s. Nearly 700 people died at the hands of lynchers between 1889 and 1893—a peak never seen before or since the crisis of the New South.

II

Southern whites—and most Northern whites, for that matter— argued that the lynching outbreak had only one cause: an epidemic of the "New Negro Crime," "brutal outrages" upon white women by "black beasts." Contemporary critics of the South and subsequent studies of the problem have generally discounted any real outbreak of rape by blacks as the cause of the wave of lynching, pointing out that newspaper accounts often revealed that "crimes" other than rape had been given as the alleged offense, that innocent men were lynched, and that white Southerners seemed to be spoiling for a fight. How, then, do we explain the timing of lynching's peak? The triggers of lynching, for all the attention devoted to it by contemporaries, sociologists, and historians, are still not known.

Everyone today agrees on the obvious, even banal, "causes" of lynching: racism, frustration, poverty, submerged political conflict, irrational white fears, a weak state. These forces, though, were constants in the postwar South. They surely existed during Reconstruction, and yet lynching did not sweep through the region; they did not end in 1900, yet lynching declined throughout the early twentieth century. What was it, then, about the early 1890s that made these few years the time of the most brutal mob violence in Southern, indeed American, history?

One obvious answer might be Populism, the political movement that threatened to unite poor whites and poor blacks, destroying white solidarity and the class rule of a few in the process. During Reconstruction, we have seen, the boundary between political violence and criminal violence often disappeared; whites hid, consciously and unconsciously, private motives of hate and greed behind appeals to white unity. There is no reason to believe that white Southerners would not do the same thing fifteen or twenty years later when, to many, the stakes seemed just as high as they had during Reconstruction. In some ways, the situation was even more threatening in the nineties, because whites had become divided among themselves in a way that had not been in the sixties and seventies.

W. B. Pattillo, editor of the Greensboro *Herald and Journal*, looked back upon 1892, when he had first come to Greene County, from the vantage point of 1899. "Seven years ago about one-half of the white citizens had become estranged from the other half, and Cuffee—corrupted—was holding the balance of power. Strife grew more bitter, and it did seem at one time that the embitterness engendered might lead to bloodshed." That crisis had passed, but a terrible seed had been planted: "The whites of Georgia have been sowing to the wind, and it looks now like we are reaping the whirlwind; for the negroes who have been debauched [with whiskey and money to buy their votes]—not altogether but partly—by the whites, are the ones that are committing the crimes against womanhood, that are so frequent and diabolical." Feelings ran high in Whitfield, too, in the early 1890s. One Dalton newspaper looked down its Democratic nose at a Populist meeting, which the paper called a "huge pile of putrid nastiness and ignorant corruption," a "hermphrodite" party, "rantankerous bigoted asses who brayed negro supremacy and undertook to array the races against each other."[31]

Political passions may have helped fuel the lynching crisis of the nineties by creating racial animosity, but overt political motives apparently accounted for little of the bloodshed. Very few observers, whatever their race, region, or politics, pointed to political coercion as the direct cause of lynching. Populism did fuel lynching, one white said, not by battles over specific elections, but by upsetting the fragile balance of racial etiquette in the South. "Political equality breeds ambition for social equality, with its train of evils which no one can understand or fully appreciate who has not lived in the midst of these unfortunate derelicts of Fate and Nature," argued an article titled "Some Co-Operating Causes of Negro Lynching." "The negro thus asserts himself, and his sense of his own importance, which was quiescent and pacific so long as he was kept in political and social subordination, becomes often offensively and insolently inflated." Black claims to respect, in other words, exceeded their bounds. Once blacks' hunger for equality was whetted by politics, whites warned, there could be only one tragic result. A Memphis newspaper ominously intoned in 1892, "The Negro as a political factor can be controlled. But neither laws nor lynchings can subdue his lusts. Sooner or later it will force a crisis. We do not know in what form it will come."[32]

The key to the lynching epidemic in the New South does not lie solely in submerged repercussions of Populism. The causes of the epidemic were both more straight forward and more pathological than politics. Defenders of lynching—and there were many in the white South—repeated the same "explanation" of lynching like a litany: white men lynched because black men raped. Opponents and analysts of lynching have not accepted this explanation, of course, and have usually portrayed lynchings either as calculated Machiavellian tactics to defend white male supremacy from the threat of Populism or as simply uncontrolled bloodlust. To deny either the irrationality or rationality of lynching, however, is to miss its essence. Lynching was madness, but with a method. Lynching was not unlike the persecution of witches in colonial New England, in that people thought they knew what they were doing: combating an elusive but terrible foe. As a lynching party in Maryland proclaimed, "Before God we believe in the existence of a higher code than that which is dignified by the great seal of a Commonwealth and that the high and holy time to exercise it is when the chastity of our women is tarnished by the foul breath of an imp from hell and the sanctity of our homes invaded by a demon." Defenders of justice in both cases had always to be vigilant for signs of the impending visitation— which had a way of appearing just when people were looking for it.[33]

Black men were lynched for other crimes, but rape was always the key: "while other crimes may renew the lynching fever in the lawless, it is the crime against female virtue that spreads the fever among those who have never had it, thereby not only feeding the ranks of the lynchers, but weakening the spirit of many who remain on the side of law and order so that their denunciation of lawlessness encourages the mob by its feebleness." It was in this way that rape, Edward Leigh Pell concluded in his 1898 article, "has a prominence in a lynching epidemic that it does not have in the published statistics." "To say that men are lynched for other crimes than that against white women, and that therefore lynching cannot be attributed to it, is to be more plausible than accurate," Clarence H. Poe argued. "It is with this crime that lynching begins; here and here only could the furious mob spirit break through the resisting wall of law and order. Once through, it does not stop. But it is only because lynching for rape is excused that lynching for any other crime is ever attempted."[34]

The fear of black rape obviously triggered something deep within the psyche of the white South. Whites had long associated blacks with sexuality, however: why did that association suddenly erupt in a

wave of lynching in the late 1880s and early 1890s? In part, that crisis
developed because a new generation of blacks and whites faced each
other across an ever-widening chasm. The "best" whites and blacks
seldom had contact with one another, as both races increasingly
withdrew into their own neighborhoods and churches. Virtually no
white man under 50 years old in 1890 would have once been master
of a slave plantation. At the time the lynching crisis hit the South no
man under 30 years old, white or black, would have any memory of
slavery at all—only of racial distrust, conflict, and bloodshed. Since
most "criminals" and most violent men have always been young,
and nowhere younger than in the postwar South, it is safe to assume
that most lynchers and lynching victims came from this new
generation. These men, white and black, feared each other with the
fear of ignorance. They saw each other dimly, at a distance.[35]

The same fear nurtured by unfamiliarity seemed even more
intense among white women. To be sure, well-to-do white women
had black servants whom they trusted and thought they knew. They
did not know "bad niggers," though, however much they might hear
and read about them. And at no time did they hear more about
black rapists than in the early 1890s. "A person can not pick up a
newspaper without an account of this 'one crime' with all its
revolting details," Charles H. Otken observed in 1894. "There is a
timidity and dread among the white women of the South, unknown
in the days of slavery." The Savannah *Morning News* made the same
complaint in 1893. Rapes of white women by black men "are
becoming so numerous and bold that accounts of one or more of
their crimes appear in the newspapers almost every day. White men
living in the country who are distant from neighbors are afraid to
leave their wives and daughters unprotected in their homes." The
New York *Herald* reminded whites outside the South to be understanding of white Southern fears, for "the difference between bad
citizens who believe in lynch law, and good citizens who abhor lynch
law, is largely in the fact that the good citizens live where their wives
and daughters are perfectly safe."[36]

In this atmosphere of fear it is hardly surprising that white women
perceived black rapists where they did not in fact exist. At the height
of the lynching epidemic in the South, for example, Mrs. Jim Kittles
of Dalton was alone at home one Sunday night while her husband
was at church. Suddenly she heard "someone prowling about the
house and believed she saw a negro trying to open the window.
Criminal assaults upon helpless white women instantly occurred to

her mind, and getting her husband's pistol, she fired several shots through the window where she thought the intruder to be." An eighteen-year-old white boy, Walter Wright, heard the shots and ran to the church to tell Kittles that someone was shooting at his house. The husband rushed home; inside the house, he took the gun from his frightened wife and fired at a form moving outside the window. The shot killed young Wright, who had followed to assist in the defense of the Kittles' home.[37]

White women in the South, their fears fueled by their white male kin and the press, undoubtedly perceived assault where none existed. Walter White, who in the 1920s investigated thousands of lynchings, many of them firsthand, suggested that a large number of lynchings might be traced to "the Southern white woman's proneness to hysteria where Negroes are concerned." White observed that "in the great majority of cases where rape or attempted rape was alleged, the women can be divided into four classes: young girls ranging from the ages of twelve or thirteen to nineteen or twenty years of age, passing through the difficult period of adolescence; second (and this includes a considerable percentage of the alleged victims of attacks), women who range in age from the middle forties upwards; third, women who have been married for many years and usually to rather unattractive husbands; fourth, spinsters." Walter White undoubtedly reflected traditional sexist assumptions in this categorization, and, perhaps wisely, backed away from spelling out the obvious connections between lynchings and tensions in these women's sexuality. It requires little imagination, however, to perceive the way the South's greatest sexual taboo attracted the attention of disturbed people of all races and genders, including white women.[38]

The fact remains, of course, that men, not women, lynched other men. Southern white men, as they repeatedly announced, consciously "elevated" their women. Elevated or not, white women found themselves bound by an amplified double standard. Respectable white women were expected to remain virginal before marriage while white men were not; furthermore, while white men might indulge in casual sexual dalliance with black women without lasting stigma, a white woman who had interracial sex in or outside marriage suffered social death. White men, historian Jacquelyn Dowd Hall has argued, knew they had "betrayed" racial purity by generations of miscegenation, and so "as absolutely inaccessible sexual property, white women became the most potent symbol of white male supremacy." Lynching thus "served as a dramatization of hierarchical power relationships based both on gender and on race. . . . Masculine guilt over miscegenation, the veiled hostility toward women in a patriarchal society, the myths of black sexuality—a dense web of sexual violation and desperate rationalization" lay behind lynching. This cluster of fears stretched on for decades before and after the crisis of the early 1890s, though, and there seems little indication that any change in gender relationships in the rural South generated the largest wave of lynchings in American history. The mysterious recesses of sex and race provided much of the fuel for the conflagration of the nineties, but not the spark.[39]

To some extent, the fires of lynching began by a sort of spontaneous combustion fed by racial and sexual fear. Thanks to the speed and thoroughness with which news of lynchings were spread by the press of the late nineteenth-century South, the crisis of one isolated county could soon fuel the fears and anger smoldering in a county hundreds of miles away. Lynchings were news in a way trials were not. As Booker T. Washington pointed out, courts in the North and South often charged white men with rape, "but, because the white man, in most cases, is punished by the regular machinery of the courts, attention is seldom attracted to his crime outside of the immediate neighborhood where the offense is committed." When white Southerners read of a widely publicized lynching, on the other hand, they automatically assumed that a rape had indeed occurred and began to look for warnings of the crime in their own community. The "insolence" of local blacks, the appearance of a "strange nigger," a rash of breaking and entering—all could be taken as evidence that an "outrage" might be imminent. Unfortunately, people looking for a criminal usually find one. Every accusation, every suspicion, every lynching of an innocent "rapist" echoed throughout the South, so that all sense of proportion disappeared.[40]

Whites, it seems fair to say, did not know they were battling a foe of their own creation. Their newspapers were filled with real fear and anger, not with fabricated excuses to buttress the racial status quo. Walter White, the light-skinned black who explored lynchings in the South in the 1920s, described the dynamics of this process: "The vast majority of whites in the states where lynchings are most frequently staged really believe that most mob murders are the results of sex crimes. Having created the Frankenstein monster (and it is no less terrifying because it is largely illusory), the lyncher lives in constant fear of his own creation and, at the same time, has by means of his creation caused more crimes against the women of his race than there would have been in a more sane and normal environment."[41]

White also suggested that "the vast amount of advertising which lynchings have given to allegations of sex crimes has induced subnormal Negroes to attempts crimes of rape, the power of suggestion being as potent as it is." How many alienated, enraged, or mentally unbalanced blacks raped white women precisely because the white community feared that crime so much can never be known, of course. It does seem likely, however, that lynch mobs often turned to blacks considered to be outsiders—whether "subnormal" or mere strangers—by both the blacks and whites of the neighborhood. The Reverend A. J. Stokes, a black minister from Montgomery, opposed lynching but argued that "there never was a respectable colored man lynched in the south, except in a case of murder. I speak from my own experience when I say that in the lynchings I have known about, the victims were always men in the community no one could say a good word for. They came out from the slums at night, like the raccoon, and stole back again." The Greensboro *Herald and Journal* assured local blacks that "no decent, well-behaved colored man is in danger of being lynched." Whitfield's paper, too, praised industrious local blacks who have "the friendship and confidence of every citizen in this community," and asked, "Does Bostonian intelligence grasp the idea that it would be foolish for southern farmers and people generally to lynch the best common labor it possesses?" "Good" blacks would be protected, but a black rapist should know that he "would be lynched incontinently." "The negroes who commit these crimes," the *North Georgia Citizen* argued on another occasion, "are vicious, uneducated and discountenanced by the respectable element of their race. The per cent of bad among the negro is very small, and is confined to those born and reared since slavery. We do not say this to justify slavery, for we think it a curse."[42]

When a "bad negro" did suddenly appear, the white community quickly closed ranks. Men of widely varying background temporarily joined in a common cause. "I believe it is generally conceded that mobs who thus deal summary justice to this debased class of criminals, are, as a rule, composed of our best citizens, who are foremost in all works of public and private good," claimed a letter to the Savannah *Morning News* in 1893, "and in this, their only act of transgression, we must accord to them a pure purpose to do the right in this time of their dire extremity, when in their honest judgment no other certain course is open to them." The judgment of Walter Hines Page in the same year lends a sense of proportion to this argument: "It is safe to say that there are not five men in every thousand in any county in all the black States who ever went forth with a mob or even lynched a man. . . . This is the simple truth; but the whole truth is even more—the nine hundred and ninety-five law-abiding and law-loving men share in the guilt as they must share in its consequences, if they show themselves unable or unwilling to put an end to it. Acquiescence is surrender."[43]

Lynch mobs began with pressure from below as well as from leaders above. "We have many classes of whites in the South, the lowest of which are little, if any, above the lower Negroes in education or morality," observed one white woman. "This class is not a large one, but it is widely scattered; and it is the most unstable element in our civilization. It is the nitrogen of the South, ready at a touch to slip its peaceful combinations, and in the ensuing explosion to rend the social fabric in every direction. It is the storm-centre of our race prejudices, and generates many a cyclone which cuts a broad swath through much that the South cherishes." If the majority of respectable whites so cherished racial peace, the question remains, why did men of power and influence not contain lynching? Because, the woman explained, "individualistic as we are, unorganized by a social consciousness, half a dozen of them can sway the weak, the excitable, the unformed among us, can fire the mob spirit, and lay the honour of thousands in the dust."[44]

The South's inability or unwillingness to control this "nitrogen" revealed, among other things, the power of "public opinion" within the South. "In a democracy with a republican form of government . . . ," James E. Cutler pointed out in 1905, "the people consider themselves a law unto themselves. They make the laws; therefore they can unmake them. . . . To execute a criminal deserving of death is to act merely in their sovereign capacity, temporarily dispensing with their agents, the legal administrators of the law." Local officials often tried to resist lynch mobs, but then again often they did not. Some were afraid of the lynchers, some were in sympathy with them. As Savannah's black newspaper charged at the height of the lynching epidemic, "The success which almost invariably attends the efforts of such lawless mobs, is nearly always the result of collusion with the officers of the law, and instances are

not infrequent when sheriffs and jailors have been passive spectators, or active participants in these deeds of violence and blood."[45]

"The cause of lynching," one Southerner agreed, "is that we are
the only Government on earth that has set up several thousand little-
bitty, small, weak, distinctive governments. . . . These tiny kingdoms
can kill their subjects like dogs if they want to, and under State rights
they know that there is no law on earth to prosecute them but their
own law; no judge ever prosecutes himself." Indeed, state or federal
governments could do little to prevent lynchings. In the late 1890s
several Southern states passed laws that made the entire county
where a lynching occurred pay from $2,000 to $10,000 to the state or
to the survivors of the victim of the lynching. The Dalton *Argus*
ridiculed a similar plan proposed by Georgia's governor: "That's
about the silliest thing we ever heard on the subject. . . . If a man had
an objectionable father or other relative, and needed a little money,
all he would have to do would be to organize a mob, lynch him, and
then collect $5000 out of the county. It would beat life insurance all
holler."[46]

The frequent claims about the inefficiency and corruption of the
courts in the South also stood as an integral part of the justification
of lynching. As the *North Georgia Citizen* flatly stated in 1893, "The
punishment of crime is too lax, it is not speedy enough—there are
too many delays and failures of the law in this particular—too many
continuances and granting of new trials in criminal cases—and
hence, in a great measure, may be attributed the number of
lynchings that are of such frequent occurrence throughout the
country." The most frequently suggested remedy for lynching, in
fact, called for speeding up the formal justice system. The Greensboro *Herald* argued in 1884, in its first discussion of lynching, that
laws be passed making "it *obligatory* on the judge of the Court having
jurisdiction, to convene his Court, as soon as possible after the
commission of the crime, in special session to try the accused and
upon conviction let the criminal be executed *instantly*. . . . Then will
the people be spared the temptation—the almost necessity—of
staining their hands in extra-judicial, though most foul blood."
Another commentator suggested that black rapists be legally
emasculated, substituting "orderly procedure for private passion
and revengeful force."[47]

Even if courts did move quickly and harshly, several intractable
obstacles prevented the "just" punishment of black rapists by the
courts. First of all, whites seemed to accept as a given that victims of

rape could not be expected to testify in court. The ravished woman placed in such a situation would find that "to add to her unspeakable woe and humiliation, her name is sounded from one end of the country to another, and she is pilloried in her anguish for the public gaze," an 1893 letter in the Savannah *Morning News* titled "Woman's Plea for Lynching" passionately argued. "Far rather would any delicate woman see her ravisher go free, than to have to testify against him and bring him to a legal punishment. Yea, far rather would she deliberately end her own life and lay down its burden of shame and disgrace. . . . Let every other crime be dealt with by law—but do you see now why lynchings are the only way to deal with this?"[48]

The laws and courts had other limitations as well. The stern Old Testament morality of many Southerners seemed to demand lynching. "At first the voice of our brother's blood may cry to us from the ground, but the voice grows weaker and weaker as time goes on," read one plea for lynching. "The legal principle, an eye for an eye and a life for a life, can be enforced only when there is a vivid realization of the victims' loss. As this becomes dimmer, the punishment of the criminal seems more and more like a new and useless effusion of blood." The Dalton *Argus* in 1897 complained that "the Atlanta preachers seem to have run entirely out of Gospel subjects to preach on. Last Sunday several of them preached against lynching, and not one of them preached against rape." In Numbers 25, verses 6 through 9, the mountain paper claimed, the city ministers could have found "an account of the first great lynching, seen the Bible condemnation for the gratification of lust, and God's commendation of the lyncher." Other defenders of lynching argued that the secular law was simply too good, too noble and dramatic, for black rapists. "The swift apprehension and slaughter of the culprit not only strikes greater dread than the regular process of justice, but does not gratify the negro's enjoyment of the pomp and ceremoney of a formal trial before a judge," argued English traveler James Bryce.[49]

Whether or not blacks "enjoyed" the pomp and ceremony of formal justice, there can be no doubt that trials and hangings did indeed stand as dramatic and long-remembered events in the lives of Southerners of both races. Thousands of people traveled long distances—sometimes on special excursion trains—to witness hangings. One landowner in Tennessee brought in over $500 selling reserved seats and barbecue at a hanging in 1880. Parents sent notes to teachers to excuse their children from school to allow them to go to a hanging. It was powerful theater. After praying with a minister, after a solemn procession to the scaffold, after a chance to exhort the crowd, after a final prayer, after the singing of "wild airs" by blacks, "a dead silence then ensues; this is broken by the falling of the drop, and as the doomed man is launched into eternity a piercing and universal shriek arises, the wildest religious mania seizes the crowd, they surge to and fro, sing and raise the holy dance." Black spectators often retrieved and cherished bits of rope as talismans.[50]

In an effort to avoid the "morbid and lamentable incidents which invariably surround such events when they are performed before the public gaze," in 1888 Greene County hanged George McDuffie, a black man who had killed another black man, within the thick stone walls of the county's venerable dungeon. If the hanging had been public, the *Herald and Journal* argued, "there would have been probably ten thousand spectators, of which ninety-five per cent would have been colored." As circumspect as the McDuffie hanging was, in fact, still "thousands of colored people poured into town by every passable and every possible road. . . . The crowd clung to the shadow and the sunshine of those walls for hours. They clung as if their own rather than the criminal's life was in peril." After the completion of the hanging had been announced, the crowd "lingered near the scene of death with an unaccountable longing to gratify an impulse they did not understand and could not satisfy." With an almost mystical wonder, the white editor watched as the black crowd "vanished into the earth, into the air, into every outlet, alley and road that led from Greensboro. . . . They had folded their fans and umbrellas and silently stolen away."[51]

The very lynchings supposedly perpetrated to avoid such "pomp," however, still seemed to some whites to bestow too much attention and glory upon the rapist. A spokeswoman of the Georgia Women's Federation wrestled with this problem in 1897. She recognized as a fact that "in the veins of the southern man there boils hot blood, and when the honor and purity of his home is invaded, personal vengeance he will have." But lynching did not act to prevent such invasions, for "there is a glamour of martyrdom about it that makes of the criminal a hero to be patterned after by his kind, and the quick death, without time to realize all the horror, is really merciful compared to the crime." She believed that "some sure, dreaded physical punishment" would act as a better deterrent than lynching. The Dalton *Argus*, which approvingly reprinted the woman leader's sentiments, missed the point, however, and praised lynching. In fact, "THE ARGUS would not object to seeing public sentiment so amend the lynching custom as to include in 'the lynching bee' some of those who sympathize with the brutal rapist, or who try to keep him from the just vengeance of the relatives, friends and neighbors of the girl or woman he has brutally outraged." Violence begot a thirst for even greater violence. Once a community tolerated lynching for any purpose, people had little trouble finding other situations in which extralegal bloodshed might be justified.[52]

Given an opportunity to act brutally, the sad fact seems to be that at least some people will. Legal officials, newspapers, and public opinion within the postwar South gave that sanction, both tacitly and explicitly, and white men took advantage of the opening. As E. L. Godkin of the *Nation* wrote in 1893, "man is the one animal that is capable of getting enjoyment out of the torture and death of members of its own species. We venture to assert that seven-eights of every lynching party is composed of pure, sporting mob, which goes nigger-hunting, just as it goes to a cockfight or a prize-fight, for the gratification of the lowest and most degraded instincts of human- ity. . . . They do not care a straw about seeing justice—even wild justice—done on a malefactor." The prominent Southern minister Atticus G. Haygood, also writing in 1893, accepted the "irration- ality" of the mob, but blamed it on the "maddening" crime of rape. " 'Emotional insanity' may dominate a thousand men as certainly and completely as it may dominate one man, driven to the wall and knowing nothing but the emergency that is upon him. And such insanity may be accomplished by the utmost deliberation in seeking its ends." No theory was necessary to explain lynching, Haygood argued, but it could be explained by "what we know of the elemental forces that control human nature throughout all time and the world over." The Dalton *Argus* put the matter more plainly in 1894: "Lynchings are human, and where human nature is found, lynch- ings will always be the reward for certain crimes."[53]

Such assertions, while obviously inadequate in themselves, do serve as a warning to latter-day interpreters not to overexplain lynching. The dark undertow of human nature—bloodlust, morbid curiosity, sexual fear, distrust of those who differ in any way from oneself—may well "explain" the feelings of thousands of Southern white men who stood and watched as a mutilated black man burned to death. At a more specific level of explanation, characteristics of societies based on honor also led to the public and ritualized bloodshed. The premium placed by all such societies upon female chastity, male virility, extralegal retribution, public humiliation, and the physical mutilation of deviants was a crucial ingredient in Southern lynching. Nevertheless, honor alone is inadequate as an explanation. In fact, the American South, whose allegiance to honor was always more qualified, distrusted, and even ridiculed than in other honor societies, turned to lynching while far more self-conscious honor-bound societies did not. Honor, although important, was not enough; we must look at factors more specific to the postwar South to explain the wave of lynching.[54]

The evidence suggests that a widespread and multifaceted crisis rocked the South in the late 1880s and 1890s. The lynching epidemic was at first a product of this crisis, and then a cause of further disorder. The crisis had as its fundamental catalyst the deep economic depression of those years. As the market economy penetrated the countryside, an ever-swelling number of people found themselves affected by dramatic swings in the business cycle. The early 1880s witnessed a tenuous period of relative economic stability—though not prosperity—in the South. But beginning in the late 1880s serious economic trouble began to appear again in the region. The percentage of business failures in the South between 1889 and 1896 outstripped the other settled parts of the nation every year except 1893, and even in that year the South nearly equaled the industrial Northeast in rate of failures.[55]

The crime wave of the late 1880s and early 1890s, from all indications, was even larger than those of 1857 and 1873. The statistical evidence shows that Southern prison populations climbed dramatically even before the climax of the 1893 panic and subsided rather sharply after 1895. Total arrest rates in cities throughout the country peaked between 1889 and 1892, and homicide arrests also rose markedly in those years to rates as high as those during Reconstruction.[56]

Familiar complaints could be heard once again in the South. As early as 1890 the Greensboro *Herald and Journal* urged readers to "put our shoulders to the wheel, pay up what we owe, give the business men an opportunity to discharge their debts . . . and thereby avert the impending crisis of a financial panic and the consequent ills which would inevitably follow it during the coming spring and summer." Several months later the paper bemoaned the appearance of an increased number of vagrants, from among whose ranks the paper believed most criminals came, and warned that "the vagrants must go—either to work or to the chaingang." Two years later the effects of the depression were still mounting, and the Greensboro paper agreed with the New York *World* that the " 'hard times do not end when the panic is over.' This is but too true, and to some the end of life has already been reached ere the wheels of commerce begin to move." In the winter of 1893 the Savannah *Morning News* sadly commented that throughout the nation, even in the largely agricultural South, "every city has a larger percentage of people who are in need of assistance than has been the case for many years. . . . Not since 1873 has there been so large a part of the working people out of employment." If the poor "are not helped through the hard times thousands of them will die from the lack of the actual necessaries of life." The city was surrounded by vagrants; they stayed out of the reach of the police, but they still frightened women and children at home alone and commited "petty thefts on every occasion to get a livelihood." As Savannah's black newpaper observed, "Hungry men out of employment are apt to become desperate."[57]

The victims of theft suffered along with those driven to steal. "Thievery among negroes, if not the cause, has been the occasion, of much violence," Charles H. Otken wrote in the midst of the depression of the early nineties. "It is difficult to appreciate the situation. Honest men that work hard to make a living, and fail in so many instances to make ends meet, and then have the little they make stolen, are certainly annoyed beyond endurance." As the *North Georgia Citizen* had observed in the depths of the depression of the 1870s, "Where a people are idle they do not only fail to prosper, but they are sure to get into trouble with each other, and then follow backbitings, quarreling, fighting and murder. . . ." Lynching did not appear on this 1874 list of mayhem resulting from forced idleness and hunger, but such a list in 1894 would have to be expanded to include this relatively new form of mass violence. "Men who can not see afar off, moving in a narrow circle, toiling hard, discouraged, despondent, in debt, the farm under mortgage, ruin and poverty staring them in the face," Otken sadly observed, "are easily led into desperate measures, and that to their own undoing." This was a portrayal of the plight of both races in the South in the nineties, both the blacks forced to travel through the countryside desperately looking for food and work, and the struggling white farmers who felt under seige from the "vagrants."[58]

A contemporary described the way such a scene appeared to a propertied white man. The great majority of the rapes of white women were "committed by the more worthless blacks—ordinarily 'strange niggers,' or members of that vagrant class of black proletariat that has sprung up since the great economic changes of recent years have transformed the South . . . ," argued "A Southern Lawyer" in 1900. "Lacking steady employment, and frequently too lazy to work even when employment is possible, these idle, vicious persons roam over the country, a prey to every brutal propensity." W.E.B. DuBois examined the crisis from a different perspective and found the same ingredients: white fear and frustration, unemployed and displaced blacks, and economic crisis. DuBois admitted that the black community had bred what others called "bad niggers" since the Civil War, "a class of black criminals, loafers, and ne'er-do-wells who are a menace to their fellows, both black and white." The relatively sudden appearance of "the real Negro criminal stirred the South deeply. The whites, despite their long use of the criminal court for putting Negroes to work, were used to little more than petty thievery and loafing on their part, and not to crimes of boldness, violence, or cunning. When, after periods of stress or financial depression, as in 1892, such crimes increased in frequency, the wrath of a people unschooled in the modern methods of dealing with crime broke all bounds and reached strange depths of barbaric vengeance and torture." The economic crisis of the nineties, in other words, produced a greater number of black "vagrants" and "criminals" at the same time that it produced angry, fearful whites.[59]

The lynching epidemic of the late 1880s and early 1890s spread like a contagious disease. The constants of Southern history in the nineteenth century—racism, sexual tensions, honor, ruralness, localistic republicanism—had created a context in which lynching could and did occur. The features of the South more specific to the postwar years—the declining faith by both races in the courts, growing alienation between new generations of blacks and whites, stereotypes and fears of "bad niggers"—increased the likelihood of frequent extralegal bloodshed. Then all these growing but inchoate fears were brought to a head by the direct and indirect effects of the depression. Battles over Populism heightened racial tension and encouraged renewed group violence. Black vagrants, "strange niggers," roamed the countryside, knocking on doors, sleeping in barns, looking for food. Reports of unsolved burglaries, arrests, and prison sentences all increased. The rape, real or alleged, of a white woman by a black man sparked a lynching in one isolated community. Southern newspapers hungrily published accounts of the rape and the lynching. White people began to see rapists behind strange black faces, began to perceive black "insolence" as bodily threats. Black communities, in an effort to protect themselves, would readily blame a black stranger when a serious crime has been committed against a local white. In such a setting, a lynching became far more likely than it had been only a few years earlier.

Greene County experienced a lynching that revealed all the characteristics of the South's wave of violence.[60] The Greensboro newspaper reported in April of 1894 that William Denham (or Ahern—he gave two names), a 21-year-old black man, "was a stranger in this place and not a single person, white or black, had ever seen him in this neighborhood before the commission of the crime for which he has paid the penalty that will always be inflicted in such cases." Stopping at a home near the railroad running through Greene County, Denham "asked Miss Ida, the 18-year-old daughter of the proprietress, for something to eat. The young girl instinctively feared the negro from his insolent manner and told him she would go inside and get something for him." Once inside, however, she locked the door behind her. "Seeing himself fooled, the brute demanded admittance, and on being refused burst the fastener and started for the terrified young woman." She fled through another door, screaming. The black man supposedly grabbed the young woman, but released her when he saw the woman's brother-in-law in the yard. The "fiend" escaped and the male relative immediately began to organize a "possee."

Meanwhile, Denham went to another house about three-quarters of a mile away, the home of W. C. Chambers. "No one was in the house at the time, but Mrs. Chambers, who was nursing her infant, not yet six weeks old, when Denham approached and demanded food." According to the newspaper, "before Mrs. Chambers could even reply the black demon had rushed into the room, snatched the babe from her breast, tossed it rudely on the bed and then overpowered the poor woman. . . . When Mr. Chambers returned from his day's work in the fields, he found his innocent wife prostrated and his young child probably injured unto death at the hands of the villainous rapist." Soon, "the whole county was to horse and in hot pursuit. Every negro quarters, the highways and by-ways were searched most diligently." Since no one knew the man, the searchers had a difficult time locating him. "Finally, however, one of the squads that were patrolling the roads, ran across a strange negro and arrested him. He was carried to Mrs. Chambers and identified and later confessed. By some means or other the sheriff got the brute and locked him in jail."

"Crowds began pouring into town as the news of the horrible crime spread in the country and by 10 o'clock Greensboro was holding more people than at any time in its recent history." Sheriff "Dutch" English called out the militia, the Greensboro Rifles, to guard the prisoner. Although the crowd was ready to lynch Denham, telegrams from relatives of the Chambers family in a neighboring county who wanted to be present convinced the crowd to wait until morning. A large contingent guarded the jail, however, to make sure the sheriff did not smuggle the prisoner out. The crowd asked Greensboro's merchants and clerks to close their stores and help ensure that the prisoner did not leave by train. "Every merchant acquiesced and at the toll of a certain bell business was suspended until the crime was avenged."

The crowd decided that men from outside Greene County should wrest the prisoner from the sheriff, "so that the new law, which handles severely those who refuse to assist the sheriff when called, could be averted." This advance force pushed their way past the sheriff on the steps on the familiar stone jail on Greensboro's main street. Meanwhile, Greensboro's mayor and the judge of the County Court promised the crowd that "speedy justice would be meted out to the confessed criminal." The crowd paid the officials "not the slightest attention." The older men of Greene, too, "pleaded with the more impulsive to wait for a jury trial," but to no avail. The militia's officers suddenly found themselves called away on "emergencies": the wife of one had taken ill, the other's house had caught fire. Without their officers, the militia rank and file joined the mob.

After the mob had finally succeeded in ramming through the heavy door of the jail with a railroad bar, the accused, according to accounts, behaved in the best "bad nigger" manner. "I reckon I'm the buck you're hunting for," he told the mob. "The gentlemen thought he was, too, and taking him from the cell he was marched a half mile down the Georgia Railroad track, tied hands and feet, pulled up to the limb of a pine tree and his body riddled with pistol bullets. There was not a word spoken and no boisterous conduct whatever. Everybody meant business, and the negro knew it. Unlike most lynchings there was not the slightest sign of liquor." The county commissioners ordered that Denham's body be taken down and buried. "They said that they knew how death was arrived at and saw no reason for a foolish investigation." Only a few hours after the outbreak, the paper reported, "no one talks of the lynching unless it is broached by some stranger, many of whom have come to the city driven by curiosity to see the remains of the wretch. The entire job was well executed in a most orderly manner and everything is quiet." The whites of the county "are lavishing in their praise of the negroes, who themselves boast of the fact that it was a stranger and not a Greene county man who perpetrated the foul crime."

No disinterested observer can help but note that much of what happened in this lynching might have resulted from mistakes, poor judgment, imagination, lies, and bad luck. We can never know if William Denham originally intended any harm to the 18-year-old girl he first asked for food, or whether he was angered at her rude refusal and obvious fear; whether the black stranger picked up on the road was actually the same man the mob was looking for; whether he "confessed"; whether he defiantly faced the mob; whether local officials could have prevented the lynching; whether the black community was as approving of the lynching as the whites wanted to believe. Every lynching was unique, inscrutable, mysterious. Yet, like all crimes, the lynchings were not unique at all, but rather depressingly similar, monotonous in their brutality, the actions of people swept up in something larger and worse than themselves.

III

While the South's black belt suffered through its crisis of lynching, the upcountry South saw its own unique crisis in the 1880s and 1890s. Honor, republicanism, and the market economy again played key roles, but the settings and the plots of the two crises often differed dramatically. The bloodshed in the mountains flared up more sporadically, manifested itself in a greater variety of ways, and attacked whites as often as blacks. The vigilante violence known as whitecapping, the famous feuds of the Southern Appalachians, and the bloody battles over moonshining all had the same roots.

Dalton and the surrounding area of North Georgia saw as much of this violence as any part of the upcountry South. In 1879 on an isolated road, a mob of men killed an elder of the Mormon Church who had been in the northern part of the Whitfield County with an aide "for several weeks proclaiming their plurality of wives doctrine, with a view to working up a colony of women to send to Utah." After a farce of a trial, all the vigilantes were found not guilty, though few local people actually approved of the murder. "While the more intelligent portion of the people of our county . . . are bitterly opposed to the teachings of Mormonism and do not want its teachers in their midst disseminating their hellish doctrines," editorialized the *North Georgia Citizen*, "they nevertheless do not think shootings its advocates down on the public highways is the way to rid the county of them."[61]

Whitfield County did not stand alone in the South in its anti-Mormon violence. In the late 1870s and 1880s Mormon missionaries were also whipped, beaten, and threatened in Alabama, Kentucky, and North Carolina. Five years after the violence in Whitfield, four Mormons died in Tennessee's "Cave Creek Massacre." In a society based on male honor and female "virtue," polygamy threatened the heart of what rural white Southerners accepted without question. In a region that rejected any outside "meddling," even by one's own government, the organized forces of Mormonism seemed a subversive nightmare. In the eyes of the rural white Southerners whose communities the Mormons visited, the missionaries threatened to destroy through nefarious seduction just as strange blacks threatened to destroy by rape.[62]

Isolated mountain people had no notion of cultural pluralism or moral relativism—only right and wrong. Mountain folk did not always agree among themselves exactly what constituted "right," and when they disagreed both sides furiously defended their beliefs. As one Virginian explained, the mob violence in the mountains in the 1890s "started out with the purpose of cleaning up the country and making people behave themselves and do things like they should do. . . . If they found too many different men going to a woman's house after night they would lay for them and whip the woman, and the man too if they weren't afraid that he might be a little too formidable for them." It was not only promiscuous women who received warnings and punishment; mobs might visit a man who mistreated his family, someone who slandered his or her neighbors, someone who allowed his livestock to trample other people's crops, or someone who drank too much.[63]

How one stood on drinking, in fact, often served as the measure of one's general moral stance. Opponents of alcohol found their justification in stern biblical moralism, while defenders of alcohol turned to the secular republican heritage of individual freedom. "Shall the best people in this county be defeated by irresponsible parties who would establish the whiskey business in our midst at the expense of truth and everything that is noble and good?" asked a letter to the *North Georgia Citizen* in 1883. "Are we not willing to work as hard for temperance and the right as they are for intemperance, street fights, lawlessness and other things done under the cover of night that disgrace our town and county?" But when voters did close Whitfield's saloons in the mid-1880s, the county's other newspaper echoed a warning Southerners had issued for decades: that the bold step of prohibition carried with it "responsibilities which few republican governments willingly assume. It is a broad sweep of Puritan Anarchism. It is an abridgement of personal freedom and privileges, the guarantee of our constitution, and the Gibraltar of our political being."[64]

Prohibition won first in Dalton and then in Whitfield County. Temperance advocates were pleased, but the banning of liquor did not effect the moral revolution many had hoped for. "It is well known that, in the main, the inhabitants of Dalton are a moral and highly cultivated people . . . ," the *North Georgia Citizen* commented in 1885. "We have voted whiskey and gambling completely out of the town. . . . All drunkenness, disorder or disturbance of any PUBLIC character is scrupulously dealt with." But troubling problems persisted. While every citizen knew that vagrancy, lewdness, attempted "outrages," and burglary flourished in Whitfield, "evidence sufficient for conviction can seldom be secured. Our Superior Court at its last session, for the want of this evidence, turned out most of the persons who had been arrested." Whitfield's good citizens fumed, and "for several months a profound sense of indignation has been felt among our people that there seemed to be no way to reach these immoral lepers that were known to exist in the place. . . . Numbers of our women and children had not slept for many weary nights on account of the depredations."[65]

Then, on one August night in 1885, a gang of masked men suddenly appeared on the streets of Dalton. The mob "proceeded in an orderly manner to visit places of some of the most notorious characters of the town, giving them notice to leave." But some of the "notorious characters" refused to flee; one was killed, three others, including one woman, received whippings. Although the mob visited whites as well as blacks, only blacks were beaten or shot. After the warnings, the shooting, and the whipping, the mob went to the home of Dalton's mayor and delivered a pronouncement:

Owl Hollow, Aug. 19, 1885.

Gentlemen: Our object is to protect the good people of Dalton, and especially the widows and orphans of the community, and what we do to-night will in our judgement afford them the best protection, and we hope the good people will approve. If there is any old fool who thinks different he had best keep his mouth closed, or we will serve him as the balance of thieves and robbers, and if there is anyone who attempts to encourage a sentiment in opposition to our projects, we shall wipe him up. . . . [We] do not want any town dudes to interfere as they have no discretion in this matter.

The manifesto portrayed the members of the mob as self-consciously rural men, protecting rural virtue from "the congregation of boot blacks and loafers, white and black," in the town. Most whitecappers, as participants in such mobs came to be called, were little different—in class or history of criminal offenses—from most residents of rural Georgia. The Atlanta press responded with disbelief and indignation at the "invasion" of Dalton by the mob, but the two local newspapers expressed mixed emotions. "Whether the actions of the Regulators was right or wrong . . . ," the *North Georgia Citizen* commented, "there is one thing that can be said, and said truthfully, and that is this: their coming has brought a wonderful change for the better in more ways than one." The *Argus* agreed that "the reformation of Dalton is notable, but it is the reformation born of terror. . . . We cannot, with impunity, sink to the level which recognizes but one means of moral reformation, and that means a menace to civil liberty."[66]

Regulators and vigilantes repeatedly emerged near Whitfield over the next decade. A riot erupted in 1887 in Dalton when Governor John B. Gordon commuted the death sentence of a white man convicted of murdering a white woman in the county. Two years later an "inoffensive, harmless negro, with scarcely half sense" living with a white woman was killed in his own house. In that same year, fifty members of the "Owl Hollow Brotherhood," which had appeared in Dalton in 1885, dressed in black hooded capes and white masks, "rode into town upon muffled hoofed steeds" to demand that the adopted son of the Whitfield state senator be turned over to them to be punished for killing the legislator. The sheriff, however, had spirited the young man out of the county.[67]

In the early nineties, mob violence in Whitfield County recurred with increasing frequency and harshness. In 1891, a notice appeared at a local building site declaring that the "Red Regulators" would not tolerate the hiring of black workmen. That same year a mob whipped a young black man accused of stealing a gun from a local magistrate—and then awakened the magistrate late one night to force him to sign a statement swearing that the earlier mob had not threatened to kill the alleged thief. In 1893, a white man convicted of raping a white woman and sentenced to twenty years was taken from jail in neighboring Murray County by a masked band of about eighty men and set free. A few months later a mob in Whitfield County broke down the door of the house of three white sisters who were apparently suspected of prostitution. "The helpless, frightened women were compelled to get up and go out in the yard in their night clothes, where they were unmercifully whipped by the White Caps." The violence reached its peak in October of 1892, when a mob of 150 disguised men came into Dalton, "extinguishing all the lights, capturing the police force as guides, firing guns and pistols to the terror of the whole population. They entered a small tenement house occupied by two families of negroes, breaking down the doors, taking one man who was raised here, and without a blemish on his character, and shot him dead at his door, whipping his wife, who attempted to give the alarm."[68]

This bloodshed did not go unchallenged. As early as 1889 Whitfield County ministers met and passed a series of resolutions denouncing vigilante violence. After admitting that the churches had not "in the past presented the sinful aspect of this subject as its importance demands," the ministers declared their belief that "civil governments, or 'the powers that be,' are ordained of God." After the mob of 1892 visited Dalton, the ministers of all the churches called for a mass meeting of the town. The mayor presided, "and when he took the stand he looked into the faces of one thousand of our citizens, who had indignation and determination depicted on their faces." The citizens raised $750 as "sinews of war" against the mob, and declared, with no hint of conscious irony, that "should another mob appear upon our streets a fusilade from a thousand guns will be turned loose upon them." Local newspapers bemoaned the effect of vigilantism on the area's prosperity. "No law abiding man wants to invest his money in a hot-bed of white caps," warned a newspaper from a small town near Dalton. The "best people of the county are moving out of it—those who can, and the others would go, if they could sell their property." The paper attacked vigilante violence as "a hoary relic of the days of reconstruction—those dark days when your wives and daughters were imperilled—then you had need of a secret, self-protecting organization, but since then this country has undergone a decided change, and this ancient order should long since have become a memory of the past."[69]

Why, in fact, did "Regulators," "ku-klux," and "Brotherhoods" rage so in the mountains of northwest Georgia in the 1880s and 1890s? As with lynchings in the black belt, certain constants played a crucial role. In the mountains, ironically, the very scarcity of blacks may have encouraged violence against them. Blacks did not constitute a crucial part of the work force in the upcountry, and so any "troublesome" black person seemed easily expendable. Too, blacks were so outnumbered that individuals could be attacked with little fear of retribution from their allies. But despite the paucity of local blacks, mountain whites shared the same phobias as low-country whites. After the 1885 killing of the Dalton black man by the mob of 150, the *Argus* explained that every action of the posse had been "guided by an incensed feeling against miscegenation, actual or by tendency. . . . They strike at a negro who is living with a white woman; at a white man who is stopping with a negro woman. They visit a mixed boarding house and den of miscegenation. They issue orders to those whose habits are tending to open outrage." Even though no white woman claimed rape, the white men of Whitfield felt compelled to make sure that any "tendency" toward rape was squelched by violence.[70]

Such racial and sexual fears did not form the only bridge between mountain and black belt violence. The weakness of legal institutions received even more of the blame for upcountry vigilantism than it did for low-country lynchings. The *Argus* spelled out the connection explicitly. Dalton in 1894 seemed filled with black and white vagrants, chicken thieves, and "low, dissolute, indecent characters," yet "the courts do not seem to be able to touch them up severely enough. They are turned loose upon payment of costs, get out on writs of habeus corpus, give small bonds, and go free to further ply their abandoned callings and indulge in their low vices." In a flagrant invitation to vigilantism, the paper counselled citizens who had failed to get satisfaction in the courts to "invent methods of your own." It seems no accident that the paper's complaint that nine-tenths of the criminals came from "the vagrant class" emerged in 1894. Dalton had long worried about the congregation of vagrants brought in by the railroad, and the panic of the nineties made things worse. Unemployment in both Atlanta and Chattanooga, larger cities to the south and north of Whitfield, created a host of "vagrants," many of whom stopped off in Dalton. Repeatedly the local press singled these transients out as the root of Dalton's problems.[71]

Troubles in the market economy also played a more direct role in the crisis of the upcountry. Many small farmers in the South made moonshine because they could not produce a profitable crop for the market economy. "We can't make cotton here, with which to get money to buy clothes and other necessaries; we can't make much wheat, and about the only crop we can make is corn. We can't sell corn here, because everybody else wants to sell corn," argued a moonshiner from North Georgia in 1896. "There is no money in cattle, and what can I do to get a little money? I am not making this whiskey to speculate on. I am only making enough to buy books for my three children and clothes for them to wear to school. . . . " This explanation, aside from the way it romanticizes the enterprise, accurately describes the plight of farmers in the most remote regions of the South; farmers closer to the railroad or on better land apparently turned to distilling when the price of other crops declined. In such counties of North Georgia, William F. Holmes has discovered, the depression in 1893 caused farmers who had not made moonshine before to begin to produce liquor for extra money. Vigilante violence followed a significant pattern: it became more serious in 1889, remained at a relatively high level from 1890 to 1892, reached a dramatic peak in 1893 and 1894, and dissipated rather quickly thereafter. This was also the trajectory of the depression in the late nineteenth century in the South, of the pattern of prison incarceration, and of the wave of lynchings.[72]

Whitfield's vigilante response to fears of miscegenation as well as to the vagrancy (and escalation of moonshining) born of national economic collapse made the county's experience similar to that of the black belt, but different from that of much of the more remote mountainous portions of the South that had no town the size of Dalton, or even a railroad. After all, few blacks could be found in the hollows of the Southern Appalachians in the 1880s and 1890s, and decades passed before many mountain counties experienced the massive social dislocation caused by their sudden integration into the international market economy brought about by coal mines and company stores. Yet the bitter feuds and the bloodshed triggered by moonshining associated with the Southern mountains did not emerge on a large scale until the 1880s and 1890s—simultaneous with the epidemic of lynching in the South. While the contexts differed dramatically, the group violence of the South's different subregions emerged when local prejudices, fears, and articles of faith confronted dramatic change brought on by outside forces. In the black belt, that outside force was the depression of the 1880s and 1890s; in the mountains, there was another force as well: the federal government.

When the representatives of that government suddenly appeared in upcountry counties and demanded that local residents pay high "luxury" taxes on whiskey, mountaineers responded with bitter resistance. The government bore down during two periods: the late 1870s to the early 1880s, and again in the early 1890s. As a federal revenue agent admitted in the midst of the earlier effort at enforcement, "thousands upon thousands" of people in the mountains disregarded the federal tax of ninety cents on every gallon of spirituous liquors. "The principal objection urged by them against it, was that their fathers before them had always been allowed to make as much liquor as they pleased, and were never disturbed, and therefore they had a right to the same liberty and privilege." Tradition, then, played a role—but so did localistic republicanism: "They also claimed that inasmuch as this is a free government—a Republic—every citizen should be allowed to make a living for himself and family as best he can; and if he does not steal, or trample upon the rights of his neighbors, the Government should not interfere with him." Others simply felt they owed no allegiance, and no taxes, to a federal government that did nothing for them except force them to pay tribute. As a mountaineer from an isolated area explained early in the twentieth century, "Thar's plenty o' men and women grown, in these mountains, who don't know that the Government is ary thing but a president in a biled shirt who commands two-three judges and a gang o' revenue officers."[73]

The worst violation of mountaineers' "inalienable rights," in their view, stemmed from the system the government used to discover moonshiners. Revenue agents paid local informers ten dollars to act as "guides" to stills. "The authorities are taking the evidence of a set of prejudiced and perjured pukes and on that evidence some of the best men we have are being incarcerated and placed under heavy bonds," reported a North Georgia paper in 1894. "Such business as this is money to the officers and to the informers, but nine out of ten

of these informers are miserable liars." Although moonshining was
undoubtedly going on, "this great government should use a more
honorable means of prosecution than that of picking up the trash of
the county and using their evidence against respectable people."
Simple greed was not the only reason people turned informer. "Oh,
sometimes hit's the wife or mother of some feller who's drinking too
much. Then, agin, hit may be some rival blockader [moonshiner]
who aims to cut off the other feller's trade, and, same time, divert
suspicion from his own self," explained one mountaineer. "But
ginerally hit's just somebody who has a gredge agin the blockader for
family reasons, or business reasons, and turns informer to git even."
Thus, almost everyone in the mountains, including the preachers,
denounced the informer system. A man who lived among the
moonshiners wrote to an Atlanta newspaper, "This entire system of
secrecy is contrary to the spirit of our institutions, a relic of the dark
ages." The secrecy, backbiting, money motive, and familial connections of the informing system bred "feuds, whipping and
sometimes homicide."[74]

Ironically, leading citizens had long blamed most of the violence in
their communities on alcohol, and thought they could reduce
violence by abolishing the sale of liquor. Prohibition, however, had
the opposite effect in the mountains. As the price of moonshine
increased along with demand, "amid a poverty-stricken class of
mountaineers, the temptation to run a secret still, and adulterate the
output, inflames and spreads," Horace Kephart observed early in
the twentieth century. One critic of whitecapping argued that the
vigilantes were "not a product of the wilderness, but an excrescence
of over-crowded communities, afflicted with an excess of blue laws
and a dearth of legitimate pastimes." The more the South wrestled
with its demons, in other words, the bloodier the South became;
every solution it tried seemed to bring more trouble.[75]

Many of the famous mountain feuds, along with many whitecapping incidents, had their specific origins in battles over moonshining. Other feuds festered in animosities bred by the Civil War,
others in obscure conflicts whose precise origins had long been
forgotten. "The southern highlander has a long memory," commented one observer. "Slights and injuries suffered by one generation have their scars transmitted to sons and grandsons." Mountain
areas bred feuds because conflicts over honor there entangled not
merely individual men, or even their immediate families, but whole
chains of families. As an early student of Southern feuds wrote in

1901, "Blood-relationship is the greatest bond of social solidarity. An affront to one member of a family is an affront to all his kin. . . . There is no such thing as a neutral ground; if not for, you are against."[76]

The local "state" often seemed, and was, merely a tool of a rival family. "You know folks are mostly related in this country," one mountaineer explained. "If I get into trouble, even if I am not to blame, there is no use going to law if the judge is kin to the other side, or if the lawyer has succeeded in getting his own men on the jury. It doesn't make any difference what the evidence is, the case goes the way they want it to go." If a man took a grievance to court and lost, the mountaineer argued, he then had only three choices: "let them throw off on me as a coward, if I stay in the county; to leave the county and give up all I own, and still be looked at as a coward; or to get my kinfolk and friends together and clean up the other crowd. What would *you* do?"[77]

Anthropologist Jacob Black-Michaud has noted that feuds tend to develop where "the concept of honour is ill-defined and consequently liable to any number of interpretations by the combatants themselves and the society at large." The feud therefore can continue indefinitely, "since as long as one of the parties is 'losing' they can always make out that their honour has not yet been satisfied and claim another life to 'equalize.' " No book or code of etiquette such as channeled the honor of elite duels ever appeared for feuds; no climactic and clear event marked the end of a feud. The general amorphousness of honor among the lower class became accentuated in the Southern mountains of the late nineteenth century. Where did "honor" come in when people received ten dollars from the federal government to inform on their neighbors? Was it honorable to make whiskey, as people had done for generations, despite blue laws passed by zealous church folk, or was it honorable to aid the government and the "good people" in stopping the manufacture of illegal and violence-provoking liquor? In such a situation, only one rule provided certainty: "My family *right* or *wrong!*" Outside authority changed, the economy changed, laws changed, but family endured.[78]

The various societies that we call "the South" underwent simultaneous crises in the late 1880s and early 1890s. The black belt bred hundreds of lynchings, the upcountry bred widespread feuds and whitecapping. The chain of events that led to the death of each victim was, of course, unique; chance and personality accounted for much bloodshed. So did apparently immutable features of the nineteenth-century South: race hatred, sexual fears, honor, intense moralism, and localistic republicanism. But the timing of the crisis seems no accident. Without the ever-widening chasm between the races in the black belt, without the attempts of the federal government to exert its authority in the mountains, and without the direct and indirect effects of the depression throughout the region, the New South might have avoided the crisis that crippled the region for generations long after the 1890s had ended.

Conclusion
"The Hurt That Honor Feels"

In 1906 Thomas J. Kernan, a lawyer from Baton Rouge, prepared a paper on the "Jurisprudence of Lawlessness" for the American Bar Association. The attorney codified for his audience the "unwritten decalogue" that prevailed within the Southern courts where he had long practiced. The first four of the ten commandments of Kernan's code turned around the "protection" of women. In the case of rape, adultery, seduction, or "slander against chastity" only one punishment, as far as public opinion was concerned, would suffice: violence at the hands of a male relative of the woman. Where crimes against women were involved few Southern men would be satisfied with a legal settlement. " 'The jingling of the guinea' never did and never will 'help the hurt that honor feels.' What surprise is it, then, that one so deeply injured should himself seek redress when the law gives him none?" Recognizing the force of this sentiment among Southern jurors, Kernan suggested that the law could actually be strengthened if it faced facts, if adultery, seduction, and slander could "be made felonies at law and their perpetrators should be clad in stripes."[1]

Challenges to the virtue of Southern women did, as Kernan argued, ignite the honor of Southern men in the 1890s as much as in the 1830s. When in 1897 a certain Mr. Kimes of West Virginia shot a Mr. Hail three times for "alienating the affections" of his wife, the assailant received the sentence of twenty-four hours in jail and a nominal fine. Kimes did not go to jail, however, or pay the fine, for

266

the governor enthusiastically pardoned him. "I remit this fine and costs with more pleasure than any word the English language can furnish me to express," the governor announced. "My only regret is that Kimes did not kill Hail. He ought to have done so." In 1893 Ellen Hunter, "a young lady of one of the best known families of Savannah" was rumored to have visited a room in the DeSoto Hotel on the Fourth of July where a well-known New York traveling man was staying. When a local minister felt compelled to tell the woman's father of the fast-flying rumors, the dishonored parent became furious. Hunter first extracted an explicit denial and alibi from his daughter and then marched with her to the hotel, where he confronted the manager and several of his clerks. The aggrieved father "was armed and evidently meant business," and the hotel men "lost no time in denying positively that they had ever made any such statements." In fact, they published cards in the Savannah *Morning News* to that effect. Hunter published his own card as well: "The base cowardly liars who can traduce a woman and stab the name of an honorable family in the back are worse than assassins. If they will take such a chance to my face I will kill them on sight." When in 1893 an Atlanta jury required only seven minutes to acquit a man accused of murder, the Greensboro *Herald and Journal* applauded the speedy verdict: "The evidence showed that the deceased man had grossly insulted Mrs. Mehan, at a time too when she was daily expecting to fulfil the God-given office of her creator, in becoming a mother. 'Vengeance is mine saith the Lord, I will repay,' but the provocation was so unusual and terribly trying to human endurance, any man less than a saint would have done as Mehan did, and the jury's verdict is a popular one with the people."[2]

The next three commandments of Thomas J. Kernan's 1906 unwritten decalogue involved "crimes" less volatile than offenses against women, but they, too, seemed to have won considerable allegiance in the late nineteenth-century South. Law Five held that the survivor of a duel must be acquitted; Law Six commanded that any man who kills another in a fair fight shall be found not guilty; and Law Seven dictated that "the lie direct and certain other well known opprobrious epithets, which constitute mortal insult, are each equal to a blow, and any of them justifies an assault."[3]

Southern courts did not confront many cases of dueling in 1906, but the practice had lingered stubbornly after the Civil War. Savannah, for its part, witnessed at least seven duels between 1868 and 1875, and the *Morning News* reported eight others in various Southern cities during the same years. "An affair of honor came off yesterday," the Savannah paper reported during Reconstruction in language that could have appeared in the 1820s. "In the course of a heated debate, words were spoken which Mr. Russell thought reflected upon the character of his father. A correspondence ensued, which originated in a challenge to mortal combat, according to the code." After a duel on the nearby Carolina shore in which neither combatant received an injury, "the seconds proposed a settlement which was agreed to, and the contending parties shook hands and with the crowd returned to the city."[4]

Mannered duels still occurred in the South after Reconstruction, but they were increasingly eclipsed by less formalized and more deadly violence. Dueling "is no longer an honorable way of killing," a Southern professor observed in 1883, but "the old spirit of so-called chivalry has not declined with the 'Code': there is the same unwillingness—in a lessening degree—to go to the law; and in this transition stage from the 'Code' to the courts we have fallen into the present lawless and cruel habit of street-fighting." "It is customary nowadays to say that the duel belongs to a barbarous age that is past, and the code duello is obsolete," Thomas J. Kernan commented in 1906. "It is true that the formal duel, with seconds and surgeons and all the punctilio of diplomatic procedure, is no longer in vogue in this country, but a much more dangerous and deadly form of it, the street duel, is still . . . too much the fashion and gives no sign of decadence." No longer were seconds necessary; aggrieved men shot each other on sight, with or without warning. Kernan's sixth unwritten commandment held that as long as the fight was "fair," no one could be blamed.[5]

Apparently, few fights failed to meet the criteria of fairness as applied by Southern juries. In 1880, H. V. Redfield described a typical trial of a Southern man accused of murder. "He kills a man in a street-fight or otherwise, but it is usually a street-fight or bar-room affray." He is arrested. He goes free on bond until the trial. But the trial, thanks to the defendant's lawyer, is continued, and then continued again. "The grass grows over the grave of the slain. . . . Public interest dies out. Some of the witnesses move off. There are a few more continuances to give other witnesses a chance to move around and see the country. The witness, however, who heard the deceased 'make threats' about the defendant never moves away." The trial finally begins. "Major A. and Colonel B. and

General C. appear for the defendent." A jury is chosen, preferably including several men who have been involved in such "shooting scrapes" themselves. "The witnesses are examined. It is proved that the deceased was seen to 'reach around behind him as if to draw a pistol,' or that he started home, presumably to get his shot-gun. The defendant had his with him. The case is argued. Authorities are cited. The defendant is acquitted." The violence and the verdict had changed little between the 1830s and the 1880s.[6]

In 1897, seventeen years after Redfield's mocking portrayal of the Southern trial for violence, a letter from "a prominent Georgian" bemoaned the persistence of this frame of mind. "Every community" in the South included men who fight on slight provocation, the correspondent complained, who "give themselves up without resistance or trouble, so confident are they of acquittal. It has come to the pass in the state of Georgia that when a man thinks his life is threatened he must act quickly in self-defense, for he knows full well that no fear of the law acts to restrain his would-be slayer." Even if a murderer did have the bad fortune to be convicted, "he can count, almost to a certainty, on securing a new trial, with all the chances for acquittal in his favor." The Savannah *Morning News* agreed that something had to be done: "there must be convictions and hangings for murder. And the hangings must not be solely of unknown and degenerate negroes. White murderers as well as black, must be brought to the gallows." But as in the Old South, a thirst for bloody retribution was one of the very reasons violent men went unpunished. Angry grand juries indicted men for murder, rather than for justifiable homicide or voluntary manslaughter, the Greensboro *Herald and Journal* pointed out in 1899, yet "the most casual review of the testimony would show that the crime was not premeditated and a verdict for murder could not be technically secured." As a result, "the culprit goes free because he was indicted for the gravest crime known to the code." Southern justice appeared to know no moderation. Just as antebellum proponents of the penitentiary had charged, Southern courts tended to impose either vengeful and dramatic punishment or no punishment at all.[7]

As in the antebellum South, too, the expectation, even dread, of violence inexorably bred violence. When in 1897 two young men were killed at a dance by an 18-year-old adversary, a North Georgia newspaper blamed the deaths on the routine way Southern men carried concealed weapons. "As a rule one does not arm himself for the specific purpose of shooting another," the paper pointed out.

"He just puts a pistol in his pocket and struts out among his fellow men to be ready for emergencies, which he generally proceeds to make. A drink or two will put him in a humor for a row, and make him sensitive to insults." As the Greensboro paper pithily put it, "An angry word, a temporary burst of passion, and out comes the ever-present weapon, and another victim is sent unshriven into eternity."[8]

"The curse and shame of the South," lamented an 1882 article on "The Influence of Homicide on Southern Progress," "is the constant presence in the minds of all classes, from childhood up, of homicide as one of the probable contingencies of ordinary social life." Robert Penn Warren remembered that in Kentucky in the early twentieth century "there was a world of violence that I grew up in. You accepted violence as a component of life. . . . You heard about violence, and you saw terrible fights . . . not violence of robbery, you see; it was another kind of violence in the air: the violence of anger, what sociologists call status homicide. . . . there was some threat of being trapped into this whether you wanted to or not and being stuck with it."[9]

Sociologists have devoted considerable attention to the persistence of Southern violence, to the fact that the region has dominated American homicide statistics throughout the twentieth century. Some explain it by reference to something undefined in Southern culture, something Raymond Gastil calls "Southernness"; others argue that more concrete conditions such as poverty and lack of education are to blame. Both interpretations hold part of the explanation. The Southern violence of the twentieth century was a product of honor, the key variable of violent "Southernness." Only culture channels the frustration of poverty into violence; millions of people have been locked into the deepest poverty without ever resorting to homicide or assault. But increasingly the violent culture of honor could live only where the forces of change, of "progress," of "dignity" did not penetrate into the character of Southerners. Lower-class whites and lower-class blacks perpetuated honor after most educated middle-class Southerners had turned away from honor and violence as archaic relics of a glorious but impractical Southern past.[10]

Hot-blooded wealthy young Southern men might still bristle over an insult in the twentieth century in a way their Northern counterparts could not understand, but they no longer resorted to the elaborate etiquette of the duel. Indeed, the duel and its formal code, the most visible and self-consciously aristocratic manifestations of honor, were the first parts of honor to be discarded, jettisoned within one generation after the end of the Civil War. Perhaps the mass slaughter of that war, the depersonalized and often senseless deaths in a losing cause, undermined Southerners' faith in ritualized violence. The laws of "civilized" combat and warfare, the glory of frontal assaults and waving flags, died a violent death, and dueling may have been a casualty of the armageddon. Men who killed and faced their own death as well may have come to place more value on "mere" life itself and less on the abstraction called honor. Perhaps, too, the defeat of the South forced members of the region's elite to reconsider before they ostentatiously engaged in a form of violence strictly reserved for an "aristocracy." Their high opinion of themselves had not necessarily diminished with their wealth, but they did realize that the war had, within their own system of values, "dishonored" the South. Although the region fought valiantly, it had been physically bested. After such a defeat, any ritualized violence that required all the regalia and etiquette of the vanquished antebellum world may have seemed evidence more of hubris than honor.

In 1889, for example, the Greensboro *Herald and Journal* rejected the formal duel as a legitimate way of settling conflict—not because violence was unjustified, but because the formality now seemed archaic and pretentious. "We can understand how a man in sudden heat of passion, before explanations can be made, will shoot another down for an insult," the paper conceded, but men did not fight duels while their blood was still hot—only after elaborate preparations. It was this calculating aspect of dueling that came to seem outmoded after the Civil War. "It does seem to us as if some of the prominent men in Georgia are bent on violating the laws and at the same time endeavoring to make themselves appear as ridiculous as possible," the paper from the black belt editorialized. Duelists who went upon the ground of battle "with all the hulabaloo and style imaginable, make themselves the laughing stock of the continent."[11]

The duel may have died, too, because of positive alternatives that emerged after the Civil War. Proponents of evangelical piety had always denounced dueling, and that piety had been given dramatic and manly form in the personae of Stonewall Jackson and Robert E. Lee. After the example offered by these men, never again would a Southern gentlemen have to renounce God's law to prove himself worthy of the highest honor his people could bestow. Even more important, new avenues to respectability appeared in the South after the Civil War. Business as well as planting now seemed to offer legitimate, if not preferred, ways to make a living, and there seemed little profit in a public ritual of bloodshed. Clients wanted men of circumspection and caution, not impetuosity and pretension.

Business values soon came to be celebrated in the South with a fervor equal to that of anywhere else in America. As early as 1882 one Southerner dreamed of a time when business and a strong state would bring the South into step with "the most highly civilized States." In such modern societies "the foremost classes give little or no attention to enemies at all. They are too busy with commerce, science, literature, and politics to bother about them. They do not care what any enemy says, and do not mind what he does, as long as he is not in debt to them. They keep up a disciplined police force to catch him and lock him up if he gets drunk, or threatens violence, or goes about calling names in the street." In 1893 Walter Hines Page saw encouraging signs that such a state of affairs was emerging in the South. The culture of business could do the South a great service, he wrote, by eradicating the "Southern bully," who with "his oaths and 'honor' . . . has strutted through all the quiet ways of Southern life, calling himself 'the South,' writing and speaking of 'our people,' and now [leading] mobs to avenge 'our women.' " Business tolerated no such nonsense. "The new spirit of industry should take him in hand. Commerce has no social illusions; it has the knack of rooting up vested social interests that stand in its way; and it has been left for commerce, by infusing its influence into the body of local public sentiment in the South, to rid us of this historic, red-handed, deformed, and swaggering villain."[12]

The Savannah *Morning News*, too, attacked "FALSE IDEAS OF HONOR" in 1894. "Is there danger of a revival of that old and false code of social ethics that prompted its holders to resort to the duel and to go 'heeled' for an emergency?" the paper asked after reporting the deaths of two young men in a fight. Surely not, for there was a better way, a more "civilized" code of values. "In these modern times, character and honor depend upon a man's own life and conduct; not upon what another may say of him. So long as the individual maintains his character spotless he has in his possession a more powerful weapon than a pistol with which to defend his reputation—the weapon of truth. Armed with truth and backed up by common sense, he is well nigh invulnerable." Here stood dignity in all its glory.[13]

These notions of just behavior gained increasing credence and allegiance throughout the middle and upper classes of the New South. The power of these new ideals grew with every widely hailed "sensible" speech by Henry Grady or Booker T. Washington, with every editorial boosting a small town or growing city, with every new clerical or managerial job in a prospering firm, with every issue of the *Nation* or the *Forum* or the *Arena* read in a Southern home, with every sermon delivered by an educated city minister before a well-to-do congregation, with every generation of Southern men who went off to learn new notions in college. A South full of enthusiastic Rotary Clubs and Chambers of Commerce came into being with startling speed in the early twentieth century, and the men who steered the South into "progress" tended to have little use for old-fashioned honor.

The men who still adhered to honor in the South at the turn of the century were usually not the sort to write articles or give speeches, and few defenders of honor made their feelings known except by their actions. Yet some Southerners who did write looked upon the diminution of honor with mixed feelings. N. S. Shaler, a Southern-born professor at Harvard, observed in 1890 that modern man had lost any but a utilitarian conception of human nature, a conception that valued mere survival over everything else. As a result, honor had no meaning: "Modernism has worked to intensify the passion for existence until those who are most under its dominion cannot well conceive how a man, except for some supreme duty, to which he is pledged by altruistic motives, can give up his own life or take that of his neighbor." Professor Shaler would not defend violence, but he did insist that the "extreme devotion to continued mundane existence which is so manifest in our modern civilization is certainly open to debate." Surely, he thought, there was some virtue in a conception of honor in which mere life itself did not constitute "a supreme good for which almost all else was to be sacrificed, but something to be taken in hand and put in the risk of the pursuit of manly ideals." Shaler, despite his perception of honor as something more than mere pretension or childish lack of control, admitted that such a code of ethics must necessarily seem "irrational and brutal" as the enlighted nineteenth century drew to a close. The Southern devotion to honor labeled the region, even to its sympathizers, a throwback to an earlier stage of civilization.[14]

Still, there were people who insisted that the older stage had been better than the new. In 1916 a minister from Nashville turned the tables on the advocates of the triumphant business civilization of America and defended honor. "The establishment of an aristocracy founded on money is not only contrary to republican ideals, but it is the lowest form of aristocracy," the Reverend James H. M'Neilly charged. All the evils of modern society could be laid at the door of monopoly and the reliance on mere money as the only measure of a man. "The debasing of character is seen in the sharpness in business which condones successful dishonesty, in the disregard of the plighted word, in the lax sense of honor, in the looseness of the marriage bond and the sexual immoralities of the social leaders, in the lack of reverence for the most sacred relations as parental, divine, and patriotic." Such a scene seemed a far cry and a marked declension from the mid-nineteenth-century South, where "a man defended the good name of the women in his family with his life, and any aspersion on his honor was resented on the instant. His word was his bond. To his mind the tricks of trade were thievery."[15]

In the twentieth century, those Southerners who sought to defend their traditional society increasingly turned to other conservative values more "American" than honor. Localistic republicanism, in the guise of states' rights, provided an ideological defense against the growing power of the national state. Intellectuals appealed to the South's heritage of Jeffersonian agrarianism as an alternative to industrial capitalism. Evangelical moralism manifested itself, among blacks as well as whites, in the shape of prohibitionism, arguments for literal biblical infallibility, and an ongoing crusade against the growing secularization of American and Southern society. Appeals to white racism served for generations, too, to impede all sorts of change. These forces together formed a matrix of conservatism in the South. Whites among all classes adhered to one or all of these articles of faith, but an acute sensitivity to insult and a propensity for violence—the manifestations of honor—came with each passing decade to be identified more and more with poor white "rednecks" and poor urban blacks.

Ironically, a white Southern man from the 1830s or 1870s, whatever his class, would understand far better than most middle-class Americans of the twentieth century can the values of today's poor urban dweller, North and South. "The significance of a jostle, a slightly derogatory remark, or the appearance of a weapon in the hands of an adversary" means something to poor blacks and whites it does not mean to the middle and upper classes, Marvin Wolfgang and Franco Ferracuti discovered in their investigation of homicide in Northern cities. "A male is usually expected to defend the name and honor of his mother, the virtue of womanhood . . . and to accept no derogation about his race (even from a member of his own race), his age, or his masculinity." In places where the justice of the state is suspect and visible only intermittently, gangs engage in feuds, use violence against informers, and generally provide their own violent "state." In turn, urban dwellers have formed their own vigilante organizations to fight the "outrages" of the urban twentieth century.[16]

It would seem that the culture of honor and its violence should have soon withered and died in the inhospitable atmosphere of Northern cities, where so many generations of Southern migrants of both races moved. "Dignity," after all, had supposedly flourished since the mid–nineteenth century among the schools, factories, and relatively active governments of the North. Indeed, historians have discovered that Northern cities, like industrialized societies in general did experience declining rates of violence from the mid-nineteenth century well into this century. The institutions of industry and state apparently acted to encourage the self-control, the incentives to postpone gratification, and the greater certainty of detection and arrest that act to reduce violence. Many migrants from the South however, especially blacks, have remained insulated from such forces, stranded in desperate Northern cities where unemployment, ineffective schooling, and dangerous neighborhoods not only allow Southern-born honor to survive, but actually generate an honor of their own. Honor has found new breeding grounds in cities, once the most advanced outposts of dignity. "Whenever the authority of law is questioned or ignored, the code of honor re-emerges to allocate the right to precedence and dictate the principles of conduct," anthropologist Julian Pitt-Rivers has observed. Honor springs up "among aristocracies and criminal underworlds, schoolboy and street-corner societies, open frontiers and those closed communities where reigns 'The Honorable Society,' as the Mafia calls itself."[17]

Just as the twentieth century has seen honor take new root in the North and dignity undergo its own tribulations—the preoccupation with self all too often collapsing into alienation and narcissicm—so has this century seen the shifting fortunes of the international market economy finally favor the South. Factories and their jobs have deserted the "Frost Belt" for the "Sun Belt." Black and white migrants from impoverished rural areas pour into Southern cities, just as they have for decades. The rural culture of a republicanism distrustful of the state, evangelical moralism, and even honor refuses to die in its new setting, however, despite the homogenizing effects of schools, time clocks, modern technology, chain stores, and television. Crime and punishment, as much as anything, measure the continuity of the South with the past: the region still leads the nation in homicide and assault rates, still holds the greatest number of men on death row, and still contains the largest number of handguns.[18] For over a century now, the South has seemed to be disappearing—yet it persists in a thousand subtle and obvious ways. The region always manages to resurrect itself in new guises, for among every new generation walk the ghosts of the old.

Appendix
Sources and Method

Throughout this study I treat all statistics as simply as possible, keeping to graphs and frequency tables. Aside from the advantages such a strategy of simplicity offers to readers unfamiliar with statistical techniques, this approach also seems the only honest way to handle data as small in absolute numbers and as suspect in origin as much of the statistical information on nineteenth-century Southern crime and punishment must necessarily be. I have even avoided the usual practice of presenting statistics of criminality in terms of rate per population. Not only do the resulting numbers give a false sense of precision, but they are actually less telling, it seems to me, than the raw numbers. The population has to be estimated between census years (and in the South in 1870 large numbers of blacks were left out of the census altogether), and as a result these computations merely introduce another element of distortion into the final figures. Urban arrest rates can profitably be figured by population rate, especially for large cities, but rural crimes and state prison statistics are best presented as straightforwardly as possible—warts and all. Although the reader should keep in mind that the general population was always growing during the period explored here, it did not grow with the same fits and starts that marked prison statistics.

I. Penitentiary Records and State Manuscript Sources

The published penitentiary records of the various Southern states are rather rare and sometimes scattered, especially for the antebellum period. In some states in some years the reports were published as parts of legislative journals; in other years in other states they were published separately. The notes to Chapters Three, Five, Six, and Seven detail in what form specific reports appeared. The Tennessee State Library possesses the most complete and most accessible penal records of any Southern state. All of Georgia's penitentiary reports for the nineteenth century have been gathered, microfilmed, and made available at the Georgia Department of

Archives and History, but antebellum reports are sometimes sketchy and reports apparently were not published for some years. The most convenient published penitentiary records for Mississippi are not in that state's archives, but in the legislative journals at the Mississippi State Law Library in Jackson. Alabama's penitentiary reports, because they were often bound apart from legislative journals, were the least accessible of those studied, and several reports from the late 1850s are missing. Alderman Library at the University of Virginia contains a full set of that state's *Annual Reports*, which include penitentiary records. The Library of Congress and the Massachusetts State Library have excellent collections of reports, especially for the Northern states. For the antebellum period, the *American Almanac* often (though not always) published annual summary statistics for the penitentiaries of several Northern and Southern states. William C. Sneed's *History of the Kentucky Penitentiary* (1860) contains a convenient collection of that state's antebellum penitentiary reports. The reports for every state vary greatly in quality from year to year. Some are mere compendiums of statistics, while others offered detailed assessments, prescriptions, and testimony.

By far the most useful state manuscript sources were those of the various governors. Usually indexed, their correspondence contains queries on penal innovation, directives to wardens, expressions of displeasure by prisoners, and letters from mayors and sheriffs requesting assistance. Every governor was besieged by petitions for pardon, and the files of postwar governors in particular bulge with such documents. For many governors, these petitions form the major part of their administration's official papers. These petitions have received no previous scholarly attention and at first seem quite forbidding. Not only are they numerous, but sometimes dates and names are missing; if they are indexed it is by the prisoner's name, which usually has no meaning for the researcher. Most of the petitions are formulaic and many are nearly illegible. But the occasional letter that allows a glimpse into the most obscure life makes the effort seem worthwhile. I examined petitions from the 1840s to the 1880s for Alabama, Mississippi, and Tennessee. Georgia possesses many such petitions—over 100 boxes, in fact—but they have been taken from the original files of the governors and alphabetized regardless of date (and most date from the early twentieth century). This method of filing makes the Georgia petitions difficult to use for the purposes of this book.

The statistical information presented in Figures 3.1 and 3.2 and in the tables in the notes to Part One comes from the following penitentiary records:

Figures:

Kentucky, 1836–59   New York, 1830–59 (with missing years)
Mississippi, 1840–59   Ohio, 1835–60

Tables in notes to Chapters Two and Three

Kentucky, 1849–59 ($n = 1112$)   Virginia, 1846, 1858 ($n = 562$)
Tennessee, 1849–59 ($n = 1072$)   Maryland, 1852, 1860 ($n = 423$)
Mississippi, 1849–59 ($n = 596$)   Texas, 1849–60 ($n = 445$)
Alabama, 1847–55 ($n = 1227$)   Michigan, 1850–60 ($n = 1247$)
Georgia, 1817–53, 1855, 1860   Eastern Pennsylvania 1851–59 ($n = 746$)
    ($n = 1740$)   Connecticut, 1850–59 ($n = 581$)

The statistics for Figures 5.1, 5.2, and 5.3 and the accompanying tables in Chapter Five, note 57 and Chapter Seven, note 56 came from these penitentiary reports:

Mississippi, 1866–1900	Texas, 1866–88
Tennessee, 1866–98	Michigan, 1866–99
Alabama, 1868–1900 (with	Massachusetts, 1872–99
missing years)	Ohio, 1866–1900
Georgia, 1869–99	Eastern Pennsylvania, 1866–99
Virginia, 1870–1900	

Some prisons did not publish records of prisoners received each year, so to compare states I have used prison population size instead for the postbellum era although this is obviously a less sensitive measure of trends in incarceration than the number of people received each year. The "years" usually ran from fall to fall.

The table in Chapter Six, note 25, uses figures from these reports:

Alabama, 1866–82 (n = 3007)	Mississippi, 1866–81 (n = 3934)
Georgia, 1872, 1874, 1877–78,	Tennessee, 1869–80 (n = 5644)
1886–88, 1895–96 (n = 2643)	

II. Local Records

The major sources for the local statistics were the Superior Court Minutes of Chatham, Greene, and Whitfield counties at the Georgia Department of Archives and History in Atlanta. I recorded each case that came before the Superior Courts between 1850 and 1900 (and in the sample years of 1835, 1838, 1841, 1844, 1847). For the years between 1850 and 1880 I converted the information on each criminal case to a code and recorded them on specially designed mimeographed sheets. From the courts records I recovered information on the date and nature of every offense, the court session, the name, gender, and usually race of each defendant, the disposition of the case by the grand jury (true bill, no bill, *nolle prosequi*, no arrest), the verdict of the petit jury, and the sentence.

I defined "criminals" as those people for whom the grand jury believed the evidence warranted a trial before the petit jury. Such a definition excluded people who might have been falsely prosecuted by neighbors or law enforcement officials, but included more people than the relatively few individuals the courts actually found guilty. As others have noted, the very fact of being successfully indicted by a grand jury is often enough to label one a criminal, and the inclusion of all against whom a true bill was found seemed the best way to define those whom contemporaries considered criminal.

I sought each defendant for whom a true bill was found in the three counties' manuscript censuses for 1850, 1860, 1870, and 1880. The manuscript census records offered information on age, family position, wealth, and nativity, and confirmed information from the court records on race and sex. The antebellum and postbellum tax digests of the three counties contained useful data on property holding. For postwar Savannah, city directories also revealed data on residence, race, and occupation. After the information available for each defendant had been gathered, I transferred the data to computer cards and analyzed them by means of the SPSS (Statistical Package for the Social Sciences) program. Along with two graduate assistants, I later tabulated all the cases before two rural Virginia courts between 1820 and 1900. As the table in note 28 in Chapter Four shows, the patterns in those Upper South counties were similar to those in Georgia before the war; after the war the usefulness of the Virginia data was weakened because the courts prosecuted many crimes labeled merely "misdemeanors" or "felonies."

I also used the manuscript censuses for the Georgia counties to take systematic random samples of the general populations of the three counties in 1860 and 1870. I sampled among men over 16 years of age—the group most likely to appear in the court records. The samples had the following characteristics:

	1860	1870
Chatham	$n = 647$	$n = 720$
Greene	$n = 387$[a]	$n = 690$
Whitfield	$n = 401$[a]	$n = 681$

[a]Confidence interval: 95% at ±5%; all others 99% at ±5%

Although I believe that this study deals with the major trends of crime and punishment in the South, studies of other locales may well discover divergent and revealing patterns. We particularly need explorations of the transition from the colonial to the antebellum South, which I slighted in my focus on the effects of emancipation.

Notes

Abbreviations Used in Notes

ADAH   *Alabama Department of Archives and History*
GDAH   *Georgia Department of Archives and History*
LSU   *Louisiana State University Press*
MDAH   *Mississippi Department of Archives and History*
TSLA   *Tennessee State Library and Archives*
UNC   *University of North Carolina Press*

Chapter 1. Honor and Its Adversaries

1. Issac Weld, *Travels through the States of North America, and the Provinces of Upper and Lower Canada, During the Years 1795, 1796, and 1797* (London: Stockdale, 1799), p. 110; Charles William Janson, *The Stranger in America, 1793–1806*, Carl S. Driver, ed. (1807; reprint, New York: Press of the Pioneers, 1935), p. 308.

2. Duelist quoted in Jerome G. Taylor, Jr., "Upper Class Violence in Nineteenth-Century Tennessee," *West Tennessee Historical Society Papers* 34 (Oct. 1980):33–34; others quoted in Charles Coleman Wall, "Students and Student Life at the University of Virginia, 1825 to 1861" (Ph.D. diss., University of Virginia, 1978), pp. 90, 95.

3. John W. DeForest, *A Union Officer in the Reconstruction*, James H. Croushore and David Potter, eds. (New Haven: Yale University Press, 1948), pp. 178–79.

4. B. J. Ramage, "Homicide in the Southern States," *Sewanee Review* 4 (1896): 213–14.

5. For police, court, and prison records, see Chapters Three, Four, Seven, and Conclusion; Other studies that find high levels of violence in the South include Sheldon Hackney, "Southern Violence," *American Historical Review* 74 (1969): 906–25; Raymond D. Gastil, "Homicide and a Regional Culture of Violence," *American Sociological Review* 36 (1971): 412–27; Colin Lofton and Robert H. Hill,

"Regional Subculture and Homicide: An Examination of the Gastil-Hackney Thesis," *American Sociological Review* 39 (1974): 714–24; H. C. Brearley, *Homicide in the United States* (Chapel Hill: UNC, 1932), pp. 17–28; H. C. Brearley, "The Pattern of Violence," in W. T. Couch, ed., *The Culture of the South* (Chapel Hill: UNC, 1935), pp. 684–85; Michael S. Hindus, *Prison and Plantation: Crime, Justice, and Authority in Massachusetts and South Carolina, 1767–1878* (Chapel Hill: UNC, 1980), p. 97; Dickson Bruce, *Violence and Culture in the Antebellum South* (Austin: Univ. of Texas Press, 1979), esp. p. 242, n. 4; Wilbur Zelinsky, *The Cultural Geography of the United States* (Englewood Cliffs, N.J.: Prentice-Hall, 1973), pp. 103–4; Henry P. Lundsgaard, *Murder in Space City: A Cultural Analysis of Houston Homicide Patterns* (New York: Oxford Univ. Press, 1977), pp. 217–18; Keith D. Harries and Stanley D. Brunn, *The Geography of Law and Justice: Spatial Perspectives on the Criminal Justice System* (New York: Praeger, 1978), p. 4; H. V. Redfield, *Homicide, North and South: Being a Comparative View of Crime Against the Person in the Several Parts of the United States* (Philadelphia: J. B. Lippincott, 1880); Rev. James A. Lyon, quoted in C. G. Parsons, *Inside View of Slavery; or, A Tour Among the Planters* (Boston: John P. Jewett, 1855), pp. 188–90.

6. Thomas Jefferson, *Notes on the State of Virginia*, William Peden, ed. (Chapel Hill: UNC, 1955), p. 162; Emily Burke, *Reminiscences of Georgia* (Oberlin, Ohio: J. M. Fitch, 1850), pp. 152–53; Parsons, *Inside View*, pp. 209–15.

7. On the effects of childrearing on Southern violence, see Bruce, *Violence and Culture*, esp. chap. 2; Bertram Wyatt-Brown, *Southern Honor: Ethics and Behavior in the Old South* (New York: Oxford Univ. Press, 1982), esp. Chaps. 5 and 6.

8. *The Papers of Frederick Law Olmsted*, vol. 2, *Slavery and the South, 1852–1857*, Charles E. Beveridge and Charles Capen McLaughlin, eds., (Baltimore: Johns Hopkins Univ. Press, 1981), p. 239. On procedural fairness for slaves, see Chapter Four.

9. Wilbur J. Cash, *The Mind of the South* (1941; reprint, New York: Vintage Books, 1969), pp. 44–45; Eugene Genovese, *Roll, Jordan, Roll: The World the Slaves Made* (1974; reprint, New York: Pantheon, 1976), pp. 43–44; John Hope Franklin, *The Militant South, 1800–1861* (Cambridge: Belknap Press of Harvard Univ. Press, 1956), pp. 14–32. On national mythology and violence, see Richard Slotkin, *Regeneration Through Violence: The Mythology of the American Frontier, 1600–1860* (Middletown, Conn.: Wesleyan Univ. Press, 1973).

10. See the elegant seminal article by Charles Sydnor, "The Southerner and the Laws," *Journal of Southern History* 6 (1940): 7–8; Robert Dykstra, *The Cattle Towns* (New York: Knopf, 1968), pp. 112–48; David J. Bodenhamer, "Law and Disorder on the Early Frontier: Marion County, Indiana, 1823–1850," *Western Historical Quarterly* 10 (July 1979): 323–36; Walter Nugent, *Structures of American Social History* (Bloomington: Indiana Univ. Pres, 1981), pp. 85–86; Werner J. Einstadter, "Robbery-Outlawry on the U.S. Frontier, 1863–1890: A Reexamination," in James A. Inciardi and Anne E. Pottieger, eds., *Violent Crime: Historical and Contemporary Issues* (Beverly Hills: Sage, 1978), p. 35; John Phillip Reid, *Law for the Elephant: Property and Social Behavior on the Overland Trail* (San Marino, Cal.: Huntington Library, 1980). On the diffusion of at least one element of Southern culture throughout the western United States by way of Texas, see Terry G. Jordan, *Trails to Texas: Southern Roots of Western Cattle Ranching* (Lincoln: Univ. of Nebraska Press, 1981).

11. Sheldon Hackney, in "Southern Violence," pp. 924–25, after offering a useful survey of older explanations of regional patterns of homicide, posits a persistent

defensiveness and sense of grievance as the heart of the problem. Dickson Bruce, in *Violence and Culture in the Antebellum South*, argues that Southerners were violent despite themselves because they believed human relations were so fragile that violence was bound to result, that passion was bound to erupt despite elaborate formalities.

12. Peter Berger, Brigette Berger, and Hansfried Kellner, *The Homeless Mind: Modernization and Consciousness* (1973; New York: Vintage Books, 1974), pp. 83–84, 88–89; Franklin, *Militant South*; Steven M. Stowe, "The 'Touchiness' of the Gentleman Planter: The Sense of Esteem and Continuity in the Ante Bellum South," *Psychohistory Review* 8 (Winter 1979): 6–17. Wyatt-Brown's *Southern Honor* brilliantly describes that culture in all its ramifications, though with a different emphasis than the present book. William J. Cooper, *The South and the Politics of Slavery* (Baton Rouge: LSU, 1980), deals with the role of honor in politics.

13. Pierre Bourdieu, "The Sentiment of Honor in Kabyte Society," in J. G. Peristiany, ed., *Honour and Shame: The Values of Mediterranean Society* (London: Weidenfeld and Nicholson, 1966), p. 212; Sydnor, "Southerner and the Laws," pp. 17–18.

14. Faux quoted in Grady McWhiney and Perry D. Jamieson, *Attack and Die: Civil War Military Tactics and the Southern Heritage* (University : Univ. of Alabama Press, 1892), p. 171; on the importance of public opinion, see Wyatt-Brown, *Southern Honor*, pp. 45–46; Taylor, "Upper Class Violence," pp. 50–52; "South Carolina Morals," *Atlantic Monthly* 33 (April 1877): 468; W. Conrad Gass, "The Misfortune of a High-Minded and Honorable Gentlemen: W. W. Avery and the Southern Code of Honor," *North Carolina Historical Review* 56 (July 1979): 278–97.

15. Redfield, *Homicide*, pp. 188–89.

16. Ysabel Rennie, *The Search for Criminal Man: A Conceptual History of the Dangerous Offender* (Lexington, Mass.: Lexington Books, 1978), p. 132; Ian R. Tyrrell, "Drink and Temperance in the Antebellum South: An Overview and Interpretation," *Journal of Southern History* 48 (Nov. 1982): 485–510; William B. Taylor, *Drinking, Homicide, and Rebellion in Colonial Mexican Villages* (Stanford: Stanford Univ. Press, 1979), pp. 70–71.

17. *Nation* 35 (Nov. 9, 1882): 400.

18. Ramage, "Homicide," p. 216.

19. William Thomson quoted in Clement Eaton, *The Waning of the Old South Civilization, 1860–1880's* (Athens: Univ. of Georgia Press, 1968), p. 4.

20. William Oliver Stevens, *Pistols at Ten Paces: The Story of the Code of Honor in America* (Boston: Houghton Mifflin, 1940), pp. 12–13, 50, 73, 77–78; David Brion Davis, *Homicide in American Fiction, 1790–1860: A Study in Social Values* (Ithaca: Cornell Univ. Press, 1957), p. 270; Jack K. Williams, *Dueling in the Old South: Vignettes of Social History* (College Station: Texas A & M Univ. Press, 1980); Wyatt-Brown, *Southern Honor*, chap. 13; Hindus, *Prison and Plantation*, pp. 42–48; Donna Andrew, "The Code of Honour and Its Critics: The Opposition to Duelling in England, 1700–1850," *Social History* 5 (Oct. 1980): 409–34.

21. Hinton Rowan Helper, *The Impending Crisis* (1857), reprinted in Harvey Wish, ed., *Ante-Bellum: Writings of George Fitzhugh and Hinton Rowan Helper on Slavery* (New York: Capricorn, 1960), pp. 209–10.

22. Stowe, " 'Touchiness'," pp. 7, 14–15.

23. Sydnor, "Southerner and the Laws" pp. 15, 17; Robert Dawidoff, *The Education of John Randolph* (New York: Norton, 1979), p. 255.

24. Timothy Flint, *Recollections of the Last Ten Years, Passed in Occasional Residence and Journeying in the Valley of the Mississippi* (1826; reprint, New York: Da Capo Press, 1968), pp. 180–81.

25. Stevens, *Pistols*, p. 40; Jack K. Williams, *Vogues in Villainy: Crime and Retribution in Antebellum South Carolina* (Columbia: Univ. of South Carolina Press, 1959), p. 243; Michael P. Rogin, *Fathers and Children: Andrew Jackson and the Subjugation of the American Indian* (1975; reprint, New York: Vintage Books, 1976), p. 58; Bruce, *Violence and Culture*, p. 27; Davis, *Homicide*, pp. 269–70.

26. Joseph G. Baldwin, *Flush Times of Alabama and Mississippi: A Series of Sketches* (New York: Appleton, 1853), pp. 58–59; Alexis de Tocqueville, *Journey to America*, trans. George Lawrence; ed. J. P. Mayer (New Haven: Yale Univ. Press, 1960), p. 103.

27. Julian Pitt-Rivers, "Honor and Social Status," in Peristiany, *Honour and Shame*, p. 30; Mrs. Jackson quoted in Rogin, *Fathers and Children*, p. 58; Baldwin, *Flush Times,* p. 58. Blackstone quoted in Wyatt-Brown, *Southern Honor*, p. 549, n. 22.

28. Beveridge and McLaughlin, *Papers of Olmsted*, 2:232–33.

29. David Macrae, *The Americans at Home* (Edinburgh: Edmonston and Douglas, 1870) 2:152; Julian Pitt-Rivers, "Honor," in *International Encyclopedia of the Social Sciences*, David L. Sills, ed. (New York: Macmillan, 1968) 6:508. On the narrowness and specificity of causes for violence in general see Albert Bandura, *Aggression: A Social Learning Analysis* (Englewood Cliffs, N.J.: Prentice-Hall, 1973).

30. On the relationship between manners and violence in the South, see Bruce, *Violence and Culture*, pp. 67–88; Wyatt-Brown, *Southern Honor*, chap. 13; Philip Greven, *The Protestant Temperament: Patterns of Child-Rearing, Religious Experience, and the Self in Early America* (New York: Knopf, 1977), p. 319.

31. Berger et al., *Homeless Mind*, pp. 83–84, 88–89, suggest the terms "honor" and "dignity."

32. S. S. MacClintock, "The Kentucky Mountaineers and Their Feuds," *American Journal of Sociology* 7 (July 1901): 171.

33. T. H. Breen, ed., *Shaping Southern Society: The Colonial Experience* (New York: Oxford Univ. Pres, 1976), p. 5; David Grayson Allen, *In English Ways: The Movement of Societies and the Transferal of English Local Law and Customs to Massachusetts Bay in the Seventeenth Century* (Chapel Hill: UNC, 1981).

34. Lawrence Stone, *The Crisis of the Aristocracy, 1558–1641* (Oxford: Oxford Univ. Press, 1965), pp. 223–25, 269.

35. Rhys Isaac, "Evangelical Revolt: The Nature of the Baptists' Challenge to the Traditional Order in Virginia, 1765 to 1775," in Breen, *Shaping Southern Society*, pp. 247–65; quote from pp. 150–51. Also see A. G. Roeber, "Authority, Law, and Custom: The Rituals of Court Day in Tidewater Virginia, 1720 to 1750," *William and Mary Quarterly*, 3rd ser., 37 (Jan. 1980): 29–52; on the self-conscious adoption of the values of the English gentry, see Bernard Bailyn, "Politics and Social Structure in Virginia," in Breen, *Shaping Southern Society*, pp. 200–201; Dawidoff, *John Randolph*, p. 72.

36. *Journal and Letters of Philip Vickers Fithian, 1773–1774: A Plantation Tutor of the Old Dominion*, Hunter Dickinson Farish, ed. (Williamsburg: Colonial Williamsburg, 1943), pp. 240–41.

37. Quoted in Charles S. Sydnor, *American Revolutionaries in the Making: Political Practices in Washington's Virginia* (1952; reprint, New York: Free Press, 1965),

p. 27. On the high rates of homicide throughout English society in the fourteenth century, see Barbara Hanawalt, *Crime and Conflict in English Communities, 1300–1348* (Cambridge: Harvard Univ. Press, 1979), pp. 96–101, 273.

38. Carl Bridenbaugh, *Myths and Realities: Societies of the Colonial South* (1952; reprint, New York: Atheneum, 1962), p. 133; biographer of Jackson quoted in Robert Kelley, *The Cultural Patterns in American Politics: The First Century* (New York: Knopf, 1979), pp. 146–47. Also see James G. Leyburn, *The Scotch-Irish: A Social History* (Chapel Hill: UNC, 1962), pp. 3, 6, 9–10, 46, 69–70, 183; E. E. Evans, "The Scotch-Irish: Their Cultural Adaptation and Heritage in the American Old West," in E.R.R. Greene, ed., *Essays in Scotch-Irish History* (London: Routledge and Kegan Paul, 1969). One the mountaineers, see Horace Kephart, *Our Southern Highlanders* (1913; reprint, Knoxville: Univ. of Tennessee Press, 1976), p. 285; Otis K. Rice, *The Allegheny Frontier: West Virginia Beginnings, 1730–1830* (Lexington: Univ. of Kentucky Press, 1970), p. 182.

39. Kelley, *Cultural Patterns*, pp. 71–74; on the similarity between assault rates in colonial North Carolina and New York, see Donna J. Spindel, "The Administration of Criminal Justice in North Carolina, 1720–1740," *American Journal of Legal History* 25 (April 1981): 161. Douglas Greenberg offers an excellent portrayal of New York, stressing the diversity of the colony, in his *Crime and Law Enforcement in the Colony of New York, 1691–1776* (Ithaca: Cornell Univ. Press, 1974).

40. David Thomas Konig, *Law and Society in Puritan Massachusetts: Essex County, 1629–1692* (Chapel Hill: UNC, 1979), pp. 190–91. On the paucity of violent crime in Puritan Massachusetts, see David H. Flaherty, "Crime and Social Control in Provincial Massachusetts," *Historical Journal* 24 (1981): 339–60; Kai T. Erikson, *Wayward Puritans: A Study in the Sociology of Deviance* (New York: Wiley, 1966), pp. 175–76; Eli Faber, "Puritan Criminals: The Economic, Social, and Intellectual Background to Crime in Seventeenth-Century Massachusetts," *Perspectives in American History* 11 (1977–78): 83–114. On the conflict that did exist in New England, see Lyle Koehler, *A Search for Power: The "Weaker Sex" in Seventeenth-Century New England* (Urbana: Univ. of Illinois Press, 1980), esp. chap. 7.

41. On Puritans and the renunciation of honor, see Julian Pitt-Rivers, *The Fate of Shechem or the Politics of Sex: Essays in the Anthropology of the Mediterranean* (Cambridge: Cambridge Univ. Press, 1977), p. 36; on Puritans and the celebration of self, see Perry Miller, *The New England Mind: The Seventeenth Century* (Cambridge: Harvard Univ. Press, 1954), p. 449; James Henretta, *The Evolution of American Society, 1700–1815: An Interdisciplinary Analysis* (Lexington, Mass: D.C. Heath, 1973), pp. 100–101.

42. On the complex relationship of the American Whig ideology and "modernity," see Daniel Walker Howe, *The Political Culture of the American Whigs* (Chicago: Univ. of Chicago Press, 1979); Kelley, *Cultural Patterns*, pp. 164–65. On the ideology of the Republicans, the classic work is Eric Foner, *Free Soil, Free Labor, Free Men: The Ideology of the Republican Party Before the Civil War* (New York: Oxford Univ. Press, 1970).

43. On the new fusion of Protestantism and capitalism in the antebellum era, see Paul E. Johnson, *A Shopkeeper's Millennium: Society and Revivals in Rochester, New York, 1815–1837* (New York: Hill and Wang, 1978). The way New England culture was spread throughout the North is well described in Whitney R. Cross,

The Burned-Over District: The Social and Intellectual History of Enthusiastic Religion in
Western New York, 1800–1850 (1950; reprint, New York: Harper Torchbook,
1965), and Foner, *Free Soil*, pp. 106–8.

44.

	Proportion of suicides to 10,000 of all deaths, 1860	Proportion of homicides to 10,000 of all deaths, 1860
Southern average	18	672
Northern average	33	502
National average	27	565

SOURCE: *Eighth Census of the United States, Mortality* (Washington, 1866), 235. Also see Hackney's article "Southern Violence," which is constructed around the concept of the suicide-homicide ratio.

45. Lewis O. Saum, *The Popular Mood of Pre-Civil War America* (Westport, Conn.:
Greenwood Press, 1980), pp. 170, 220; Ronald G. Walters, "The Erotic South:
Civilization and Sexuality in American Abolitionism," *American Quarterly* 25
(1973): 177–201.

46. On such opinions held by many Northerners concerning the South, see Foner,
Free Soil, pp. 40–72.

47. Wyatt-Brown, *Southern Honor*, pp. 15–17.

48. J. Davis explains the necessity of smallness of scale, undiversified economy, and
stratification to honor in his *People of the Mediterranean: An Essay in Comparative
Social Anthropology* (London:Routledge and Kegan Paul, 1977), pp. 77–78, 98–99,
101–7; on the corrosive effect of pluralism on honor, see Pitt-Rivers, *Fate of
Shechem*, pp. 1–2; Orlando Patterson, *Slavery and Social Death: A Comparative Study*
(Cambridge: Harvard Univ. Press, 1982), p. 99. The phrase "unthinking
decision" is from Winthrop Jordan, *White Over Black: American Attitudes Toward the
Negro, 1550–1812* (Chapel Hill: UNC, 1968). Stephen Innes has explored the
patterns of patronage that preceded free labor capitalism in the colonial North
in his *Labor in a New Land: Economy and Society in Seventeenth-Century Springfield*
(Princeton: Princeton Univ. Press, 1983).

49. Richard Lyle Power, *Planting Corn Belt Culture: The Impress of the Upland Southerner
and Yankee in the Old Northwest* (Indianapolis: Indiana Historical Society, 1953),
pp. 122, 84. On the failure of the market to dominate the rural North, see
Nugent, *Structures of American Social History*, pp. 80–81.

50. Rhys Isaac, *The Tranformation of Virginia, 1740–1790* (Chapel Hill: UNC, 1982),
esp. p. 120; Isaac's groundbreaking work has significantly altered our
understanding of the colonial South. As Samuel Hill, Jr., has pointed out, the
evangelical South and a self-conscious South came into being simultaneously;
religion has been a crucial part of the region as long as the South has considered
itself a unique society: *The South and the North in American Religion* (Athens: Univ.
of Georgia Press, 1980), chap. 2. For a fuller account of religion in the
antebellum South, see Chapter Four.

51. Donald B. Mathews, *Religion in the Old South* (Chicago: Univ. of Chicago Press,
1977), pp. 37–38. Along with that of Mathews, Anne C. Loveland's work is
crucial for an understanding of Southern religion. Her *Southern Evangelicals and
the Social Order, 1800–1860* (Baton Rouge: LSU, 1980) stresses the fatalistic
outlook of the ministers of Southern Protestantism. On changes in Northern
religion and culture, see Ann Douglas, *The Feminization of American Culture* (New
York: Knopf, 1977).

52. On women and evangelical religion, see Mathews, *Religion in the Old South*, pp. 101–24; Catherine Clinton, *The Plantation Mistress: Woman's World in the Old South* (New York: Pantheon Books, 1982), pp. 95–96, 160–63.
53. Rev. Arthur Wigfall, "Sermon Upon Duelling," *Southern Presbyterian Review* 10 (1857–58): 130.
54. Ibid., pp. 126–28.
55. *Watchman and Observer*, Jan. 27, 1848, p. 95, quoted in Loveland, *Southern Evangelicals*, pp. 181–82; "The Tabor Duel," *Central Presbyterian*, Jan. 10, 1857.
56. Wigfall, "Sermon," pp. 131, 129; *Watchman and Observer*, June 19, 1851, p. 178, and Feb. 3, 1848, p. 97, quoted in Loveland, *Southern Evangelicals*, p. 182; *Central Presbyterian*, Jan. 10, 1857; comment on Wigfall in *Southern Presbyterian Review* 10 (1857–58): 131. Loveland concludes, "Evangelicals employed a good deal of argumentation in an effort to discredit the code of honor which sustained dueling in the Old South." The antebellum South witnessed the formation of a number of antidueling societies, largely led by evangelicals: see John Christie Dann, "Humanitarian Reform and Organized Benevolence in the Southern United States, 1780–1830" (Ph.D. diss., College of William and Mary, 1975), pp. 283–84; Joanne V. Hawks, "Social Reform in the Cotton Kingdom, 1830–1860" (Ph.D. diss., Univ. of Mississippi, 1969), p. 85, n. 142.
57. Sydnor, "Southerner and the Laws"; Cash, *Mind of the South*, pp. 34–35.
58. Edward W. Phifer, "Slavery in Microcosm: Burke County, North Carolina," in Elinor Miller and Eugene D. Genovese, eds., *Plantation, Town, and County: Essays on the Local History of American Slavery* (Urbana: Univ. of Illinois Press, 1974), pp. 78–79. As Rhys Isaac has written of the courts in colonial Virginia, "A society dominated by landholders, jealous of their independence and litigious in the defense of their boundaries and entitlements, could not but attach great importance to the arena in which conflicts over matters of this kind were joined and their issue determined": *Tranformation*, p. 90. Dickson Bruce also stresses the positive role of law in the antebellum South: *Violence and Culture*, pp. 80–81. On an actual overabundance of lawyers in at least part of the South, see E. Lee Shepard, "Breaking into the Profession: Establishing a Law Practice in Antebellum Virginia," *Journal of Southern History* 48 (Aug. 1982): 393–410.
59. Beveridge and McLaughlin, *Papers of Olmsted* 2:155–56; Sydnor, "Southerner and the Laws," pp. 7–8. There was sufficient opposition to dueling among influential men in the South that the state constitutions of at least four states barred duelists from office. See Ralph A. Wooster, *Politicians, Planters, and Plain Folk: Courthouse and Statehouse in the Upper South, 1850–1860* (Knoxville: Univ. of Tennessee Press, 1975), pp. 6, 9, 12, 16.
60. J.F.H. Claiborne, *Mississippi as a Province, Territory and State* (Jackson: Power and Barksdale, 1880) 1:482; Reuben Davis, *Recollections of Mississippi and Mississippians* (Boston: Houghton Mifflin, 1889), p. 104.
61. Lawrence Friedman, *A History of American Law* (New York: Touchstone Books, 1973), p. 253; Davis, *Homicide*, pp. 300–301. Michael Hindus in *Prison and Plantation* stresses the inefficiency of Southern justice, as does Robert M. Ireland in "Law and Disorder in Nineteenth-Century Kentucky," *Vanderbilt Law Review* 32 (1979): 281–99; but see the important correctives offered by Mary K. B. Tachau immediately following, pp. 301–4. In Marion County, Indiana (surely more typical of the North than Massachusetts, offered by Michael Hindus as an archetype of efficient Northern criminal justice), over half of all indictments

failed to reach a decision; 40 percent simply disappeared. See Bodenhamer, "Law and Disorder," p. 335 and n. 36. Roger Lane, in *Violent Death in the City: Suicide, Accident, and Murder in Nineteenth-Century Philadelphia* (Cambridge: Harvard University Press, 1979), pp. 66–67, has detailed the low rates of conviction for violent crimes in nineteenth-century Philadelphia. Southern justice, by modern standards, *was* rather lax, but its laxity needs to be kept in historical perspective.

62. For a fuller description of the role of the state in the South, see Chapters Two, Three, and Four. The relationship between honor and the law is also described in the Conclusion, esp. note 3.

Chapter 2. The Penitentiary in the Old South

1. Hawthorne quoted in Tom Wicker, *A Time to Die* (1975; reprint, New York: Ballantine Books, 1976), p. 421. In their classic work, *Punishment and Social Structure* (New York: Columbia University Press, 1939), pp. 6–7, Georg Rusche and Otto Kirchheimer argue, "Only a specific development of the productive forces permits the introduction or rejection of corresponding penalties." In other words, a society supposedly adopts only those forms of punishment it can "incorporate . . . as integral parts of the whole social and economic system." On the surface, at least, the Southern penitentiary would seem to be an exception.

2. For decades, historians perceived the penitentiary as a dramatic improvement over the past. The two most influential books on the American penitentiary written from this perspective were Orlando F. Lewis, *The Development of American Prisons and Prison Customs, 1776–1845* (Albany: Prison Association of New York, 1922), and Blake McKelvey, *American Prisons: A Study in American Social History Prior to 1915* (Chicago: Univ. of Chicago Press, 1936). Both books are still useful. W. David Lewis's account of prisons in New York challenged the older view of penal reform and offered what is still the most rounded treatment of the penitentiary in the antebellum United States: *From Newgate to Dannemora: The Rise of the Penitentiary in New York, 1796–1848* (Ithaca: Cornell Univ. Press, 1965). David Rothman, by showing how the American penitentiary was part of a broad movement toward institutionalization in the Jacksonian era, heightened and altered historians' perception of the phenomena dramatically; see his *Discovery of the Asylum: Social Order and Disorder in the New Republic* (Boston: Little, Brown, 1971). Rothman stressed the "social control" function of the penitentiary and thus reflected a growing disenchantment with the institution. The strongest critique of all sorts of asylums, however, came from Michel Foucault, whose *Madness and Civilization: A History of Insanity in the Age of Reason*, trans. Richard Howard (1965; reprint, New York: Vintage Books, 1973), and *Discipline and Punish: The Birth of the Prison*, trans. Alan Sheridan (New York: Pantheon, 1977), offered a vision of institutions as part of a vast network of incarceration symptomatic of modern society.

3. See Michael Ignatieff, *A Just Measure of Pain: The Penitentiary in the Industrial Revolution, 1750–1850* (New York: Pantheon, 1978), which deals with the rise of the institution in England, and Dario Melossi and Massimo Pavarini, *The Prison and the Factory: Origins of the Penitentiary System*, trans. Glynic Cousin (1977; trans. London: Macmillan, 1981).

4. J. Thorsten Sellin, *Slavery and the Penal System* (New York: Elsevier, 1976), pp. 70–112; on the state of these institutions in England at the time of the birth of the penitentiary, see Ignatieff, *Just Measure*, pp. 29–43; on workhouses in colonial America, see Drew R. McCoy, *The Elusive Republic: Political Economy in Jeffersonian America* (Chapel Hill: UNC, 1980), pp. 116–17; on their presence in Virginia, see John Patrick Shevock, "Poor Relief in Colonial Virginia" (Master's thesis, University of Virginia, 1979), pp. 45–56.

5. John K. Alexander, *Render Them Submissive: Responses to Poverty in Philadelphia, 1760–1800* (Amherst: Univ. of Massachusetts Press, 1981), pp. 61–85, 165–66.

6. John Howard, *The State of the Prisons in England and Wales*, 4th ed. (London: Printed for J. Johnson, C. Dilly, et al., 1792); Ignatieff, *Just Measure*, pp. 44–79.

7. W. D. Lewis, *From Newgate to Dannemora*, pp. 16–23; Foucault, *Discipline and Punish*, pp. 236–37.

8. Samuel Walker, *Popular Justice: A History of American Criminal Justice* (New York: Oxford Univ. Press, 1980), pp. 48–49; Jefferson quoted in Terrence M. Slaven, "Curing the Moral Disease: The Penitentiary in Jeffersonian Virginia" (Master's thesis, Univ. of Virginia, 1972), pp. 7–9.

9. Rothman, *Discovery*, pp. 88–94.

10. "The 'Penitentiary House,' " *Virginia Cavalcade* 6 (Summer 1956): 11–17; Slaven, "Curing the Moral Disease"; Orlando Lewis, *Development*, pp. 210–15; Norman Johnston, *The Human Cage: A Brief History of Prison Architecture* (New York: Walker, 1973), p. 21.

11. Gov. George M. Troup, quoted in Edward J. Harden, *The Life of George M. Troup* (Savannah: E. J. Purse, 1859), pp. 227–28; John Christie Dann, "Humanitarian Reform and Organized Benevolence in the Southern United States, 1780–1830" (Ph.D. diss., College of William and Mary, 1975), pp. 265–66; William C. Sneed, *A Report on the History and Mode of Management of the Kentucky Penitentiary* (Frankfort: J. B. Major, State Printer, 1860), pp. 15–16, 21, 46; Marvin Gettleman, "The Maryland Penitentiary in the Age of Tocqueville, 1828–1842," *Maryland Historical Magazine* 61 (1961): 269–90.

12. Rothman, *Discovery*, pp. 79–108.

13. Gustave de Beaumont and Alexis de Tocqueville, *On the Penitentiary System in the United States and Its Application to France* (1833; reprint, Carbondale: Southern Illinois Univ. Press, 1964), p. 65.

14. W. D. Lewis, *From Newgate to Dannemora*, p. 28; Christopher Lasch, "Origins of the Asylum," in *The World of Nations: Reflections on American History, Politics, and Culture* (New York: Knopf, 1973), pp. 3–17. I have been greatly influenced by Lasch's elegant and suggestive essay.

15. Foucault, *Discipline and Punish*, pp. 232–33; Lasch, "Origins," p. 17.

16. Beaumont and Tocqueville, *On the Penitentiary System* p. 79; Louis Hartz, *The Liberal Tradition in America: An Interpretation of American Political Thought Since the Revolution* (New York: Harvest Books, 1955), pp. 56–57; on the ideals and tensions surrounding the moral state of a republican people, see Gordon Wood, *The Creation of the American Republic, 1776–1787* (1969; reprint, New York: Norton, 1972), pp. 68, 91–124.

17. On the various meanings of republicanism, see Robert Kelley, *The Cultural Patterns in American Politics: The First Century* (New York: Knopf, 1979), pp. 83–85;

Robert Shalhope, "Thomas Jefferson's Republicanism and Antebellum South-ern Thought," *Journal of Southern History* 42 (1976): 533; Dorothy Ross, "The **Liberal Tradition Revisited and the Republican Tradition Addressed**," in John Higham and Paul K. Conkin, eds., *New Directions in American Intellectual History* (Baltimore: John Hopkins Univ. Press, 1979), pp. 116–31.

18. George McDuffie, quoted in William Freehling, *Prelude to Civil War: The Nullification Controversy in South Carolina, 1816–1836* (1966; reprint, New York, Harper Torchbook, 1968), p. 330. On Southern republicanism and slavery, see Edmund S. Morgan, *American Slavery-American Freedom: The Ordeal of Colonial Virginia* (New York: Norton, 1975), esp. pp. 381–85; J. Mills Thornton, *Politics and Power in a Slave Society: Alabama, 1800–1860* (Baton Rouge: LSU, 1978); Michael F. Holt, *The Political Crisis of the 1850s* (New York: Wiley, 1978); Harry L. Watson, *Jacksonian Politics and Community Conflict: The Emergence of the Second American Party System in Cumberland County, North Carolina* (Baton Rouge: LSU, 1981); Fred Siegel, "The Paternalist Thesis: Virginia as a Test Case," *Civil War History* 25 (Sept. 1979): 246–61. On democracy in the antebellum South, see George Fredrickson, *The Black Image in the White Mind: The Debate on Afro-American Character and Destiny, 1817–1914* (New York: Harper, 1971), pp. 61–70; Fletcher Green, *Constitutional Development in the South Atlantic States, 1776–1860* (Chapel Hill: UNC, 1930); Charles Sydnor, *Development of Southern Sectionalism, 1819–1848* (Baton Rouge: LSU, 1948), esp. pp. 275–93. For important correctives, see **Eugene Genovese, "Yeoman Farmers in a Slaveholder's Democracy,"** *Agricultural History* 44 (1975): 331–42, and Joyce Appleby, "The Social Origins of American Revolutionary Ideology," *Journal of American History* 64 (March 1978): 935–58.

19. Rep. Thomas F. Fletcher, *Nashville Whig*, Dec. 2, 1826, in Robert H. White, ed., *Messages of the Governors of Tennessee* (Nashville: Tennessee Historical Commission, 1952–59) 2:161–62; also see *North Carolina Standard* (Raleigh), June 3, 1846; E. Bruce Thompson, "Penal Reform in Tennessee, 1820–1850," *Tennessee Historical Quarterly* 1 (1942): 297–98.

20. Mississippians quoted in E. Bruce Thompson, "Reforms in the Penal System of Mississippi," *Journal of Mississippi History* 7 (1945), 59–60; (Milledgeville) *Georgia Journal*, Jan. 12, 1829, speech of Rep. Sturges of Upson County; Boynton Merrill, Jr., *Jefferson's Nephews: A Frontier Tragedy* (1976; reprint, New York: Avon Books, 1978), p. 232. Such concerns highlight the importance of geographic mobility in the antebellum South, a mobility that may have created a perceived need for a state-level penal institution. The stocks and pillory depended upon a stable population and the presumed necessity of a good reputation. Public ridicule or humiliation did little good when no one knew the transient culprit or expected to see him again. See Rothman, *Discovery*, p. 50; Sydnor, *Development of Southern Sectionalism*, pp. 250–59; James B. Oakes, *The Ruling Race: A History of American Slaveholders* (New York: Knopf, 1982), pp. 76–95.

21. *Greensborough* (N. C.) *Patriot*, May 16, 1846: (Huntsville, Ala.)*Southern Advocate*, Sept. 24, 1833; Jan. 28, 1834.

22. (Milledgeville) *Georgia Journal*, Jan. 5, 1829; Virginia *House Journal*, 1823–24, p. 155.

23. *Greensborough Patriot*, May 9, 1846; April 25, 1846.

24. Reprinted in *Hillsborough* (N. C.) *Recorder*, March 18, 1846; *North Carolina Standard*, Oct. 8, 1845. For a summary of the reasons a republican government

needed to build a penitentiary, see "Giles," in *North Carolina Standard*, March 11, 1846; also see *Nashville Whig*, Oct. 10, 1829, in White, *Messages* 2:270; "Pineville," *Mobile Commercial Appeal and Patriot*, July 11, 1834.

25. Sneed, *Kentucky Penitentiary*, p. 591.

26. Rep. Holmes of McIntosh County, in *Georgia Journal*, Dec. 11, 1828.

27. Rep. Lewis Reneau of Sevier county in *Nashville Whig*, Dec. 2, 1826, in White, *Messages* 2:168, 279; Lacey quoted in Guion Griffis Johnson, *Ante-Bellum North Carolina: A Social History* (Chapel Hill: UNC, 1937), p. 663. For a detailed account of opposition to the penitentiary in South Carolina, see Michael Hindus, *Prison and Plantation: Crime, Justice, and Authority in Massachusetts and South Carolina, 1767–1878* (Chapel Hill: UNC, 1980), pp. 215–25. Also see Jack K. Williams, *Vogues in Villainy: Crime and Retribution in Antebellum South Carolina* (Columbia: Univ. of South Carolina Press, 1959), p. 129. The case of Delaware is also instructive: Robert G. Caldwell, *The Penitentiary Movement in Delaware, 1776 to 1829* (Wilmington: Historical Society of Delaware, 1946).

28. *Southern Recorder*, Nov. 22, 1859; Rep. Miller of Chatham County, *Georgia Journal*, Jan. 5, 1829; Lewis Reneau in White, *Messages* 2:168; "Onslow," *North Carolina Standard*, May 13, 1846; see South Carolina committee report in Hindus, *Prison and Plantation*, pp. 285–86.

29. Reneau in White, *Messages* 2:168; "Capital Punishment," *Southern Presbyterian Review*, Dec. 1847, p. 10.

30. *Georgia Journal*, Jan. 5, 1829, speech of Rep. Holt of Clark County; Jan. 19, 1829, speech of Rep. Nesbit of Morgan County.

31. *Georgia Journal*, Jan. 5, 1829, speech of Rep. Sturges; Tennessee *House Journal*, 1821, pp. 146–47; Gov. Adair, message to the Kentucky Legislature, 1821, in Sneed, *Kentucky Penitentiary*, p. 116. On the travails of the Georgia penitentiary, see "Report of the Penitentiary Committee," Georgia *Senate Journal*, 1823, pp. 183, 187, 214; James C. Bonner, "The Georgia Penitentiary at Milledgeville, 1817–1868," *Georgia Historical Quarterly* 55 (1971): 307.

32. *Greensborough Patriot*, Feb. 21, 1846.

33. *North Carolina Standard*, April 22, 1846.

34. Ibid.

35. *Mobile Commercial Register and Patriot*, Nov. 20, Nov. 27, Dec. 11, 1833; Joanne V. Hawks, "Social Reform in the Cotton Kingdom, 1830–1860" (Ph.D. diss., Univ. of Mississippi, 1969), pp. 61–62. On the vote, see *Southern Advocate*, Aug. 12, 1834; *Mobile Commercial Register and Patriot*, Aug. 6, 1834; for Gov. Gayle's remarks, *Southern Advocate*, Nov. 23, 1834. As far as I could discover, the final tally was never published.

36. Johnson, *Ante-Bellum North Carolina*, pp. 661–73; *North Carolina Standard*, Sept. 10, 1845; (Raleigh) *Star*, Oct. 15, 1845; *North Carolina Standard*, Sept. 24, 1845.

37. Computed from returns in North Carolina Legislative Papers, 1846–47 (L.P. 628), *Greensborough Patriot*, Aug. 22, 1846, and *North Carolina Standard*, Aug. 12, 19, 1846. The three counties that returned majorities in favor of the penitentiary were Pasquotank (87.7%), Perquimons (71.0%), and Craven (59.2%). Out of a total vote of 66,829, only 14,891 voted in favor of a penitentiary.

38. *North Carolina Standard*, June 24, 1846; Sept. 16, 1846. Whigs did support other institutions in North Carolina. In 1844–45, only one year before the vote on the penitentiary, over 90 percent of the legislative votes for an insane asylum and

over 75 percent of the votes in favor of a school for the deaf and dumb came
from Whigs. See Marc W. Kruman, *Parties and Politics in North Carolina, 1836–
1865* (Baton Rouge: LSU, 1983), pp. 57–63. The penitentiary was neglected
in relation to these institutions in Georgia as well, as Peter Wallenstein shows in
his "From Slave South to New South: Taxes and Spending in Georgia from
1850 Through Reconstruction" (Ph.D. diss., John Hopkins Univ., 1973), p. 180.
Mental institutions in the South, unlike penitentiaries, were inspired by outside
reformers, especially Dorothea Dix, who "commented that the South taken as a
region showed little contrast to other sections of the country she had visited":
Elizabeth Wisner, *Social Welfare in the South: From Colonial Times to World War I*
(Baton Rouge: LSU, 1970), pp. 53–66. By 1860 all Southern states except
Florida had established mental hospitals. See Clark R. Cahow, entry for
"Mental Health," *Encyclopedia of Southern History* (Baton Rouge: LSU, 1979), p.
812.

39. Robert B. Gilliam to William A. Graham, March 29, 1846, quoted in Kruman,
Parties and Politics, p. 62. On the amorphousness of party identity in the South,
see Thornton, *Politics and Power*, p. 97; on the complex relationship between
politics and penitentiary in Georgia, see Paul Murray, *The Whig Party in Georgia,
1825–1853* (Chapel Hill: UNC, 1948), pp. 37–38, 98, 198. A. Fulcher's story is
told in Mary Patricia Walden, "History of the Georgia Penitentiary at
Milledgeville, 1817–1868" (Master's thesis, Georgia State Univ., 1974), p. 50.
For the Charles H. Nelson affair, see the *Southern Banner* (Athens), Aug. 29,
1844, citing the *Southern Whig*, Dec. 16, 1843. I would like to thank Gayle Martin
for calling this and the Crawford quote in the next note to my attention.

40. George W. Crawford to John M. Berrien, Jan. 1, 1845, in John M. Berrien
Papers, microfilm at the University of Virginia; on the turnover in principal
keepers, see Walden, "Georgia Penitentiary," pp. 49–50. The role of Southern
governors is described in Thompson, "Reforms in Mississippi," pp. 60–61;
Thornton, *Politics and Power*, p. 83; Hindus, *Prison and Plantation*, pp. 211–13.

41. *Southern Advocate*, Jan. 28, 1834.

42. *Savannah Georgian*, Jan. 1, 1829; Gov. William Carroll in White, *Messages* 2:142;
for a defense of the penitentiary in view of "the difficulties . . . attendant upon
all great and novel undertakings," see Gov. Gilmer's comments in Georgia
Senate Journal, 1831, p. 16. The distinction between "cosmopolitan" and
"localistic" seems to explain much of the alignment on the penitentiary. As
Jackson Turner Main has written in his *Political Parties Before the Constitution* (1973;
reprint, New York: Norton, 1974), "To the commercial-cosmopolitans almost
everything that governments did was beneficial as long as they themselves
exercised power—as, in one way or another, they generally could. . . . The kind
of democracy advocated by the other side they regarded as menacing, because it
meant government by narrow men, who possessed little or no property, were
unfit to rule, and really sought no government at all" (p. 395). This pattern
intersected with both class and geography: "large landowners, lawyers, and
traders voted with the Cosmopolitans regardless of where they lived, but . . . the
political preference of artisans depended upon their residence, not their
occupation"(p. 374). I suspect that this was the pattern in the antebellum South
as well.

43. *North Carolina Standard*, Oct. 8, 1845; Olmsted quoted in William L. Barney, *The
Secessionist Impulse: Alabama and Mississippi in 1860* (Princeton: Princeton Univ.

Press, 1974), pp. 41–42. For a sophisticated statement of the connection between humanitarianism and class legislation in general, see William A. Muraskin, "The Social Control Theory in American History: A Critique," *Journal of Social History* 9 (Summer 1976): 559–68. The striving for "benevolence" in the South—as elsewhere—was often part of the process by which a dominant class establishes hegemony over others in a society. "Hegemony" in this sense is a system of values held throughout society which sanctions and supports the existing social order. The concept was developed by Antonio Gramsci and has been applied to the South by Eugene Genovese; see "On Antonio Gramsci," in Genovese's *In Red and Black: Marxian Explorations in Southern and Afro-American History* (New York: Pantheon, 1971), and *Roll, Jordan, Roll: The World the Slaves Made* (1974; reprint, New York: Vintage Books, 1976), esp. pp. 25–49, 148–49. For the clearest and most succinct statement of the meaning of hegemony and ideology as intended here, see David Brion Davis, *The Problem of Slavery in the Age of Revolution, 1770–1823* (Ithaca: Cornell Univ. Press, 1975), pp. 349–50.

44. Barney, *Secessionist Impulse*, p. 53. On elsewhere in the South, see Ralph A. Wooster, *Politicians, Planters, and Plain Folk: Courthouse and Statehouse in the Upper South, 1850–1860* (Knoxville: Univ. of Tennessee Press, 1975), p. 33; Oakes, *The Ruling Race*, p. 61. Sir William Blackstone, *Commentaries on the Laws of England* (New York: W. E. Dean, 1852) 2:1–13; on Blackstone's influence, see Walker, *Popular Justice*, p. 44; Dennis R. Nolan, "Sir William Blackstone and the New American Republic: A Study of Intellectual Impact," *New York University Law Review* 51 (Nov. 1976): 731–68; on Blackstone and prison reform, see David H. Lockmiller, *Sir William Blackstone* (Chapel Hill: UNC, 1938), pp. 128–31.

45. *North Carolina Standard*, Oct. 8, 1845; Virginia *House Journal*, 1823–24, pp. 31–32.

46. On grand juries, see Hindus, *Prison and Plantation*, p. 213. Subscription records show that 23 citizens from Tennessee and 72 from Kentucky supported the Boston Prison Discipline Society (BPDS) in 1843: *Eighteenth Report*, BPDS (1843), pp. 326–30; other examples of Southern knowledge of and concern for "advanced" thinking on the penitentiary include glowing comments on Francis Lieber's translation of Beaumont and Tocqueville's book on American prisons (*Southern Advocate*, Sept. 3, 1833); visits by Virginia officials to the Pennsylvania penitentiary (Virginia *House Journal*, 1830–31, doc. 1, pp. 12–13); and the presentation of the reports of penitentiaries in other states ([Raleigh] *Star*, Feb. 25, 1846; *Hillsborough Recorder*, March 4, 1846; *Greensborough Patriot*, March 7, 1846). Jack K. Williams believed "public opinion" in South Carolina wanted a penitentiary: *Vogues in Villainy*, p. 131. Although E. Bruce Thompson believed that in Tennessee "the greatest demand for reform came from the artisans and the yeoman farmers" who considered prepenitentiary punishment "reminiscent of the medieval system of privilege and inconsistent with the spirit of republican government" ("Penal Reform," pp. 291–92), Peter Wallenstein seems closer to the mark when he shows that in Georgia "it was the representatives of the wealthier counties—the black belt and the towns—and not those of the poorer districts who provided most of the votes to enlarge state education and welfare expenditures" ("Slave South to New South," p. 186). Marc Kruman helps us understand the scattered pattern of support for the penitentiary in North Carolina when he demonstrates that "local notables" often shaped voting patterns more than did "socioeconomic and geographic

conditions," and that "these opinion-shapers, more than others, were likely to
be aware of and have a personal interest in the economic and constitutional
conflicts of the day" (*Parties and Politics*, pp. 16–18). Some local leaders
apparently opposed the penitentiary, perhaps for the same reason members of
the English ruling class in the eighteenth century opposed legal reform: they
were more interested in defending their *authority*, their control over local justice,
than in rationalizing the law to protect their property. This comparison actually
serves to highlight the extent to which Southern elites (at least those who sought
and attained office) partook of cosmopolitan republican ideology rather than
purely local power. See Douglas Hay, "Property, Authority and the Criminal
Law," in Hay et al, eds., *Albion's Fatal Tree: Crime and Society in Eighteenth-Century
England* (London: Allen Lane, 1975).

47. Plumer quoted in Anne C. Loveland, *Southern Evangelicals and the Social Order,
1800–1860* (Baton Rouge: LSU, 1980), pp. 163–64; Lieber quoted in Frank
Freidel, *Francis Lieber: Nineteenth-Century Liberal* (Baton Rouge: LSU, 1947), p.
259; *Watchman of the South*, Feb. 10, 1842, p. 98; "Capital Punishment," *Southern
Presbyterian Review*, Dec. 1847, pp. 8, 13.

48. On the resistance of Southern evangelicals to "secular" reform, see Loveland,
Southern Evangelicals, pp. 125–29; Donald G. Mathews, *Religion in the Old South*
(Chicago: Univ. of Chicago Press, 1978), pp. 1–38; Williams, *Vogues in Villainy*,
pp. 129–30.

49. Gov. Hugh McVay, Alabama *Senate Journal*, 1837, p. 8; *Mobile Commercial Register
and Patriot*, July 18, 1834.

50. Williams, *Vogues in Villainy*, p. 113; Perry quoted in Lillian A. Kibler, *Benjamin F.
Perry: South Carolina Unionist* (Durham: Duke Univ. Press, 1946), p. 231.

51. James M. Banner, Jr., "The Problem of South Carolina," in Stanley Elkins and
Eric McKitrick, eds., *The Hofstadter Aegis: A Memorial* (New York: Knopf, 1974),
pp. 60–93; Hawks, "Social Reform," p. 81; Green, *Constitutional Development*, pp.
249–51; Freehling, *Prelude*, pp. 89–91. My interpretation differs from that of
Michael Hindus, who posits a more elaborate argument for the failure of South
Carolina to build a penitentiary. The reasons he offers—the absence of a
"culture of reform," the incompatibility of a reform ideology with the dominant
Southern ideology, the lack of a demand for change in the South, a political
structure unresponsive to reformers—apply as much to Southern states that did
build penitentiaries. See Hindus, *Prison and Plantation*, pp. 215–25, for a
summary of his argument. The failure of Florida to build a penitentiary seems
to require less explanation. It did not become a state until 1845, and in 1860
had a population smaller than that of New Orleans. See Emory M. Thomas, *The
Confederate Nation, 1861–1865* (New York: Harper, 1979), p. 51. "Echoes" of
penal reform reached the Florida territory, Arthur W. Thompson notes, "but
few were noticeably moved": *Jacksonian Democracy on the Florida Frontier* (Gainesville: Univ. of Florida Press, 1961), p. 40.

52. Beaumont and Tocqueville, *Penitentiary System*, p. 65. The account here is a
composite of several Southern penitentiaries: rules for the Alabama institution
are in the "Penitentiary" file, 1842, at ADAH; Kentucky rules described in a
letter in 1826 to Gov. William Carroll of Tennessee in Carroll Correspondence,
TSLA; White, *Messages* 3:116; Lewis, *American Prisons*, pp. 265–68.

53. Augustus Kuhlman, "Crime and Punishment in Missouri: A Study of the Social

Forces in the Trial and Error Process of Penal Reform" (Ph.D. diss., Univ. of Chicago, 1929) 2:41–43; Mississippi revolt described in *Savannah Republican*, Oct. 5, 1860; on burning, see Bonner, "Georgia Penitentiary," pp. 310, 315; on conversation, see George Thompson, *Prison Life and Reflections* (Hartford: A. Work, 1847), p. 151; on obscene songs, Gettleman, "Maryland Penitentiary," p. 284.

54. Chaplain's Report, Tennessee *Senate Journal*, 1849–50, appendix; Leroy M. Lee, D. D., *The Life and Times of the Reverend Jesse Lee* (Richmond: John Early, 1848), pp. 482–84; A. Pomroy, chaplain, Mississippi *House Journal*, 1854, p. 70; *Alabama Penitentiary Board of Inspectors' Report*, Oct. 1, 1852, pp. 8–9. See Joseph M. Hawes, "Prisons in Early Nineteenth-Century America: The Process of Convict Reformation," in idem, ed., *Law and Order in American History* (Port Washington: Kennikat Press, 1979), pp. 37–52.

55. W. H. Wharton, Tennessee *Senate and House Journals*, 1857–58, appendix, p. 84; P. Lane, "Chaplain's Report," Mississippi *House Journal*, 1861–62; Charles S. Morgan, Virginia *Annual Reports*, 1849–50, doc. 7, p. 7; Sneed, *Kentucky Penitentiary*, p. 586.

56. Cobb quoted in Daniel Flanigan, "The Criminal Law of Slavery and Freedom, 1800–1868" (Ph.D. diss., Rice Univ., 1973), p. 21; Flanigan discusses slaves and imprisonment on pp. 21–24. Maryland and Arkansas also admitted slaves briefly. See Gettleman, "Maryland Penitentiary," pp. 276–277; Sellin, *Slavery and Penal System*, p. 144.

57.

	White Males	Black Males	White Females	Black Females
Tennessee	95.6	3.5	0.8	0.1
Alabama	98.0	1.1	0.9	0
Georgia	99.0	0	1.0	0
Kentucky	90.2	8.0	1.6	0.2
Mississippi	98.6	1.1	0	0.3
Virginia	67.4	29.5	1.1	2.0
Maryland	47.6	43.8	0.8	7.8
Louisiana[a]	68.8	5.0	1.2	3.6

[a]21.4% of the inmates of Louisiana's penitentiary were slaves
SOURCE: See Appendix, Part I.

58. Quoted in Ira Berlin, *Slaves Without Masters: The Free Negro in the Antebellum South* (1974; reprint, New York: Vintage, 1976), p. 323; Gov. James Pleasants, Virginia *House Journal*, 1824, pp. 1–2; Gov. William B. Giles, Virginia *House Journal*, 1827, pp. 4–5.

59. Virginia *House Journal*, 1848–49, pp. 22–23; Virginia *House Journal*, 1857–58, doc. 1, pp. cxlix–cl.

60. Gov. William B. Giles, Virginia *House Journal*, 1828, pp. 4–5; *Alabama Penitentiary Board of Inspectors' Report*, Oct. 1850, p. 6; letter from Thomas B. Ives, Jan. 19, 1841, "Prison Correspondence," MDAH.

61. "Report of the Joint Standing Committee on the Penitentiary, 1845," (Milledgeville) *Federal Union*, Dec. 30, 1845; Gov. Steward quoted in Kuhlman, "Missouri" 2:195. On women in Northern penitentiaries see Estelle Freedman, *Their Sisters' Keepers: Women's Prison Reform in America, 1830–1930* (Ann Arbor: Univ. of

Michigan, 1981); Nicholas Fischer Hahn, "Female State Prisoners in Tennessee: 1831–1979," *Tennessee Historical Quarterly* 39 (Winter 1980): 475–97.

62. Unpaged manuscript, Pardon Docket book, Herschel V. Johnson, Executive Papers, GDAH—figures tabulated from Jan. 1854 to Nov. 1857. Also see "Executive Pardon from Feb. 20th 1836 to August 31st 1843," Govs. William Schley and George R. Gilmer, GDAH, which shows clemency granted 98 times, refused only 14.

63. Governor's Records, John Pettus, 1860, MDAH, petition for James Halladay (first quote) and A. F. Tucker (second quote); also see petition of John Moore, Sept. 25, 1854, in Gov. Isham G. Harris Papers, box 4, folder 5, TSLA, who promised if pardoned to go to Texas because the North and "this part of the west is so overrun and taken up by Monopoly that a poor man has no chance to get along."

64. *Greensborough Patriot*, Feb. 14, 1846.

65. Virginia *House Journal*, 1827, appendix, Joint Committee to Examine the Penitentiary Institution, p. 2. In 1828, 1,760 visitors came to the Virginia penitentiary: Virginia *House Journal*, 1828, Report of Joint Committee, p. 2; Gov. Newton Cannon, in White, *Messages* 3:263.

66. Gov. G. Gilmer, Georgia *Senate Journal*, 1831, pp. 16–17. For a caustic comment that more "industry" might be found in the penitentiary than in the executive's mansion from which such pronouncements emanated, see Anne N. Royall, *Mrs. Royall's Southern Tour, or Second Series of the Black Book* (Washington: n.p., 1831) 2:124–25. On the importance of work in prisons elsewhere, see Dario Malossi, "Institutions of Social Control and Capitalist Organization of Work," trans. John Lee, in Bob Fine et al., *Capitalism and the Rule of Law: From Deviancy Theory to Marxism* (London: Hutchinson, 1979), pp. 90–99; Patricia O'Brien, *The Promise of Punishment: Prisons in Nineteenth-Century France* (Princeton: Princeton Univ. Press, 1982), pp. 150–51.

67. *Athens* (Ala.) *Chronicle*, reprinted in *Greensborough Patriot*, Nov. 22, 1845; *Federal Union*, April 15, 1845. Another correspondent asked, "Are not the monopolists the veritable criminals?": *Greensborough Patriot*, Jan. 24, 1846.

68. Gov. Andrew Johnson in White, *Messages* 4:550–52; Gov. Herschel V. Johnson, Georgia *House Journal*, 1855–56, pp. 18–19; *Georgia Banner* reprinted in *Federal Union*, April 15, 1845. On the influence of Andrew Johnson's artisan background and his problems with the penitentiary, see H. Blair Bentley, "Andrew Johnson and the Tennessee State Penitentiary, 1853–1857," *East Tennessee Historical Society Publications* 47 (1975): 28–45.

69. *Southern Recorder*, Dec. 14, 1858; John Hebron Moore, "Mississippi's Ante-Bellum Textile Industry," *Journal of Mississippi History* 16 (1954): 91–94; Thompson, "Penal Reform in Mississippi," p. 74; *Alabama Penitentiary Board of Inspectors' Report*, 1851, pp. 19–20; William Schley to Gov. Clay, Oct. 17, 1836; Penitentiary Records, 1836–39, ADAH.

70. Berlin, *Slaves*, pp. 323–24; White, *Messages* 5:122, 152–53, 155; Wallenstein, "Slave South to New South," pp. 183–84.

71. *Federal Union*, Nov. 23, 1856; for attacks, see *Southern Banner*, Jan. 6, 1846; *Federal Union*, Nov. 25, 1845; on quarrying stone, *Southern Recorder*, Dec. 14, 1858; on draining the swamp, *Southern Recorder*, Dec. 14, 1858.

72. *Southern Recorder*, Aug. 24, 1858; Gov. Joseph E. Brown, Georgia *House Journal*, 1858, p. 27; Sneed, *Kentucky Penitentiary*, pp. vii–viii, 15–16, 21, 46; Kuhlman, "Missouri" 2:9–17; Mark Carleton, *Politics and Punishment: The History of the Louisiana State Penal System* (Baton Rouge: LSU, 1971), p. 9.

73. Fletcher Green, "Some Aspects of the Convict Lease System in the Southern States," in Green, ed., *Essays in Southern History Presented to Joseph Gregoire de Roulhac Hamilton* (Chapel Hill: UNC, 1949), p. 117; *Alabama Penitentiary Board of Inspectors' Report*, 1847, p. 21; 1849, p. 9; 1851, pp. 18–19; 1855, p. 3; Gov. John A. Watson, in Alabama *Senate Journal*, 1857, p. 22.

74. *Southern Recorder*, Jan. 8, 1850; *North Carolina Standard*, Jan. 7, 1846.

75. *Greensborough Patriot*, Feb. 21, 1846; *Southern Recorder*, Dec. 14, 1858; Thompson, *Prison Life*, pp. 128–32.

76. *Alabama Penitentiary Board of Inspectors' Report*, Oct. 1, 1850, p. 5; 1847, p. 21.

77. Boston Prison Discipline Society *Report*, 1850, p. 486; Tocqueville, *Journey to America*, p. 128; Saum, *Popular Mood*, pp. 162–64; on conditions in Northern prisons, see W. D. Lewis, *Newgate to Dannemora*, pp. 178–200; Beaumont and Tocqueville, *American Prisons*, pp. 69–70; John Phillips Resch, "Ohio Adult Penal System, 1850–1900: A Study in the Failure of Institutional Reform," *Ohio History* 81 (Autumn 1972): 236–62; Lawrence Friedman and Robert Percival, *The Roots of Justice: Crime and Punishment in Alameda County, California, 1870–1910* (Chapel Hill: UNC, 1981), pp. 289–90; Rothman, *Discovery*, pp. 101–2; Glen A. Gildemeister, "Prison Labor and Convict Competition with Free Workers in Industrializing America, 1840–1890" (Ph.D. diss, Northern Illinois Univ., 1977).

78. See Melossi and Pavarini, *Prison and Factory*, pp. 185–86; Ignatieff, *Just Measure*, pp. 62–63.

Chapter 3. The City

1. George White, *Statistics of the State of Georgia, Including an Account of Its Natural, Civil and Ecclesiastical History* (Savannah: W. Thorne Williams, 1849), pp. 85–86; Chatham County Superior Court Minutes, February term, 1861, microfilm at GDAH.

2. Of the 234 people convicted in the Chatham County Superior Court between 1850 and 1860, 88.5% (207) were prosecuted alone rather than with one or more codefendants.

3. Chatham County Superior Court Minutes, May 18, 1850, pp. 31–32, GDAH. Thomas Gamble, Jr., *A History of the City Government of Savannah, Georgia from 1790 to 1901* (Savannah: City Council, 1901), pp. 198, 239. On New Orleans's jail, see Robert C. Reinders, *End of an Era: New Orleans, 1850–1860* (New Orleans: Pelican, 1964), pp. 71–72; on Richmond's, see Clement Eaton, *The Growth of Southern Civilization* (1961; reprint, New York: Harper Torchbooks, 1961), p. 283.

4. Savannah City Council Minutes, Jan. 1854, Georgia Historical Society, Savannah. For descriptions of the jail, see Presentment, Superior Court Minutes, 1850, pp. 31–32; Savannah *Republican*, March 3, 1855.

5.

Chatham County Superior Court Indictments, 1850–1860

	Property	Violent	Order	Deceit	Slave	Other
1850	18	27	16	2	1	6
1851	17	14	3	6	1	2
1852	14	33	15	14	5	8
1853	17	59	15	14	5	8
1854	7	40	10	4	5	5
1855	7	19	4	9	3	4
1856	8	47	5	11	5	4
1857	7	41	4	1	1	8
1858	23	10	7	6	9	13
1859	13	32	7	6	9	23
1860	26	22	11	4	5	8
Total	157	344	97	77	44	89
% Total	19.4	42.6	12.0	9.5	5.4	11.0

NOTE: In this table, 126 (80.2%) of the property offenses were larcency; 190 (55.2%) of the violent offenses were assault and battery and 120 (34.9%) were assault with intent to murder; 37 (84.1%) of the slave offenses involved whites accused of trading with slaves; 63 (70.8%) of the "other" offenses were labeled only "misdemeanors" in the court minutes.
SOURCE: In this and all following tables the sources are those described in the Appendix.

6. A sample of earlier years (1835, 1838, 1847; N = 101) showed the following pattern. The percentages registered in the 1850s appear in parentheses.

Offense		Offense	
Property	23.8 (19.3)	Deceit	8.9 (8.1)
Violent	48.5 (42.3)	Slave	5.9 (5.6)
Order	8.9 (11.9)	Other	3.9 (12.7)

7. All the slaves were accused of murder. For a discussion of the statistics on race, nativity, gender, occupation, and property holding of the criminal defendants, see Appendix, Part II.

8.

Nativity of Defendants in Savannah, 1850–60 (Percentages)

South		North		Europe	
GA	23	CT	1	Ireland	31
SC	11	NY	5	Scotland	2
NC	3	PN	1	England	5
TN	1	MA	3	France	2
VA	1	NH	1	Germany	7
		MD	1		
		IN	1		

NOTE: $N = 98$.

9. Of the 92 men for whom I could find occupations, 33 were unskilled laborers, 29 were artisans, 18 were clerks or agents, 7 were professional men, and 5 were farmers or planters. I could determine the ages of 101 defendants (by using penitentiary records in addition to the census records):

Age	#	%	Age	#	%
15–20	10	9.9	41–50	12	11.9
21–25	20	19.8	51–60	4	4.0
26–30	17	16.8	60+	1	1.0
31–40	37	36.6			

Of the 59 men for whom I could determine property holding, 49 (or 83.1%) owned nothing; the rest were scattered in insignificant numbers throughout various levels of wealth.

10.

Verdicts and Punishments Accorded Different Types of Crime in Savannah
(Percentages)

	Property	Violence	Order	Slavery	Deceit	Other
Guilty	57.8	64.4	72.7	66.7	64.3	55.5
Not Guilty	41.0	32.2	27.3	22.2	35.7	44.4
N	83	90	22	9	14	16
Fine	2.1	67.2	81.3	66.7	0	100.0
Penitentiary	54.2	13.8	6.3	0	88.9	0
N	27	47	14	4	8	3

NOTE: Figures on verdicts do not total 100.0% due to mistrials.

While people accused of theft or burglary accounted for only 19.3% of all defendants brought before the grand jury, they accounted for 38.5% of those passed to the petit jury; the proportion of those accused of a violent crime before the grand jury (42.3%), on the other hand, declined to 35.0% by the time they reached the petit jury.

11.

Nativity of Penitentiary Inmates, 1850–60
(Percentages)

	KY	TN	MS	AL	GA	VA	MD	TX	MI	PN
Native	34	46	12	14	55	76	61	7	7	46
Southern	21	43	46	60	33	6	5	39	2	7
Northern	24	3	18	8	4	10	10	17	59	14
Foreign	21	8	24	18	8	8	24	37	32	34

Ratio of Foreign Population to Foreign Inmates

	KY	TN	MS	AL	GA	VA	MD	TX	MI	PN
	1:3	1:4	1:12	1:9	1:4	1:3	1:2	1:4	1:2	1:2

12.

Urban Origins of Southern Penitentiary Inmates, 1850–60

	Percentage of State Inmates	Percentage of State Pop.	Ratio of Population Inmates
Mobile	32.9	4.2	1:7.8
Montgomery	7.5	2.4	1:3.1
Vicksburg	20.5	1.7	1:12.1
Natchez	9.9	1.6	1:6.2
Memphis	18.5	3.0	1:6.2

(Continued next page)

(Continued from previous page)

	Percentage of State Inmates	Percentage of State Pop.	Ratio of Population Inmates
Nashville	13.4	3.6	1:3.7
Louisville	26.9	7.2	1:3.7
Covington	6.6	3.4	1:1.9
Savannah	11.2	2.3	1:4.9
Augusta	6.4	1.7	1:3.8

NOTE: I have used only the two largest cities of each state; had I included all large towns and smaller cities, the state ratios would be even more skewed.

13.

Offenses of Southern Penitentiary Inmates, 1850–60

	AL	GA	MS	TN	VA	MD	LA[a]
Property	46.5	52.1	54.1	52.0	48.6	54.5	40.4
Violent	30.0	32.5	24.9	27.3	29.0	26.7	42.9
Deceit	8.8	11.3	6.5	9.4	12.5	3.8	5.3
Other	14.7	4.1	14.5	11.3	9.9	15.0	11.4

[a]Whites only.

14. Several recent studies have begun to reevaluate the place of the city in the slave South. See David R. Goldfield, *Urban Growth in the Age of Sectionalism: Virginia, 1847–1861* (Baton Rouge: LSU, 1977); idem, *Cotton Fields and Skyscrapers: Southern City and Region, 1607–1980* (Baton Rouge: LSU, 1982); Leonard P. Curry, "Urbanism and Urbanization in the Old South: A Comparative View," *Journal of Southern History* 40 (1974): 43–60; Blaine Brownell, "Urbanization in the South: A Unique Experience?" *Mississippi Quarterly* 26 (1973): 105–201.

15. Average percent population growth from 1850 to 1860 for a cross section of Southern cities (Charleston, Louisville, Memphis, Nashville, Mobile, Montgomery, and Vicksburg): 49.3; Savannah: 45.6; average population in 1860, same eight cities, 22,893; Savannah, 22, 292; average percent foreign-born in 1860, 21.2; Savannah, 29.0. Source: *Report of Social Statistics of Cities, Part II* (Washington: U.S. Census Office, 1887). Average ratio of prisoners to population in 1850s, 1:5.5; Savannah 1:4.9. Source: Penitentiary reports (see Appendix).

16. On the history of the city's economic growth, see Richard H. Haunton's excellent "Savannah in the 1850s," (Ph.D. diss., Emory University 1968), pp. 34–35; *Republican*, Nov. 4, 1854; tables in Alan Smith Thompson, "Mobile, Alabama, 1850–1861: Economic, Political, Physical, and Population Characteristics" (Ph.D. diss., Univ. of Alabama, 1979), pp. 15–16. The city also produced manufactured goods in 1860 valued at almost $2 million—the largest in Georgia, but not as large in relation to other Georgia cities as its population size would have dictated. See Fred Siegel, "Artisans and Immigrants in the Politics of Late Antebellum Georgia," *Civil War History* 27 (Sept. 1981): 221–30; Haunton, "Savannah," pp. 130–31.

17. On spatial expansion, see Haunton, "Savannah," pp. 16–23; Savannah *Morning News*, March 12, 1851; Ian Davey and Michael Doucet, "The Social Geography

of a Commercial City, ca. 1853," appendix 1 of Michael B. Katz, *The People of Hamilton, Canada West: Family and Class in a Mid-Nineteenth-Century City* (Cambridge: Harvard Univ. Press, 1975), p. 330; on Savannah's population growth, see Haunton, "Savannah," pp. 63–66; Herbert Weaver, "Foreigners in Ante-Bellum Savannah," *Georgia Historical Quarterly* 37 (1953): 1–2.

18. In 1860, only 11.3% of the city's adult free inhabitants owned real estate, and half of that 11.3% owned 91.5% of the city's real property; 3.2% of the free residents held 46.3% of all personal property; and 20.0% of the slaveholders held 57.7% of the slaves: Haunton, "Savannah," pp. 34–37. For the concentration of wealth elsewhere, see Goldfield, *Urban Growth*, and Edward Pessen, *Riches, Class and Power Before the Civil War* (Lexington, Mass.: D. C. Heath, 1973), pp. 169–201.

19. Emily P. Burke, *Reminiscences of Georgia* (Oberlin, Ohio: J. M. Fitch, 1850), pp. 63–64; William Harden, *Recollections of a Long and Satisfying Life* (1934; reprint, New York: Negro Univ. Press, 1968), pp. 35–36.

	Percentage of White Males Aged 20–30 in City Pop.	Percentage of White Males Aged 20–30 in State Pop.
Mobile	25.0	17.5
Montgomery	20.8	
Vicksburg	20.7	17.9
Natchez	20.4	
Memphis	30.6	18.0
Nashville	22.6	
Louisville	21.5	17.5
Covington	18.6	
Savannah	27.3	17.3
Augusta	21.2	

SOURCE: 1860 federal census.

20. On wages, see Haunton, "Savannah," pp. 52–54; for other reassessments of the place of the white workingmen in the urban antebellum South, see Ira Berlin and Herbert G. Gutman, "Free Workers and Slaves: The Composition of the Urban Male Laboring Population in the Antebellum South," unpublished paper; Siegel, "Artisans and Immigrants." I am grateful to Professors Berlin and Gutman for sharing their work with me.

21. William M. Baker, *The Life and Labours of the Reverend Daniel Baker* (Philadelphia: W. W. and A. Martien, 1858), pp. 30–31; on the number of prostitutes, see Bertram Wyatt-Brown, *Southern Honor: Ethics and Behavior in the Old South* (New York: Oxford Univ. Press, 1982), pp. 547–48, n. 2; on the location of the brothels, see Haunton, "Savannah," p. 18; on the "bachelor-transient subculture" and its effect on crime, see John C. Schneider, *Detroit and the Problem of Order, 1830–1880: A Geography of Crime, Riot, and Policing* (Lincoln: Univ. of Nebraska Press, 1980), esp. pp. 36–52. I have found Schneider's spatial emphasis extremely suggestive and illuminating. An article that provides useful comparisons on urban merchant community, police reform, and nativism as well as prostitution is Richard Tansey, "Prostitution and Politics in Antebellum New Orleans," *Southern Studies* 18 (Winter 1979): 449–79.

22. C. G. Parsons, *Inside View of Slavery; or, A Tour Among the Planters* (Boston: John P. Jewett, 1855), p. 23; on slaves and free blacks, see Joseph Bancroft, *Census of the City of Savannah* (Savannah: E. C. Councell, 1848), p. 9; Haunton, "Savannah," pp. 76–78.

23. Report of the chief of police, in *Republican*, March 24, 1855.

24. Of 43 property crimes recorded in the Savannah *Morning News* between 1850 and 1860, 28 were committed in the city's central business district. Of 20 reported violent crimes, only 2 occurred in the center of town.

25. See Sarah L. Boggs, "Urban Crime Patterns," *American Sociological Review* 30 (Dec. 1965): 908; for a similar pattern in the North see David R. Johnson, **"Crime Patterns in Philadelphia, 1840–70," in Allen F. Davis and Mark H.** Haller, eds., *The Peoples of Philadelphia: A History of Ethnic Groups and Lower-Class Life, 1790–1940* (Philadelphia: Temple Univ. Press, 1973), pp. 91–96, and idem, *Policing the Urban Underworld: The Impact of Crime on the Development of the American Police* (Philadelphia: Temple Univ. Press, 1979), pp. 72–77. Davey and Doucet, "Social Geography," suggest the term "commercial city" and define its major characteristics, esp. pp. 321–22. On similarities of Northern and Southern cities, see Goldfield, *Urban Growth*, p. xxii; Curry, "Urbanism and Urbanization," p. 58; Edward Pessen, "The Social Configuration of the Antebellum City: An Historical and Theoretical Inquiry," *Journal of Urban History* 2 (1976): 271. On great population density in cities of this era, see Sam Bass Warner, Jr., *The Private City: Philadelphia in Three Periods of Urban Growth* (Philadelphia: Univ. of Pennsylvania Press, 1967), pp. 16, 56–57; on poor living on periphery, see Blaine H. Brownell and David R. Goldfield, *The City in Southern History: The Growth of Urban Civilization in the South* (Port Washington, N.Y.: Kennikat Press, 1977), p. 149; on juxtaposition, see David Ward, "The Internal Spatial Differentiation of Immigrant Residential Districts," in idem, ed., *Geographical Perspectives on America's Past: Readings on the Historical Geography of the United States* **(New York: Oxford Univ. Press, 1979), pp. 335–43.** On intermingling of immigrants in Southern cities, see Herbert Weaver, "Foreigners in Ante-Bellum Towns of the Lower South," *Journal of Southern History* 13 (1947): 67–68. On **residential patterns of other Southern cities, see Reinders,** *End of an Era*, pp. 32, 68, 95; Thompson, "Mobile," chap. 5; **Gary Lawson Browne,** *Baltimore in the Nation, 1789–1861* (Chapel Hill: UNC, 1980), pp. 190–93.

26. Berlin and Gutman, "Free Workers and Slaves"; Haunton, "Savannah," pp. 52–54.

27. Haunton, "Savannah," pp. 58–59; Manuscript Census Schedules, Population, Chatham County, 1860. Roger Shugg, *Origins of Class Struggle in Louisiana: A Social History of White Farmers and Laborers during Slavery and After, 1840–1875* (Baton Rouge: LSU, 1939), p. 40, quoting *New Orleans Creole*, Jan. 29, 1857; Samuel A. Cartwright, "Prevention of Yellow Fever," *Medical and Surgical Journal* 10 (Nov. 1853): 315, in Reinders, *End of an Era*, p. 95.

28. Quote on Irish men in Berlin and Gutman, "Free Workers and Slaves," p. 23; on the connection between spatial development and the rise of the police, see Schneider, *Detroit*; for dates American police were uniformed (though not necessarily established), see Eric A. Monkkonen, *Police in Urban America, 1860–1920* (Cambridge: Harvard Univ. Press, 1981), Appendix A. Monkkonen argues that the police's "introduction and dispersion throughout the country was not a

function of elite demands for class control, changing urban riots, or rising crime." Police, he argues, simply "swept down the size hierarchy of U. S. cities, from large to small, in forty-year period" (pp. 53–56). Southern cities were "deviant" in this regard, for they adopted police earlier than their mere size would suggest. Monkkonen argues that the police developed in Savannah and other Southern cities because those cities performed urban functions befitting cities of much larger population and because of the need to control slaves. I agree that Southern cities were more important and complex than their size alone would suggest, but would stress that police developed in the South because commercial capitalism developed in those cities an internal structure and diversity that created a perceived need for the police. On other Southern police, see William C. Evitts, *A Matter of Allegiances: Maryland from 1850 to 1861* (Baltimore: Johns Hopkins Univ. Press, 1971), pp. 112–13; Goldfield, *Urban Growth*, pp. 145–46; Reinders, *End of an Era*, pp. 64–68. Charleston's police, established in 1857, were modeled on Savannah's: see Michael Hindus, "The Contours of Crime and Justice in Massachusetts and South Carolina, 1767–1878," *American Journal of Legal History* 21 (1977): 229; D. Clayton James, *Antebellum Natchez* (Baton Rouge: LSU, 1968), p. 263; Richard C. Wade, *Slavery in the Cities: The South, 1820–1860* (New York: Oxford Univ. Press, 1964), pp. 100–101; Shugg, *Origins of Class Struggle*, p. 58; Jack K. Williams, *Vogues in Villainy: Crime and Retribution in Ante-bellum South Carolina* (Columbia, 1959), p. 73; Ira Berlin, *Slaves Without Masters: The Free Negro in the Antebellum South* (New York: Vintage, 1974), pp. 330–31.

29. Quote on Charleston from Louis F. Tasistro in Wade, *Slavery*, p. 98; Samuel Walker, *Popular Justice: A History of American Criminal Justice* (New York: Oxford Univ. Press, 1980), pp. 3–4; see Dennis C. Rousey, "The New Orleans Police, 1805–1884: A Social History" (Ph.D. diss., Cornell Univ. 1978); John P. Radford, "Race, Residence, and Ideology: Charleston, South Carolina, in the Mid-Nineteenth Century," in Ward, *Geographical Perspectives*, p. 346; Kenneth G. Alfers, *Law and Order in the Capital City: A History of the Washington Police, 1800–1886* (Washington, D.C.: George Washington Univ. Press, 1976). On the expectations surrounding the police in a democracy, see Allen Silver, "The Demand for Order in Civil Society: A Review of Some Themes in the History of Urban Crime, Police and Riot," in David J. Bordua, ed., *The Police: Six Sociological Essays* (New York: Wiley, 1967), pp. 1–24.

30. Harden, *Recollections*, pp. 17–18; *Republican*, Dec. 1, 1855; *Evening Journal*, Jan. 18, 1853, in Richard H. Haunton, "Law and Order in Savannah, 1850–1860," *Georgia Historical Quarterly* 56 (1972): 1–24.

31. *Republican*, Feb. 2, 4, 1853; *Republican*, Jan. 24, 1851; Report of R. D. Arnold, Mayor, 1860, p. 8; Gamble, *History of the City Government*, pp. 198, 239–40; Report of John Ward, Mayor, in *Republican*, Nov. 21, 1854; April 2, 21, 1855.

32. Frederic Bancroft, *Slave-Trading in the Old South* (Baltimore: J. H. Furst, 1931), pp. 222–31; William A. Byrne, "The Burden and Heat of the Day: Slavery and Servitude in Savannah, 1733–1865" (Ph.D. diss., Florida State Univ., 1979), pp. 229–30; *Republican*, June 7, 1854.

33. George Mercer Diary, Nov. 7, 1859, quoted in Haunton, "Savannah," pp. 202–3; C. C. Jones, Jr., to Rev. and Mrs. C. C. Jones, Oct. 6, 1859, in Robert Myers, ed., *The Children of Pride: A True Story of Georgia and the Civil War* (New Haven:

Yale Univ. Press, 1972), pp. 523–24. On the role of businessmen elsewhere in support of police, see Goldfield, *Urban Growth*, p. 146; Robert Dykstra, *The Cattle Towns* (New York: Knopf, 1973), pp. 114–15; Haunton, "Savannah," pp. 200–204, 48–49.

34. Savannah *Daily Georgian*, March 5, 1856; also see May 21, 22, 1856; Report of Edward C. Anderson, Mayor, 1855, in *Republican*, Nov. 22, 1855; June 5, 6, 30, July 3, 1855; Savannah *Morning News*, Nov. 10, 11, 1854; June 16, 20, 1860.

35. Savannah *Morning News*, Dec. 12, 1857; *Republican*, Aug. 5, 1854; also see Haunton, "Law and Order," pp. 13–14; *Republican*, Aug. 2, 1854; Sept. 11, 14, 23, 1857; for similar complaints in other cities, see Wade, *Slavery*, pp. 100–101.

36. Letter reprinted in *Georgian*, Feb. 22, 1856.

37. "Report of the Chief of Police," *Republican*, March 24, 1855.

38. Savannah City Council Minutes, Aug. 1860, Georgia Historical Society.

39. *Republican*, July 26, 1854; Dec. 1, 1855; also see Nov. 20, Dec. 2, 3, 4, 1854; *Morning News*, Dec. 5, 1854; also see Roger Lane, *Policing the City: Boston, 1822–1905* (Cambridge: Harvard Univ. Press, 1967), and James F. Richardson, *The New York Police: Colonial times to 1901* (New York: Oxford Univ. Press, 1970).

40. Richard D. Arnold to Col. John W. Farney, Dec. 18, 1850, in Richard H. Shryock, ed., *Letters of Richard D. Arnold, M.D., 1808–1876* (Durham: Duke Univ. Press, 1929), pp. 46–47; *Republican*, June 7, 1854; *Morning News*, April 4, 19.

41. Savannah *Morning News*, April 18, July 11, 1856; Haunton, "Savannah," pp. 229–30; *Morning News*, Oct. 15, 16, 18, 1856. On the Irish in Savannah politics, see Siegel, "Artisans and Immigrants," pp. 226–27; for other cities see Thompson, "Mobile," p. 168; Reinders, *End of an Era*, pp. 63–64.

42. Wilbur Miller, *Cops and Bobbies: Police Authority in New York and London, 1830–1870* (Chicago: Univ. of Chicago Press, 1977); James Stirling, *Letters from the Slave States* (London: J. W. Parker and Son, 1857), pp. 146–47. On problems of police authority, see Walker, *Popular Justice*, pp. 16–17; Mark Haller, "Historical Roots of Police Behavior: Chicago, 1890–1925," *Law and Society Review* 10 (1976): 303–23.

43. *Morning News*, June 16, 1860.

44. See note 6; *DeBow's Review* 18 (1855): 418–19; E. Merton Coulter, ed., *The Other Half of Old New Orleans, Sketches of Characters and Incidents from the Recorder's Court* (Baton Rouge: LSU, 1939), p. 2.

45. Between 1850 and 1860 the Chatham Superior Court indicted an average of 14 people per year for property crimes; in 1858 the number was 23 and in 1860 it was 26. The yearly average number of penitentiary sentences for Southern cities for which I have records are as follows:

	1848–57	*1858*
Vicksburg	14	36
Memphis	40	84
Nashville	32	45
Louisville	29	51

Property incarcerations increased from 1.6 prisoners per thousand in Mississippi and 1.5 in Tennessee in 1857, to 2.8 and 2.7, respectively, in 1858. Incarcerations for violent crime increased only from 0.7 to 1.0 in Mississippi and 1.0 to 1.2 in Tennessee. See Appendix, Part I.

| | Prisoners Received | | | | | |
| | North | | | South | | |
	MA	MI	CT	VA	TX	TN
1850	221	50	64	60	13	67
1851	169	83	31	92	36	65
1852	177	87	60	89	39	72
1853	159	72	49	109	33	76
1854	151	103	75	107	41	101
1855	141	141	31	127	45	61
1856	146	137	63	103	38	102
1857	160	170	63	111	66	95
1858	198	195	74	—	46	147[a]
1859	163	211	71	121	85	147[a]

[a]Biennial report showed 294 prisoners received in 1858 and 1859.
SOURCE: See Appendix, Part I.

46. See Theodore Ferdinand, "The Criminal Patterns of Boston Since 1849," *American Journal of Sociology* 73 (1967):84–99, esp. 97; Elwin H. Powell, *The Design of Discord: Studies of Anomie* (New York: Oxford Univ. Press, 1970), p. 121; David J. Bodenhamer, "Crime and Criminal Justice in Antebellum Indiana: Marion County as a Case Study" (Ph.D. diss., Indiana Univ. 1977), pp. 160, 167. In New York courts, the percentage increase in criminal conviction rates was higher during the 1853–57 and 1858–62 periods than at any other time in the nineteenth century: Estelle Freedman, *Their Sisters' Keepers: Women's Prison Reform in America, 1830–1930* (Ann Arbor: Univ. of Michigan Press, 1981), Appendix A, p. 161.

47. Daniel R. Hundley, *Social Relations in Our Southern States* (New York: H. B. Price, 1860), p. 262. Fluctuations in food supply had long led to waves of theft in rural Europe. See V.A.C. Gatrell and T. B. Hadden, "Criminal Statistics and Their Interpretation," in Anthony Wrigley, ed., *Nineteenth-Century Society* (London: Cambridge Univ. Press, 1972); J. M. Beattie, "The Pattern of Crime in England, 1660–1800," *Past and Present* 62 (1974); 84–95, esp. 92–95; Barbara Hanawalt, *Crime and Conflict in English Communities, 1300–1348* (Cambridge: Harvard Univ. Press, 1979), pp. 238–60; Howard Zehr, *Crime and the Development of Modern Society: Patterns of Criminality in Nineteenth-Century Germany and France* (London: Croom Helm, 1976), esp. p. 82; Ted Robert Gurr et al., *The Politics of Crime and Conflict: A Comparative History of Four Cities* (Beverly Hills: Sage, 1977), esp. p. 763. For a survey of the older literature on the subject as it pertains to the United States, see Thorsten Sellin, *Research Memorandum on Crime in the Depression* (New York: Social Science Research Council, 1937), esp. pp. 20–62; for a more recent attempt to link violence with business cycles, see Andrew F. Henry and James F. Short, Jr., *Suicide and Homicide: Some Economic, Sociological, and Psychological Aspects of Aggression* (Glencoe, Ill.: Free Press, 1954).

48. William Sparks, *The Memories of Fifty Years* (Philadelphia: Claxton, Remsen, and Haffelflinger, 1872), p. 365. On the bad roads and difficulty of transport, see Everett Dick, *The Dixie Frontier: A Social History of the Southern Frontier from the First Transmontane Beginnings to the Civil War* (New York: Capricorn Books, 1964), pp. 225–35. The only other two Southern states for which records exist for the

1830s and 1840s are Tennessee and Virginia, and they show some, but relatively little, response to the economic crisis:

Prisoners Received

	TN	VA		TN	VA
1830	—	57	1840	59	52
1831	36	49	1841	68	52
1832	42	43	1842	66	58
1833	33	40	1843	82	55
1834	50	54	1844	64	33
1835	44	63	1845	66	—
1836	52	64	1846	82	—
1837	64	71	1847	68	53
1838	49	56	1848	66	33
1839	53	59	1849	76	56

SOURCE: See Appendix, Part I.

49. John Stover, *Iron Road to the West: American Railroads in the 1850s* (New York: Columbia Univ. Press, 1978), pp. 59–61. On the general transformation of the South, see J. Mills Thornton, *Politics and Power in a Slave Society: Alabama, 1800–1860* (Baton Rouge: LSU, 1978). Percentage urban:

	1840	*1860*
Alabama	2.2	5.1
Georgia	3.6	7.1
Kentucky	3.9	10.5
Mississippi	1.1	2.6
Tennessee	0.8	4.2
Virginia	6.9	9.5
Maryland	24.2	33.9

SOURCE: *Historical Statistics of the United States, Colonial Times to 1970* (Washington, 1975).

George Van Vleck, *The Panic of 1857: An Analytical Study* (New York: Columbia Univ. Press, 1943), pp. 6–7; *Morning News*, Nov. 22, 1853; also see *Republican*, Aug. 23, 1854.

50. *Hunt's Merchant's Magazine* 44 (1857), quoted in Robert R. Russel, *Economic Aspects of Southern Sectionalism, 1840–1861* (Chicago: Univ. of Illinois, 1922), pp. 102–3; letter by Amasa Walker to editor, *Hunt's Merchant's Magazine* 37 (1857): 533; *New Orleans Crescent* in *Republican*, Oct. 7, 1857; *New Orleans Commercial Bulletin*, in *Republican*, Oct. 9, 1857. On the complexity of lines of influence and patterns of specie suspension even in the Panic of 1837, see Allen R. Pred, *Urban Growth and the Circulation of Information: The United States System of Cities, 1790–1840* (Cambridge: Harvard Univ. Press, 1973), pp. 246–55; also see Samuel Rezneck, *Business Depressions and Financial Panics: Essays in American Business and Economic History* (Westport, Conn.: Greenwood, 1968), pp. 103–25.

51. Van Vleck, *Panic*, pp. 75–76; in its *Annual Report*, the New York Association for Improving the Condition of the Poor observed that in the winter of 1857–58 the city "presented a more appalling picture of social wretchedness than was probably ever before witnessed on this side of the Atlantic" (p. 22).

52. Peter Temin, in his "Anglo-American Business Cycles, 1820–1860," *Economic History Review* 27 (May 1974): 221, discounts the long-term importance of the panic entirely, and Douglass C. North, *The Economic Growth of the United States, 1790–1860* (1961; reprint, New York: Norton, 1966), p. 214, stresses the relative lack of impact of the panic on the South. Browne, *Baltimore*, p. 171; John T. O'Brien, "Factory, Church, and Community: Blacks in Antebellum Richmond," *Journal of Southern History* 44 (Nov. 1978): 517–18; Berlin and Gutman, "Free Workers and Slaves," p. 41.

53. *Morning News*, Oct. 15, 16, 1857; *Republican*, Dec. 24, 1857; William W. Gordon to Eleanor L. Kinzie, Oct. 17, 1857, in Haunton, "Savannah," p. 123; also see C. C. Jones, Jr., to Rev. and Mrs. C. C. Jones, Sept. 26, Oct. 10, Oct. 15, 1857, in Myers, *Children of Pride*, pp. 369–70, 374, 375; *Republican*, Oct. 16, 1857; quote on prosperous times from *News*, Sept. 13, 1850; *Republican*, Oct. 23, Dec. 11, 25, 1857; *News*, May 9, 1853; Sept. 5, 16, 1850.

54. *Republican*, Dec. 8, 4, 1857; Nov. 5, 1857; Mississippi *House Journal*, 1835–36, pp. 192–93; note on an 1839 manuscript, file of Report of the Board of Inspectors, Bookkeeper and Other Officials, 1820–1873, Penitentiary Records, GDAH.

55. *Republican*, Oct. 13, Nov. 20, 1860; also see Oct. 18, Nov. 23, Dec. 14; for other cities, see Evitts, *Matter of Allegiances*, p. 170; Reinders, *End of an Era*, p. 243. First citizen quoted in James David Griffin, "Savannah, Georgia, During the Civil War" (Ph.D. diss., Univ. of Georgia, 1963), pp. 42–43. Dr. John S. Law to Rev. C. C. Jones, Dec. 19, 1860, in Myers, *Children of Pride*, p. 635.

56. Rezneck, *Business Depressions*, pp. 103–6; *Republican*, Feb. 6, 1855.

57. Alexandria paper quoted in Goldfield, *Urban Growth*, p. 179; Baltimore journal quoted in Rezneck, *Business Depressions*, p. 106. Also see Van Vleck, *Panic*, p. 83; on 1860, see Browne, *Baltimore*, p. 214.

58. Daniel R. Hundley, *Work and Bread; or, The Coming Winter and the Poor* (Chicago: James Barnet, 1858), pp. 14–16; Dobb quoted in Michael B. Katz, "Origins of the Institutional State," *Marxist Perspectives* 4 (Winter 1978): 15–17. Criminologists do not agree on the effect of unemployment on crime. A 1979 study argues that "the unemployment rate alone explains 54 percent of the variation in the prison population sentenced during the years from 1952 through 1978," while a 1980 rebuttal argues that "unemployment may affect the crime rate, but even if it does, its general effect it too slight to be measured." Both essays—the first by Matthew Yeager and the second by Thomas Orsagh—are in the *Journal of Criminal Law and Criminology* 70 (1979): 586–88; 71 (1980): 181–83.

59. For a useful overview of these findings, see David Cohen and Eric A. Johnson, "French Criminality: Urban-Rural Differences in the Nineteenth Century," *Journal of Interdisciplinary History* 12 (Winter 1982): 477–501; also see note 66 below. On the South, see Michael S. Hindus, *Prison and Plantation: Crime, Justice, and Authority in Massachusetts and South Carolina, 1767–1878* (Chapel Hill: UNC, 1980), pp. 74–75; Robert M. Saunders, "Crime and Punishment in Early National America: Richmond, Virginia, 1784–1820," *Virginia Magazine of History and Biography* 86 (Jan. 1978): 33–44; Arthur F. Howington, "Violence in Alabama: A Study of Late Ante-Bellum Montgomery," *Alabama Review* 27 (July 1974): 213–31.

60. *Republican*, May 18, 1854.

61. *Morning News*, Nov. 15, 1859; *Republican*, Sept. 11, 1855; *Morning News*, July 7,

1856; Thomas Gamble, Jr., *Savannah Duels and Duellists, 1733–1877* (1923; reprint, Spartanburg, S.C.: Reprint Co., 1974), pp. 183–90, 229–300.

62. Parsons, *Inside View*, p. 135; James Silk Buckingham, *The Slave States of America* (London: Fisher, Son, 1842) 1:286–87; Joseph Holt Ingraham, *The South-West, By a Yankee* (New York: Harper and Bros., 1835) 2:167–68.

63. Haunton, "Law and Order," p. 12; Gresham Sykes, *Criminology* (New York: Harcourt Brace Jovanovich, 1978), p. 160.

64. Occupation and Prosecution for Crime (Percentages)

	Property	Violent	Order	Slavery	Deceit	Other
Merchants, Professionals, and Planters (N = 10)	25.0	50.0	0	12.5	12.5	0
Clerks and Proprietors (N = 18)	5.5	38.9	27.8	16.7	11.1	0
Artisans (N = 29)	27.6	44.8	6.9	3.4	6.9	10.4
Unskilled Workers (N = 35)	51.4	25.7	5.7	0	2.8	14.2

SOURCE: See Appendix, Part II.

65. Savannah resident quoted in Griffin, "Savannah During Civil War," p. 18: Northern visitor quoted in Haunton, "Law and Order," p. 11. Also see Samuel Clark, *Social Origins of the Irish Land Wars* (Princeton: Princeton Univ. Press, 1979), pp. 66–74; E. P. Thompson, *The Making of the English Working Class* (1963; reprint, New York: Vintage, 1966), pp. 433–37; Earl Niehaus, *The Irish in New Orleans* (Baton Rouge: LSU, 1965), pp. 66–69.

66. The most sustained argument that urbanization and violent crime are not causally related in Eric Monkkonen, *The Dangerous Class: Crime and Poverty in Columbus, Ohio, 1860–1885* (Cambridge: Harvard Univ. Press, 1975); also see Roger Lane, "Crime and Criminal Statistics in Nineteenth-Century Massachusetts," *Journal of Social History* 2 (Winter 1968): 156–63; idem, *Violent Death in the City: Suicide, Accident, and Murder in Nineteenth-Century Philadelphia* (Cambridge: Harvard Univ. Press, 1979). Conventional wisdom is also questioned in Abdul Lodhi and Charles Tilly, "Urbanization, Crime, and Collective Violence in Nineteenth-Century France," *American Journal of Sociology* 79 (1973): 296–336; Gurr et al., *Politics of Crime*. Also see the Conclusion of the present book.

67. Out of 485 slaves in Savannah's jail in 1857 and 1859, 277 (57.1%) were there for safekeeping, 158 (32.6%) for running away, 14 (2.9%) for larceny, and the other 7.4% for a wide variety of scattered offenses. Manuscript records of Savannah City Jail, Georgia Historical Society.

68. Boston Prison Discipline Society, *Report*, 1844, p. 439. The jail was in Louisville. Fredrika Bremer, trans. Mary Howitt, *The Homes of the New World: Impressions of America* (New York: Harper and Bros., 1853) 2:210–11.

69. Burke, *Reminiscences*, pp. 43–46; Ralph B. Flanders, *Plantation Slavery in Georgia* (Chapel Hill: UNC, 1933), pp. 263–64; also see Howell M. Henry, *Police Control of the Slave in South Carolina* (Emory, Va.: Emory and Henry College, 1914), pp. 46–47; Willie Lee Rose, *A Documentary History of Slavery in North America* (New York: Oxford Univ. Press, 1976), p. 243.

70. Richmond paper quoted in Berlin, *Slaves Without Masters*, p. 334; *Morning News*, July 17, 1851.

71. Quoted in Haunton, "Law and Order," pp. 3, 4, 5; also see Whittington B. Johnson, "Free Blacks in Antebellum Savannah: An Economic Profile," *Georgia Historical Quarterly* 44 (Winter 1980): 420–21.

72. Byrne, "Burden," pp. 114–15, 119–20, 254; quote in Wade, *Slavery*, p. 106; Berlin, *Masters Without Slaves*, pp. 317–32; Haunton, "Law and Order," pp. 3–4; idem, "Savannah," pp. 63–64.

73. Manuscript records of Savannah City Jail, January through June, 1859, Georgia Historical Society.

74. Richard D. Arnold to Col. John W. Forney, Dec. 18, 1850, in Shryock, *Letters*, pp. 44–45; *Republican*, June 20, 1855; Berlin, *Slaves Without Masters*, p. 262; Harden, *Recollections*, pp. 45–46. For other accounts of urban slave theft, see Hindus, "Contours," p. 229; Robert S. Starobin, *Industrial Slavery, in the Old South* (New York: Oxford Univ. Press, 1970), p. 80; Buckingham, *Slave States of America* 2:68; Frederick Law Olmsted, *The Cotton Kingdom*, Arthur Schlesinger, ed. (New York: Knopf, 1953), pp. 82–83.

75. Wade, *Slavery*, esp. chap. 9; Claudia Dale Goldin, *Urban Slavery in the American South, 1820–1860* (Chicago: Univ. of Chicago Press, 1976). There were few free blacks in Savannah, so little was said of them; fortunately we have two histories that deal substantively with the plight of free blacks and their relationship to law and crime: Ira Berlin's *Slaves Without Masters* and Leonard P. Curry, *The Free Black in Urban America, 1800–1850: The Shadow of the Dream* (Chicago: Univ. of Chicago Press, 1981), pp. 261, 114–18.

Chapter 4. The Black Belt and the Upcountry

1. (Greensboro) *Weekly Gazette*, Sept. 21, 1859.

2. H. V. Redfield, *Homicide, North and South: Being a Comparative View of Crime Against the Person in the Several Parts of the United States* (Philadelphia: J. B. Lippincott, 1880), p. 20.

3. William Sparks, *The Memories of Fifty Years* (Philadelphia: Claxton, Remsen and Haffelfinger, 1872), p. 93.

4. Quoted in an article by Thaddeus B. Rice in Greensboro *Herald-Journal*, March 7, 1941, in T. B. Rice Collection, GDAH. The spelling of Greensboro changed over the years; I have used the current spelling throughout.

5. Arthur F. Raper, *Tenants of the Almighty* (New York: Macmillan, 1943), pp. 32, 50–51; T. B. Rice, *History of Greene County, Georgia, 1786–1886*, Carolyn White Williams, ed. (Macon: J. W. Burke, 1961), p. 312, appendix, pp. 438–41; *Weekly Gazette*, Aug. 17, 1859; *Ninth Census of the United States, Population* (Washington, 1866), pp. 58–77; ibid., *Manufactures*, pp. 68, 78–79.

6. Raper, *Tenants*, pp. 50–51, 32; (Greensboro) *Planter's Weekly*, Sept. 5, 1860; on the general process, see James C. Bonner, "Profile of a Late Antebellum Community," *American Historical Review* 49 (July 1944); 663–80, reprinted in Elinor Miller and Eugene D. Genovese, eds., *Plantation, Town, and County: Essays on the Local History of American Slave Society* (Urbana: Univ. of Illinois Press, 1974), esp. p. 33; Gavin Wright, *The Political Economy of the Cotton South: Households, Markets, and Wealth in the Nineteenth Century* (New York: Norton, 1978), pp. 26–33.

7. J. T. Whitman, quoted in Helen Shope, "Dalton's First Family," *Conasauga: North Georgia's Magazine* 2 (1979): 11.

8. The median wealth in Greene in 1860 was $2,560; in Whitfield, only $1,557. The median real estate holding in Greene was also higher: $2,187, versus $1,744 for Whitfield. See Appendix, Part II. Percentage in Whitfield with 1 or 2 slaves was 38.0% (*n* = 178): *Eighth Census, Manufactures*, pp. 68, 78–79. Exact figures on farms over 500 acres: Greene, 24.8% (*n* = 95); Whitfield, 0.8% (*n* = 4).

9. Raper, *Tenants*, pp. 33–35; (Dalton) *North Georgia Citizen*, July 7, 1881, "Reminiscences"; Whitfield County History Commission, *Official History of Whitfield County, Georgia* (Dalton: A. J. Showalter, 1936), pp. 50–51.

10. On the relation of the rural antebellum South to the market economy, see Steven Hahn, "The Roots of Southern Populism: Yeoman Farmers and the Transformation of Upper Piedmont Georgia, 1850–1890" (Ph.D. diss, Yale Univ., 1979), chap. 1; John T. Schlotterbeck, "Plantation and Farm: Social and Economic Change in Orange and Greene Counties, Virginia, 1716 to 1860" (Ph.D. diss., Johns Hopkins Univ., 1980).

11. Paul Murray, *The Whig Party in Georgia, 1825–1853* (Chapel Hill: UNC, 1948), pp. 178–85.

12. Thomas R. R. Cobb, *A Digest of the Statute Laws of the State of Georgia* (Athens: Christy, Kelsea and Burke, 1851) 2:832–43, 1121. "It is well known," writes Theodore Ferdinand, "that the police of small, cohesive communities are considerably more effective in detecting and solving crime than the police of large, urban communities": "The Criminal Patterns of Boston Since 1849," *American Journal of Sociology* 73 (July 1967): 85.

13. From personal observation and historical marker on Main Street in Greensboro, Georgia.

14. Whitfield County Superior Court Minutes, April 30, 1859, p. 342; Oct. 29, 1859, p. 437; Joseph G. Baldwin, *Flush Times of Alabama and Mississippi: A Series of Sketches* (New York: Appleton, 1853), p. 59.

15. Raper, *Tenants*, pp. 16, 47; *Weekly Gazette*, May 25, 1859; *Planter's Weekly*, March 28, 1860.

16. Out of 91 defendants in Greene in the 1850s, 50 appeared in one of the censuses; in Whitfield, only 20 out of 50 were in the census records. On mobility, see James B. Oakes, *The Ruling Race: A History of American Slaveholders* (New York: Knopf, 1982), pp. 77–78. Jack K. Williams has observed that in antebellum South Carolina, "had grand juries not summarily disposed of about one-third of the criminal indictments the situation would have been hopeless. As things stood there was a constant complaint that sessions dockets were too crowded, with juries overworked and justice ill-served as a result": *Vogues in Villainy: Crime and Retribution in Antebellum South Carolina* (Columbia: Univ. of South Carolina Press, 1959), p. 80. Williams's book is a groundbreaking and fascinating study.

17. Superior Court Minutes, manuscript census returns, Georgia Penitentiary Records, GDAH.

18. In the 1850s, the Greene County court levied 50 fines, 44 of them under $10, 1 for $25, 1 for $75; of Whitfield's 7 fines, 6 were for under $10, the other $25; Jim Byrd, Valle Crucis, North Carolina, in Laurel Shackelford and Bill Weinberg, eds., *Our Appalachia: An Oral History* (New York: Hill and Wang, 1977), pp. 24–25.

19. Quoted in Robert M. Ireland, "Law and Disorder in Nineteenth-Century Kentucky," *Vanderbilt Law Review* 32 (1979): 281–99, esp. 282; Daniel H. Calhoun, "Branding Iron and Retrospect: Lawyers in the Cumberland River Country," in *Professional Lives in America: Structure and Aspiration, 1750–1850* (Cambridge: Harvard Univ. Press, 1965).

20. Sparks, *Memories*, p. 74; Superior Court Minutes, Greene and Whitfield County Tax Digests, manuscript census returns, 1850, GDAH.

21. (Milledgeville) *Southern Recorder*, Dec. 14, 1858; quote in Ireland, "Law and Disorder," p. 291; *Hinds County Gazette*, Sept. 27, 1854.

22. Greene County Superior Court Minutes, March 1852, p. 500; manuscript census returns, tax digests, 1852, GDAH.

23. Madison *Visitor* in *Southern Recorder*, May 24, 1859.

24. Raper, *Tenants*, pp. 42, 17.

25. A. R. Newsome, ed., "The A. S. Merrimon Journal, 1853–1854," *North Carolina Historical Review* 8 (July 1931): 300–330; quote, p. 324.

26. Penfield *Temperance-Banner*, Jan. 27, 1855.

27. Cobb, *Digest* 2:811; Superior Court Minutes.

28. Crimes by Category, Five Counties (Percentages)

	Greene[a]	Whitfield[a]	Louisa[b]	Shenandoah[b]	Chatham[c]
Property	3.7	6.4	13.3	16.3	19.8
Violence	24.3	31.3	26.6	43.4	42.9
Order	15.3	36.0	13.3	6.5	11.6
Slavery	10.0	0.2	10.1	0	5.7
Deceit	3.0	3.9	0.7	1.8	8.2
Liquor	11.3	2.6	10.1	20.6	0.7
Gaming	18.7	9.2	21.1	2.5	0.1
Sexual	5.3	3.8	4.7	2.8	1.3
Other	8.4	6.6	0.1	6.1	9.7
N	300	1,000	128	325	915

[a]Includes 1835, 1838, 1841, 1844, 1847, 1850–60 (figures for Whitfield before 1852 are from Murray County, from which Whitfield was made in 1852).
[b]1820–60; does not include prosecutions for failure to do road duty.
[c]1835, 1838, 1847, 1850–69 (other records missing).
SOURCE: See Appendix, Part II.

According to Guion Griffis Johnson, in *Ante-Bellum North Carolina: A Social History* (Chapel Hill: UNC, 1937), p. 658, 60% of all crimes punished by North Carolina's county courts were assault and battery or affray, and these figures do not include felonies. Michael Hindus, in his article, "The Contours of Crime and Justice in Massachusetts and South Carolina, 1767–1878," *American Journal of Legal History* 21 (1977): 218, shows that in South Carolina between 1800 and 1860, crimes against persons comprised 61.5% of recorded crimes (and this figure does not include riot and affray); for the North, Hindus found that in Massachusetts from 1833 to 1858 only 17.8% of crimes were violent. There was also little violence in Marion County (Indianapolis), Indiana, in the antebellum period. See David J. Bodenhamer, "Law and Disorder on the Early Frontier: Marion County, Indiana, 1823–1850," *Western Historical Quarterly* 10 (July 1979): 330.

29. Percent of propertyless criminals: Greene, 38.0 (n = 50); Whitfield, 35.3 (n = 17); Chatham, 83.1 (n = 59): See Appendix, Part II.

30. It is revealing that 77.8% of the defendents found in Greene had been born in Georgia, while only 22.2% of Whitfield's had; the latter, a much younger and apparently more fluid society, drew 29.6% of its defendants from South Carolina and 33.3% from other Southern states.

31. Exact percentages married: Greene: 74.0 (n = 50); Whitfield: 90.0 (n = 20); Chatham: 52.8 (n = 72).

32. "Relation of Education to the Prevention of Crime," *DeBow's Review* 18 (1855): 418–19; Kai T. Erikson, *Wayward Puritans: A Study in the Sociology of Deviance* (New York: Wiley, 1966).

33. In antebellum North Carolina, retailing liquor, bastardy, fornication, and adultery accounted for 16.6% of crime. See Johnson, *Ante-Bellum North Carolina*, p. 658. David Bodenhamer, in "Law and Lawlessness in the Deep South: The Local Response to Antebellum Crime" (Paper presented at the Organization of American Historians Convention, 1978), abridged version in Walter J. Fraser, Jr., and Winfred B. Moore, Jr., eds., *From the Old South to the New: Essays on the Transitional South* (Westport: Greenwood, 1981), pp. 109–19, found in other Georgia counties that moral crimes accounted for from 17.7% to 41.9% of all crime.

34. Whitfield County Superior Court Minutes, Oct. 1859, p. 438. Fluctuations in the prosecution of moral crimes also accounted for the major fluctuations of crime rates in at least parts of the North: see Bodenhamer, "Law and Disorder," and Hindus, "Contours."

35. Whitfield Superior Court Minutes, 1852, pp. 53–55; Penfield *Temperance-Banner*, Jan. 26, 1854; W. J. Rorabaugh, "The Sons of Temperance in Antebellum Jasper County," *Georgia Historical Quarterly* 64 (Fall 1980): 263–79. Also see Chapter One, note 16 of the present study.

36. Letter to *Biblical Recorder*, July 10, 1832, quoted in C. C. Pearson and J. Edwin Hendricks, *Liquor and Anti-Liquor in Virginia, 1619–1919* (Durham: Duke Univ. Press, 1967), pp. 69–70. For similar resistance of some Southern church members to reform, see Bertram Wyatt-Brown, "The Anti-Mission Movement in the Jacksonian South: A Study in Regional Folk Culture," *Journal of Southern History* 36 (1970).

37. Rhys Isaac, "Evangelical Revolt: The Nature of the Baptists' Challenge to the Traditional Order in Virginia, 1765 to 1775," in T. H. Breen, ed., *Shaping Southern Society: The Colonial Experience* (New York: Oxford, 1976), pp. 247–65, 258–59. Raper, *Tenants*, pp. 23–24.

38. Donald G. Mathews, *Religion in the Old South* (Chicago: Univ. of Chicago Press, 1977), pp. 82–83; Rhys Isaac, *The Transformation of Virginia, 1740–1790* (Chapel Hill: UNC, 1982), p. 309.

39. " 'Whitfield County's Tunnel Hill' is Topic of Paper Read by Mrs. Gowin for Historians,' *Dalton Citizen*, Dec. 20, 1951.

40. Mrs. W. M. Sapp, Sr., "History of the [Dalton First Baptist] Church," Dalton, 1947, microfilm at GDAH; L. W. Richardson, "A Glimpse of Dalton in 1853," *Whitfield-Murray Historical Society Quarterly* 5 (April 1981): 7–10.

41. Rice, *History of Greene County*, p. 118; Cortland V. Smith, "Church Organization as an Agency of Social Control" (Ph.D. diss., Univ. of North Carolina, Chapel Hill, 1967), pp. 201–2.

42. T. P. Jones to the Baptist Church at Bethesda, in Bethesda Church Minutes, 1833–66, microfilm at GDAH; second quote in entry for March 6, 1864, Bethesda Minutes. Luther Addington in Shackelford and Weinberg, *Our Appalachia*, pp. 44–45. For a church in North Carolina the major offenses were, in declining order, drunkenness, disputing with a member, neglecting church service, being "out of the way," sexual immorality, fighting, and becoming angry: see Johnson, *Ante-Bellum North Carolina*, pp. 450–51.

43. *The Papers of Frederick Law Olmsted*, vol. 2, *Slavery and the South, 1852–1857*, Charles E. Beveridge and Charles Capen McLaughlin, eds., (Baltimore: Johns Hopkins Univ. Press, 1981), p. 208; *Southern Evangelical Intelligencer*, May 8, 1819, quoted in Anne C. Loveland, *Southern Evangelicals and the Social Order, 1800–1860* (Baton Rouge: LSU, 1980), p. 160. In her superb study, Loveland stresses the fatalism of Southern evangelical ministers; see esp. pp. 125–29.

44. Penfield Baptist Church Minutes, Feb. 1850; Johnson, *Ante-Bellum North Carolina*, p. 450.

45. *Methodist Quarterly Review* 9 (Jan. 1855): 85, quoted in Loveland, *Southern Evangelicals*, p. 110; *Southern Presbyterian Review* 10 (1857–58): 132; minutes of Siloam, Bethesda, and New Hope Baptist churches, microfilm at GDAH.

46. *Weekly Gazette*, Aug. 10, 1859.

47. Ibid.; Rice, *History of Greene County*, pp. 121–22; Raper, *Tenants*, pp. 52–53; Penfield Baptist Church Minutes, Sept. 1856; *Mary Chesnut's Civil War*, C. Vann Woodward, ed., (New Haven: Yale Univ. Press, 1981), p. 259; Ralph B. Flanders, *Plantation Slavery in Georgia* (Chapel Hill: UNC, 1933), pp. 269–70. Slave religion has received a great deal of attention from historians; see especially John Blassingame, *The Slave Community: Plantation Life in the Antebellum South* (rev. ed., New York: Oxford Univ. Press, 1979); Eugene Genovese, *Roll, Jordan, Roll: The World the Slaves Made* (New York: Pantheon, 1974); Mathews, *Religion*; and for a recent synthesis, Albert J. Raboteau, *Slave Religion: The "Invisible Institution" in the Antebellum South* (New York: Oxford Univ. Press, 1978).

48. Siloam Baptist Church Minutes, 1828–69, GDAH, June 1850; August 1850; Bethesda Baptist Church Minutes, Dec. 19, 1853; also see New Hope Baptist Church Minutes, GDAH, Nov. 1856, the case of Isaac. William B. Posey, cited in Genovese, *Roll, Jordan, Roll*, p. 599, argues that theft was the most commonly disciplined offense among slaves who were church members; also see Mathews, *Religion*, p. 147; Smith, "Church Organization," p. 177; Joseph C. Robert, "Excommunication, Virginia Style," *South Atlantic Quarterly* 40 (July 1941): 243–58. John T. O'Brien has discovered that autonomous urban black churches in Richmond maintained a rigorous discipline similar to that of white congregations: "Factory, Church, and Community: Blacks in Antebellum Richmond," *Journal of Southern History* 44 (Nov. 1978): 528–29.

49. Bethesda Baptist Church Minutes, July 1856, Aug. 1858; George P. Rawick, ed., *The American Slave: A Composite Autobiography* (Westport, Conn.: Greenwood Press, 1972): *Arkansas Narratives* 8(2):190.

50. Rawick, *American Slave*: 8(1):35, 12(2):131; Raper, *Tenants*, p. 53.

51. Rawick, *American Slave: Ga. Narr., Suppl.* 3:70; also see Frederick Law Olmsted, *The Cotton Kingdom: A Traveller's Observations on Cotton and Slavery in the American Slave States*, Arthur Schlesinger, ed., (New York: Knopf, 1953), p. 76. Frederick Douglass, *The Heroic Slave* (1853), quoted in Ronald T. Takaki, *Violence in the Black*

Imagination: Essays and Documents (New York: Putnam, 1972), p. 50; Josiah Henson, *Father Henson's Story of His Own Life* (1858; reprint, New York: Corinth Books, 1962), pp. 21–23. Stealing and other forms of resistance are much more prominent in slave autobiographies than in the WPA narratives: see David Thomas Bailey, "A Divided Prism: Two Sources of Black Testimony on Slavery," *Journal of Southern History* 46 (Aug. 1980): 381–404.

52. Ex-slave quoted in Paul D. Escott, *Slavery Remembered: A Record of Twentieth-Century Slave Narratives* (Chapel Hill: UNC, 1979), p. 77; Escott lists citations for 14 other comments on theft in Rawick, *American Slave*. Song in William F. Cheek, *Black Resistance Before the Civil War* (Beverly Hills: Sage, 1970), p. 58. On the slave tales, see Lawrence Levine, *Black Culture and Black Consciousness: Afro-American Folk Thought From Slavery to Freedom* (New York: Oxford Univ. Press, 1977), p. 130; also see the "John tales" in Harold Courlander, *A Treasury of Afro-American Folklore* (New York: Crown, 1976), p. 431.

53. Olmsted, *Cotton Kingdom*, p. 83; S. A. O'Ferrall, *A Ramble of Six Thousand Miles Through the United States of America* (London: E. Wilson, 1832), p. 203; Rawick, *American Slave: Ga. Narr.* 12(2):119.

54. Charles L. Perdue, Jr., Thomas E. Borden, and Robert K. Phillips, eds., *Weevils in the Wheat: Interviews with Virginia Ex-Slaves* (Charlottesville: Univ. of Virginia Press, 1976), pp. 266, 245, 124; Lunsford Lane, *The Narrative of Lunsford Lane* (Boston: J. G. Torrey, 1842), p. 19; Rawick, *American Slave: Ga. Narr.* 12(2):235.

55. Rawick, *American Slave: Ga. Narr.* 12(2):310; *Miss. Narr., Suppl.* 9:1388–89; Frances Anne Kemble, *Journal of a Residence on a Georgia Plantation in 1838–1839* (New York: Longman, Roberts and Green, 1863), pp. 193–94.

56. Recent studies show that age curves are one of the most accurate predictors of crime trends. See Ted Robert Gurr, "On the History of Violent Crime in Europe and America," in Hugh D. Graham and Ted R. Gurr, eds., *Violence in America: Historical and Comparative Perspectives* (rev. ed., Beverly Hills: Sage, 1979), pp. 366–69. On the youth of slaves, see Oakes, *Ruling Race*, pp. 249–50.

57. Frederick Douglass, *My Bondage and My Freedom* (1855; reprint, New York: Dover, 1969), pp. 188–90.

58. Ibid.

59. Genovese, *Roll, Jordan, Roll*, pp. 607–8; Levine, *Black Culture and Black Consciousness*, p. 117; Gresham Sykes, *Criminology* (New York: Harcourt Brace Jovanovich, 1978), pp. 308–13.

60. Peter Wood, *Black Majority: Negroes in South Carolina from 1670 to the Stono Rebellion* (New York: Norton, 1974), pp. 216–17; Gerald Mullin, *Flight and Rebellion: Slave Resistance in Eighteenth-Century Virginia* (New York: Oxford Univ. Press, 1972), pp. 60–61; D. R. Hundley, *Social Relations in Our Southern States* (New York: H. B. Price, 1860), pp. 228–30. On theft by planters, see Rawick, *American Slave: Ga. Narr.* 13(4):134, 185; 12(2):52, 317; *Fla. Narr.* 16:191–92.

61. Penfield *Temperance-Banner*, Nov. 10, 1853, Sept. 16, 1854; Augusta *Dispatch*, Nov. 29, 1859, in *Weekly Gazette*, Dec. 7, 1859.

62. Olmsted, *Cotton Kingdom*, pp. 195, 65–66, 258; *State v. Hale*, 9 *NC* 325, 327 (1823), quoted in Daniel F. Flanigan, "The Criminal Law of Slavery and Freedom, 1800–1868" (Ph.D. diss., Rice University 1973), p. 167. For the best

figures on slave violence, see Flanigan's dissertation, pp. 47–48, 50, table on 404–5, expanded from figures in U. B. Phillips, "Slave Crime in Virginia," *American Historical Review* 20 (1915): 336–40.

63. Nehemiah Adams, *A South-Side View of Slavery; or, Three Months at the South, in 1854* (Boston: B. B. Mussey, 1854), pp. 41–42; U. B. Phillips, *American Negro Slavery* (1918; reprint, New York: LSU, 1966), p. 463; "On the Management of Negroes," *Southern Agriculturist* 7 (1834): 369, in Genovese, *Roll, Jordan, Roll*, p. 635; Rev. C. C. Jones, *Religious Instruction of the Negroes of the United States* (Savannah: T. Purse, 1842), p. 136; George Fredrickson, *The Black Image in the White Mind: The Debate on Afro-American Character and Destiny, 1817–1914* (New York: Harper, 1971), pp. 53–56; quote from Dr. Samuel Cartwright, "Negro Freedom: An Impossibility Under Nature's Laws," *DeBow's Review* 30 (1861), in Federickson, *Black Image*, p. 55.

64. *Weekly Gazette*, May 18, 1859; Blassingame, *Slave Community*, pp. 318–30; Escott, *Slavery Remembered*, pp. 85–94; Takaki, *Violence in the Black Imagination*. The notion of reciprocal rights is central to Genovese's *Roll, Jordan, Roll*: see esp. p. 91.

65. Hundley, *Social Relations*, p. 332; Rawick, *American Slave: Ga. Narr.* 12(1):80.

66. Rawick, *American Slave: Miss. Narr., Suppl.* 6:179; *Ga. Narr.* 12(1):310; 13(4):293–94; also on stripping see *Ga. Narr.* 13(4), 291–30; *Mo. Narr., Suppl* 12(4):243; Willie Lee Rose, *Slavery and Freedom*, William Freehling, ed. (New York: Oxford Univ. Press, 1982), pp. 32–34.

67. There is an extensive literature on the law of slavery. A. E. Keir Nash helped begin the recent debate with a series of articles stressing the fairness of Southern courts. See, for example, "Fairness and Formalism in the Trials of Blacks in the State Supreme Courts of the Old South," *Virginia Law Review* 56 (1970): 62–100. Nash defends his interpretation against all detractors in a long essay, "Reason of Slavery: Understanding the Judicial Role in the Peculiar Institution," *Vanderbilt Law Review* 32 (1979): 7–218. Daniel Flanigan, in his excellent dissertation "Criminal Law" and in his article "Criminal Procedure in Slave Trials in the Antebellum South," *Journal of Southern History* 40 (1974): 537–64, also stresses procedural fairness in higher courts in the South; Meredith Lang, in *Defender of the Faith: The High Court of Mississippi, 1817–1875* (Jackson: Univ. Press of Mississippi, 1977), pp. 158–59, sees the criminal law of slavery as "sympathetic, almost indulgent." Mark Tushnet's detailed study, *The American Law of Slavery, 1810–1860: Considerations of Humanity and Interest* (Princeton: Princeton Univ. Press, 1981), emphasizes the relative autonomy and internal dynamics of the legal system. Arthur Howington has investigated the treatment of blacks in the county courts in "According to Law: The Trial and Punishment of Black Defendants in Antebellum Tennessee" (Paper read at the Organization of American Historians annual meeting, New York City, April 12, 1978); he argues that black defendants were treated much the same as whites. But Michael Hindus, in "Black Justice Under White Law: Criminal Prosecutions of Blacks in Antebellum South Carolina," *Journal of American History* 63 (1976): 573–99, examined even lower courts for two counties in South Carolina and found that blacks were treated very harshly at that level. Other studies have examined fewer cases in more detail and reveal the importance of the nature of the

offense, the circumstances, and the climate of race relations. See John C. Edwards, "Slave Justice in Four Middle Georgia Counties," *Georgia Historical Quarterly* 57 (1973): 265–73; Royce Gordon Shingleton, "The Trial and Punishment of Slaves in Baldwin County, Georgia, 1812–1826," *Southern Humanities Review* 8 (1974): 67–73. Older accounts, while anecdotal and tending to focus on the unique, offer greater detail and are quite useful. The chapters on law and crime in Flanders, *Plantation Slavery in Georgia*, pp. 233–279, are outstanding, as are those in James B. Sellers, *Slavery in Alabama* (University, Ala.: Univ. of Alabama Press, 1950). H. M. Henry's *Police Control of the Slave in South Carolina* (Emory, Va.: Emory and Henry College, 1914) is still worth consulting, and so is Helen T. Catterall's monumental *Judicial Cases Concerning American Slavery and the Negro*, 5 vols. (Washington: Carnegie Institution, 1929–37). Leon Higginbotham, Jr.'s, *In the Matter of Color: Race and the American Legal Process: The Colonial Period* (New York: Oxford Univ. Press, 1978) provides necessary background. In a brief and useful essay, "Approaches to the Study of the Law of Slavery," *Civil War History* 25 (1979): 329–38, Mark Tushnet synthesizes much of the recent work on the law of slavery.

68. Rev. C. C. Jones to C. C. Jones, Jr., Dec. 10, 1859, and C. C. Jones, Jr., to Rev. and Mrs. C. C. Jones, Dec. 12, 1859, in Robert Myers, ed., *The Children of Pride: A True Story of Georgia and the Civil War* (New Haven: Yale Univ. Press, 1972), pp. 544–46. Genovese's chapter in *Roll, Jordan, Roll* on "The Hegemonic Function of the Law" has greatly influenced my argument. Also see Douglas Hay, "Property, Authority and the Criminal Law," in Hay et al., eds., *Albion's Fatal Tree: Crime and Society in Eighteenth-Century England* (New York: Allen Lane, 1975), esp. p. 33.

69. Olmsted, *Cotton Kingdom*, p. 262; Flanigan, "Criminal Law," pp. 145–46, 164, 167; Genovese, *Roll, Jordan, Roll*, pp. 46–47. Greene County Superior Court Minutes, March 1851; also see March 1853 for the similar punishment of another slave.

70. Douglass, *Bondage and Freedom*, p. 64; J.D.B. DeBow quoted in Richard C. Wade, *Slavery in the Cities: The South, 1820–1860* (New York: Oxford Univ. Press, 1964), p. 249; (Raleigh) *North Carolina Standard*, Sept. 17, 1845.

71. Catherine Hewey, quoted in Edwards, "Slave Justice," p. 267.

72. John Horrey Dent Diary, microfilm at GDAH, 5:61–62, May 1859. The use of this valuable diary is greatly facilitated by Ray Mathis and Mary Mathis, *Introduction and Index to the John Horrey Dent Farm Journals and Account Books, 1840–1892* (University, Ala: Univ. of Alabama Press, 1977). On hangings, also see Johnson, *Ante-Bellum North Carolina*, p. 677; Williams, *Vogues in Villainy*, p. 101; E. Merton Coulter, "Hanging as a Socio-Penal Institution in Georgia and Elsewhere," *Georgia Historical Quarterly* 57 (1973): 22.

73. George Fitzhugh, *Sociology for the South*, in Eric McKitrick, ed., *Slavery Defended: The Views of the Old South* (Englewood Cliffs, N.J.: Prentice-Hall, 1963), pp. 47–48; also see "The North and the South," *DeBow's Review* 7 (1849): 309: "So much for the States of the North, agricultural, manufacturing, and commercial, old and new, as compared with those of the South, in crime. The results are uniformly and largely in favor of the South."

Chapter 5. War and Reconstruction

1. (Greensboro) *Planter's Weekly*, Nov. 21, 1860; Allen D. Candler, ed., *The Confederate Records of the State of Georgia* (Atlanta: State Printer, 1909) 1:68–79. For the connection between honor and secession, see William J. Cooper, Jr., *The South and the Politics of Slavery* (Baton Rouge: LSU, 1978), esp. pp. 69–74; Don E. Fehrenbacher, *The South and Three Sectional Crises* (Baton Rouge: LSU, 1980), pp. 64–65.

2. James David Griffin, "Savannah, Georgia, During the Civil War" (Ph.D. diss., Univ. of Georgia, 1963), pp. 57–59; also see Michael P. Johnson, *Toward A Patriarchial Republic: The Secession of Georgia* (Baton Rouge: LSU, 1977), p. 40.

3. Whitfield County History Commission, *Official History of Whitfield County, Georgia* (Dalton: A. J. Showalter, 1936), p. 55; Whitfield County Superior Court Minutes, GDAH, May 1861, p. 135.

4. Arthur Raper, *Tenants of the Almighty* (New York: Macmillan, 1943), pp. 62–75.

5. Ibid., pp. 63–64; Whitfield County Superior Court Minutes, May 1861, p. 166.

6. Griffin, "Savannah During Civil War," pp. 211–12.

7. Ibid., pp. 43, 193.

8. John Trowbridge, *The South: A Tour of Its Battlefields and Ruined Cities* (Hartford: L. Stebbing, 1866), p. 167; Steven Hahn, "The Roots of Southern Populism: Yeoman Farmers and the Transformation of Upper Piedmont Georgia, 1850–1890," (Ph.D. diss., Yale Univ. 1979), p. 206; Emory Thomas, *The Confederate Nation, 1861–1865* (New York: Harper, 1979), pp. 202–5; Paul D. Escott, *After Seccesion: Jefferson Davis and the Failure of Confederate Nationalism* (Baton Rouge: LSU, 1978), p. 128.

9. Cains quoted in Hahn, "Roots," p. 204; Seddon quoted in Escott, *After Secession*, pp. 107–10.

10. Whitfield County Superior Court Minutes, 1861–65, GDAH; C. Mildred Thompson, *Reconstruction in Georgia: Economic, Social , Political, 1865–1872* (1915: reprint, Savannah: Beehive Press, 1972), pp. 22–23; Hahn, "Roots," p. 205. During the war, 139 (67.1%) of the defendants were prosecuted with at least one other defendant, while only 68 were prosecuted individually. Between 1856 and 1860, on the other hand, 116 (43.3%) of the defendants were prosecuted in groups, while 152 were not. For whatever reason, Whitfield prosecuted more people as groups than did Greene or Chatham counties.

11. Both quoted in James L. Roark, *Masters Without Slaves: Southern Planters in the Civil War and Reconstruction* (New York: Norton, 1977), p. 64, and also see p. 55; Bell Irvin Wiley, *The Plain People of the Confederacy* (Baton Rouge: LSU, 1944), pp. 64–66.

12. *Official History of Whitfield*, pp. 56–61.

13. Bell Irvin Wiley, *The Life of Johnny Reb* (1943: reprint, Baton Rouge: LSU, 1978), p. 53; Wiley, *Plain People*, pp. 62–63.

14. *Official History of Whitfield*, pp. 60–61.

15. Thompson, *Reconstruction*, p. 15; Raper, *Tenants*, pp. 70–71; Bell Irvin Wiley, *Southern Negroes, 1861–1865* (1938; reprint, Baton Rouge: LSU Press, 1965), pp.

246–47. On slaves' response to the war, see Leon Litwack, *Been in the Storm So Long: The Aftermath of Slavery* (New York: Knopf, 1979), esp. pp. 5, 142; Wiley, *Plain People*, pp. 70–74, 78–81; C. Peter Ripley, *Slaves and Freedmen in Civil War Louisiana* (Baton Rouge: LSU Press, 1976), p. 13.

16. William A. Byrne, "The Burden and Heat of the Day: Slavery and Servitude in Savannah, 1733–1865" (Ph.D. diss., Florida State Univ., 1979), pp. 308, 316–17; Savannah *Morning News* (hereafter *SMN*), Sept. 27, 1864.

17. Raper, *Tenants*, pp. 74–75.

18. Ibid., pp. 72–73. The Greensboro *Herald* published a revealing account of emancipation by humorist Bill Arp on Dec. 19, 1872: "The whole thing cum upon us so sudden—so collapsy. It was like we all had moved to another country. . . . If we could have slid into it quietly and slantendikular, if slavery could have sorter tapered in, everybody could have got used to it. . . . Talk about manners and customs and statisticks! Why we wasent the same people."

19. See Theodore B. Wilson, *The Black Codes of the South* (University, Ala.: Univ. of Alabama Press, 1965); Donald G. Nieman, *To Set the Law in Motion: The Freedman's Bureau and the Legal Rights of Blacks* (Millwood, N. Y.: KTO, 1979), pp. 72–98; for Georgia, see Thompson, *Reconstruction*, pp. 143–45; Alan Conway, *The Reconstruction of Georgia* (Minneapolis: Univ. of Minnesota Press, 1966), pp. 55–57.

20. Quoted in Litwack, *Been in the Storm*, pp. 286–87; Charles Stearns, *The Black Man of the South and the Rebels; or, The Characteristics of the Former, and the Recent Outrages of the Latter* (1872; reprint, New York: Kraus Reprint Co., 1969), pp. 70–71. For the unbounded faith in contract and legality, see Daniel A. Novak, *The Wheel of Servitude: Black Forced Labor after Slavery* (Lexington: Univ. of Kentucky Press, 1978), p. 11. On the nature of legal change after the war, see Daniel J. Flanigan, 'The Criminal Law of Slavery and Freedom, 1800–1868" (Ph.D. diss., Rice Univ., 1973); Harold D. Woodman, "Post–Civil War Southern Agriculture and the Law," *Agricultural History* 53 (1979): 319–37; William Cohen, "Negro Involuntary Servitude in the South, 1865–1940: A Preliminary Analysis," *Journal of Southern History* 42 (1976): 31–60; John B. Meyers, "The Freedman and the Law in Post-Bellum Alabama, 1865–1867," *Alabama Review* 23 (Jan. 1970): 55–69.

21. George R. Bentley, *A History of the Freedmen's Bureau* (Philadelphia: Univ. of Pennsylvania Press, 1944), pp. 152–68; Thompson, *Reconstruction*, pp. 50–51; Paul A. Cimbala, "The 'Talisman Power': Davis Tillson, The Freedmen's Bureau, and Free Labor in Reconstruction Georgia, 1865–1868," *Civil War History* 28 (June 1982): 153–71; freedmen quoted in Nieman, *To Set the Law in Motion*, p. 27.

22. Nancy Bowman to Gen. John Pope, May 2, 1867, Bureau of Refugees, Freedmen, and Abandoned Lands: Records of the Assistant Commissioner for the State of Georgia, National Archives RG 105, microcopy 798 [herafter FB-Ga], Letters Received, reel 14; L. P. Gudger to Col. C. C. Sibley, Sept. 13, 1867, FB-Ga, Letters Received, reel 18.

23. Gen. Tillson to Brt. Major Gen. Brannon, March 5, 1866, FB-Ga, Endorsements, reel 18, p. 117; Jonathan T. Dawson to Assistant Commissioner, Feb. 23, 1866, FB-Ga, Letters Received, reel 11, pp. 107–8.

24. Joseph Williams and five others to Col. C. C. Sibley, June 17, 1867, FB-Ga, Letters Received, reel 19; Abram Colby and 32 others to Gen. John Pope, Aug.

15, 1867, ibid., reel 17; the order for the investigation appears in Endorsements, Aug. 21, 1867, 3:377.

25. Thompson, *Reconstruction*, p. 36; A. G. Brown to Assistant Commissioner, May 12, 1866, FB-Ga, Endorsements, reel 8, p. 211; James Grant to Assistant Commissioner, April 24, 1866, Letters Received, reel 11, p. 170; Abram Winfield and ten others to Assistant Commissioner, Jan. 27, 1866, ibid., reel 11, pp. 514–15; Gen. Tillson to Gen. O. O. Howard, March 12, 1866, Endorsements, reel 8.

26. "Condition of Affairs in the Southern States—Georgia," House of Representatives, *Miscellaneous Documents*, 3d sess. 40th Cong. 1868–69, p. 138; Nieman, *To Set the Law in Motion*, pp. 27–28; Jesse Parker Bogue, Jr., "Violence and Oppression in North Carolina During Reconstruction, 1865–1873" (Ph.D. diss., Univ. of Maryland, 1973); Thomas D. Morris, "Equality, 'Extraordinary Law,' and Criminal Justice: The South Carolina Experience, 1865–1866," *South Carolina Historical Magazine* 83 (Jan. 1982): 15–33. Most of the energies of the courts were spent on wages and contracts—only about one-quarter of the cases involved criminal charges: Henry August Volz III, "The Administration of Justice by the Freedmen's Bureau in Kentucky, South Carolina, and Virginia" (Master's thesis, Univ. of Virginia, 1975), pp. 34–40, appendices A and B; Conway, *Reconstruction*, pp. 77–82.

27. Greensboro *Herald* (herafter *GH*), March 25, 1875.

28. Ibid., Dec. 3, April 2, Oct. 22, Oct. 29, 1868.

29. *Report of the Joint Select Committee to Inquire into the Condition of Affairs in the Late Insurrectionary States* (Washington, 1872), *House Reports*, 42d Cong., 2d sess., no. 22 (hereafter *KKK Report*), Georgia, pp. 695–707.

30. Ibid., pp. 700–701.

31. *GH*, Nov. 16, 1867.

32. Ibid., Aug. 26, 1869.

33. Ibid., April 2, 1868; Thompson, *Reconstruction*, pp. 351–52.

34. *GH*, Oct. 29, Nov. 12, Nov. 19, Dec. 3, 1874.

35. Thompson, *Reconstruction*, pp. 338–41. Vigilante violence did not begin immediately after the war, but only after Southern whites lost control of the state legal apparatus. See Conway, *Reconstruction*, p. 74; Charles L. Flynn, Jr., "White Land, Black Labor: Property, Ideology, and the Political Economy of Late Nineteenth-Century Georgia" (Ph.D. diss., Duke Univ., 1980), pp. 39–44.

36. Thompson, *Reconstruction*, p. 368.

37. Ibid., p. 340.

38. *KKK Report*, Georgia, pp. 567–580.

39. Ibid., pp. 571, 573–74.

40. See Chapter Seven.

41. Litwack, *Been in the Storm*, pp. 280–81; Jack D. L. Holmes, "The Underlying Causes of the Memphis Race Riot of 1866," *Tennessee Historical Quarterly* 17 (Sept. 1958): 195–221; Bobby L. Lovett, "Memphis Riots: White Reaction to Blacks in Memphis, May 1965–July 1866," *Tennessee Historical Quarterly* 38 (Spring 1979): 9–33; William S. McFeely, *Yankee Stepfather: General O. O. Howard and the Freedmen* (1968; reprint, New York: Norton, 1970), pp. 272–87.

42. "South Carolina Morals," *Atlantic Monthly* 33 (April 1877): 474.

43. Thompson, *Reconstruction*, pp. 173–74, 356. Also see Joseph P. Reidy, "Aaron A.

Bradley: Voice of Black Labor in the Georgia Lowcountry," in Howard N. Rabinowitz, ed., *Southern Black Leaders of the Reconstruction Era* (Urbana: Univ. of Illinois Press, 1982). pp. 281–308.

44. Conway, *Reconstruction*, pp. 175–76.

45. John C. Reed, "What I Know of the Ku Klux Klan," *Uncle Remus Magazine*, Jan.–Nov. 1868, quoted in Thompson, *Reconstruction*, p. 357; *KKK Report*, Georgia, pp. 1113–14.

46. Robert Somers, *The Southern States Since the War, 1870–71* (1871; reprint, University: Univ. of Alabama Press, 1965), pp. 153–54; *KKK Report*, Georgia, pp. 190–93; testimony of W. W. Paine, Savannah. The standard work on the Klan is Allen W. Trelease, *White Terror: The Ku Klux Klan Conspiracy and Southern Reconstruction* (New York: Harper and Row, 1971). On the interconnectedness of the objects of Klan violence, see J. C. A. Stagg, "The Problem of Klan Violence: The South Carolina Up-Country, 1868–1871," *Journal of American Studies* 8 (1974): 303–18. For a view from the black side, see Gladys-Marie Fry, *Night Riders in Black Folk History* (Knoxville: Univ. of Tennessee Press, 1975).

47. See Edmund S. Morgan, *American Slavery—American Freedom: The Ordeal of Colonial Virginia* (New York: Norton, 1975), pp. 380–87.

48. **GH, Nov. 4, 1869. See Raper, *Tenants*, pp. 78, 369–70, for accounts of conflict** between a worker and employer and a copy of an early contract in Greene County.

49. See Roark, *Masters Without Slaves*, pp. 142–45; Greene County Court Minutes, 1866, GDAH.

50. On the transformation of the Southern economy, see Harold D. Woodman, "Sequel to Slavery: The New History Views the Postbellum South," *Journal of Southern History* 43 (Nov. 1977): 523–54, esp. pp. 550–54—an article crucial to understanding the postwar South; Woodman, "Post–Civil War Southern Agriculture"; Gavin Wright, *The Political Economy of the Cotton South: Households, Markets, and Wealth in the Nineteenth Century* (New York: Norton, 1978); Jonathan M. Wiener, *Social Origins of the New South: Alabama, 1865–1885* (Baton Rouge: LSU, 1978); Roger L. Ransom and Richard Sutch, *One Kind of Freedom: The Economic Consequences of Emancipation* (Cambridge: Cambridge Univ. Press, 1977); Lawrence N. Powell, *New Masters: Northern Planters During Civil War and Reconstruction* (New Haven: Yale Univ. Press, 1980); Cohen, "Negro Involuntary Servitude."

51. Raper, *Tenants*, p. 51. On the economic transformation of the upcountry, see Hahn, "Roots of Southern Populism."

52. *North Georgia Citizen* (hereafter *NGC*), May 29, 1879; for the sources of the numbers, see Appendix, Part II.

53. Wright, *Political Economy*, p. 181; contemporary observer, ibid.; *Montgomery Daily Advertiser*, Jan. 24, 1883, quoted in Wiener, *Social Origins*, pp. 97–98.

54. *GH*, Jan. 14, 1875; Aug. 12, 1875; Nov. 28, 1878.

55. *NGC*, June 25, 1874; Nov. 26, 1874; Jan. 28, 1874; also see Dec. 3, 1874; Jan. 18, 1875; Nov. 18, 1875; March 18, 1875; April 6, 27, 1876; Jan. 25, 1877; May 29, **1879. John Horrey Dent Diary, Microfilm at GDAH, 12:23, 149 (Feb. and Nov. 1876);** also see 13:229.

56. *NGC*, Nov. 26, 1874; April 1, 1875.

57. Indictments in Greene, Whitfield, and Chatham Counties, 1850–79
(Percentages)

	Greene		Whitfield		Chatham	
	1850s	*1866–79*	*1850s*	*1866–79*	*1850s*	*1866–79*
Property	2.8	27.4	5.5	19.0	19.3	35.4
Violence	23.0	19.5	28.1	27.0	42.3	36.6
Order	12.1	15.8	32.5	7.6	11.9	3.2
Morality	6.4	8.3	5.5	11.7	1.3	1.2
Deceit	1.2	3.5	4.9	2.2	8.1	13.2
Misdemeanor	9.2	10.3	8.9	22.9	0	6.7
Vagrancy	0	6.4	0	3.7	0	0.2
Arson	0	2.8	0	1.3	0	0.9
Other	45.2	5.7	14.5	4.6	17.0	2.4
N	248	456	616	814	815	1383

NOTE: Antebellum "other" includes gaming and crimes of slavery (see Chapter Three, note 5 for more detailed antebellum figures for Chatham County; Chapter Four, note 28 for Greene and Whitfield). All columns may not total 100% due to rounding. Also see note 60 below.
SOURCE: For the sources of this and subsequent tables, see Appendix, Part II.

States not included in Figure 5.1 and 5.2 show the same pattern of growth in prison population:

	South		North			South		North	
	TN	*TX*	*MI*	*MA*		*TN*	*TX*	*MI*	*MA*
1866	311	434	506	—	1873	—	937	660	586
1867	485	—	585	—	1874	963	1461	703	643
1868	394	429	625	—	1875	—	1471	790	695
1869	551	439	649	—	1876	997	1702	836	728
1870	—	503	669	—	1877	—	1559	802	744
1871	739	520	634	—	1878	1153	1564	804	768
1872	—	752	592	545	1879	—	1708	777	770

SOURCE: See Appendix, Part I.

58. Gov. James M. Smith, Georgia *Senate Journal*, 1872, pp. 138–39; Gov. John C. Brown, Message of 1875, in Robert H. White, ed., *Messages of the Governors of Tennessee* (Nashville: Tennessee Historical Commission, 1952–59) 6:379. Mississippi's infamous "pig law" of 1876 made the theft of any domestic animal a penitentiary offense with a sentence of up to five years. Arkansas's first Democratic legislature made the theft of anything worth over $2 punishable by one to five years in the state penitentiary. Alabama lawmakers made the theft of any property worth over $25 grand larceny; the previous figure had been $100. See Vernon L. Wharton, *The Negro in Mississippi, 1865–1890* (1947; reprint, New York: Harper Torchbook, 1965), p. 237–38; Garland Bayliss, "The Arkansas State Penitentiary Under Democratic Control, 1874–1896," *Arkansas Historical Quarterly* 34 (1975): 189–99; *Alabama Acts*, 1874–75, pp. 237–39, 259–60, 452–54; *Georgia Acts*, 1875, p. 26; *Tennessee Acts*, 1870–71, ch. 36; 1875, ch. 39; also see James Oakes, "A Failure of Vision: The Collapse of the Freedmen's Bureau Courts," *Civil War History* 25 (March 1979): 66–77. Counteracting the tendency these acts would have of sending more convicts to state penal institutions,

however, were laws designed to keep more convicts in the counties. Georgia passed a law "which reduced a large number of offences to a lower grade so as to increase the number of offenders who were eligible for work on the [county] chain gang": James C. Bonner, "The Georgia Penitentiary of Milledgeville, 1817–1874," *Georgia Historical Quarterly* 55 (Fall 1971): 320–1. In Tennessee, "by raising the amount constituting grand larceny from $10 to $30 and by declaring petit larceny to be a misdemeanor, the law makers paved the way for the punishment of more petty criminals in the county of the crime": Jesse Crawford Crowe, "Agitation for Penal Reform in Tennessee, 1870–1900" (Ph.D. diss., Vanderbilt Univ., 1954), p. 59. The warden of the Alabama penitentiary actually complained that "the courts are sentencing all able bodied convicts to hard labor for the counties, and giving the penitentiary the old and feeble, the extreme young, the imbecile and the blind": J. H. Bankhead, *Biennial Report of the Inspectors of the Alabama Penitentiary, From Sept. 30, 1880, to Sept. 30, 1882*, p. 13. Thus legal change alone cannot account for the region-wide increase in commitments to state-level penal institutions after the Civil War.

59. Chatham County Superior Court Minutes, GDAH; *SMN*, Oct. 22, 1867; 90.8% of the blacks owned no property in 1870 (see Appendix, Part II); Ransom and Sutch, *One Kind of Freedom*, pp. 62–63; John Kellogg, "Negro Urban Clusters in the Postbellum South," *Geographical Review* 67 (July 1977): 310–21; Howard N. Rabinowitz, *Race Relations in the Urban South, 1865–1890* (1978; reprint, Urbana: Univ. of Illinois Press, 1980), pp. 18–30, 97–124; Litwack, *Been in the Storm*, pp. 310–22; John Blassingame, "Before the Ghetto: The Making of the Black Community in Savannah, Georgia, 1865–1880," *Journal of Social History* 6 (1973): 409–48; Paul B. Worthman, "Working Class Mobility in Birmingham, Alabama, 1860–1914," in Tamara K. Hareven, ed., *Anonymous Americans: Explorations in Nineteenth-Century Social History* (Englewood Cliffs, N.J.: Prentice Hall, 1971), pp. 172–213; Richard J. Hopkins, "Status, Mobility, and the Dimensions of Change in a Southern City: Atlanta, 1870–1910," in Kenneth T. Jackson and Stanley K. Schultz, eds., *Cities in American History* (New York: Knopf, 1972), pp. 216–31.

60. *SMN*, June 20, 1867.

Property Crimes Indicted

	1866	1867	1868	1869	1870	1871	1872	1873	1874	1875	1876	1877	1878	1879
Greene	1	7	6	8	7	5	13	7	11	18	15	24	15	22
Whitfield	15	12	10	3	2	8	3	7	8	21	23	12	14	17
Chatham	9	11	17	21	10	25	27	43	66	52	22	15	20	14

Penitentiary Sentences

	1866	1867	1868	1869	1870	1871	1872	1873	1874	1875	1876	1877	1878	1879
Greene	0	4	3	3	3	3	1	2	5	12	6	7	3	4
Whitfield	2	0	0	0	0	1	0	0	2	7	4	1	2	2
Chatham	3	23	13	21	12	23	28	32	49	50	24	12	22	12

SOURCE: See Appendix, Part II.

Savannah's black newspaper, the *Tribune*, complained of the "great amount of work given and money paid the horde of foreigners from Canada, and according to the spirit of the times, from New York," Nov. 25, 1876. According to Blaine H. Brownell and David R. Goldfield, the South suffered more than the North during the depression of the 1870s: *The City in Southern History: The Growth of Urban Civilization in the South* (Port Washington: N.Y.: Kennikat Press, 1977), p.

102. On the impact of the depression of 1873 in New Orleans, see Roger Shugg, *Origins of Class Struggle in Louisiana: A Social History of White Farmers and Laborers During Slavery and After, 1840–1875* (Baton Rouge: LSU, 1939), pp. 296–97. For the effect of the depressions on 1873 and the early 1890s on Savannah's arrest rates, see W. E. B. DuBois, ed., *Some Notes on Negro Crime, Particularly in Georgia*, no. 9 of *Atlanta University Publications* (1904; reprint, New York: Arno Press, 1968), p. 51.

61. Savannah *Mayor's Report*, 1866, 4–5; *SMN*, Oct. 21, 1869; for praise of the force, see *SMN*, Jan. 11, May 18, Nov. 1, Dec. 20, 1869; Dec. 19, 1878.

62. *SMN*, Nov. 22, 1865; May 31, 1888; Edward King, *The Southern States of North America* (London: Blackie and Son, 1875), p. 369. For another ecstatic description of the Savannah police, see Somers, *Southern States*, pp. 74–75. On Southern police and black officers, see Rabinowitz, *Race Relations*, pp. 41–43.

63. *KKK Report*, Georgia, p. 178.

64. Savannah *Tribune* (hereafter *ST*), July 15, 1876; Judge W. B. Flemming, in Chatham County Superior Court Minutes, 1866, 205; *SMN*, March 11, 1869; *ST*, Jan. 15, June 3, 1876.

65. See Howard N. Rabinowitz, "The Conflict Between Blacks and the Police in the Urban South, 1865–1900," *The Historian* 39 (Nov. 1976): 62–76; on the spread of fundamentally similar police forces in nineteenth-century America, see Eric H. Monkkonen, *Police in Urban America, 1860–1920* (Cambridge: Cambridge Univ. Press, 1981), pp. 63–64.

66. Charles Nordhoff, *The Cotton States in the Spring and Summer of 1875* (New York: D. Appleton and Co., 1876), p. 24.

67. *NGC*, Oct. 14, 1875; Nashville *Banner*, March 1, 1884, quoted in Rabinowitz, *Race Relations*, p. 40; John R. Dennett, *The South As It Is: 1865–1866*, Henry M. Christman, ed. (New York: Viking, 1965), p. 132; also see Litwack, *Been in the Storm*, p. 287; Flanigan, "Criminal Law," pp. 307–28; Whitelaw Reid, *After the War: A Tour of the Southern States, 1865–1866*, C. Vann Woodward, ed. (1866; reprint, New York: Harper and Row, 1965), p. 516.

68. *GH*, Sept. 7, 1867, quoting Louisville *Journal*.

69. Flanigan, "Criminal Law," pp. 307–28; song in Lawrence Levine, *Black Culture and Black Consciousness: Afro-American Folk Thought From Slavery to Freedom* (New York: Oxford Univ. Press, 1977), p. 257; Arthur Raper, *Preface to Peasantry: A Tale of Two Black Belt Counties* (Chapel Hill: UNC, 1936), p. 285; Superior Court Minutes.

Verdict by Race, 1866–79 (Percentages)

	Black	White	Antebellum
Greene			
guilty	80.3	60.4	74.7
not guilty	19.7	39.6	24.2
N	218	48	
Whitfield			
guilty	69.4	44.5	51.0
not guilty	30.6	55.5	49.0
N	49	137	
Chatham			
guilty	77.1	57.2	63.0
not guilty	22.0	41.8	33.9
N	463	208	

(Continued next page)

(Continued from previous page)

NOTE: Columns do not total 100% due to rounding, and in the case of Chatham, to mistrials. "Antebellum" column includes both races, although the number of blacks was very small.

70. "South Carolina Morals," p. 474; *NGC*, July 2, 1868; William D. Waters to Abigail Waters, Aug. 12, 1866, in Powell, *New Masters*, pp. 104–6.

Verdict by Crime, 1866–79 (Percentages)

	Property	*Violent*
Greene		
guilty	82.9	69.0
not guilty	17.1	31.0
N	146	71
Whitfield		
guilty	74.0	48.4
not guilty	26.0	51.6
N	50	64
Chatham		
guilty	76.8	63.9
not guilty	22.4	35.3
N	357	238

71. *GH*, Aug. 5, 1872; May 22, 1873. The Georgia legislature, in response to such crowding and delay, passed a law allowing counties to establish a "County Court" to handle misdemeanors and minor civil cases. The surviving records of these courts in Greene and Whitfield suggest that they met intermittently, and a correspondent to the Greensboro *Herald* noted that "there are scarcely any two counties now in the State which have County Courts exactly alike in their structure" (March 23, 1877). Since all records of these courts are fragmentary, it is impossible to know what effect they may have had on the Superior Court's activities, other than reducing their business—which hardly affects the basic change in crime after the war: a large increase in the number of cases before the **Superior Court. Figures from Greene's County Court listed in the Greensboro** *Herald-Journal* between 1890 and 1899 show the same patterns as appear in Superior Court records: out of 129 cases, 83 involved blacks, 3 involved whites, and in 43 cases race was not mentioned; 74 defendants were found guilty, 27 not guilty, and in 28 cases no verdict was specified. The chain gang was the punishment for 63 of the 74 people convicted. Forty cases involved theft, 19 **involved violence, and the rest were scattered. See** *Georgia Acts,* 1865–66, pp. 64–71; 1866, pp. 52–54; 1871–2, pp. 288–98; Albert B. Saye, *A Constitutional History of Georgia, 1732–1968*, rev. ed. (Athens: Univ. of Ga. Press, 1970), pp. 267–79, 286, 300; records of Greene County Court Minutes, 1866–71, Greene County Court House, Greensboro, and on microfilm at GDAH; Whitfield County Court Minutes, 1866, Whitfield County Court House, Dalton. On the chain gang, see *Georgia Acts*, 1866, p. 26; 1874, p. 29; Bonner, "Georgia Penitentiary," pp. 320–21. By the 1880s, nearly all Southern states allowed the hiring out of defendants convicted of misdemeanors or felonies: see Novak, *Wheel of Servitude*, p. 34; also see *Second Annual Report of the Commissioner of Labor, 1886, Convict Labor* (Washington, 1887), pp. 8–10, 18–20; Gov. John C. Brown, Message of 1873, in

White, *Messages* 6: 308; *Tennessee Acts*, 1875, pp. 121–22; Crowe, "Agitation for Penal Reform in Tennessee," p. 59; *Alabama Acts*, 1875–76, p. 287; Allen Going, *Bourbon Democracy in Alabama, 1874–1890* (University: Univ. of Alabama Press, 1951), p. 174; Gov. Benjamin G. Humphreys in Mississippi *House Journal*, 1866–67, p. 14.

72. *GH*, June 3, 1869; *SMN*, May 9, 1866; *GH*, Feb. 1, 1876.

73. *Biennial Report of the Inspectors of the Alabama Penitentiary*, 1884–86, pp. 24, 51, 80; New Orleans *Tribune*, Nov. 29, 1865, quoted in Litwack, *Been in the Storm*, p. 286. On the imperatives of the system to encourage arrests, see Jesse F. Steiner and Roy M. Brown, *The North Carolina Chain Gang* (Chapel Hill: UNC, 1927).

74. *GH*, Sept. 16, 1875.

75. *GH*, Sept. 13, 1877; also see DuBois, *Some Notes*, pp. 45, 46, 47, 48.

76. Dennett, *South As It Is*, p. 151; Monroe N. Work, "Negro Criminality in the South," *Annals of the American Academy of Political and Social Science* 49 (Sept. 1913): 78.

77. William H. Thomas, "The Negro and Crime" (Address before the Southern Sociological Congress, Nashville, May 7–10, 1912), p. 7, Auburn University Library; *NGC*, April 17, 1873; Oct. 21, 1875; April 23, 1874.

Offense by Race, 1866–79 (Percentages)

	Black	*White*
Greene		
property	61.9	16.7
violence	21.6	43.8
N	218	48
Whitfield		
property	44.9	10.2
violence	16.3	30.7
N	49	137
Chatham		
property	61.3	35.1
violence	30.3	46.2
N	463	208

78. See note 57, this chapter. Some of the misdemeanors recorded in the table showing indictments were probably for gaming and liquor; concern with such offenses may well have reasserted itself when other crimes seemed to slacken in any given year.

79. Penfield Baptist Church Minutes, June 8, 1866, GDAH. The later pronouncement, a resolution of the Georgia Baptist Association, was unanimously adopted; White Plains Baptist Church Minutes, March 1870, GDAH.

80. Bethesda Baptist Church Minutes, Jan. 1867, GDAH; also see Dr. John D. Mill, of Bairdstown (Baptist) Church, in T. B. Rice, *History of Greene County, Georgia, 1786–1886*, Carolyn White Williams, ed. (Macon: J. W. Burke, 1961), pp. 125–27.

81. *NGC*, Sept. 11, 1873; *GH*, Aug. 16, 1877; *GH*, April 10, 1879; *NGC*, Nov. 18, 1875. Between 1864 and 1880, blacks in Savannah established ten churches: Robert E. Perdue, *The Negro in Savannah, 1865–1900* (New York: Exposition Press, 1973). In 1871 an African Baptist Church was founded in Dalton—see

"History of New Hope Baptist Church," by Dr. Bettie M. Smith, Aug. 12, 1977, typescript at Whitfield-Murray Historical Society, Dalton, Georgia. Also see James C. Bonner, *Georgia's Last Frontier: The Development of Carrol County* (Athens: Univ. of Georgia Press, 1971), p. 61.
82. W.E.B. DuBois, *Souls of Black Folk* (1903; reprint, New York: American Library, 1969), pp. 199–201.

Chapter 6. The Convict Lease System

1. Margaret Mitchell, *Gone With the Wind* (New York: Macmillan, 1936), pp. 741–43, 759–61.
2. Hilda Jane Zimmerman, "Penal Systems and Penal Reform in the South Since the Civil War" (Ph.D. diss., Univ. of North Carolina at Chapel Hill, 1947), pp. 50–55.
3. Joseph H. Parks, *Joseph E. Brown of Georgia* (Baton Rouge: LSU, 1977), p. 318; James C. Bonner, "The Georgia Penitentiary at Milledgeville, 1817–1874," *Georgia Historical Quarterly* 55 (Fall 1971): 303–28; Peter Wallenstein, "From Slave South to New South: Taxes and Spending in Georgia from 1850 Through Reconstruction" (Ph.D. diss., Johns Hopkins University, 1973), p. 286.
4. Georgia *Senate Journal*, 1865–66, pp. 136–37; Howell Cobb, Mark Cooper, and John Fitten to Gov. Jenkins, November 2, 1866, in Executive Department Correspondence, Dec. 1865–Jan. 1868, GDAH.
5. A. Philips to Gen. A. M. Durant, June 26, 1865, in Gov. William Sharkey Papers, vol. 69, MDAH.
6. Bonner, "Georgia Penitentiary," pp. 321–22; *Report* of Overton H. Walton, Principal Keeper of the Georgia Penitentiary, 1868, pp. 27–28; Director's Report, Tennessee *House Journal*, 1867–68, appendix, p. 310. See the Appendix to the present volume for locations of prison reports.
7. Albert D. Oliphant, *The Evolution of the Penal System of South Carolina from 1866 to 1916* (Columbia: State Co., 1916); George B. Tindall, *South Carolina Negroes, 1877–1900* (Columbia: Univ. of South Carolina Press, 1952), pp. 265–76; Blake McKelvey, *American Prisons: A Study in American Social History Prior to 1915* (Chicago: Univ. of Chicago Press, 1936), p. 168; Zimmerman, "Penal Systems," pp. 79–80, 111.
8. Daniel A. Novak, *The Wheel of Servitude: Black Forced Labor After Slavery* (Lexington: Univ. of Kentucky Press, 1978), pp. 23–24; Garland Bayliss, "The Arkansas State Penitentiary Under Democratic Control, 1874–1896," *Arkansas Historical Quarterly* 34 (1975): 196–98; Jack P. Maddex, *The Virginia Conservatives, 1867–1879: A Study in Reconstruction Politics* (Chapel Hill: UNC, 1970), pp. 224–28; Wallenstein, "Slave South," pp. 290–92; Allen Going, *Bourbon Democracy in Alabama, 1874–1890* (University: Univ. of Alabama Press, 1951), pp. 170–1.
9. Mississippi *Senate Journal*, Called Session, Oct. 1866, pp. 95–96; *Annual Report* of the Superintendent of the Mississippi Penitentiary, 1875, p. 5.
10. It is clear that the convict lease was not the invention of the Bourbon Democrats. On the complicated politics of the system, see Thomas Holt, *Black Over White: Negro Political Leadership in South Carolina During Reconstruction* (Urbana: Univ. of Illinois Press, 1977), p. 169; Mark Carleton, *Politics and Punishment: The History of the Louisiana State Penal System* (Baton Rouge: LSU, 1971), pp. 18–19,

65–66; Edmund L. Drago, *Black Politicians and Reconstruction in Georgia: A Splendid Failure* (Baton Rouge: LSU, 1982), pp. 71–72; Wallenstein, "Slave South," pp. 290–21; Bonner, "Georgia Penitentiary," pp. 321–22, 324; Jesse Crowe, "The Origin and Development of Tennessee's Prison Problem, 1831–1871," *Tennessee Historical Quarterly* 15 (1956): 128–30; Vernon L. Wharton, *The Negro in Mississippi, 1865–1890* (1947; reprint New York: Harper Torchbook, 1965), p. 235; J. H. Jones, "Penitentiary Reform in Mississippi," *Publications of the Mississippi Historical Society* 6 (1902): 111–12; William C. Harris, *Day of the Carpetbagger: Republican Reconstruction in Mississippi* (Baton Rouge: LSU, 1979), pp. 353–61; Edward C. Williamson, *Florida Politics in the Gilded Age, 1877–1893* (Gainesville: Univ. of Florida Press, 1976), pp. 28–29; Robert G. Crawford, "A History of the Kentucky Penitentiary System, 1865–1937" (Ph.D. diss., Univ. of Kentucky, 1955), p. 100; Zimmerman, "Penal Systems," p. 59.

11. Kentucky, North Carolina, South Carolina, and Texas used the Public Account system (convicts did not produce for the market), plus the Contract system (the state contracted the produce goods for the market, but supervised the convicts themselves); Maryland, Virginia, and West Virginia used the Contract system alone; and Missouri combined Public Account with Contract and the Piece Price system, a variant of the latter; McKelvey, *American Prisons*, pp. 179–80; *Second Annual Report of the Commissioner of Labor, 1886. Convict Labor* (Washington, 1887), pp. 266–67, 380–81; Archie Green, *Only a Miner: Studies in Recorded Coal-Mining Songs* (Urbana: Univ. of Illinois Press, 1972), p. 119.

12. Harold Woodman, "Sequel to Slavery: The New History Views the Postbellum South," *Journal of Southern History* 43 (1977): 550; William Cohen, "Negro Involuntary Servitude in the South, 1865–1940: A Preliminary Analysis," *Journal of Southern History* 42 (1976): 31–60; Pete Daniel, *The Shadow of Slavery: Peonage in the South, 1901–1969* (Urbana: Univ. of Illinois Press, 1972); Novak, *Wheel of Servitude*; George Fredrickson, *White Supremacy: A Comparative Study in American and South African History* (New York: Oxford Univ. Press, 1981), p. 214; Matthew J. Mancini, "Race, Economics, and the Abandonment of Convict Leasing," *Journal of Negro History* 63 (1978): 339–52.

13. Woodman, "Sequel," p. 549. Significantly, leasing appeared in the West as well as in the South, along with greedy lesees, negligent state officials, overcrowding, poor clothing, and total disregard for reform. See George Thomson, "The History of Penal Institutions in the Rocky Mountain West, 1846–1900" (Ph.D. diss., Univ. of Colorado, 1965), esp. pp. 103–115.

14. On the labor shortage in the South, see Jonathan Wiener, *Social Origins of the New South: Alabama, 1865–1885* (Baton Rouge: LSU, 1978); Fredrickson, *White Supremacy*, pp. 200–201; C. Vann Woodward, *Origins of the New South, 1877–1913* (Baton Rouge: LSU, 1951), p. 226, 416; Dutton quoted in Williamson, *Florida Politics*, pp. 34–35, and Williamson also drew the cotton gin analogy, on p. 136; Crowe, "Tennessee's Prison Problem," p. 132.

15. On antebellum railroads, Robert S. Starobin, *Industrial Slavery in the Old South* (New York: Oxford Univ. Press, 1970), pp. 28–29; Rebecca Hunt Moulder, "Convicts as Capital," *East Tennessee Historical Society Publications* 48 (1976): 57–59.

16. Thorsten Sellin, *Slavery and the Penal System* (New York: Elsevier, 1976), p. 148.

17. Such a description fits many of the leading industrialists of the New South. See Maury Klein, *The Great Richmond Terminal: A Study in Businessmen and Business Strategy* (Charlottesville: Univ. of Virginia Press, 1970), pp. 13–14; Justin Fuller, "History of the Tennessee Coal, Iron, and Railroad Company, 1852–1907" (Ph.D. diss., Univ. of North Carolina at Chapel Hill, 1966). Henry DeBardeleben, a major employer of convicts and a central figure in Southern industrialization, proclaimed, "Life is one big game of poker": Woodward, *Origins*, p. 310. Fittingly, Thomas O'Connor, lessee of Tennessee convicts from 1871 to 1883, was a professional gambler before and after his tenure as lessee: Moulder, "Convicts," p. 41.

18. Statement of T. L. Thomas in appendix to Jones, "Penitentiary Reform," p. 126; testimony of Hubbard Cureton, *Proceedings of the Joint Committee Appointed to Investigate the Condition of the Georgia Penitentiary* (Atlanta, 1870), pp. 117–18; *Convict Labor*, p. 303; J. G. Bass in *Annual Report of the Inspectors of the Alabama Penitentiary*, 1877, pp. 8–9.

19. Quoted in Crowe, "Tennessee's Prison Problem," pp. 134, 127; Isabel C. Barrows, "Life in Southern Prisons," *Harper's Weekly* 34 (Aug. 2, 1890): 605.

20. W. A. Milliken quoted in *American Iron and Steel Association Bulletin* 20 (Dec. 29, 1886): 347, quoted in Fuller, "Tennessee Coal, Iron, and Railroad Company," p. 310; T. J. Hill, General Manager, Tennessee State Coal Mines, in National Prison Association *Proceedings*, 1897, pp. 389, 390; Albert D. Kirwan, *Revolt of the Rednecks: Mississippi Politics, 1876–1925* (Lexington: Univ. of Kentucky Press, 1951), pp. 167–68; Wharton, *Negro in Mississippi*, p. 239; Going, *Bourbon Democracy*, pp. 177–80; Darrell Roberts, "Joseph E. Brown and the Convict Lease System," *Georgia Historical Quarterly* 44 (1960): 400.

21. Atticus Haygood, *Two Sermons: Prison Reform; The Good and the Bad* (Macon: J. W. Burke, 1887), p. 9. When three positions as penitentiary inspector were to be filled in Alabama in 1881, over thirty applications were received. The job was a choice political plum: little work and high pay. See folder marked "Inspectors of Penitentiary—Applications for Appointments, 1881," Gov. Rufus W. Cobb Papers, ADAH. For the terrible conditions in postwar Northern prisons, see David Rothman, *Conscience and Convenience: The Asylum and Its Alternatives in Progressive America* (Boston: Little, Brown, 1980), pp. 17–40; Glen A. Gildemeister, "Prison Labor and Convict Competition with Free Workers in Industrializing America, 1840–1890" (Ph.D. diss., Northern Illinois Univ., 1977), pp. 35–36.

22. Rebecca Latimer Felton, "The Convict Lease System of Georgia," *Forum* 2 (1886–87): 486; Roberts, "Joseph E. Brown," pp. 404–5; A. F. McKelway, "The Convict Lease System of Georgia," *Outlook* 90 (1908): 68–69; J. G. Bass to Gov. Rufus Cobb, May 1879, in folder marked "Leasing of the State Penitentiary, 1879" in Cobb Papers, ADAH; Testimony of J. G. Bass in *Joint Special Committee on the Alabama Penitentiary, Report*, 1880–81, pp. 22–23; Crawford, "Kentucky Penitentiary," pp. 122–25; Rufus K. Boyd to Robert McKee, Feb. 26, 1883, McKee Correspondence; Robert McKee to Thomas R. Roulhac, February 25, 1883, McKee Letterbook, 1882–83, ADAH, both partially quoted in Woodward, *Origins*, p. 215.

23. R. H. Dawson, "The Convict System of Alabama—As It Was and As It Is," in Saffold Berney, ed., *Hand-Book of Alabama*, 2d ed. (Birmingham: Roberts and Son, 1892), p. 257; *Proceedings of the Joint Committee on the Georgia Penitentiary*, 1870,

p. 196. Also see the "Annual Report of the Physician" of the Mississippi State Penitentiary, in *Mississippi Annual Report*, 1875, p. 10; *Report* of John T. Brown, Principal Keeper of the Georgia Penitentiary, 1875, pp. 4–5. George Washington Cable tellingly described a report from Tennessee: "As the eye runs down the table of deaths, it finds opposite the names, among other mortal causes, the following: Found dead. Killed. Drowned. Not given. Blank. Blank. Blank. Killed. Blank. Shot. Killed. Blank. Blank. . . . "A chaplain preaching at this camp reported that the prisoners " 'seemed to enjoy the services very much'; and this is all he has to say of the place where men were being 'found dead,' and 'killed,' and 'drowned,' and '——'-ed." *The Silent South: Together with the Freedman's Case in Equity and the Convict Lease System* (New York: Scribner's Sons, 1885), pp. 130–31, 137; Arlin Turner, ed., *The Negro Question, A Selection of Writings on Civil Rights in the South by George Washington Cable* (Garden City, N.Y.: Doubleday, 1958), pp. 69–70.

24. *Convict Labor*, pp. 266–67, 380–81. The inspectors of the Tennessee penitentiary in 1869 reckoned that the lease system actually cost the state a great deal. They found that 232 of the 510 convicts in the prison were there for petit larceny, their thefts averaging less than $5 each. Thus their total theft was only about $1,000. The inspectors estimated that it cost the state between $50,000 and $60,000 just to transport these criminals from their home counties to Nashville. "Report of the Directors of the Tennessee Penitentiary to the General Assembly of the State," *Tennessee House Journal*, 1867–68, appendix, pp. 307–8. And see the *Annual Report of the Inspectors of the Alabama Penitentiary*, 1870–71, pp. 1–4.

25.

Southern Cities and Incarceration, 1866–80

	Percentage of State Inmates	Percentage of State Population	Ratio of Population to Inmates
Mobile	16.7	4.3	1:3.9
Montgomery	8.7	4.2	1:2.1
Savannah	10.3	3.2	1:3.2
Atlanta	6.7	3.0	1:2.2
Augusta	4.3	2.2	1:1.9
Macon	6.5	1.8	1:3.6
Vicksburg	7.6	3.0	1:2.5
Natchez	2.1	2.1	1:1.0
Memphis	20.6	5.5	1:3.7
Nashville	14.9	5.1	1:2.9
Knoxville	5.4	2.4	1:2.2

SOURCE: See Appendix, Part I.

Punishment by Race, Chatham County Superior Court, 1866–79 (Percentages)

	Black	*White*
Fine	14.1	49.2
Chain gang	6.5	4.2
Penitentiary	76.4	44.9
Hanged	3.1	1.7
	(N = 356)	(N = 118)

SOURCE: See Appendix, Part II.

26. The average percentage of white prisoners of foreign birth in the antebellum era for Alabama, Mississippi, Tennessee, and Kentucky stood at 17.6; the postbellum average fell to 11.1 See Appendix, Part I.

27. R. M. Cunningham, "The Convict System of Alabama In Its Relation to Health and Disease," National Prison Association *Proceedings*, 1889, p. 137.

28. Howell Cobb, Mark Cooper, and J. Fitten to Gov. C. Jenkins, Nov. 2, 1866. Gov. Jenkins agreed on the necessity of racial separation—see his letter to Senators and Representatives, Nov. 12, 1866, in Executive Department Correspondence, Dec. 1865–Jan. 1868, GDAH; on the leveling effect of the lease system, *Christian Index*, 1879, quoted in Roberts, "Joseph E. Brown," p. 409; testimony of Hubbard Cureton in *Proceedings of the Joint Committee Appointed to Investigate the Georgia Penitentiary*, 1870, p. 123; also see John V. Ryan, quoted in Jesse C. Crowe, "Agitation for Penal Reform in Tennessee, 1870–1900" (Ph.D. diss., Vanderbilt Univ. 1954), p. 161.

29. Dr. H. H. Tucker, "Prison Labor, a Speech Before the National Prison Congress" (Atlanta, 1886), pp. 19–20, Georgia State Library; Gov. John C. Brown, Message of 1875 to Tennessee Legislature in Robert H. White, ed., *Messages of the Governors of Tennessee* (Nashville: Tennessee Historical Commission, 1952–59) 6:380.

30. Savannah *Morning News*, Nov. 21, 1893.

31. Greensboro *Herald*, March 24, 1881; Tennessee *House Journal*, 1871, appendix, p. 393. In Chatham, 51.5% of defendants were less than 25 years old, but only 40.6% of Greene's and 41.5% of Whitfield's were that young; before the war, only 29.7% of Chatham's defendants had been that young. The average percentage of the general population between the ages of 15 and 24 for the states of Alabama, Georgia, Mississippi, and Tennessee was 29.2 in 1860, but declined markedly to 21.9 in 1870 and 20.0 in 1880; meanwhile, the percentage of those states' prisoners under 30 grew from 57.8% before the war to 76.2% afterward. The percentage changed hardly at all in Michigan, Pennsylvania, and Ohio, from an average of 65.5 to 68.0. *Historical Statistics of the United States, Colonial Times to 1976* (Washington, 1970), and reports described in Appendix, Part I. Also see Mancini, "Convict Leasing," pp. 343–44.

32. "Report of the General Agent of the Virginia Penitentiary," pp. 58–59, Virginia *Annual Reports*, 1882–83; Tennessee *House Journal*, 1889, pp. 322–25, quoted in Zimmerman, "Penal Systems," p. 163.

33. *Report* of John T. Brown, Principal Keeper of the Georgia Penitentiary, 1874, p. 11; Georgia *House Journal*, 1878, p. 391; Crawford, "Kentucky Penitentiary," pp. 109–10.

34. *Testimony Before the Joint Committee... Alabama, 1888–89*, p. 117; Jerome Cochran, State Health Officer, *Alabama Penitentiary Report*, 1884, p. 250; *Report* of John T. Brown, Principal Keeper of the Georgia Penitentiary, 1875, p. 9; Jones, "Penitentiary Reform," appendix, p. 127; "Louisiana Tiger" to Gov. J. C. Brown, Nov. 21, 1871, Gov. Brown Papers, TSLA.

35. "Report of the Committee on the Penitentiary," *Georgia House Journal*, 1878, p. 389; Roberts, "Joseph E. Brown," p. 404. (In Texas, the number of escapes tripled when the penitentiary was first leased in 1871: Lawrence D. Rice, *The Negro in Texas, 1874–1900* (Baton Rouge: LSU, 1971), pp. 245–50.) "Senator Brown's Argument Before the Governor," pp. 4–5, Joseph E. Brown Papers at

Atlanta Historical Society; "Louisiana Tiger" to Gov. Brown, Nov. 21, 1871. Records of punishment show that lashes were frequently dispensed for fighting, gambling, resisting punishment, and burning shoes—the last a particularly effective and infuriating form of resistance, since it destroyed the lessees' property. See "Monthly Reports of Corporal Punishment, Diet and Condition of Convicts, 1884–1886, 1889," Penitentiary Records, GDAH.

36. On convict amusements, see testimony of T. Alexander, Lessee, in *Proceedings of Joint Committee to Investigate Georgia Penitentiary,* 1870, p. 180; on religion, see Mississippi *House Journal,* 1866–67, appendix, p. 24; *Georgia Penitentiary Report,* 1872–73, p. 5; religion and guard quote, Alexander testimony, p. 179. See Michael Ignatieff, *A Just Measure of Pain: The Penitentiary in the Industrial Revolution, 1750–1850* (New York: Pantheon, 1978), pp. 38–42, on the concept of inmate subculture.

37. *Testimony before the Joint Committee . . . Alabama,* 1888–89, p. 120; "Louisiana Tiger" to Gov. Brown, Nov. 21, 1871.

38. Harold Courlander, *A Treasury of Afro-American Folklore* (New York: Crown, 1976), pp. 381, 408. For a sensitive and extensive study of these songs in the modern South, see Bruce Jackson, *Wake Up Dead Man: Afro-American Worksongs from Texas Prisons* (Cambridge: Harvard Univ. Press, 1972).

39. J. G. Bass, Warden, *Alabama Penitentiary Report,* 1874–75, p. 5. It was argued that "the convict . . . who is working on levees, or cultivating cotton, receives a much less severe punishment than the law intended": Gov. Adelbert Ames, Message to the Legislature, Mississippi *House Journal,* 1876, pp. 14–15. Gov. Charles T. O'Ferrall, Virginia *House Journal,* 1897–98, p. 25; *Second Report,* Tennessee State Board of Health, p. 308.

40. Reginald Heber Dawson Diary, 1883–87, ADAH. Dawson was President of the Board of Inspectors, Alabama Convict System. The quotes are from, respectively, May 25, July 5, and March 13, 1883.

41. Gov. Alvin Hawkins, Message of 1883, in White, *Messages* 6:712–13.

42. Petition for Van Massar, Sept. 1868 in Governors' Records, vol. 70, MDAH; petition in file of Gov. Patton, "Petitions and Pardons, 1866," ADAH; petition of J. J. Broughton to Gov. A. Ames, Aug. 1868, Governors' Records, vol. 70, MDAH; petition of David Miller, Nov. 5, 1876, in Gov. James Porter Papers, box 13, TSLA.

43. Petition of Phillip Hopkins, undated, in Gov. Porter Papers, box 13, TSLA; petition for pardon, name missing, Gov. John Brown Papers, box 7, 1871, TSLA; petition for Wilson Jordan, May 6, 1872, ibid.; W. D. Highlander, Feb. 19, 1875, Gov. Porter Papers, box 10, TSLA. Highlander was pardoned four days later.

44. Petition for pardon, June 15, 1872, Gov. John Brown Papers, box 7, TSLA; petition for Gideon Barnes, 1873, ibid., box 10.

45. Joseph A. Smith, Dec. 1866 to Gov. Robert M. Patton, in file labeled "Pardons and Petitions, 1866," ADAH.

46. Petition for pardon of Wilson Boykin, May 26, 1869, in Gov. A. Ames's Records, vol. 70, MDAH; petition for pardon, 1866, Gov. William Brownlow's Records, box 6, TSLA; petition for pardon, 1868, Gov. Robert Patton, in file labeled "Pardons and Petitions, 1868," ADAH.

47. Petition for Lucinda Banks, June 8, 1872, Gov. John Brown Papers, box 7,

TSLA. Also see Lester D. Stephens, "A Former Slave and the Georgia Convict Lease System," *Negro History Bulletin* 39 (1976): 505–7.

48. Petition for pardon, Sept. 1869, Gov. A. Ames's Records, vol. 70, MDAH; L. Milles Bentley, Sept. 7, 1875 to Gov. James Porter, Porter Papers, box 11, TSLA.

49. F. W. Bowie to Gov. Robert B. Lindsay, June 12, 1871, in "Pardons and Petitions—1871," ADAH; *Annual Report of the Inspectors of the Alabama Penitentiary*, 1873–74, p. 3.

50. J. O. Keener, Chaplain, *Alabama Penitentiary Report*, 1876–77, pp. 13–14; J. M. Sharpe, Chaplain, in *Tennessee Penitentiary Report*, 1876–78, pp. 15–16. The warden of the Tennessee penitentiary flatly commented in 1880 on the reforming capability of the institution he presided over: "Some few, perhaps, go out wiser if not better men, none go out with an improved character." L. Blizard, Warden, in *Tennessee Penitentiary Report*, 1878–80, p. 15.

51. *Alabama Penitentiary Report*, 1890, pp. 34–35; "Report of the Board of Inspectors of the Tennessee State Penitentiary to the General Assembly," Tennessee *House Journal*, 1871, appendix, pp. 397–404; Sir George Campbell, *White and Black: The Outcome of a Visit to the United States* (New York: R. Worthington, 1879), p. 169.

52. Woodward, *Origins*, p. 215.

53. *Tennessee House Journal*, appendix, 1871, pp. 394–95; *Alabama Penitentiary Report*, 1880–82, p. 15; "Louisiana Tiger" to Gov. J. C. Brown, Nov. 21, 1871.

54. William H. Felton in Rebecca Felton, *My Memoirs of Georgia Politics* (Atlanta: Index Pub. Co., 1911), p. 590; *Mississippi Penitentiary Report*, 1876, p. 6; *Alabama Penitentiary Report*, 1882–84, pp. 78–79.

55. J. B. Anderson, Chaplain, *Alabama Penitentiary Report*, 1880–82, p. 30; John D. Brown, Principal Keeper, *Georgia Penitentiary Report*, 1876, p. 7. Also see T. J. Hill's speech in National Prison Association *Proceedings*, 1897, p. 391.

56. Tucker, "Prison Labor," pp. 21–22; National Prison Association *Proceedings*, 1890, p. 121; C. B. Benson, Secretary, North Carolina Office Board of Public Charities, letter to National Prison Association *Proceedings*, 1894, p. 264.

57. Campbell, *White and Black*, p. 169; John T. Brown, Principal Keeper, *Georgia Penitentiary Report*, 1875, p. 14; address by George T. Winton, National Prison Association *Proceedings*, 1891, p. 292.

58. Adjutant Gen. J. J. Dickerson quoted in Noel Gordon Carper, "The Convict–Lease System in Florida, 1866–1923" (Ph.D. diss., Florida State Univ., 1964), pp. 60–61.

59. *Convict Labor*, p. 301; testimony of Henry DeBardeleben in *Testimony Before the Joint Committee of the General Assembly, Appointed to Examine into the Convict System of Alabama, Session of 1888–89*, p. 39; *Fort Payne* (Ala.) *Herald* quoted in Woodward, *Origins*, p. 232; *Report of the Industrial Commission on Prison Labor* (Washington, 1900), p. 20.

60. U.S. Commissioner of Labor *Report*, 1886, quoted in *Industrial Commission*, p. 23.

61. *North Georgia Citizen*, June 29, 1893; "Dawson" quoted in Herbert Gutman, "Black Coal Miners and the Greenback-Labor Party in Redeemer Alabama, 1878–1879: The Letters of Warren D. Kelley, Willis Johnson Thomas, 'Dawson,' and Others," *Labor History* 10 (Summer 1969): 516–17, 526–27.

62. Fuller, "Tennessee Coal, Iron, and Railroad Company," p. 282; T. J. Hill, National Prison Association *Proceedings*, 1897, p. 393; Moulder, "Convicts," p. 57.

63. Going, *Bourbon Democracy*, pp. 187–88; Atlanta *Constitution* in Greensboro *Herald*, May 23, 1884; Roberts, "Joseph E. Brown," pp. 402–3.

64. "Report of the Board of Inspectors of the Tennessee State Penitentiary to the General Assembly," *Tennessee House Journal*, 1871, appendix, pp. 397–404. Statement and miner quoted in William W. Rogers and Robert D. Ward, *Labor Revolt in Alabama: The Great Strike of 1894* (University, Ala.: Univ. of Alabama Press, 1965), p. 46.

65. There are several accounts of this struggle: Arthur C. Hutson, "The Coal Miners' Insurrection of 1891 in Anderson County, Tennessee," *East Tennessee Historical Society Publications* 7 (1935): 105–15; idem, "The Overthrow of the Convict Lease System in Tennessee," ibid. 8 (1936): 82–103; Green, *Only a Miner* (Univ. of Illinois Press, 1972), pp. 153–239; Pete Daniel, "The Tennessee Convict War," *Tennessee Historical Quarterly* 34 (1975): 273–92; Woodward, *Origins*, p. 232–34.

66. *Nashville Daily American*, Aug. 23, 1892, quoted in Woodward, *Origins*, pp. 232–33; Rogers and Ward, *Labor Revolt*, pp. 25–26.

67. Hutson, "Coal Miners' Insurrection," pp. 83, 107, 113; Rogers and Ward, *Labor Revolt*, p. 71; Green, *Only a Miner*, pp. 169, 110–11, 114.

68. Anne Gary Pannell and Dorothea E. Wyatt, *Julia S. Tutwiler and Social Progress in Alabama* (University: Univ. of Alabama Press, 1961), pp. 108–16; Arlin Turner, *George Washington Cable: A Biography* (Durham: Duke Univ. Press, 1956). A Prison Association of Virginia formed in 1890 to help youthful offenders; with a judge's permission, a felon under 21 years of age might be sent to the Association for work and guidance. By 1899, it had 112 young men—all white—under its wing, divided into "families." See *First Annual Report of the Bureau of Labor and Industrial Statistics of the State of Virginia* (Richmond, 1899), p. 357.

69. *Third Biennial Report of the Inspectors of the Alabama Penitentiary*, 1890, pp. 31–32; Carleton, *Politics and Punishment*, pp. 50–51, comments on the powerlessness of humanitarian reformers; guard quoted in Clarissa Olds Keeler, *American Bastiles* (Washington: Carnaham Press, 1910), p. 15; *Second Report* of the State Board of Health of the State of Tennessee, 1880–84, pp. 313–14; J. B. Anderson, Chaplain, *Biennial Report of the Alabama Penitentiary*, 1880–82, p. 29.

70. Greensboro *Herald*, June 5, 1879; *North Georgia Citizen*, June 23, 1881.

71. Greensboro *Herald*, July 28, 1881; June 30, 1881; Dalton *Argus*, March 27, 1886.

72. "Senator Brown's Argument Before the Governor," p. 39.

73. W. D. Lee, Inspector of Convicts, "The Lease System of Alabama," National Prison Association *Proceedings*, 1890, p. 106; George C. Burney to George Washington Cable, 1886, quoted in Turner, *George Washington Cable*, p. 245.

74. Lee, "Lease System of Alabama," p. 116; Tucker, "Prison Labor," p. 19.

75. Sims, National Prison Association *Proceedings*, 1890, pp. 120–21; Cunningham, ibid., 1889, pp. 138–39; ibid., 1888, p. 79; T. J. Hill, ibid., 1897, p. 391.

76. Enoch C. Wines and Theodore W. Dwight, *Report on the Prisons and Reformatories of the United States and Canada* (Albany: Van Benthuysen and Sons, 1867), p. 289; John Phillips Resch, "Ohio Adult Penal System, 1850–1900: A Study in the Failure of Institutional Reform," *Ohio History* 81 (Autumn 1972): 244–48, 250–53.

77. *Convict Labor*, pp. 141, 163; Samuel Walker, *Popular Justice: A History of American*

Criminal Justice (New York: Oxford Univ. Press, 1980), pp. 72, 85–86.

78. Zimmerman, "Penal Systems," p. 211–77.

79. Quoted in *Fourth Annual Report of the Bureau of Labor and Industrial Statistics of the State of Virginia*, p. 136. See Mancini, "Convict Leasing."

80. Hilda Jane Zimmerman, "The Penal Reform Movement in the South during the Progressive Era, 1890–1917," *Journal of Southern History* 17 (1951): 462–92; Cohen, "Involuntary Labor," pp. 57–58; George B. Tindall, *Emergence of the New South, 1913–1945* (Baton Rouge: LSU, 1967), pp. 213–14.

Chapter 7. The Crisis of the New South

1. *Greensboro Herald and Journal* (hereafter *GHJ*), Jan. 4, 1889; Oct. 1, 1897; *North Georgia Citizen* (hereafter *NGC*), Sept. 15, 1893.

2. Computed from lists of grand jurors listed in *GHJ*. In Chatham County, 34.2% were indicted for property crimes, 31.6% for violent crimes, and the remaining 34.2% for misdemeanors and scattered other offenses (N = 2,832). A comparison of these figures with note 57 in Chapter Five reveals no significant change in any county between the era of Reconstruction and the last twenty years of the century.

Indictments in Greene and Whitfield Counties, 1881–1900 (Percentages)

	Greene	*Whitfield*
Property	33.5	26.4
Violence	29.2	29.5
Order	9.1	10.6
Morality	17.8	3.2
Misdemeanors/Other	10.5	30.3
N	439	716

SOURCE: Appendix, Part II.

3. *Savannah Morning News* (hereafter *SMN*), Feb. 3, Feb. 23, 1894; July 18, 1893; on technology, see *SMN*, Jan. 26, 27, 31, 1890; May 30, 1893; Thomas R. Gamble, *History of the City Government of Savannah, 1790–1901* (Savannah City Council, 1901), pp. 319–20, 411, 412; *SMN*, Nov. 7, 1894. For descriptions of other Southern police forces late in the nineteenth century that show the similarities of all, see Laylon Wayne Jordan, "Police and Politics: Charleston in the Gilded Age, 1880–1900," *South Carolina Historical Magazine* 81 (Jan. 1980): 35–50; Joy J. Jackson, *New Orleans in the Gilded Age: Politics and Urban Progress, 1880–1896* (Baton Rouge: Louisiana Historical Association, 1969), pp. 232–57; Eugene J. Watts, "The Police in Atlanta, 1890–1905," *Journal of Southern History* 39 (May 1973): 165–82.

Total Police per 100,000 in Major Cities

	1880	1890	1900	Mean Rate of Arrests, 1880–1900
South	.1441	.1591	.1607	7.4
North	.2585	.6185	.4665	12.5
Midwest	.1157	.3899	.2080	6.9

The data used in the above table were made available by the Inter-University Consortium for Political and Social Research. The data for the study of "Police Departments, Arrests, and Crime in the U.S., 1860–1920," were originally collected by Eric Monkkonen with funding provided by the Univ. of North Carolina and the Univ. of California Academic Senate. Neither the collector of the original data nor the Consortium bear any responsibility for the analyses or interpretations presented here. I have recoded some of the data to allow regional comparisons. I would like to thank the staff of the University of Virginia Computing Center for their help in this task.

4. Presentments in Greensboro *Herald* (hereafter *GH*), Sept. 22, 1881; article, Sept. 29, 1881. For another account of a convict dying and a three-day trial of the guard (in which he was found not guilty), see Aug. 25, 1893.

5. *GH*, May 19, 1881, June 2, 1881. Whitfield County did not have enough convicts to maintain its own chain gang: *NGC*, April 16, 1896; March 27, 1897.

6. *Biennial Report of the Inspectors of the Alabama Penitentiary, 1884–1886*, pp. 24, 51, 80. Georgia Gov. W. J. Northern also argued that county convicts endured worse conditions than state convicts: *GHJ*, Nov. 3, 1893.

7. *SMN*, July 30, 1893; Feb. 18, 1894; Jan. 31, 1894; April 28, 1894.

8. *Savannah Tribune* (hereafter *ST*), Nov. 17, 1894; May 11, 1889. Also see Feb. 11, 18, 25, April 15, 1893. The *SMN* warned on May 1, 1894, "It will be impossible . . . to handle convicts much longer as they are now being handled. They are nearly all negroes, and they are steadily becoming more restive."

9. *GHJ*, Jan. 19, 1895.

10. Dalton *Argus*, July 9, 1887; *SMN*, June 16, 1897; Aug. 3, 1894; May 29, 1897. A prominent Birmingham lawyer warned, "Cruel, brutal, inexcusable murders of Negroes do not even excite public comment much less conviction, and we have thus had our sense of justice blunted until it is almost destroyed, and wonder that things can be so. It is manifest that we have carried our own, the white people's interest too far. Nothing else seems to have concerned us, and by the inevitable law we are reaping our reward." Alex T. London, in Birmingham *Age-Herald*, July 5, 1904, quoted in Martha Mitchell Bigelow, "Birmingham's Carnival of Crime, 1871–1910," *Alabama Review* 3 (April 1950): 128.

11. *SMN*, June 24, 1893. The *GHJ* on April 2, 1897, attacked the state judiciary: any able judges and solicitors "are more accidental than intentioned. . . . The question is never asked in the Legislature what a candidate's qualifications are. If he can assure the others that he has an influential 'pull' behind him, that settles his case. He is 'in it.' "

12. *ST*, July 22, 1893; Richmond *Planet*, Jan. 5, 1895.

13. *ST*, July 6, 1895; Jan. 13, 1894; Richmond *Planet*, Jan. 19, May 11, 1895.

14. *History of the Savannah Police Department* (Savannah: Savannah Policemen's Benevolent Association, 1897), p. 67; *SMN*, Nov. 30, 1888; *Atlanta Constitution*, Aug. 17, 22, 1883, quoted in Howard N. Rabinowitz, "The Conflict Between Blacks and the Police in the Urban South, 1865–1900," *Historian* 39 (Nov. 1976): 72–73; Richmond *Planet*, June 15, 1895; Watts, "Police in Atlanta," p. 172; Leon Litwack, *Been in the Storm So Long: The Aftermath of Slavery* (New York: Knopf, 1979), p. 288.

15. Philip A. Bruce, *The Plantation Negro as a Freeman: Observations on His Character,*

Condition, and Prospects in Virginia (New York: G. P. Putnam's Sons, 1889), pp. 90–92.

16. Bruce, *Plantation Negro*, p. 82. In Savannah between 1889 and 1892 69 assaults were listed in the *SMN*; of these, 37 involved two blacks, 16 involved two whites, 11 involved black assailants and white victims, 6 involved white assailants and black victims. Numbers less subject to distortion by the newspaper itself show the same pattern: of the 42 homicides recorded by the coroner in Savannah between 1895 and 1898, 28 of the victims were blacks, 14 white. All but 4 of the whites had been killed by other whites, all but 5 of the blacks by other blacks. Savannah *Annual Reports*, 1895, 1896, 1897, and 1898. For later patterns see Thomas F. Pettigrew and Rosalind B. Spier, "The Ecological Structure of Negro Homicide," *American Journal of Sociology* 67 (May 1962): 621–29. The pattern persists. As Gresham Sykes notes, "In a survey of 17 large cities it was found that of the criminal homicides for which data was available, 24 percent involved whites killing whites and 66 percent involved blacks killing blacks. Only 10 percent of the homicides revealed an interracial relationship." *Criminology* (New York: Harcourt Brace Jovanovich, 1978), p. 134.

17. W.J.M. In *Nation* 35 (Nov. 9, 1882): 399–400; Howard N. Rabinowitz, *Race Relations in the Urban South, 1865–1890* (1978; reprint, Urbana: Univ. of Illinois Press, 1980), p. 351, n. 57. Southern police saying quoted in Raymond Fosdick, *American Police Systems* (1920; reprint, Montclair, N.J.: Patterson Smith, 1972), p. 45. Also see James Borchert, *Alley Life in Washington: Family, Community, Religion and Folklife in the City, 1850–1970* (Urbana: Univ. of Illinois Press, 1980), pp. 189–95.

18. *SMN*, Feb. 1, 1893. The paper complained three years earlier (Sept. 13, 1890), "It is an every Sunday affair for the colored railroad laborers and dock hands to spend Sundays in the saloons of Yamacraw and the Old Fort. They congregate in these saloons, drink, quarrel and fight, and spend the greater portion of their week's wages in drink."

19. *SMN*, April 14, 1894. Smalls was arrested in Baltimore, brought back to Savannah, and, after two trials, executed: Gamble, *City Government*, p. 411. The *SMN* praised the retrial because "the colored people are inclined to think there is one kind of justice for them and another kind for white people. . . . It is important not only that they should be dealt with justly, but that they should feel that they are so dealt with" (Sept. 1, 1895).

20. Lawrence Levine, *Black Culture and Black Consciousness: Afro-American Folk Thought from Slavery to Freedom* (New York: Oxford Univ. Press, 1977), pp. 408, 407–20.

21. Levine, *Black Culture*, pp. 408–9; Greil Marcus, *Mystery Train: Images of America in Rock 'n' Roll Music* (1975; reprint; New York: Dutton, 1976), p. 33. Also see Charles E. Silberman, *Criminal Violence, Criminal Justice* (1978; reprint, New York: Vintage, 1980), p. 415.

22. *GHJ*, Dec. 19, 1980; Bruce, *Plantation Negro*, p. 81; William Alexander Percy, *Lanterns on the Levee: Recollections of a Planter's Son* (1941; reprint, Baton Rouge: LSU, 1973), pp. 23, 300–301.

23. H. C. Brearley, "The Pattern of Violence," in William T. Couch, ed., *The Culture of the South* (Chapel Hill: UNC, 1935), pp. 690–91; Arthur F. Raper, *Preface to Peasantry: A Tale of Two Black Belt Counties* (Chapel Hill: UNC, 1936), pp. 285–87; John C. Dollard, *Caste and Class in a Southern Town* (1937; reprint, New York:

Harper and Bros., 1949), p. 269. On homicide and suicide; Austin Porterfield, "Indices of Suicide and Homicide by States and Cities: Some Southern—Non-Southern Contrasts with Implications for Research," *American Sociological Review* 14 (1949): 488.

24. On deprived groups being outside the law, see Julian Pitt-Rivers, *The Fate of Shechem or the Politics of Sex: Essays in the Anthropology of the Mediterranean* (Cambridge: Cambridge Univ. Press, 1977), pp. 9–10. Brearley, "Pattern of Violence," pp. 690–91; Charles S. Johnson, *Shadow of the Plantation* (Chicago: Univ. of Chicago Press, 1934), pp. 191–92.

25. "South Carolina Morals," *Atlantic Monthly* 33 (April 1877): 470; Tennesseean quoted in Litwack, *Been in the Storm*, p. 278.

26. Wright quoted in Jacquelyn Dowd Hall, *Revolt Against Chivalry: Jessie Daniel Ames and the Women's Campaign Against Lynching* (New York: Columbia Univ. Press, 1979), pp. 143–44.

27. *GHJ*, July 30, 1896; Charles H. Smith, "Have American Negroes Too Much Liberty?" *Forum* 16 (1893): 179.

28. *Fisk Herald* quoted in Rabinowitz, *Race Relations*, p. 335; Booker T. Washington, "Education Will Solve the Race Problem. A Reply," *North American Review* 171 (Aug. 1900): 227; W.E.B. DuBois, *The Souls of Black Folk* (1903; reprint, New York: New American Library, 1969), pp. 190–91.

29. Clifton R. Breckenridge, in *Race Problems of the South* (1900; reprint, New York: Negro Universities Press, 1969), pp. 172–73; Walter Hines Page, "The Last Hold of the Southern Bully," *Forum* 16 (1893): 303.

30. Ida B. Wells-Barnett, *On Lynching: Southern Horrors, A Red Record, Mob Rule in New Orleans* (1892, 1895, 1900; reprint, New York: Arno Press, 1969), "Red Record," pp. 8–12; NAACP, *Thirty Years of Lynching in the United States* (New York: National Association for the Advancement of Colored People, 1919), p. 8.

31. *GHJ*, Aug. 25, 1899; *Argus*, Oct. 8, 1892.

32. Henderson M. Somerville, "Some Co-Operating Causes of Negro Lynching," *North American Review* 167 (Oct. 1903): 510; Memphis *Daily Commercial* quoted in Wells-Barnett, *Lynching* ("Southern Horrors"), p. 17. Through the use of "boundary theory" developed by Emile Durkheim and Kai T. Erikson, James M. Inveriarity has attempted to explain lynching as a response to the challenge offered to the boundary of the white community by the threat of the third political party: "Populism and Lynching in Louisiana, 1889–1896: A Test of Erikson's Theory of the Relationship Between Boundary Crises and Repressive Justice," *American Sociological Review* 41 (April 1976): 262–80. He is effectively critiqued by Ira M. Wasserman, Whitney Pope, Charles Rogin, and others, ibid. 42 (1977): 359–69. Except in Louisiana, lynchings and years of elections did not coincide very closely.

33. On witchcraft, most suggestive in this regard are Kai T. Erikson, *Wayward Puritans: A Study in the Sociology of Deviance* (New York: Wiley, 1966); John Demos, *Entertaining Satan: Witchcraft and the Culture of Early New England* (New York: Oxford Univ. Press, 1982); quote from Baltimore *American*, June 15, 1875, in Winfield Collins, *The Truth About Lynching and the Negro in the South* (New York: Neale, 1918), pp. 57–58.

34. Edward Leigh Pell, "The Prevention of Lynch-Law Epidemics," *Review of Reviews* 17 (March 1898): 321; Charles H. Poe, "Lynching: A Southern View," *Atlantic Monthly* 93 (Feb. 1904): 156. On the prevalence of offenses other than rape as the

cause for lynching, see *Thirty Years of Lynching*, p. 37; Hall, *Revolt*, p. 149. All evidence on lynching is necessarily imprecise and ambiguous; the disjunction between the statistical indicators that downplay rape and the almost complete monopolization of debate on lynching by rape makes the fascination with rape even more telling.

35. See David Herbert Donald, "A Generation of Defeat," in Walter J. Fraser, Jr., and Winfred B. Moore, Jr., eds., *From the Old South to the New: Essays on the Transitional South* (Westport, Conn.: Greenwood, 1981), pp. 3–20; Rabinowitz, *Race Relations*, pp. 329–39.

36. Charles H. Otken, *The Ills of the South; or, Related Causes Hostile to the General Prosperity of the Southern People* (New York: G. P. Putnam's Sons, 1894), p. 231; *SMN*, Aug. 1, 1893; *Herald* quoted in W. Cabell Bruce, "Lynch Law in the South," *North American Review* 155 (1892): 380.

37. *NGC*, May 26, 1892.

38. Walter White, *Rope and Faggot: A Biography of Judge Lynch* (1929; reprint: New York, Arno Press, 1969), pp. 57–58.

39. Hall, *Revolt Against Chivalry*, pp. 155–56, 147–48.

40. Washington, "Education," p. 226; Arthur F. Raper, *The Tragedy of Lynching* (Chapel Hill: UNC, 1933), pp. 29–30.

41. White, *Rope and Faggot*, pp. 56–57.

42. Quoted in *SMN*, March 29, 1897; *GHJ*, Oct. 13, 1893; *NGC*, June 1, 1899; June 15, 1899.

43. L.W.R. in *SMN*, Nov. 21, 1893; Page, "Southern Bully," p. 313.

44. Lily H. Hammond, *In Black and White: An Interpretation of Southern Life* (New York: Fleming H. Revell, 1914), pp. 60–61.

45. James E. Cutler, *Lynch-Law: An Investigation into the History of Lynching in the United States* (New York: Longmans, Green, 1905), p. 269; *ST*, Jan. 2, 1892.

46. *Manufacturer's Record* 76 (Dec. 25, 1919): 113, quoted in George B. Tindall, *Emergence of the New South, 1913–1945* (Baton Rouge: LSU, 1967), p. 172; Dalton *Argus*, Aug. 7, 1897. Lynching legislation was passed in Georgia (1893, 1895), North Carolina (1893), South Carolina (1895, 1896), Tennessee (1897), Kentucky (1897, 1902), Texas (1897), and Alabama (1901): James E. Cutler, "Proposed Remedies for Lynching," *Yale Review* 13 (Aug. 1904): 194–212; Pell, "Prevention," p. 323.

47. *NGC*, Feb. 23, 1893, *GH*, Aug. 1, 1884; William H. Thomas, *The American Negro: What He Was, What He Is, and What He May Become; A Critical and Practical Discussion* (New York: Macmillan, 1901), pp. 234–36.

48. *SMN*, Nov. 16, 1893. Edward Leigh Pell charged that this common charge was hypocritical, for "the class of men" who lynch instead of calling for circumspect and private cross-examination of alleged rape victims "are the very men who are most insistent upon crowding into court on every such occasion, to leer upon the victim and to devour every unclean suggestion that comes in the way": "Prevention," p. 322.

49. Poe, "A Southern View," p. 158; *Argus*, July 31, 1897; James Bryce quoted in Alton Hornsby, comp., *In the Cage: Eyewitness Accounts of the Freed Negro in Southern Society, 1877–1929* (Chicago: Quadrangle, 1971), p. 218.

50. E. Merton Coulter, "Hanging as a Socio-Penal Institution in Georgia and

Elsewhere," *Georgia Historical Quarterly* 57 (Spring 1973): 17–55; Crowe, "Penal Reform," pp. 130–31; "A South Carolinian," *Atlantic Monthly* 39 (June 1877): 681–82.

51. *GHJ*, May 11, May 18, 1888.

52. *Argus*, July 24, 1897.

53. E. L. Godkin, "Judge Lynch as an Educator," *Nation* 57 (Sept. 28, 1893): 222–23; Atticus Haygood, "The Black Shadow Across the South," *Forum* 16 (1893): 167–68; *Argus*, Jan. 6, 1894. On the limitations of any model to explain lynching, see James R. McGovern, *Anatomy of a Lynching: The Killing of Claude Neal* (Baton Rouge: LSU, 1982), p. 157. As C. Vann Woodward has shown in relation to disfranchisement, "What happened toward the end of the century was an almost simultaneous—and sometimes not unrelated—decline in the effectiveness of restraint that ·had been exercised by all three forces: Northern liberalism, Southern conservatism, and Southern radicalism": *The Strange Career of Jim Crow*, 3d rev. ed. (1955; reprint, New York: Oxford Univ. Press, 1974), p. 69. As I have tried to show, other "permissions to hate" developed as well: growing generational and residental fragmentation, stereotypes of black criminality, erosion of faith in the power of the law. It may well be that lynching itself played an active role in creating the climate for disfranchisement that followed so quickly after the lynching epidemic. One Georgia newspaper actually argued for disfranchisement in 1899 by asserting that "the floater in politics makes the rapist in fact." The *GHJ* made a revealing rebuttal: "it is not altogether clear to us that the one crime of which ignorant, vicious negroes are guilty, and which is fast lashing the minds of the whites into such a frenzy that they are not willing to consign the punishment of rape fiends to the law, will be lessened by depriving such men . . . of the ballot": Aug. 4, 1899.

54. Bertram Wyatt-Brown has portrayed the role of honor in lynchings and charivari before the Civil War: *Southern Honor: Ethics and Behavior in the Old South* (New York: Oxford Univ. Press, 1982), esp. chap. 16.

55.

Percentage of Business Failures

Region	1889	1890	1891	1892	1893	1894	1895	1896	1897	1898	1899	1900
East	1.31	1.11	1.10	1.00	1.80	1.42	1.03	1.50	1.49	1.64	1.51	1.71
Middle	0.86	0.88	0.92	0.70	1.15	1.51	1.12	1.45	1.08	1.03	1.63	0.80
South	1.35	1.26	1.71	1.49	1.71	1.69	1.59	1.61	1.66	1.39	1.00	1.04
West	0.86	0.80	0.77	0.64	0.95	0.78	0.80	1.03	0.84	0.80	0.59	0.69
Pacific Territories	1.69	1.89	2.21	1.75	2.28	2.26	1.99	2.08	1.89	1.78	1.48	1.40

SOURCE: *Statistical Abstracts of the United States,* 1891 (p. 12), 1892 (p. 2), 1895 (p. 336), 1898 (p. 365), 1900 (p. 391). This compilation did not include business failures before 1889; there was also economic trouble earlier in the 1880s, but it did not seem to lead to the same level of disruption as did the depressions of the 1870s and 1889–96.

C. Vann Wodward notes that "the Panic of 1893 did not mark the beginning of the depression of the South, for there the proportion of failures was exactly the same in 1891 that it was two years later. The panic, however, did bring home to the cities and industrial towns of the South as never before the distress that had gripped the surrounding countryside for years": *Origins of the New South, 1877–1913* (Baton Rouge: LSU, 1951), p. 264.

56. See Figures 5.1, 5.2, and 5.3.

	Prison Populations				Total Arrests/100,000			Homicide Arrests/100,000		
	TN	*NC*	*MI*	*MA*	*South*	*North*	*Midwest*	*South*	*North*	*Midwest*
1880	1241	464	778	750	6.9	8.6	4.4	.0090	.0024	.0045
1881		395		702	7.0	8.4	4.6	.0079	.0029	.0075
1882	1336	461	578	665	7.2	8.0	4.7	.0116	.0071	.0043
1883		432		611	7.4	7.6	4.3	.0049	.0026	.0045
1884	1323	490	670	561	7.6	7.3	4.3	.0053	.0043	.0044
1885		565		490	8.1	7.0	3.9	.0046	.0054	.0032
1886	1216	593	796	522	7.9	6.7	4.2	.0070	.0062	.0034
1887		602	787	546	7.7	6.5	4.6	.0041	.0057	.0042
1888	1363	528		556	7.3	a	4.5	.0082	.1245	.0041
1889		534	749	575	7.9	24.2	21.1	.0082	.0156	.0147
1890	1448	481		586	8.0	18.0	13.2	.0118	.0101	.0073
1891		347	722	612	8.2	15.8	10.6	.0097	.0101	.0083
1892	1442	461	768	649	8.2	13.3	9.9	.0137	.0092	.0059
1893		607	800	669	8.0	12.0	8.9	.0113	.0084	.0057
1894	1630	442	833	667	7.9	11.1	7.6	.0146	.0087	.0076
1895		520	860	683	6.9	10.5	6.6	.0047	.0098	.0063
1896		520	833	759	7.0	30.7	6.4	.0136	.0076	.0071
1897		478	830	823	6.7	16.7	5.8	.0084	.0210	.0046
1898	1525	455	836	840	6.6	15.9	5.3	.0124	.0241	.0052
1899		393	820	845	6.1	11.9	5.0	.0074	.0187	.0059

[a]Apparent distortion in data; there is a large discrepancy between the number here and all other figures.
SOURCE: See Appendix, Part I for prison data, and acknowledgment to Eric Monkkonen and the Inter-University Consortium for Political and Social Research in note 3 above for arrest data.

As early as 1904, Monroe Work, an associate of W.E.B. DuBois, discovered that "police arrest, jail, workhouses and penitentiary commitments appear to have increased during the period from 1890 to 1892–1896. The highest rates of arrests and commitments were about 1893. Since 1894–1896 the tendency of both arrests and commitments to decrease has been notable": in W.E.B. DuBois, ed., *Some Notes on Negro Crime, Particularly in Georgia* (Atlanta: Atlanta Univ. Press, 1904), pp. 18–32. Work later commented that "the number of lynchings reached its highest point about the same period that Negro crime reached its highest point": "Negro Criminality in the South," *Annals* 41 (Sept. 1913): 75–76. Also see *Annual Report of the Board of Public Charities of North Carolina for the Year 1896* (Winston, 1897), pp. 47–49. There was a large increase in the number of people arrested for larceny in Charleston between 1890 and 1895 and a decrease thereafter: Jordan, "Police and Politics," p. 48.

57. *GHJ,* Nov. 28, 1890; July 3, 1891; Aug. 11, 1893; *SMN,* Dec. 23, 1893; Jan. 15, 1894; *ST,* Sept. 15, 1894. Also see *SMN,* Feb. 22, March 13, May 23, Aug. 12, 15, 20, Dec. 22, 1893; May 4, 1894; *ST,* May 4, 1895.

58. Otken, *Ills,* p. 46; *NGC,* June 25, 1874; Otken, *Ills,* p. 32.

59. A Southern Lawyer, "Remedies for Lynch Law," *Sewanee Review* 8 (Jan. 1900): 3; W.E.B. DuBois, "The Spawn of Slavery: The Convict-Lease System in the

South," *Missionary Review of the World* 24 (Oct. 1901): 742; DuBois, *Notes on Negro Crime*, p. 6.

60. The account of Denham's lynching is taken from *GHJ*, April 14, 1894. The paper contained two long articles, one by the local editor and one by the Augusta *Chronicle*, which sent a reporter to the scene. Not surprisingly, they agree on what happened.

61. *NGC*, Sept. 11, 1879. A detailed and interesting account of this murder was written by the elder's aide, who escaped—only to be imprisoned for polygamy in the Utah penitentiary, where he narrated his version of the story to another inmate: John Nicholson, *The Martyrdom of Joseph Standing; or, The Murder of a "Mormon" Missionary* (Salt Lake City: Deseret News, 1886).

62. Gene A. Sessions, "Myth, Mormonism, and Murder in the South," *South Atlantic Quarterly* 75 (Spring 1976): 212–25.

63. W.J. Wright, Pound, Va., in Laurel Shackelford and Bill Weinberg, eds., *Our Appalachia: An Oral History* (New York: Hill and Wang, 1977), pp. 58–59. See **William F. Holmes, "Whitecapping: Agrarian Violence in Mississippi,** 1902–1906," *Journal of Southern History* 35 (May 1969): 165–85.

64. *NGC*, June 28, 1883; *Argus*, June 2, 1883. Temperance was a major topic in Whitfield and Greene from the 1860s through the 1890s: see *NGC*, Aug. 26, 1869; Whitfield Superior Court Minutes, April 1874, p. 105; Oct. 1874, pp. 218–219; *GH*, Nov. 20, 27, 1885; *GHJ*, Aug. 17, 1895.

65. *NGC*, Aug. 27, 1885.

66. *Argus*, Aug. 23, 29, Sept. 5, 1885; *NGC*, Aug. 27, 1885. William F. Homes has studied the backgrounds of mob members in this and other instances of vigilante violence in north Georgia and provides a useful overview of the phenomenon. See his "Moonshining and Collective Violence: Georgia, 1889–1895," *Journal of American History* 67 (Dec. 1980); 589–611; also see Steven Hahn, "The Roots of Southern Populism: Yeoman Farmers and the Transformation of the Upper Georgia Piedmont, 1850–1890" (Ph.D. diss., Yale Univ., 1979), p. 400.

67. *NGC*, July 14, 1887; Oct. 3, 1889; June 27, 1889.

68. *Argus*, May 9, Sept. 12, 1891; *NGC*, March 2, 1893; Sept. 8, 1892; Oct. 13, 1892.

69. *NGC*, July 25, 1889; Oct. 17, 1892; Spring Place *Jimplecute*, quoted in *Argus*, April 8, 1893. For other denunciations, see *NGC*, Nov. 3, 1892; Jan. 3, Feb. 2, 1895.

70. *Argus*, Aug. 29, 1885.

71. *Argus*, March 31, 1894; "Law and Order," in *Argus*, Jan. 12, 1895. The same issue also pointed out that "the Atlanta papers say many people in that city have no food or fuel, and not enough clothes to keep them warm." A letter from a resident of Whitfield asked for money: "My Dear Friends:—Our poor demand your attention. The weather and other circumstances have produced suffering in many homes" (Jan. 5, 1895). In 1886 "a tramp who came to our place [Dalton] last week, in quest of work, failing, died suddenly in his room. . . . To the general public this man was only as the thousands of others who go from place to place seeking work" (*Argus*, April 17, 1886).

72. Atlanta *Constitution*, Aug. 10, 1896; Holmes, "Moonshining," p. 601.

73. [George Wesley Atkinson], *After the Moonshiners, By One of the Raiders* (Wheeling:

Frew and Campbell, 1881), pp. 13–14; mountaineer quoted in Horace Kephart, *Our Southern Highlanders* (New York: Outing Pub. Co., 1913), pp. 120–21.

74. *NGC*, Dec. 20, 1894, quoting Spring Place *Jimplecute*; Kephart, *Highlanders*, pp. 171–72; John P. Fort to Editor, Atlanta *Constitution*, Feb. 26, 1896. Also see Atlanta *Constitution*, Dec. 13, 1891; William F. Holmes, "Whitecapping in Georgia: Carroll and Houston Counties, 1893," *Georgia Historical Quarterly* 44 (Winter 1980): 388–404, esp. 391–92.

75. Kephart, *Highlanders*, pp. 185–90; F. L. Oswald, "Lynch Epidemics," *North American Review* 165 (July 1897): 119–21.

76. Kephart, *Highlanders*, pp. 171–72; S. S. MacClintock, "Kentucky Mountaineers and Their Feuds," *American Journal of Sociology* 7 (July 1901): 1–28, 171–87; quote on pp. 172–73.

77. John C. Campbell, *The Southern Highlander and His Homeland* (New York: Russell Sage, 1921), pp. 111–12; also see Kephart, *Highlanders*, pp. 387–89; Otis K. Rice, *The Allegheny Frontier: West Virginia Beginnings, 1730–1830* (Lexington: Univ. of Kentucky Press, 1970), p. 16; James C. Klotter, "Feuds in Appalachia: An Overview," *Filson Club History Quarterly* 56 (July 1982): 290–317.

78. Jacob Black-Michaud, *Cohesive Force: Feud in the Mediterranean and the Middle East* (Oxford: Basil Blackwell, 1975), p. 143; also see Samuel Clark, *Social Origins of the Irish Land Wars* (Princeton: Princeton Univ. Press, 1979), pp. 74–75; N. S. Shaler, "The Peculiarities of the South," *North American Review* 151 (1890): 484.

Conclusion: "The Hurt That Honor Feels"

1. Thomas J. Kernan, "The Jurisprudence of Lawlessness," *American Bar Association Report*, 1906, pp. 450–67; quotes from pp. 451–53, 459. The unwritten code did stipulate that those accused of the relatively minor offense of slander "must first be given an opportunity to deny and disprove the charge, or to retreat and apologize" (p. 452). "Laws" 5, 6, and 7 are discussed later in the Conclusion. Law 8 held that "in prosecutions for stealing horses, cattle or hogs, the presumption of innocence is shifted in favor of the live stock"; Laws 9 and 10 dictated that corporations and employers were to be "held liable in suits brought by 'natural persons.' " It may not be an exaggeration to see these last two as corollaries of a localistic republicanism distrustful of monopoly and fictitious wealth.

2. *Savannah Morning News* (hereafter *SMN*), Aug. 16, 1897; July 15, 1893; Greensboro *Herald and Journal* (hereafter *GHJ*), Dec. 22, 1893.

3. Kernan, "Lawlessness," p. 451–53. Kernan noted, "Under the theory of the old common law only cowards were permitted to kill in self-defense; a man was compelled to flee like a craven and be cornered like a rat in a hole before he could legally deliver the *coup de grace* to his adversary. The refinements of the bench and the rough-edged administration of justice from the jury box finally succeeded in amending that absurd law, and now flight is no longer necessary, but the person attacked may pursue and kill his adversary if necessary to his own protection" (p. 462). Indeed, the law did change in that way. In 1895 the Supreme Court of Ohio ruled that "a true man, who is without fault, is not obliged to fly from an assailant who by violence or surprise maliciously seeks to take his life, or to do him enormous bodily harm." The U.S. Supreme Court

approvingly quoted this decision and followed it, but just two years later ruled that a man who was attacked could kill his adversary only after he had used "all the means in his power otherwise to save his own life . . . such as retreating as far as he can." As Joseph H. Beale, Jr., noted in 1903, the two views of the Supreme Court were contradictory and "have pretty evenly divided the jurisdictions of this country." The interpretations of this law did divide the country, but not solely along North-South lines; East-West divisions were just as important. Seven states in the South (out of 15 in the nation) ruled that a person attacked could stand his ground (Arkansas, Georgia, Kentucky, Mississippi, Missouri, Texas, and Virginia), but 4 (out of 13 in the nation) demanded retreat first (Alabama, North Carolina, South Carolina, and West Virginia). The Alabama court in 1892 delivered as harsh an attack on honor as could be imagined: "No balm or protection is provided for wounded pride or honor in declining combat, or sense of shame in being denounced as cowardly. Such thoughts are trash, as compared with the inestimable right to live" (*Springfield* v. *State*, 96 Ala. 81, 11 So. Dep. 250). This pattern shows two things: first, the very real persistence of honor in the South (and West) into the twentieth century, and second, the perpetuation of the tension between honor and the state, a tension in which the state could dominate as well as be dominated. The values of individual jurists and legislators could be of great (if misleading) importance. In any case, the South was divided. See Joseph H. Beale, Jr., "Retreat from a Murderous Assault," *Harvard Law Review* 16 (June 1903): 567–82. Also see Richard Maxwell Brown, "Southern Violence—Regional Problem or National Nemesis? Legal Attitudes Toward Southern Homicide in Historical Perspective," *Vanderbilt Law Review* 32 (1979): 225–50, and the important critique by Dennis K. Nolan, pp. 251–59. Jerry L. Butcher, "A Narrative History of Selected Aspects of Violence in the New South, 1877–1920" (Ph.D. diss., Univ. of Missouri, 1978), shows that the South was divided as well on the right to carry concealed weapons if one had been threatened (pp. 129–32).

4. *SMN*, May 22, 1868; also see *SMN*, Aug. 20, 1870; Oct. 21, 1872; Dec. 25, 1874; Greensboro *Herald* (hereafter *GH*), Jan. 23, 1873; June 1, 1875. Also see James T. Moore, "The Death of the Duel: The *Code Duello* in Readjuster Viriginia, 1879–1883," *Virginia Magazine of History and Biography* 83 (1975): 259–66.

5. F. C. Woodward of Wofford College, South Carolina, in *Nation* 36 (Feb. 22, 1883): 170; Kernan, "Lawlessness," p. 460. Also see Edward King, *The Southern States of North America* (London: Blackie and Son, 1875), pp. 777–78; C. Vann Wodward, *Origins of the New South, 1877–1913* (Baton Rouge: LSU, 1951), pp. 158–60.

6. H. V. Redfield, *Homicide, North and South: Being a Comparative View of Crime Against the Person in Several Parts of the United States* (Philadelphia: J. B. Lippincott, 1880), pp. 163–64.

7. *SMN*, May 17, 1897; *GHJ*, Aug. 4, 1899.

8. *North Georgia Citizen* (hereafter *NGC*); Feb. 18, 1897; *GHJ*, Aug. 4. 1899.

9. *Nation* 35 (Oct. 26, 1882): 349–50; Robert Penn Warren memoir, 1974, quoted in Daniel Joseph Singal, *The War Within: From Victorian to Modernist Thought in the South, 1919–1945* (Chapel Hill: UNC, 1982), p. 346.

10. Raymond D. Gastil, "Homicide and a Regional Culture of Violence," *American*

American Historical Review 74 (Feb. 1969): 906–25. Colin Lofton and Robert H. Hill (see Chapter One, note 5) argue that Gastil and Hackney statistically overstate the role of culture in Southern violence, and the criticism seems well taken. Hackney and Gastil defined "culture" largely as everything they could not otherwise quantify, and Lofton and Hill argue that "situational variables"—such as class and education—are more important than Hackney and Gastil admit. But if, as is argued here, violence was largely the product of a traditional folk culture of honor, then one should expect to find "pockets" of that culture in those groups least affected by the homogenizing effects of modern mass culture: the poorest members of both races. The approach followed here, as in Chapter One, assumes that culture, class, and state are all crucial, all interdependent, all inseperable parts of the South. It also assumes that culture has its own "weight," but that it is changed by changes in the structure of society and economy—just as culture exerts its own force upon those variables. The key is historical specificity and context. On this debate, also see William G. Doerner, "The Deadly World of Johnny Reb: Fact, Foible, or Fantasy," in James A. Inciardi and Anne E. Pottieger, eds., *Violent Crime: Historical and Contemporary Issues* (Beverley Hills: Sage, 1978), pp. 91–98; H. David Allen and William B. Bankston, "Another Look at the Southern Culture of Violence Hypothesis: The Case of Louisiana," *Southern Studies* 20 (Spring 1981): 55–66.

11. *GHJ*, Aug. 16, Sept. 13, 1889.

12. *Nation*, Jan. 18, 1883, p. 51; Walter Hines Page, "The Last Hold of the Southern Bully," *Forum* 16 (1893): 313–14.

13. *SMN*, April 24, 1894; also see *SMN*, Sept. 11, 1897. C. Vann Woodward quotes Southerners asking in the 1870s of a state's honor, "Can honor set a leg?" and announcing that "Honor won't buy breakfast": *Origins*, p. 94.

14. N. S. Shaler, "The Peculiarities of the South," *North American Review* 151 (1890): 485.

15. James H. M'Neilly, "The Failure of the Confederacy—Was It a Blessing?" *Confederate Veteran* 24 (April 1916): 162–63.

16. Marvin Wolfgang, *Patterns in Criminal Homicide* (1958), pp. 188–89, quoted in idem and Franco Ferracuti, *The Subculture of Violence: Towards an Integrated Theory of Criminology* (London: Tavistock, 1967), pp. 153–54. On the importance of Southern background to this "subculture of violence," see Thomas F. Pettigrew and Rosalind B. Spier, "The Ecological Structure of Negro Homicide," *American Journal of Sociology* 67 (May 1962): 621–29. On honor within the twentieth-century Southern black community, see Allison Davis, Burleigh B. Gardner, and Mary R. Gardner, *Deep South: A Social Anthropological Study of Caste and Class* (Chicago: Univ. of Chicago Press, 1941), pp. 526–27. Claude Brown remembered that in Harlem in the 1940s "they used to say on the streets, "Don't mess with a man's money, his woman, or his manhood. . . . It wasn't the value of the money. It couldn't have been. It was just that these things symbolized a man's manhood or principles. . . . It went deep. . . . A man was respected on the basis of his reputation": *Manchild in the Promised Land* (New York: Macmillan, 1965), pp. 253–56. I wish to be clear: of course poverty, class, exploitation, police and judicial discrimination are of crucial importance; they feed violence, and create situations where violence seems necessary. But an honor partially

brought from the South, partially created in the atmosphere of Northern poverty is the crucial variable for black violence. As Charles E. Silberman shows, Hispanics in Northern cities are even poorer than blacks, but register significantly lower rates of violence. He, too, places great emphasis on black culture, but argues that it is the erosion—rather than persistence—of a black traditional folk culture that accounts for high rates of black violence today. See *Criminal Violence, Criminal Justice* (1978; reprint, New York: Vintage, 1980), pp. 159–67, 206, and chap. 5 in general.

17. Julian Pitt-Rivers, "Honor," in *International Encyclopedia of the Social Sciences*, ed. David L. Sills (New York: Macmillan, 1968) 6:509–10. For the clearest statements of the important thesis about declining violence in the industrial world, see Roger Lane, *Violent Death in the City: Suicide, Accident, and Murder in Nineteenth-Century Philadelphia* (Cambridge: Harvard Univ. Press, 1979), and Ted Robert Gurr, "Historical Trends in Violent Crime: A Critical Review of the Evidence," in Norval Morris and Michael Tonry, eds., *Crime and Justice: An Annual Review of Research* 3 (1981): 295–353. Gurr argues that the reason for the decline in homicide in the nineteenth century is "simple and singular": "The further down the class and status ladder, past and present, the more common is interpersonal violence, because the lower classes did not assimilate and still have not wholly assimilated the aggression-inhibiting values of the middle and upper class." This is especially true for blacks, he says, because among them "the barriers of discrimination and segregation have fostered a subculture which encourages aggressive behavior" (p. 343). My argument is compatible with this view, and tries to give historical content to the abstractions of "aggression-inhibiting values" (dignity) and a "subculture which encourages aggressive behavior" (honor).

18. On the persistence of rural culture in the urban South, see David R. Goldfield, "The Urban South: A Regional Framework," *American Historical Review* 86 (Dec. 1981): 1009–34, esp. 1018–21; William D. Miller, "Myth and New South Murder Rates," *Mississippi Quarterly* 26 (1973): 143–54; John Shelton Reed, "Below the Smith and Wesson Line: Southern Violence," in *One South: An Ethnic Approach to Regional Culture* (Baton Rouge: LSU, 1982): 137–53, esp. 148. Joseph Balogh, "Crime," in David C. Roller and Robert W. Twyman, eds., *Encyclopedia of Southern History* (Baton Rouge: LSU, 1979); Keith D. Harries and Stanley D. Brunn, *The Geography of Law and Justice: Spatial Perspectives on the Criminal Justice System* (New York: Praeger, 1978), p. 4. Recent studies do suggest that the criminal patterns of North and South are becoming more alike as the regions become more alike: see Alvin L. Jacobson, "Crime Trends in Southern and Non-southern Cities: A Twenty-Year Pespective," *Social Forces* 54 (Sept. 1975): 226–42. Another study finds homicide rates stabilizing while suicide rates increase in present-day North Carolina—just the pattern we would expect as dignity establishes its dominance: John A. Humphrey and Stuart Palmer, "Homicide and Suicide in North Carolina: An Emerging Subculture of Self-Violence?" in Inciardi and Pottieger, *Violent Crime*, pp. 99–110.

Index

Alabama: antebellum convict leasing in, 68–69; antebellum penitentiary in, 34; convict leasing in, 189, 190, 193, 194–95, 195–96, 200–201, 202, 203, 204, 209, 212, 213, 214–15, 217; corporal punishment in penitentiary, 70; county penal systems in, 226; criticism of penal labor in, 65–66; debate over penitentiary in, 43, 53; pardon requested in, 206; penitentiary chaplain in, 60; penitentiary referendum in, 49; prison industry in, 67; state farm penal system in, 221; violence in antebellum era, 17; women in penitentiary, 62

alcohol: and crime, 14, 117–18; debate over, in mountains, 256–57, 263; and violence, 99–100, 114–15. *See also* temperance

Alexandria (Virginia), and depression of 1850s, 97

Alfriend, Laura, 144

Allen, Jim, 225

Allen, Rev. W. B., 126

Anderson, Edward C., 86, 173–74

Anderson, R. H., 173, 224

Anthony, Rev. J. P., 120

Anti-Convict League, 214

Arkansas: origins of convict leasing in, 189; penitentiary of, during Civil War, 186

Arnold, Richard, 104

Auburn (New York) Penitentiary, 39

Baker, Daniel, 79–80

Baldwin, Joseph G., 17, 110

Baltimore, and depression of 1850s, 95, 97

Bankhead, John H., 195

Banks, Lucinda, 206

Barnes, Gideon, 205

Beaumont, Gustave de, 39, 58

Beccaria, Cesare, 37, 54

Bentham, Jeremy, 37, 38

Birmingham, and convict leasing, 213

Black codes, of Mississippi and South Carolina, 151. *See also* law

Black-Michaud, Jacob, 264

blacks (postbellum): alienated from white law, 335n14; attitudes toward law, 228–30; in convict lease system, 197–200, 210–11; and courts, 177–79; and honor, 344–45n16; in postwar cities, 172–73; stereotype of "bad nigger," 231–33; and theft, 176–77; violence among, 336n16; violence against other blacks, 231–33; and whitecapping, 260. *See also* slaves

Blackstone, Sir William, 18, 32, 54–55

Bland, Henry, 133

blues, and black heroes, 233

Boston, violent crime in, 99

Boston Prison Discipline Society, 101

Bourdieu, Pierre, 13

Boykin, Wilson, 206

Bradley, Aaron A., 162

Brearley, H. C., 234

Breckenridge, Clifton R., 237

Bremer, Fredrika, 101–2

Bridenbaugh, Carl, 22

Brinson, Charles, 231

Brown, John C., 169